Textual and Bibliographical Studies in Older Scots Literature

SCOTTISH
TEXT
SOCIETY

THE SCOTTISH TEXT SOCIETY

The Methuen Cup. Scotland, circa 1550. Silver gilt, rock crystal. Height: 7 in. (17.78 cm) with cover; bowl diameter: 4 1/2 in. (11.43 cm). Los Angeles County Museum of Art, William Randolph Hearst Collection (49.14.6a-b).
Photo © Museum Associates/ LACMA.

TEXTUAL AND BIBLIOGRAPHICAL STUDIES IN OLDER SCOTS LITERATURE

Selected Essays of Priscilla Bawcutt

Edited by
Janet Hadley Williams

The Scottish Text Society

2022

First published 2022 by The Scottish Text Society, Edinburgh

ISBN 978-1-89797-647-0

A Scottish Text Society publication
Published by The Boydell Press
an imprint of Boydell & Brewer Ltd
PO Box 9, Woodbridge, Suffolk IP12 3DF, UK
and of Boydell & Brewer Inc.
668 Mt Hope Avenue, Rochester, NY 14620–2731, USA
website: www.boydellandbrewer.com

The publisher has no responsibility for the continued existence or accuracy of URLs for external or
third-party internet websites referred to in this book, and does not guarantee that any content on such
websites is, or will remain, accurate or appropriate

A CIP catalogue record for this book is available
from the British Library

This publication is printed on acid-free paper

Printed and bound in Great Britain by TJ Books Limited, Padstow, Cornwall

Contents

CONTENTS

Foreword

Priscilla Bawcutt is one of the most significant scholars of Older Scots literature and culture of the last fifty years. She possessed a calm but devastating authority that was founded on immense scholarship, both broad and deep, in Scottish and English literatures, critical reading, book history and editorial practice. She was, in addition, tremendously generous in sharing that scholarship with others in the field, supporting established scholars and inspiring new ones.

Bawcutt was the expert editor – none better – of the Scottish Text Society's editions of Gavin Douglas's *Shorter Poems* and his magisterial *Eneados*, setting a gold standard for other editors to follow. For many years, she also served as a Council member and as Editorial Convenor, selflessly lending her scholarly rigour and editorial expertise to the process of vetting proposals, monitoring work in progress and ensuring that published editions were the best that they could be.

This volume collects together a number of Bawcutt's essays concerned with editing, textual scholarship and book history, all at the core of the work of the Scottish Text Society. They all represent important contributions to the discipline, bringing Older Scots literature to the attention of new audiences and changing the way we look at these materials. We are very grateful to Janet Hadley Williams for taking on the editing and publication of this volume under the auspices of the Society.

Nicola Royan and Rhiannon Purdie
President and Editorial Secretary, Scottish Text Society

Acknowledgements

To Priscilla Bawcutt, I wish I could say, '3he war the caus tharof'. All of us who pursue studies in early Scottish literature are beneficiaries of her huge contribution to the field.

Priscilla's husband, Dr Nigel Bawcutt, supported and encouraged the preparation of this book. His intelligent kindness made all the difference.

The help of the Scottish Text Society Council has been important. STS President Nicola Royan and Editorial Secretary Rhiannon Purdie generously advised along the way and at the rather difficult final stages. Of my fellow members of Council, Vice President Alasdair MacDonald was a fount of information on many diverse matters; Honorary President Rod Lyall consulted his papers on a difficult point; Hector MacQueen shared his legal expertise; Emily Wingfield, with goodwill and efficiency, drew on her networks for two particular queries; Pamela King, ever sane, made practical suggestions; Kees Dekker helped on a publishing permission; Tony Edwards gave valuable support at the beginning and proofread nine essays.

The wise and forbearing Caroline Palmer and her editorial team at Boydell & Brewer have been the very best.

All publishers gave permissions to reprint with great courtesy. For the earlier essays, where the process was not straightforward, they expended much effort on my behalf. I warmly thank Hugh Andrews, Birlinn; Alastair Arthur, Enlighten Team, University of Glasgow; Gerard Carruthers, Department of Scottish Literature, University of Glasgow; Cairns Craig, Aberdeen University Press; Duncan Jones, Association for Scottish Literature; Ourania Kalogeri, Cambridge Scholars Publishing; Caroline Palmer, Rachel Reeder and Elizabeth McDonald, Boydell & Brewer; Stephanie Peeters, Peeters; Stephen Pink and Corinne Saunders, *Medium Ævum*; Derek Taylor, Edinburgh Bibliographical Society; and Marta Werner, *Textual Cultures*.

Special thanks go to Nicholas Bawcutt, Alexander Broadie, Margaret Mackay, Kate Flaherty, Caitlin Flynn, Phoebe Garratt, Kathy Hobkirk, Conor Leahy, Emily Lyle, Tricia McElroy, John McGavin, John Mark Philo, Jamie Reid Baxter, Lado Shay, Sebastiaan Verweij, Greg Walker, and Elspeth Yeo.

My husband Ian has given much loving encouragement and sage advice throughout the preparation of this volume; I can never thank him enough.

Editor's Note

These essays are reproduced as Priscilla Bawcutt presented or published them. Full references to the conference or publication in which they were first presented or appeared, and the permissions to reprint them are appended, together with editorial notes (shown in the text by lettered notes) updating the material where necessary. Original page numbering is recorded within each essay within square brackets; for example: [25]. A consistent style, however, is applied to abbreviated forms, the spelling of proper names, shelfmarks, forms of citation of manuscripts and early printed books, spelling more generally, and to notes originally in the author-date form within the text. All additions within the text have been placed in square brackets.

Abbreviations

Aldis	Harry G. Aldis, *A List of Books Printed in Scotland before 1700* (Edinburgh, 1970)
ASLS	Association for Scottish Literary Studies (*now* ASL)
B	Bannatyne Manuscript
Bd	Bannatyne Draft Manuscript
BL	British Library
Crum	*First-Line Index of English Poetry 1500–1800 in Manuscripts of the Bodleian Library, Oxford*, ed. Margaret Crum, 2 vols (Oxford, 1969)
CSD	*Concise Scots Dictionary*
CUL	Cambridge University Library
DNB	*Dictionary of National Biography*
DOST	*A Dictionary of the Older Scottish Tongue* (http://www.dsl.ac.uk)
EEBO	*Early English Books Online* (http//eebo.chadwyck.com/home)
EETS	Early English Text Society
	ES Extra Series; OS Ordinary Series
EUL	Edinburgh University Library
Fox and Ringler	*The Bannatyne Manuscript. National Library of Scotland Advocates' MS 1.1.6*, introd. Denton Fox and William A. Ringler (London, 1980)
IMEV	Carleton Brown and Rossell Hope Robbins, *The Index of Middle English Verse* (New York, 1943)
May and Ringler	Steven May and William A. Ringler, *Elizabethan Poetry: A Bibliography and First-Line Index of English Verse, 1559–1603*, 3 vols (London, 2004)
MED	*Middle English Dictionary*
NAS	National Archives of Scotland *see* NRS
NIMEV	Julia Boffey and A. S. G. Edwards, *A New Index of Middle English Verse* (London, 2005)
NLS	National Library of Scotland
NRS	National Records of Scotland
ODNB	*Oxford Dictionary of National Biography*
OED	*Oxford English Dictionary*

ABBREVIATIONS

PMLA	*Publications of the Modern Language Association*
Ringler, TM	William A. Ringler, *Bibliography and Index of English Verse in Manuscript 1501–1558*, prepared and completed by Michael Rudick and S. J. Ringler (1992). [TM = Early Tudor manuscript transcription]
Ringler, TP	William A. Ringler, *Bibliography and Index of English Verse Printed 1476 1558* (1988) [TP = Tudor Print, 1501–58]
RMS	*Registrum Magni Sigili Regum Scotorum*
SHS	Scottish History Society
SND	*Scottish National Dictionary*
SRS	Scottish Record Society
STC	Alfred W. Pollard, G. R. Redgrave, William A. Jackson, F. S. Ferguson and Katharine F. Pantzer, *A Short-Title Catalogue of Books Printed in England Scotland and Ireland, and of English Books Printed Abroad, 1475–1640*, 3 vols (London, 1976–91)
STS	Scottish Text Society
Supplement	Rossell Hope Robbins and John L. Cutler, *Supplement to the Index of Middle English Verse* (Lexington, 1965)
TLS	*Times Literary Supplement*
TNA	The National Archives
Whiting	B. J. Whiting with Helen W. Whiting, *Proverbs, Sentences and Proverbial Phrases from English Writings mainly before 1500* (Cambridge, MA, 1968)
Whiting, 'Proverbs'	B. J. Whiting, 'Proverbs and Proverbial Sayings from Scottish Writings before 1600' (Parts I and II), *Medieval Studies*, 11 (1949), 123–205; 13 (1951), 87–164

Introduction:
'Restoring the authour's works to their integrity'

These essays celebrate Priscilla Bawcutt's immense contribution to early Scottish literary studies. In her editing, criticism, analytical surveys and investigations into book history and culture, Professor Bawcutt's publications have illuminated the field over more than fifty years. To the Scottish Text Society – formed to encourage the study and teaching of Scottish literature through the publication of original texts – Bawcutt's major editions of the works of William Dunbar and Gavin Douglas have been of particular importance. By showing the value of vigilance in textual and linguistic matters, of taking account of the larger context, and of succinct, instructive notes, they have changed the way in which editors of early Scottish texts approach their tasks.[1] Bawcutt understood that '[i]nformed criticism depends upon the availability of good editions';[2] she saw that, through the influence of editorial tradition, the power of editors was 'possibly greater than that of critics'.[3] She took these matters very seriously, placing her emphasis, like Samuel Johnson, on 'restoring the authour's works to their integrity'.[4]

The essays here have been chosen to show the breadth and depth of Bawcutt's achievement, with a preference given to those now more difficult to obtain. Essays 1 to 5 are selected for their many insights into editing. In the first, previously unpublished, Bawcutt has drawn on the work of the great early editors as well her own, directly addressing the nature of the discipline and its challenge to leave nothing obscure. Her relaxed, witty discussion both disguises and reveals the authority, acquired through years of editing, that underlies the astute commentary on the pleasures and problems the editor encounters.

The value of proof in editing, and in all scholarly practice, has been a topic of longstanding importance to Bawcutt; in the second essay, she links it to the particular activity of identifying echoes, sources and influences in literary writing. Characteristically, she draws on the unintended humour of Fluellen's assurances to Gower in *Henry V* to make her point that scepticism is always needed. Her checklist, designed to help preserve a scholar's objectivity in the face of temptation, mentions,

---

[1] This is no vague claim: nine of the Scottish Text Society editors in the current Fifth Series, for example, have acknowledged directly Bawcutt's constructive reading, shared expertise, advice and support.

[2] Priscilla Bawcutt, review of *Ane Resonyng of ane Scottis and Inglis Merchand betuix Rowand and Lionis*, ed. Roderick J. Lyall (Aberdeen, 1985), *Scottish Literary Journal, Supplement*, 22 (1985), 2–4 (4).

[3] See her full discussion in essay 1 herein.

[4] *The Plays of William Shakespeare, with the Corrections and Illustrations of Various Commentators; To Which Are Added Notes by Sam. Johnson*, 8 vols (London, 1765), I, Preface, p. lxiv.

1

for instance, the usefulness of establishing the order of precedence of text and purported source; accessibility of a source to the author whose text is said to echo it; consideration of corroborative evidence, and plausibility of the proposed debt. In the more impartial 'map' of parallels that results, Bawcutt's multitude of telling examples demonstrates the scholarly rewards of resisting a leap to wrong conclusions.

It must be added that the presence of this second essay represents others Bawcutt has written, all with a theme to which she returned throughout her career – though it cannot have made her life easy at times. This was a deep concern for the standards and reputation of critical work in Older Scots literature, and of the scholar's obligation to take no assumption for granted. 'James VI's Castalian Band: A Modern Myth' is among more easily accessible examples in which Bawcutt carefully prunes or weeds an undergrowth to reveal afresh some long-unqueried terms.[5]

As editor, Bawcutt knew and frequently addressed the reader's need for a longer perspective, or a generic framework, within which both the small details of line or word and the larger elements of stanzas and whole text can best be understood. Her helpful mini-studies on types or traditions can be found in many of her headnotes to commentaries on individual poems in her edition of Dunbar – those, for instance, on the mock testament, or the vision of hell.[6] A bravura piece on another type is her 1983 lecture, 'The Art of Flyting', which Bawcutt presented on the centenary celebration of the Scottish Text Society.[7]

In the third essay here, she examines a literary type that was especially congenial in early Scotland. With the facts she has gathered from English as well as Scottish material (*Eneados*, VIII.Prol.17 in particular), she aptly names this the 'elrich fantasy'. Bawcutt discusses the linguistic and metrically ingenious responses of Dunbar and others to the demands of this tradition, distinguishing Dunbar's 'elrich fantasyis' by their tonal differences and structural control.

Professor Bawcutt's willingness to share her editing skills and knowledge is evident in the fourth essay, which might be described as a class on how to edit fragmentary or imperfect material. Taking the case of John Rolland's *Court of Venus*, she closely studies and discusses the work of its early editors and commentators, and the 'highly imperfect' witnesses of *The Court* (to which she adds two more in the course of her investigation). Bawcutt's approach demonstrates why Rolland's long poem has been undervalued and, more broadly, why it is always important for an editor to look closely at the early text itself (rather than a transcript made by others). The meticulous list of corrected readings that she appends offers readers of *The Court of Venus* interim assistance (until a new edition can be prepared), so that a better assessment of the hitherto hidden merits of Rolland as writer can be made at once.

Bawcutt frequently sought to show the value of heeding all the evidence, however inconsequential it might appear to be. Early charms, saved by chance, perhaps seen

---

5   'James VI's Castalian Band: A Modern Myth', *Scottish Historical Review*, 80(2).210 (2001), 251–59. See also, for example, her article, 'A Note on the Term "Morality"', *Medieval English Theatre*, 28 (2006), 171–74.

6   *The Poems of William Dunbar*, ed. Priscilla Bawcutt, 2 vols, ASLS 27, 28 (Glasgow, 1998), 'I maister Andro Kennedy' (B 19), II, p. 328, and 'Off Februar the fyiftene nycht' (B 47), II, p. 383.

7   'The Art of Flyting', *Scottish Literary Journal*, 10.2 (1983), 5–24.

as scraps with a dubious relationship to their manuscript contexts – the records of kirk session, a trial or abbey land acquisitions – are the basis of essay 5. Bawcutt teases out tiny details and connections, discussing the uses of these charms in everyday life and noting the qualified regard for them shown by the medieval Church. Yet it is by carefully editing versions of charms in several witnesses that she shows how their differences can shed further light on both religious attitudes and the linguistic puzzles of ancient idioms and now-uncommon expressions.

The state of Older Scots literature and the need to describe it more systematically were among Bawcutt's far-seeing interests. Paying tribute to 'the great *Index of Middle English Verse*', she proposed a 'First-Line Index of Early Scottish Verse'.[8] She praised the facsimile of the Bannatyne Manuscript, by which William Ringler, together with Denton Fox, 'revolutionized our understanding of [its] makeup and contents'.[9] Essays 6 and 7, forming the central group in the present collection, illustrate this facet of her work. Essay 6, her own analytical survey of the manuscript miscellany in Scotland, is the first of its kind.[10] A most valuable source for repeated consultation, the survey records the similarities and differences between the Scottish compilations – of their size and physical makeup; date; contents, including later additions; overall organization; internal thematic groupings; and of scribes and owners. Often Bawcutt also suggests the paths for future research. Within her survey, the place of the Bannatyne Manuscript (NLS, Adv. MS 1.1.6) is tempered, the ideological purpose later imposed on it set aside.[11] Professor Bawcutt gives the manuscript a codicological context in which distinctive aspects and those it shares with others can be better assessed.

Bawcutt does not wish to deny the importance of the Bannatyne Manuscript.[12] In the second of the two central essays (7), she continues the pioneering work of Fox and Ringler, updating and correcting their findings. Her new information on fifty-seven of the poems in Bannatyne is another major advance that no scholar of early Scottish literary studies can ignore. She reports discoveries of new texts and new sources, and exposes diverse literary and cultural interactions, many of her concise notes meriting treatment as independent essays. One such set of comments updates information about Bannatyne no. 112, the quatrain, 'He þat thy freind hes bene rycht lang.' While Fox and Ringler had already identified another version of the verse in the Maxwell Manuscript, Bawcutt adds two more. Her first is found on a small silver-gilt object known as the Methven Cup.[13] Bawcutt argues that the cup's size suggests a secular

---

8 'A First-Line Index of Early Scottish Verse', *Studies in Scottish Literature*, 26.1 (1991), 254–70 (268). Sebastiaan Verweij has taken up this project and is preparing a prototype 'First-Line Index of Older Scots Verse'.

9 'A First-Line Index', 268.

10 This was noted by Sally Mapstone, 'Introduction: Older Scots and the Sixteenth Century', in *Older Scots Literature*, ed. Sally Mapstone (Edinburgh, 2005), pp. 175–88 (175–79).

11 On this, see, for instance, Walter Scott, *Memorials of George Bannatyne*, [ed. David Laing], Bannatyne Club (Edinburgh, 1829), p. 10, where George Bannatyne is described as 'a national benefactor'.

12 See 'The Earliest Texts of Dunbar', in *Regionalism in Late Medieval Manuscripts and Texts: Essays Celebrating the Publication of 'A Linguistic Atlas of Late Mediaeval English'*, ed. Felicity Riddy (Cambridge, 1991), pp. 183–98 (194–97).

13 For an image, see the cover and frontispiece of this volume: The Methuen Cup, Scotland, *c.* 1550, silver gilt, rock crystal; height: 7 in. (17.78 cm) with cover; bowl diameter 4 ½

rather than religious purpose, and that this might be related to the three bands of lettering incised on the vessel's cover and bowl, which, when grouped together, form a version of the quatrain in Bannatyne. Bawcutt links her second version (copied in the margin of a thirteenth-century Latin Bible owned by a Dumfries notary) to that on the Cup, noting that these two are closer to each other than to Bannatyne. In another example, 'Robeyn's Iok come to wow our Iynny' (Fox and Ringler no. 201), Bawcutt changes completely the idea that a poem is 'unique' to the Bannatyne Manuscript. Her notes expose continuities and inter-relationships. Bawcutt cites 'The Country Wedding' in *Watson's Choice Collection* as deriving ultimately from the text copied by Bannatyne; adding, invaluably, 'a closely contemporary analogue', the early example in Bodleian, MS Ashmole 48 (*c.* 1557–65). Bawcutt's notes on Fox and Ringler no. 289, 'Lanterne of lufe and lady fair of hew', look more rigorously at the topic of authorship, here to Bannatyne's ascription of the poem to 'Steill'. Fox and Ringler had suggested that this is James V's servitor, George Steill, but Bawcutt demonstrates succinctly that previous assumptions cannot be sustained.

In the final group of essays (8–12), Bawcutt combines in-depth textual and codicological studies with richly informative explorations – into personal libraries; habits of reading; compilers; annotators; and book circulation within family groups, across borders or over time. Elsewhere, Bawcutt has discussed Gavin Douglas's close involvement with one manuscript, Cambridge, Trinity College Library MS O.3.12;[14] in essay 8, she takes on a fascinating larger challenge: the re-creation – with various forms of proof – of Douglas's mental or 'imaginary' library in its extent and variety. She identifies those many works on which Douglas undoubtedly drew, and – of more importance – examines how he read them. She finds that he named some authors directly (sometimes to dismiss, as Caxton or Guido), and left others unidentified, simply paraphrasing or echoing their work. Bawcutt notes in detail that Douglas's mental reference collection included classical, medieval and humanistic authors, but points out that recently published works were among them: Henryson's *Orpheus* (1508), for instance; Mair's more controversial Latin *History of Greater Britain* (1521); and the commentaries on Virgil by Douglas's own contemporaries, Landino (1487ff) and Ascensius (1501). Such a reconstruction from evidence of different kinds is the scholarly feat upon which Bawcutt's revised edition of Douglas's *Eneados* is founded.

But essay 9 is another achievement, rescuing from obscurity the common-place book of John Maxwell. Since the early unpublished work of the manuscript's transcriber, M. L. Anderson – valuable, but flawed by an uncritical assumption that most of the contents were Maxwell's own compositions – Bawcutt's has been the only full study. It continues to spark the interest of other scholars.[15] By identifying

in. (11.43 cm), Los Angeles County Museum of Art, William Randolph Hearst Collection (49.14.6a–b). Photo © Museum Associates / LACMA. I wish to thank Ms Piper Severance, Los Angeles County Museum of Art, for her kind help.

[14] See, for example, 'The Cambridge Manuscript (C)', in *The Eneados: Gavin Douglas's Translation of Virgil's Aeneid*, ed. Priscilla Bawcutt with Ian Cunningham, STS, 5th ser. 17 (Edinburgh, 2020), I, pp. 9–13.

[15] See, for example, Sebastiaan Verweij, *The Literary Culture of Early Modern Scotland: Manuscript Production and Transmission 1560–1625* (Oxford, 2016), pp. 189–91.

Maxwell's sources (including Pettie's *A Petite Pallace* (1576), Lyly's *Euphues* (1578), Montgomerie's 'Can Goldin Titan', Rolland's *Seuin Seages* and various classical authors), she has in part recreated another 'library'. This one is that of a young man who enjoyed collecting long-known adages and proverbial sayings as well as popular rhymes and verse games, perhaps some of these last his own compositions. Profitably, she links Maxwell's inclusions to their occurrence elsewhere: other commonplace books comparable to his own; also the Bannatyne Manuscript. This is a rare depiction of the everyday or popular (rather than deeply scholarly) literary interests of one person, perhaps also of those belonging to a regional social network.

Bawcutt's study of the mid-fifteenth-century manuscript, Boston Public Library, MS f. med. 94 (essay 10), has a different balance, with her interests in manuscript history and culture playing a larger role. Scrupulously, she begins with the Boston manuscript's main contents (Lydgate's *Siege of Thebes*), its English scribe (Dodesham), and first (unknown) owner, but she quickly focuses on the manuscript's later moves, across the border into Scotland and from owner to owner. Through external sources and internal inscriptions, she explores the fortunes of the first Scottish owners, the Lyle family. She charts the passing of the manuscript to other hands; eventually, in the later sixteenth century, to the ownership of Duncan Campbell, seventh laird of Glenorchy, and possibly earlier Campbell family, who also had notable literary interests.

It is in the following part of her essay that Bawcutt combines with these investigations in book history her skills as editor. She describes and contextualizes six pieces of verse casually added to the blank leaves of the manuscript. Each is in a different hand and ink; all are in Scots with varying peculiarities; some are by known authors (Scott, Gower, Bellenden), others by writers otherwise unknown. Bawcutt produces edited transcriptions – even of the 'hasty scribble' that she identifies as a line by Alexander Scott – with commentaries and glosses. These editions are an important contribution to Older Scots literary studies, making possible further scholarship on poems that are either unknown or known elsewhere in different forms. Though she says that the history of the Boston manuscript is 'not as "coherent"' as one would like', Bawcutt has indeed found connections between these poems and other versions in the early manuscript miscellanies. She has recognized the implications of their inclusion in this one, whether as evidence of the popularity of a theme, proof of Scottish readership of certain texts, or in the use of a metrical form that elsewhere is associated with music.

Bawcutt takes a different, yet just as instructive approach in essay 11, giving a central position to the life and interests of Sir William Howard of Naworth (1563–1640), and leaving until a final section her discussion of one of his books, now BL, MS Arundel 285. She begins with Howard's privileged yet rather difficult upbringing as ward of William Cecil, Lord Burghley; his early advantageous marriage and family life; involvement, as a Catholic, in contemporary politics; antiquarian activities; and tastes as book collector. She also mentions, revealingly, what he might have been expected to own and did not. Howard's Scottish books are separately treated, before, in the last part of her essay, she singles out one item in Howard's collection, MS Arundel 285. With such a mass of carefully ordered material preceding it, the discussion of Arundel 285, as a Scottish manuscript that probably played a role in Howard's daily devotions, could not have been better introduced. Calling attention to J. A. W. Bennett's edition of Arundel 285,[16] Bawcutt looks in more detail at items of particular value – the unique copies of Dunbar's *Maner of Passyng to Confessioun* (B 41) and Kennedie's *Passioun of Christ*, for example, or the item known as 'The Lang Rosair', with its complicated printing history. She moves to broader issues, pointing out Arundel 285's value as evidence of the religious sensibility of this mid-century period. She also recognizes the manuscript's linguistic worth, with its archaisms and, probably, the 'oldest known Scottish devotional poem' among its contents. She studies the decoration, especially the woodcuts; and speculates on how Thomas Howard might have come to own the manuscript. Bawcutt's inclusive approach is never simply descriptive, but always seeks to find significance.

Gavin Douglas has been Priscilla Bawcutt's enduring interest, from her earliest postgraduate study of *The Palice of Honour* and the anonymous *King Hart*,[17] to her most recent work, the revised edition of his *Eneados* for the Scottish Text Society. It is no surprise that her impressive early essay on Douglas's imaginary inner 'library' (8 herein) can be matched by a late one that is equally so. In essay 12, Bawcutt focuses on how Douglas's translation became part of the mental, and physical, libraries of others. She opens with notes on the textual history of the *Eneados*, referring to the several excellent early manuscripts, one of them copied in Douglas's lifetime. She chooses to look more closely, however, at the circulation and readership of the first printed edition of the *Eneados*, produced by William Copland in London in 1553. Earlier editor David F. C. Coldwell described this print as inaccurate, partially anglicized, and adjusted to conform to Protestant dogma, but Bawcutt looks more attentively at the ways in which the 1553 print departs from the manuscript tradition, and explains the defective absence, or correct presence, of the extra leaf in some copies. Much of the essay concerns her argument that the impact of 1553, especially in England, but also in Scotland, is still not fully recognized. She illustrates it most persuasively, noting, for example, the use made of 1553 by George Bannatyne in his manuscript miscellany, and the remark of David Hume of Godscroft, that his text was not 'rightly printed and corrected', showing that he, too, used the print. The large number of extant copies of the 1553 print, Bawcutt observes, establishes that these two early owners were among many others. She gathers new information about some of these owners, including two Scotswomen. (Elsewhere, too, Bawcutt gives proper regard to the roles played by women in the history of books – of Marie Maitland, Esther Inglis and Lady Margaret Wemyss in essay 6; Mariota Lyle and Catherine Ruthven in 10; Elizabeth Dacre (mother and daughter) and Mary Howard in 11.)[18] Her commentary on the owner W. Barnesley and his lively interest in Douglas's vocabulary illustrates the richness of the material in this essay. Barnesley's notes,

---

[16] *Devotional Pieces in Verse and Prose from MS Arundel 285 and MS Harleian 6919*, ed J. A. W. Bennett, STS, 3rd ser. 33 (Edinburgh, 1955).

[17] See the early essays, written as Priscilla Preston: 'Did Gavin Douglas Write *King Hart*?', *Medium Aevum*, 28 (1959), 31–47; and 'Gavin Douglas: Some Additions to O.E.D. and D.O.S.T.', *Notes and Queries*, 10.8 (1963), 289–90.

[18] See also her 'Images of Women in the Poems of Dunbar', *Études écossaises*, 1 (1992), 49–58; and '"My bright buke": Women and Their Books in Medieval and Renaissance Scotland', in *Medieval Women: Texts and Contexts in Late Medieval Britain; Essays for Felicity Riddy*, ed. Jocelyn Wogan-Browne et al. (Turnhout, 2000), pp. 17–34.

Bawcutt points out, anticipated those of the great scholar Francis Junius, on whose own annotated copy of 1553 she also writes knowledgeably. Typically, Bawcutt adds an Appendix of extant copies of 1553 known to her, listing locations and shelfmarks.

For the scholar in Older Scots literature, especially the new editor, here is treasure-trove.

Janet Hadley Williams

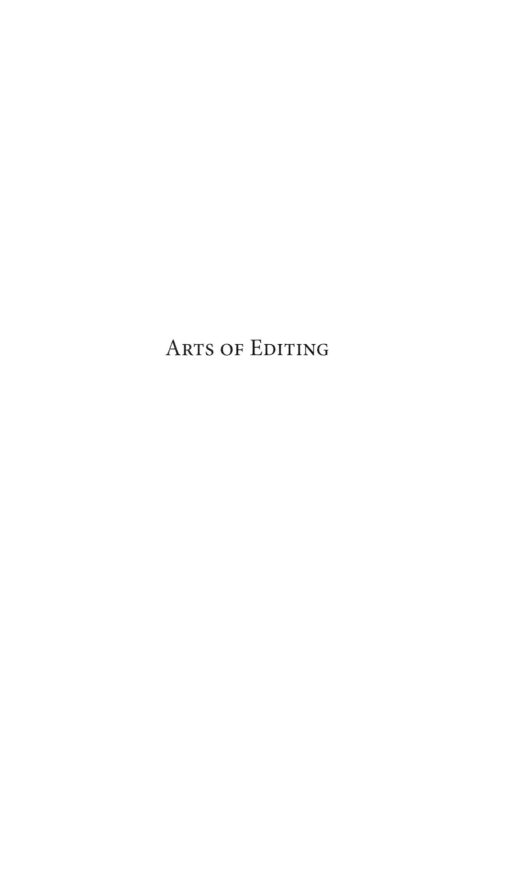

ARTS OF EDITING

1

'Let us now be told no more of the dull duty of an editor!'

This is a talk that has had several different titles.[a] I first envisaged 'Notes as necessary evils' – since despite the enormous mass of words devoted to the theory of editing, comparatively little attention has been paid to annotation. But when I learnt that my chairman expected me to offer 'some wider reflections' on Scottish editing, annotation seemed perhaps too narrow a topic. I then toyed with 'Every blur is a challenge', Kenneth Sisam's rallying call to medieval textual scholars, and one that has long served me as a kind of motto or watchword.[1] Eventually I have ended with something upbeat – Samuel Johnson's indignant response to Alexander Pope: 'Let us now be told no more of the dull duty of an editor.'[2]

In 1725, in the Preface to his edition of Shakespeare, Pope had remarked: 'I have discharged the dull duty of an Editor to my best judgment, with more labour than I expect thanks …'[3] Forty years later, in the Preface to his own edition of Shakespeare, Johnson perceptively noted that Pope 'seems to have thought [the work of editing] unworthy of his abilities, being not able to suppress his contempt of *the dull duty of an editor*'.[4] Johnson does not deny that some editorial tasks may seem tedious, but proceeds to argue that a good editor requires 'qualities very different from dullness', notably 'knowledge and taste' – in modern terms, these might be rendered as scholarship and critical ability.[5]

Editing has never seemed to me a dull task, though it has sometimes proved difficult. Editing ancient Scottish texts – far older than Shakespeare – calls for a remarkable range of abilities. One needs not only bright ideas but also stamina, or *Sitzfleisch*. A good editor has something in common with a good translator – each becomes remarkably close to their chosen author or text, immersed in small details of words and phrasing, yet not losing a sense of the relationship between the parts and the work as a whole. Editor and translator also have similar duties – fidelity to

---

1   *Fourteenth Century Verse and Prose* (Oxford, 1921; rev. ed. 1967), ed. Kenneth Sisam, p. xliii.
2   *The Plays of William Shakespeare, with the Corrections and Illustrations of Various Commentators; To Which Are Added Notes by Sam. Johnson*, 8 vols (London, 1765), I, p. xlix.
3   *The Works of Shakespeare … Collated and Corrected by the Former Editions, by Mr. Pope*, 6 vols (London, 1723–25), I (1725), p. xxii.
4   *Plays of Shakespeare*, ed. Johnson, I, p. xlviii.
5   *Plays of Shakespeare*, ed. Johnson, I, p. xlix.

the original must be balanced with awareness of the needs of new or ignorant readers. The balance, one feels, is occasionally lost in over-learned editions. Editing can give various kinds of pleasure: it is very satisfactory to illuminate a passage that has long been misunderstood, or to solve a difficult textual crux, or to be led by one's author into exploring new and unfamiliar topics – 'Of shoes – and ships – and sealing wax.'[6] Editing Dunbar took me into diverse areas – including claret and games of dice, soap-making and the symptoms of syphilis; so too did the witchcraft passages in *The Flyting of Polwart and Montgomerie*.

Editors also have remarkable power, for good or ill – the placing of a comma, or a conjectural emendation may determine how a passage is read for centuries. Their power is greater possibly than that of critics. Critical books are highly susceptible to the vagaries of fashion; but some editions (not all, of course, the great exception being those of Shakespeare) have had surprisingly long lives. The shape of the 'Riverside Chaucer' derives ultimately from F. N. Robinson's edition first published in 1933, and conceived, I believe, before the end of the nineteenth century. The first editor of any text has an awesome responsibility, since one editor often follows after another like a line of sheep I observed recently in the Isle of Skye. A spectacular instance is Allan Ramsay's treatment of the ending of Dunbar's 'Thrissill and Rois' – Ramsay's title, incidentally.[7] Ramsay substituted for Dunbar's lines ('And thus I wret, as ȝe haif hard toforrow, / Off lusty May vpone the nynt morrow') two of his own: 'Callt to my Muse, and for my Subjeck chose / To sing the Ryal Thistle and the Rose.'[8] Lord Hailes prided himself on being more accurate than Ramsay, yet nonetheless adopted this couplet, calling Dunbar's lines 'bald and prosaic';[9] they appeared in all subsequent editions of the poem until that of David Laing in 1834.

Editorial tradition – some might call it sloth or inertia – is also responsible for erroneous readings in the marginal Commentary to Douglas's *Eneados*. The note to [Book] I. [chapter] v.[line] 76, for instance, printed in Coldwell's edition, tells us that Ascanius was 'the fifth sone' of Hector.[10] This would surprise any classicist, I'm sure, and presumably worried Coldwell, since in his Glossary he made the desperate and implausible suggestion that 'fift' here meant not 'fifth' but 'enfeefed' (from the rare word *feft*).[11] In fact, the manuscript reads not 'fift' but 'sistr' (fol. 14ᵛ), and the phrase as a whole is 'sister son', which makes excellent sense: Ascanius was the nephew, not

6 Lewis Carroll, *Through the Looking Glass* (1871), chapter 4, ['The Walrus and the Carpenter'], [line 63].

7 *The Ever Green, Being a Collection of Scots Poems Wrote by the Ingenious before 1600*, ed. Allan Ramsay, 2 vols (Edinburgh, 1724), I, p. 15: 'The Thistle and the Rose, O'er Flowers and Herbage green, By Lady Nature chose, Brave King and lovely Queen'.

8 *The Poems of William Dunbar*, ed. Priscilla Bawcutt, 2 vols, ASLS 27, 28 (1998), I, lines 188–89 (B 52); *Ever Green*, ed. Ramsay, I, p. 26.

9 *Ancient Scottish Poems, Published from the Manuscript of George Bannatyne MDLXVIII*, ed. [David Dalrymple, Lord Hailes] (Edinburgh, [1770]), p. 7 ('Callt to my Muse, and for my subject chois / To sing the Ryel Thrissill and the Rose') and p. 226, note on stanza 27.

10 *Virgil's 'Æneid' Translated into Scottish Verse by Gavin Douglas*, ed. D. F. Coldwell, 4 vols, STS, 3rd ser. 25, 27, 28, 30 (Edinburgh, 1957–64), II, p. 37.

11 *Virgil's 'Æneid'*, ed. Coldwell, I, Glossary, *fift*, p. 310.

the son, of Hector.[12] Many years ago, when I discussed this and other misreadings,[13] I assumed that it was Coldwell who was responsible for mistranscribing the text. In one sense, this is true, but I now realize that he was over-influenced by two of his predecessors: George Dundas, who first published the Cambridge manuscript of the *Eneados* (Trinity College, MS O.3.12) in the Bannatyne Club edition of 1839,[14] and John Small in the 1874 edition of Douglas's works.[15]

I would never argue that we cannot learn much from past editors, many of whom were great scholars and achieved marvels, quite without the resources – dictionaries, indexes, computers – that today we take for granted. We cannot perpetually attempt to re-invent the wheel, but we should not read unthinkingly, or surrender our own critical judgements. I recall that one reviewer mocked the claim of Felicity Riddy and myself in *Longer Scottish Poems* to have 'freshly edited' each piece from the specified manuscript or print.[16] Why on earth, he implied, was it necessary to do that? But I also recall the stern command of my supervisor not to look at Craigie's edition of the Maitland Folio when I was working on *King Hart* for an MA thesis, and making my own transcript. This was a counsel of perfection, yet she was right. I was plunged in at the deep end, and learnt the hard way to cope with Scottish secretary. Along the way, however, I was able to make a few small discoveries, and in one or two places to correct Craigie's basically excellent transcript.[17] Editorial tradition is very powerful. Even when the manuscript is in front of one, it is all too easy to see it through the eyes of previous editors.

It is always worthwhile for any reader of Older Scots, but particularly an editor, to pause and reflect over oddities in words and passages. 'Every blur is a challenge …' Does the accepted reading of the text make sense? Does it fit the metrical or alliterative pattern? Might there be a different and better interpretation? Or is there a variant reading that would improve the sense? Such apparently isolated occurrences sometimes link with others, to form part of a much wider network or pattern – for example, the persistence in Scots poetic diction of ancient alliterative formulae, or the challenge to longstanding dogmas and beliefs by the Reformation.

---

[12] See *The 'Eneados': Gavin Douglas's Translation of Virgil's 'Aeneid'*, ed. Priscilla Bawcutt with Ian Cunningham, STS, 5th ser. 17 (Edinburgh, 2020), I, p. 71.

[13] 'Text and Context in Middle Scots Poetry', *Actes du 2e Colloque de Langue et de Littérature Ecossaises (Moyen Age et Renaissance)*, ed. Jean-Jacques Blanchot and Claude Graf (Strasbourg, 1978), pp. 26–33 (28).

[14] *The Æneid of Virgil Translated into Scottish Verse by Gawin Douglas Bishop of Dunkeld*, [ed. George Dundas], 2 vols, Bannatyne Club (Edinburgh, 1839), I, p. 39, line 6; II, p. vi, 39n: 'Pepill Hectorean, hardy as Hector, or of the kinrent and blude of Hector; for this Ascanyus was his fift son'.

[15] *The Poetical Works of Gavin Douglas*, ed. John Small, 4 vols (Edinburgh, 1874), II, p. 37, line 6; p. 290, note, '*P*. 37, *l*. 6. Pepill Hectorean, hardy as Hector, or of the kinrent and blude of Hector; for this Ascanyus was his fift son'.

[16] *Longer Scottish Poems: Volume One; 1375–1650*, ed. Priscilla Bawcutt and Felicity Riddy (Edinburgh, 1987), p. xxi; for the review (by Walter Scheps) see *Studies in Scottish Literature*, 24.1 (1989), 252–54 (254).

[17] *The Maitland Folio Manuscript*, ed. W. A. Craigie, 2 vols, STS, 2nd ser. 7 and 20 (Edinburgh, 1919, 1927); *The Shorter Poems of Gavin Douglas*, ed. Priscilla Bawcutt, STS, 5th ser. 2, 2nd edn (Edinburgh, 2003); see, for example, *King Hart*, notes to lines 29 and 47.

Let me give an example from a curious poem by Henryson, 'Sum Practysis of Medecyne', of which the Bannatyne manuscript preserves the sole copy.[18] Line 80 has regularly been transcribed as: 'I haif no come at this tyme langer to tary'. Long ago, I felt that there was something wrong with this line, and specifically with the word *come*. Although the first four words could be interpreted as 'I have not come', the sense of the whole line was clumsy and the alliteration defective. I suggested to Denton Fox that a far better reading here would be *tome* – this is perfectly possible palaeographically, it would fit alliteratively, and improves the sense considerably. Perhaps I should briefly digress on this word, which has nothing to do with modern English *tome*, 'book, volume', but means 'leisure, opportunity', and derives from ON *tóm* – it can be an advantage for Scottish editors to have studied Old Norse in their youth. The word commonly appears with a *u*-spelling, as in Douglas's *Palice of Honour*, 295, where it rhymes with *blume, dume* and *grume* (that is, Scots vowel no. 7). The line might be translated, 'I have no leisure at this time to tarry longer'. I use this illustration, because although Fox accepted my suggestion, and adopted it in his much reduced 1987 edition of Henryson,[19] it is not present in the full edition of 1981,[20] and so will not be known to many readers of Henryson.

Three copies exist of another substantial comic poem, usually known as 'Roull's Cursing'. Despite its considerable interest, this has received little attention, and only now is a scholarly edition in preparation by Janet Hadley Williams.[21] In the Bannatyne text of the poem, there is a tiny blur, apparently so trivial as to be meaningless.[22] At the beginning of line 79, the words 'Salbe' are deleted, a phenomenon apparently similar to other small deletions by Bannatyne elsewhere in this copy of the poem (for example in lines 36, 67 and 194). However, if one looks at the line's context in Bannatyne, and then compares it with the corresponding passage in the Maitland text of the poem, the deletion begins to look more significant than first appeared. Bannatyne has:

> Sua thay mak plane confessioun
> Thair gud will and contritioun
> Salbe Confessand þame to þair curatt ... (77–79)

Maitland has:

> Sua þai mak plane confessioun
> Than gud will and contritioun
> Salbe þair saulis remissioun
> That will schryf þame with þair curat ... (81–84)[23]

---

[18] NLS, Adv. MS 1.1.6, fols 141[V]–142[V].

[19] Robert Henryson, *The Poems*, ed. Denton Fox (Oxford, 1987).

[20] *The Poems of Robert Henryson*, ed. Denton Fox (Oxford, 1981).

[21] 'Devyne poware of michtis maist', in *'Duncane Laideus Testament' and Other Comic Poems in Older Scots*, ed. Janet Hadley Williams, STS, 5th ser. 15 (Edinburgh, 2016), pp. 57–73.

[22] This appears on fol. 105[r]; see *The Bannatyne Manuscript Writtin in Tyme of Pest 1568*, ed. W. Tod Ritchie, 4 vols, STS, 2nd ser. 22, 23 26, 3rd ser. 5 (Edinburgh, 1928–34), II, p. 279.

[23] *Maitland Folio*, ed. Craigie, I, p. 163.

B's deletion strongly suggests to me that his exemplar contained a line similar to MF's 'Salbe þair saulis remissioun.'

This passage is not wholly coherent in either witness, and we cannot be sure what the original contained, but Bannatyne seems to have been uneasy about its doctrinal implications. On the whole, the Scottish Reformers at this time were most exercised about the Mass and the intercessory role of the Virgin Mary. There is a fascinating example of this in the Bannatyne copy of the Moralitas to Henryson's 'Trial of the Fox', where we can see how he altered 'O Mary myld, medeator of mercy' to 'O lord eternall, medeator for ws mast meke' (*Fables*, 1139).[24] But penance was also a contentious issue for many Protestants, who rejected the stress laid by the medieval Church on the necessity for confession to be full and complete.[25] Remission, or salvation, proceeded from the sinner's faith in Christ's Passion, not from the words of a priest.

Behind Bannatyne's corrections of 'The Cursing', there seems a double anxiety, not only about the attribution of remission solely to the act of penance, but also about the word 'shrive' (note his preference for 'Confessand' in line 79). Elsewhere in the Bannatyne Manuscript, for instance, is a copy of Dunbar's 'Tabill of Confessioun'.[26] Here Bannatyne retains 'shrive' in rhyme position, but in some lines substitutes 'repent' (4) or 'confes' (25). The word 'shrive' practically ceased to be used in Scotland in the second half of the sixteenth century, largely because it was so strongly associated with papistry. It was a tarnished word, rather like 'Volk' and other German words that were so associated with Nazism that even today people seem reluctant to use them.

Let me turn to a rather different kind of textual 'blur' or puzzle from a fascinating poem in the *Liber Pluscardensis*: the 'Playnt', that is, complaint or lament, for Princess Margaret, dauphine of France and sister of James II. This is yet another neglected poem: the only critical study – as far as I know – is my own article concerning the discovery of its French source, published twenty years ago.[27] There still exists no modern edition,[28] and most readers probably encounter the poem in Felix J. Skene's edition of the *Liber Pluscardensis*.[29] My query concerns the nature of the very first word in the poem, which differs in Skene from that recorded in both the *Index of Middle English Verse* [*IMEV*][30] and *A New Index of Middle English Verse* [*NIMEV*],[31] item 3430: 'The michti Makar of the Major munde'. At this point, I must give a brief and highly simplified account of a complicated textual

[24] *Bannatyne Manuscript*, ed. Ritchie, IV, p. 181 (fol. 317ᵛ).

[25] For a useful exposition: *Poems of Dunbar*, ed. Bawcutt: *The Maner of Passyng to Confessioun*, I, pp. 136–38 (B 41).

[26] *Bannatyne Manuscript*, ed. Ritchie, II, pp. 42–47 (fols 17ᵛ–19ᵛ); *Poems of Dunbar*, ed. Bawcutt, I, pp. 267–73 (B 83).

[27] 'A Medieval Scottish Elegy and Its French Original', *Scottish Literary Journal*, 15.1 (1988), 5–13.

[28] For a recent annotated edition: *Six Scottish Courtly and Chivalric Poems, Including Lyndsay's 'Squyer Meldrum'*, ed. Rhiannon Purdie and Emily Wingfield (Kalamazoo, MI, 2018), pp. 33–72.

[29] Felix J. H. Skene, ed., *Liber Pluscardensis*, 2 vols (Edinburgh, 1877–78), I, pp. 382–88.

[30] Carleton Brown and Rossell Hope Robbins (New York, 1943).

[31] Julia Boffey and A. S. G. Edwards (London, 2005).

situation. The complete text of the poem survives in only two early manuscripts of the *Liber Pluscardensis*: Bodleian, Fairfax 8, 188ʳ–90ᵛ, which is usually dated 1489; and Brussels, Bibliothèque royale, 7396, 229ʳ–230ᵛ, dated before 1500. Skene chose a third manuscript as his text for the whole *Liber*, now in Glasgow's Mitchell Library 308876, because it was 'the most easy of access'.[32] This, unfortunately contained only the first two lines of the poem, so from line 3 onwards Skene's text is based on the Fairfax MS. As Skene indicates in not very clear textual notes, the Mitchell text of the poem begins with *He*; Fairfax begins with *Thee* – the first line runs, 'Thee myti makar of ye maior monde'; and the Brussels text (which I have not seen) is also said to begin with *The*.

What then is the editorial problem? Essentially, the syntactic relationship of the first line to the rest of the stanza. The stanza, as I see it, consists of one long rhetorical sentence: it is not a statement about God, the mighty maker, but an address to God, the first of a series of apostrophes or petitions to him, to *ger* (4), that is, 'cause', all sorts of things to happen. *He*, meaning 'high, lofty', makes excellent sense here – and this spelling for the word occurs elsewhere in line 191 of the poem – whereas it is surely difficult to find an appropriate sense for *The[e]*, whether one takes it as definite article or personal pronoun. There is confirmation for this interpretation in the French *Complainte pour la mort de Madame Marguerite d'Ecosse* that was the source for the Scots poem. It too begins by addressing 'Dieu' directly with a prayer: 'Faictes aux nues espuiser …' and so on.

Yet I still have some residual doubts, since the Mitchell text of the *Liber Pluscardensis* is said to be a copy of that in the Fairfax manuscript. Should one assume that its scribe, at this point, corrected his exemplar? A less important query is this: which text did the compilers of the *Index of Middle English Verse* use for their first line? One might have expected it to derive from the Fairfax manuscript, yet the spelling of some words is closer to that printed in Skene than Fairfax's 'Thee myti makar of the maior monde'. I have a suspicion that they used Skene, but perhaps misconstrued the neo-Gothic capital in *He*.[33]

A Brief Excursus on Annotation

Why did Johnson say that 'Notes are often necessary, but they are necessary evils'? Here is part of his typically forthright explanation:

> Let him, that is yet unacquainted with the powers of Shakespeare … read every play from the first scene to the last, with utter negligence of all his commentators … Let him read on through brightness and obscurity … let him preserve his comprehension of the dialogue and his interest in the fable. And when the pleasure of novelty have ceased, let him attempt exactness; and read the commentators.

---

[32] *Liber Pluscardensis*, ed. Skene, p. xviii.
[33] A printed representation of the decorative capital appears in *Liber Pluscardensis*, p. 382.

He continues:

> Particular passages are cleared by the notes, but the general effect of the work is weakened. The mind is refrigerated by interruption ... (61–62)[34]

I have sympathy with this view, much though I love to immerse myself in a copiously annotated edition, such as Denton Fox's *Henryson*. Turning aside to consult notes or a glossary may indeed destroy the excitement of first reading a poem or other literary work, and tend to 'refrigerate' the mind. Somewhat similar is the preference of many readers, at first acquaintance with a work, not to read the Introduction until the end.

Nonetheless notes are necessary, especially when dealing with a literature that is even more remote from us than Shakespeare; 'particular passages' must be 'cleared', or clarified.[35] But precisely what topics demand annotation has been interpreted very differently over the centuries. In an article entitled 'Why Editors Should Write More Notes', John Pitcher is scathing on the subject of 'editorial silences about Renaissance texts', and editorial 'indolence'.[36] I think he would approve of Denton Fox's remark in his Preface that he had not 'knowingly passed over any difficulties in silence', and Fox's apt quotation from Francis Bacon's *Advancement of Learning*: 'in Annotacions ... it is ouer usual to blaunch the obscure places and discourse vpon the playne'.[37] I leave to your own imagination what either Pitcher or Fox would have thought of Agnes Latham, editor of *The Poems of Sir Walter Raleigh*. In her brief note on the very obscure and fragmentary 'Ocean to Cynthia', she writes:

> I have not attempted to interpret difficult passages. ... The problems are simply problems of interpretation; matters for the most part upon which a reader prefers his own opinion to anyone else's. The meaning in several places is very dark and I cannot claim that I am more enlightened than another.[38]

If one looks back over the past at the practice of famous Scottish editors – I am thinking particularly of Allan Ramsay, Lord Hailes, David Laing – their editorial excisions and silences can be both amusing and tantalizing. Many concern sexual topics: thus Lord Hailes firmly announced that 'The Evergreen contains many indecent pieces which ought not to be explained'.[39] Sometimes, however, the absence of annotation derives not from the indecency of a passage, but from its very unfamiliarity to contemporary readers. What could be more infuriating to a modern editor than this comment by Lord Hailes on stanza 5 ('Sum castis swmmondis and sum exceppis') of Dunbar's 'Ane murelandis man of vplandis mak',[40] which he calls 'Tydingis fra the Sessioun'?

---

34 *Plays of Shakespeare*, ed. Johnson, I, pp. lxix–lxx.
35 *Plays of Shakespeare*, ed. Johnson, I, p. lxx.
36 *Shakespeare Studies*, 24 (1996), 55–62 (58, 61).
37 Francis Bacon, *The Tvvoo Bookes of Francis Bacon: Of the Proficience and Aduancement of Learning, Diuine and Human* (London, 1605), Book II, sig. Ss1 (69^{v}).
38 *The Poems of Sir Walter Ralegh*, ed. Agnes M. C. Latham (London, 1951), p. 127.
39 *Ancient Scottish Poems*, ed. [Lord Hailes], p. vi.
40 *Poems of Dunbar*, ed. Bawcutt, I, pp. 39–40 (B 2).

> This stanza will be both intelligible and entertaining to those who are acquainted with the forms of procedure in the court of session; to those who are not, a commentary would be nearly as obscure as the text.[41]

It is a commonplace that the needs and expectations of readers change over time. In the first half of the twentieth century, for instance, an editor could still take for granted that educated readers would have some acquaintance with the Bible and classical history and mythology, and would probably not need translations of quotations in Latin and French. This is clearly no longer the case. Modern editors also have their own personal tastes and preferences in their choice of what to annotate. In my edition of Dunbar, I attempted to 'clarify not only the literal sense of his words, but their connotations and figurative uses, as well as legalisms, poetic archaisms, proverbs, puns, and other wordplay'.[42] Not all editors, however, would necessarily share this interest in style and language.

Can one be prescriptive about what constitutes a good note? The basic task is to elucidate difficulties in the text, and to indicate an author's topical references and literary allusions. Beyond that, I find most impressive those editors who manage to be not only informative, but succinct; those who know the art of selection – one should never put in everything that one knows, only what is relevant – and those who are honest when there is no easy answer to a problem. If they highlight its existence, some later scholar may find the answer.

Pitfalls and Problems?

One of the most tricky problems for editors of many early Scottish texts is to date them. Very few poets give us as much information as does Gavin Douglas, and it is characteristic that this information about the *Eneados* is to be found in a kind of Epilogue to that work on 'the tyme, space and dait of the translatioun'. Yet prologues and epilogues and colophons are precisely the parts of a manuscript or print most exposed to wear and tear; in a number of Scottish works, possibly vital details about date or author or scribe have been lost in this way. The manuscript containing the metrical translation of Hector Boece's *Scotorum Historia* (Cambridge University Library, Kk.2.16) ends with what William Turnbull, its nineteenth-century editor, called a 'most infelicitous dilaceration'[43] – what could be more poignant than that proud but incomplete 'BE ME …'!'[44] In fact, immediately above the colophon, the date of the completion is given more fully as 29 September 1535, and other internal evidence suggests that the author was the poet William Stewart. In this particular case therefore the problem is less acute than first appears, yet much still remains to be done on dating the paper and the hand of this manuscript.

This is no trivial problem: most of us would like to know the order in which Dunbar composed his poems, and to learn whether Henryson's *Morall Fabillis*

---

[41] *Ancient Scottish Poems*, p. 248.
[42] *Poems of Dunbar*, ed. Bawcutt, I, p. ix.
[43] *The Buik of the Croniclis of Scotland; or A Metrical Version of the History of Hector Boece; by William Stewart*, ed. William B. Turnbull, 3 vols (London, 1858), I, p. vi.
[44] *Buik of the Croniclis*, III, p. 563.

preceded *The Testament of Cresseid*, or whether *The Goldyn Targe* exerted a stylistic influence on *The Palice of Honour*, or vice versa. Chronology is an important part of literary history. The problem occurs in all periods – and is not, of course, confined to Scottish writings – but it is particularly acute during the second half of the fifteenth century, a period exceptionally rich in poetry. To take a single example: we are still uncertain when the romance *Lancelot of the Laik* was composed. In the past, it was variously dated between 1460 and *c.* 1500; the researches of R. J. Lyall suggest that the paper of the manuscript that contains it (that is, section 7 of CUL Kk.1.5) should be dated between 1485 and 1490,[45] but I am not wholly confident that this helps much in dating the poem's composition. Establishing the date of *Lancelot of the Laik* has more than intrinsic value. It would be useful to those wishing to chart the introduction of the decasyllabic couplet to Scotland, and the development of the curious diction that has been termed 'Anglo-Scots'.

Any editor trying to date a Scottish poem in this period usually has to make a sensitive assessment of a range of factors: the date of the earliest witness (where this is known), topical allusions within the work, or mention of the work by other writers. To take 'Roull's Cursing', mentioned a little earlier. Was Roull indeed the author? Lord Hailes crisply commented: 'Whether written by him, or only in his name, I know not'.[46] If Roull was the author, as seems likely, he was one of the two makars of that name mentioned by Dunbar in 'I that in heill wes', and probably died before 1505. The poem itself also provides clues as to its date, the most useful of which is a reference to an 'Alexander' as the present pope (6–8). This was presumably the Borgia pope, Alexander VI (1492–1503). Slightly more debatable is the mention of 'grit glengoir' (63) – the earliest Scottish references to syphilis being from 1496 onwards.

Analysis of distinctive features of style and language perhaps holds out most hope for the future. Jack Aitken certainly was optimistic that careful study of the rhyme schemes of early Scottish poems, using what he called 'the method of rhyming sets', would help to answer questions of date and authorship.[47] The research of Keith Williamson into the historical dialectology of Older Scots also sounds extremely promising, but I am not sufficiently familiar with it to comment further.[48]

Some people, however, might regard the greatest problem facing editors of Scottish texts as the Scots language itself. The grammar and vocabulary of Older Scots are highly distinctive and can pose difficulties not only for experienced Middle English scholars but even for native speakers of Scots. One of the latter was recently floored

45 These dates were advanced by Professor Roderick J. Lyall in an unpublished paper, 'The Textual Tradition of *Lancelot of the Laik*', presented to the Glasgow University Medieval Group in 1978.

46 *Ancient Scottish Poems*, p. 272.

47 A. J. Aitken, 'Progress in Older Scots Philology', *Studies in Scottish Literature*, 26.1 (1991), 19–37 (22–23).

48 See K. Williamson, *A Linguistic Atlas of Older Scots*: LAOS, Phase 1, 1380–1500, University of Edinburgh (published online 2013); and Keith Williamson, '*DOST* and LAOS: A Caledonian Symbiosis?', in *Perspectives on the Older Scottish Tongue: A Celebration of DOST*, ed. Christian Kay and Margaret A. Mackay (Edinburgh, 2005), pp. 178–98.

by the idiom *bot and*, which he wished to emend to *both and*. *DOST* and *CSD* in fact record this expression as having the following senses: 'besides, as well as, and also'. Whether or not it survives in modern Scots I am not sure, but it was apparently still current a century ago, according to A. F. Mitchell's note on a line from the *Gude and Godlie Ballatis*: 'Christ thow art the lycht, bot and the day'.[49] This Scotticism seems still to linger about Dundee, as the following lines from a plaintive ballad published in the Dundee *Evening Telegraph* will show: 'My Jamie's gane afore me – he / My stey *but an'* my pride! …'

There is no need to demonstrate to an audience such as this how rich and varied is the vocabulary of Older Scots, and also how difficult it can be, particularly in the more colloquial registers. But it is depressing to see how little effort some critics or editors make to understand the literal sense of what they have read, giving no impression that they have consulted dictionaries or glossaries. I have lost count of the number of times that the Boar in *The Talis of the Fyve Bestes* has been interpreted as a bear – despite a vivid descriptive passage that mentions not only his bristly coat, but 'scheldis', and 'tuskis scharpe þat he with schure' (282–86).[50] Even the 'bair busteous' (401) in Henryson's 'The Cock and the Fox' sometimes metamorphoses into a bear.[51] Those who wish to know more should consult Regina Scheibe, who devoted twenty pages of her thesis to an exhaustive study of the topic.[52] I recall a critical article on Dunbar in which the poet's *panton* [soft shoes] was explained as 'pants' – this would cast new and distressing light on the line: 'He trippit quhill he tint his panton' ('Sir Ihon Sinclair begowthe to dance', 27, B 70). *Swan quhit*, a beautiful and poetic compound epithet for the ladies in Dunbar's *Tretis* (243, B 3), was taken by the same man to be an 'uncouth' verb, meaning 'drank deep', or even 'got drunk'. The most scandalous instance of such editorial ignorance, of course, occurs in the recent TEAMS edition of Dunbar by John Conlee – but I will refrain from repeating my remarks on the topic, since some of you heard them in Edinburgh.[53]

The root of the problem lies in the spelling of Older Scots. Many years ago, scholars such as Gregory Smith and H. Harvey Wood spoke of the 'uniformity in the practice of Middle Scots',[54] but A. J. Aitken put more stress on its variety and inconsistency. He

---

[49] *A Compendious Book of Godly and Spiritual Songs Commonly Known as 'The Gude and Godlie Ballatis'*, ed. A. F. Mitchell, STS, 1st ser. 39 (Edinburgh, 1897), p. 144: *Christe qui lux*, line 1.

[50] See *The Asloan Manuscript*, ed. W. A. Craigie, 2 vols, STS, 2nd ser. 14, 16 (Edinburgh, 1923–25), II, pp. 127–40 (fols 229ʳ–235ᵛ); and Priscilla Bawcutt, 'Bear or Boar in *The Tales of the Five Beasts*', *Scottish Literary Journal, Supplement*, 12 (1980), 11–12.

[51] See, for example, I. Carruthers, 'Henryson's Use of Aristotle and Priscian in the Moral Fables', *Actes du 2e Colloque de Langue et de Littérature Ecossaises (Moyen Age et Renaissance)*, ed. Jean-Jacques Blanchot and Claude Graf (Strasbourg, 1978), pp. 278–96 (279–80).

[52] Regina Scheibe, *A Catalogue of Amphibians and Reptiles in Older Scots Literature* (Frankfurt am Main, 1996), pp. 535–56.

[53] 'Editing William Dunbar: Some Afterthoughts on the Decade 1998–2008', in *Fresche fontanis: Studies in the Culture of Medieval and Early Modern Scotland*, ed. Janet Hadley Williams and J. Derrick McClure (Newcastle upon Tyne, 2013), pp. 115–25.

[54] G. Gregory Smith, *Specimens of Middle Scots* (Edinburgh, 1902), p. xi; *The Poems and Fables of Robert Henryson*, ed. H. Harvey Wood (Edinburgh, 1933), p. xxxi.

described its spelling system as 'a perhaps extreme example of a common medieval European type, in which free variation was a prominent and important feature';[55] he also noted that 'The dictionary record manifests this continuing tolerance of spelling variation – virtually every common Middle Scots word of more than one syllable possessed numerous alternative spellings'.[56]

Those long familiar with Scottish writing from this period eventually become used to this 'free variation'. But for newcomers to Scottish poetry or those who are merely ignorant, it clearly poses a great obstacle to understanding and enjoyment; and editors have a responsibility of removing – or lessening – that obstacle.

One further consequence of such variant spellings is that it necessitates an inordinate amount of cross-referencing with a Glossary, and therefore tends to increase the length of both the Glossary and the edition. This is particularly the case for an editor of Dunbar, whose poems are preserved in a number of different prints and manuscripts, whose dates straddle more than a century. To a limited extent, it would seem that some Scottish scribes and compositors had their own spelling systems.

To conclude on a more positive note, and pass from problems to prospects for the future. A number of interesting works are already in preparation for the Scottish Text Society. But I would like to call attention to other editorial projects that might appeal to bright young scholars. Here are some desiderata, in roughly chronological order.

The first originates in a suggestion once made to me by Sally Mapstone: that the STS should publish a volume entitled 'Poems of the Reign of James II'. The three envisaged are 'The Playnt for the Dauphine Margaret', accompanied, if possible, by the French *Complainte*; an important 'advice to princes' poem, sometimes known as *De regimine principum*, extant in several copies, including some manuscripts of the *Liber Pluscardensis*; and *The Buke of the Howlat*.[57] All three have great historical literary interest, yet none is easily accessible to modern readers in a good scholarly edition.

A less demanding task would be to re-edit *The Thre Prestis of Peblis*. The STS edition by T. D. Robb,[58] based on the Asloan manuscript and an imperfect copy of the Charteris print, is clearly unsatisfactory. A modern editor should be able to provide a better text, taking account of the more perfect copies of the print that were unknown to Robb, together with the fragment, Edinburgh, National Records of Scotland, MS RH 13/35.

A much more ambitious but desirable project concerns *The Contemplacioun of Synnaris*, the long devotional poem by William of Touris. This is extant in a Wynkyn de Worde print (1499), as well as several Scottish manuscripts. Although increasing attention has been paid to this work in the last fifty years, it is far from easy for

---

55 A. J. Aitken, 'Variation and Variety in Written Middle Scots', in *Edinburgh Studies in English and Scots*, ed. A. J. Aitken, Angus McIntosh and H. Pálsson (London, 1971), pp. 177–209 (181).

56 Aitken, 'Variation and Variety', p. 183.

57 This suggested project has been taken up in part. See the recent editions, Richard Holland, *The Buke of the Howlat*, ed. Ralph Hanna, STS, 5th ser. 12 (Woodbridge, 2014); and, for the 'The Playnt for the Dauphine Margaret', *Six Scottish Courtly and Chivalric Poems*, ed. Purdie and Wingfield, pp. 33–72.

58 *The Thre Prestis of Peblis*, ed. T. D. Robb, STS, 2nd ser. 8 (Edinburgh, 1920).

scholars to compare and evaluate the different versions of the text. Some form of parallel-text edition would be extremely valuable. The existence of a good edition might make *The Contemplacioun of Synnaris* better known, and perhaps counter English ignorance concerning its nationality – Norman Blake, Susan Powell and other respected scholars have taken the work to be English, presumably because we know only the Wynkyn de Worde print.[59]

A new edition of Rolland's *Court of Venus* is imperative: the 1884 edition by Walter Gregor, which is probably the worst ever to be published by the Scottish Text Society,[60] is full of ludicrous misreadings.[61] This is particularly sad, since the poem is much more accomplished than the pedestrian *Seuin Seages*.

Lastly, there is a case to be made for a parallel-text edition of Alexander Craig's *The Pilgrime and Heremite*, a romance printed posthumously in 1631. Fox went too far in calling it a 'pastiche' of the *Howlat*, but its use of alliterative metre is interesting. Michael Spiller has recently revealed the existence of a fascinating later manuscript copy (NLS, Adv. 35.4.14) – this apparently supplies the text where the print is defective, and contains lines that are much more strikingly alliterative than those in the print.[62]

Editorial Note

[a] This lecture, presented at the Conference on Scholarly Editing, De Montfort University, Leicester, 2008, is here published for the first time, by kind permission of Dr Nigel Bawcutt. Notes have been added by JHW.

---

[59] An edition by Alasdair A. MacDonald and J. Craig McDonald is to be published in 2022 by Brill.

[60] *Ane Treatise Callit the Court of Venus Deuidit into Four Buikis, Newly Compylit be Iohne Rolland in Dalkeith, 1575*, ed. Walter Gregor, STS, 1st ser. 3 (Edinburgh, 1884).

[61] See '"Mankit and Mutillait": The Text of John Rolland's *Court of Venus*' herein.

[62] See Michael R. G. Spiller, 'Found in the Forest: The Missing Leaves of Alexander Craig's *The Pilgrime and the Heremite*', in *Fresche fontanis: Studies in the Culture of Medieval and Early Modern Scotland*, ed. Janet Hadley Williams and J. Derrick McClure (Newcastle upon Tyne, 2013), pp. 377–94.

2

Source-Hunting: Some *Reulis* and *Cautelis*

I tell you, Captain, if you look in the maps of the 'orld, I warrant you sall find in the comparisons between Macedon and Monmouth, that the situations, look you, is both alike. There is a river in Macedon, and there is also moreover a river at Monmouth – it is called Wye at Monmouth, but it is out of my prains what is the name of the other river; but 'tis all one, 'tis alike as my fingers is to my fingers, and there is salmons in both.

William Shakespeare, Henry V, IV.vii.22ff.

I am using 'source-hunting' as a comprehensive label for the kind of scholarly activity that notes not only sources but echoes, influences, imitations, the resemblances, great or small, conscious or unconscious, between one literary work and another.[a] This type of study is sometimes regarded as inferior to other branches of literary scholarship that are more purely critical. I see no reason to despise it, however, particularly when it is allied to perceptive criticism. 'Source-hunting' in its widest sense provides us with maps – it helps chart the history of ideas, and follows the rise and fall of literary reputations; it can illuminate the taste of individual writers, and sometimes clarify their own writing. Middle Scots does not lack valuable studies of this kind. One of the pioneers was Janet M. Smith's *The French Background of Middle Scots Literature* (Edinburgh, 1934). In the last [86] two decades, we have seen articles on a host of topics; one of the most pertinent to the present paper is R. J. Lyall's 'Henryson and Boccaccio: A Problem in the Study of Sources', *Anglia*, 99 (1981), 38–59. There have also appeared two ambitious books: R. D. S. Jack's *The Italian Influence on Scottish Literature* (Edinburgh, 1972), and Gregory Kratzmann's *Anglo-Scots Literary Relations 1430–1550* (Cambridge, 1980).

The subject raises interesting aesthetic questions and is inter-linked with other issues, such as plagiarism or the nature of literary originality. Today, however, what primarily interests me is the question of proof. Kenneth Muir has wittily remarked that 'One man's parallel is another man's coincidence'.[b] The subjectivity of literary criticism is notorious, yet surely the branch of study is one where subjectivity should not reign, where facts should be sacred, where a possible influence should not be simply a matter of assertion, but a proposition, argued rationally and carefully scrutinized. Some recent studies, however, have been so lacking in rigour that they bring the subject into disrepute and tend to confirm those all too ready to think literary scholars woolly-minded.

Any perceptive reader will frequently be struck by resemblances between one work and another. The scholar, however, should not rest content with perceptions.

He plays the role of both detective and advocate. He has to investigate his case, test it to the best of his ability, and then persuade not a jury but *us*, the scholarly audience, of its credibility. Scholars have a responsibility both to their subject and their audience. They have a natural desire to present their case in the best light possible, but a duty to set out all the relevant evidence and not suppress awkward facts. The more obscure the postulated source, the more important it becomes to put one's audience in the picture: to 'place' the work in its literary milieu, to date it, even to give its approximate length. (Such information should be less necessary, if one [87] is dealing with well-known authors.) Again, if we suggest a borrowing from a foreign author, we should surely quote in the original language, as well as supplying a translation for the 'lewed'.

What steps can one take to validate a hunch? I have no magic touchstone, but suggest that one turns oneself into a sceptic and asks a few questions:

1.   Do we know definitely that one work preceded another? This chiefly affects authors who are close contemporaries and has bedevilled discussion of the relationship between Dunbar and Douglas. There are stylistic resemblances between *The Goldyn Targe* and *The Palice of Honour*, but we still do not know which was the earlier poem.

2.   The second question is an offshoot from the first: even if there is a century or more between two poets, can we assume that the works of the former were easily accessible to the latter? An illustration is afforded by Burns and Dunbar. Burns's fragmentary *The Night was still* (Kinsley, no. 133) contains a slight verbal similarity to Dunbar's 'Off benefice, Sir, at everie feist' (Kinsley, no. 40).[1] But Dunbar's poem was not in print till 1786 (in John Pinkerton, *Ancient Scotish Poems* [(London), I, pp. 104–05, 'Quha nathing hes can get nathing']), the year when Burns's poem is thought to have been composed. I suspect the resemblance is coincidental. The case is different with Burns's *Poem on Life* (Kinsley, no. 517); there seems an echo of *The Lament for the Makars* ['I that in heill wes and gladnes'] in these lines on 'Dame Life' (15–18):

> Oh! flickering, feeble and unsicker
>   I've found her still,
> Ay wavering like the willow wicker,
>   'Tween good and ill.

Dunbar's poem purports to be written in sickness and fear of death; Burns's poem belongs to 1796, when he was indeed dying, 'Surrounded thus by bolus pills / And potion glasses' (5–6). We know that *The Lament for the Makars* was easily available not only in Ramsay's *Evergreen* of 1724 [88] but in other eighteenth-century editions. The probability thus seems very much higher that Burns is here recalling Dunbar.

---

[1]   References are to *Burns: Poems and Songs*, ed. James Kinsley (Oxford, 1969), and *The Poems of William Dunbar*, ed. James Kinsley (Oxford, 1979).

3.   A further and related question: is there any evidence, outside the given poem, that one poet was acquainted with the work of another? We know, for instance, that Burns was deeply moved by the eighteenth-century version of *The Wallace*. In his letters, he often quotes from English poets, he refers to Gavin Douglas, but does he ever mention Dunbar?

4.   How plausible is the suggested borrowing? Some years ago, an article was published that alleged that Keats's *Ode on a Grecian Urn* was indebted to Douglas's *Palice of Honour*.[2] Even if the parallels were convincing – which they are not – is there not something inherently improbable in this suggestion? More interesting is the resemblance between the opening lines of *The Palice of Honour*, which speak of pale Aurora and 'Hir russat mantill borderit all with sable', and Horatio's speech in *Hamlet* (I.i.166):

> But look the morn in russet mantle clad
> Walks o'er the dew of yon high eastern hill …

I should like to think that Shakespeare found Douglas worth imitating, but it seems unlikely, despite the sixteenth-century prints of *The Palice*, one indeed of which was published in Fleet Street. Dawn descriptions formed a poetic topos of great antiquity, and Douglas and Shakespeare, writing in the same tradition, may have used the same phrase quite independently.

The next questions are the fundamental ones.

5.   Do the resemblances really exist? This may seem absurd, but sometimes – as with Keats and Douglas – it is less a case of 'there is salmons in both' than 'there is salmon in one, and a herring in the other'.

6.   If the resemblances exist, can they be more plausibly [89] accounted for by joint indebtedness to a common source?

7.   If the resemblances exist, are they significant? By this, I mean: are they so distinctive that they can only be accounted for by imitation, or some form of borrowing from a specific source? Here I will invoke an 'auctoritee', whose name is well known, though not in this connection. Discussing a related issue, P. G. Wodehouse says:

> The best plagiarism story I know was the one Guy Bolton told me about Owen Davis, the American playwright. He had a show on in New York, a melodrama, and a tailor claimed that it was stolen from a play which he – the tailor – had dashed off in the intervals of tailoring. Davis got together with him, and asked him just what he based his accusation on. The tailor said his play was about a man accused of murder and all the time he was innocent, and so was Davis's. Davis then took him round to some of the other plays

---

[2]   James A. S. McPeek, 'Keats and *The Palice of Honour*', *Philological Quarterly*, 27 (1948), 273–76.

running on Broadway at the moment – *The Crimson Alibi, At 9.45, The Sign
on the Door*, etc. – and pointed out that these too were about men accused of
murder and by golly in the end they turn out not to have done it after all. But
you can't down an author with evidence of that sort. 'They've ALL stolen my
play!' was his only comment.

Performing Flea (Harmondsworth, 1953), p. 154

This anecdote – possibly apocryphal – illustrates clichés of plot or theme. Any
well-informed scholar must be aware of the parallels to this in the medieval and
Renaissance period: the topos, the folk-tale motif, the conventional cluster of ideas.
It must be conceded that one poet's handling of a topos is sometimes so masterly
that it seems to dominate later writers. I'm thinking of Chaucer's use of the 'Go, little
book' theme, or his pastoral image of the 'lytel herde-gromes / That kepen bestis in
the bromes' (*House of Fame*, 1225–26). This couplet bobs up again and again in later
poets as diverse as Lydgate, Douglas and Spenser.[3]

Wodehouse tells another funny story, involving clichés of a verbal kind. Twentieth-
century readers should [**90**] have no difficulty recognizing twentieth-century clichés.
But the further back in time we go, the more difficult it becomes to spot the commonplace. Words and phrases often seem striking and distinctive to us today that would
not have had the same effect on their first audience. Some modern scholars, for
instance, have argued that Henryson's tale of *The Two Mice* influenced Wyatt's telling
of the same fable in one of his Satires.[4] The evidence for this seems pretty thin, but
one of their arguments is that Wyatt's mice, like Henryson's, cry *pepe*. Nowadays we
expect mice to squeak, and *pepe* or *peep* seems strange and therefore significant.
But, as far as I can see, during the fifteenth and sixteenth centuries, in both Scots
and English, *peep* was the normal word for the thin cry of a small animal or bird:
'Polwart, 3e peip like a mouse amongst thornes' (Montgomerie, *Flyting*, 1).[c] Indeed,
if Wyatt and Henryson had both made their mice squeak, it would in this period
have been verbally more unusual and perhaps more conclusive.

As a general rule, we should examine the nature of verbal similarities very
carefully before jumping to conclusions. Medievalists in particular should be aware
of the futility of using as evidence various kinds of stock phrase: common similes;
rhyme-tags, asseverations, like 'the sooth to say'; inclusive formulae, like 'al and sum';
emotional intensifiers, like 'pity was to see'. All these – along with common proverbs
or biblical quotations – help to characterize a style, and are evidence that two authors
are writing in a shared tradition, but nothing more.

Any hint of alliteration should put one on the alert, and suggest the possibility of
a formula, the common property of many poets. The alliterative tradition was alive
and flourishing in Scotland, well into the sixteenth century. Here, too, a phrase not
familiar today – like *tait and trig*, which is found in both Henryson (*Fables*, [**91**]

---

3 See lines 417–19 of the 'Compleynt', which appears in some manuscripts of Lydgate's
   Temple of Glas; Douglas, *Eneados*, VII.Prol.77–78; Spenser, *Shepheardes Calendar*,
   February, 35–36.
4 [See *Sir Thomas Wyatt: Collected Poems*, ed. Joost Daalder (Oxford, 1975), pp. 104–08,
   Satire 2; l. 42]; Kratzmann, *Anglo-Scottish Literary Relationships*, p. 103; cf. P. Thomson,
   Sir Thomas Wyatt and his Background (Stanford, 1964), p. 266.

1410) and Douglas (*Eneados*, XII.Prol.184) – may be a false clue as to influence. In Douglas's Prologue XII, there is another alliterative line: 'Swannys swouchis throw out the rysp and redis' (152). It has recently been pointed out that in *The Goldyn Targe* (56) there occurs a similar phrase, *rispis and redis*, 'sedges and reeds'.[5] Prologue XII is a mosaic of literary allusions, and it is not implausible that Douglas might mingle echoes of Dunbar along with Chaucer and Ovid. But weighed against this is the formulaic nature of both halves of his line: swans 'swouch' or make a rustling noise in *The Howlat* (171); and the phrase *risp and redis* occurs elsewhere in the *Eneados*, where the likelihood of Dunbar's influence seems low.

Even at the other end of the linguistic spectrum – the learned and Latinate – we cannot assume that what is unusual today was so in the past. Let me take an example from *The Palice of Honour*. The dreamer hears approach the procession of Minerva, 'Quhilk mouit fra the plague septentrionall' (195). The striking phrase, *plague septentrionall* does not refer to the Black Death nor to a Scottish seaside resort, but simply means the north. Now the same phrase also occurs in Lyndsay's *Testament of the Papyngo* (751). I used to assume that Lyndsay had filched this aureate phrase from Douglas, whom he knew and admired. But this now seems unlikely, because the phrase is found in medieval Latin, in writers as diverse as Alexander Neckam and Boccaccio. *Plague septentrionall* appears to be a technical and scientific term, signifying either the northern quarter of the heavens or the northern zone of the earth. As such, it would be familiar to both Douglas and Lyndsay, and they probably adopted it quite independently. The case is rather different with this echo of Douglas in a poem by Hugh MacDiarmid addressed to F. G. Scott: [**92**]

> Can ratt-rime and ragments o' quenry
> And recoll of Gilha' requite
> Your faburdoun, figuration and gemmell,
> And pricksang's delight?

The musical terms are today so unusual that I would argue that MacDiarmid probably derived them ultimately from the passage on music in *The Palice of Honour*, 500–01. (Even here, I cautiously say 'ultimately', as Dr Ruth McQuillan has suggested that MacDiarmid's immediate source may have been an entry in Jamieson's Dictionary.)[d]

To all those interested in this subject, I would recommend certain basic precautions. Check the currency of a word or phrase in the relevant dictionaries, not only in *DOST* but also in *OED*, *MED* and *SND*. Even Jamieson – though sometimes inaccurate – clearly still has his uses. If a passage has a sententious flavour, check dictionaries of proverbs and proverbial phrases. Particularly useful for this period are M. P. Tilley's *A Dictionary of the Proverbs in England in the Sixteenth and Seventeenth Centuries* (Ann Arbor, 1950), and [B. J. and H. W.] Whiting's *Proverbs, Sentences, and Proverbial Phrases … before 1500* (Cambridge, MA, 1968); to which should be added [B. J.] Whiting's two articles on Scottish proverbs in *Medieval Studies*, 11 and 13 (1949, 1951). For common alliterative formulae, the best repository

5   A. K. Nitecki, 'A Note on Dunbar and Douglas', *Notes and Queries*, 27.5 (1980), 389–90.

is probably still J. P. Oakden's *Alliterative Poetry in Middle English: A Survey of the Traditions* (Manchester, 1935). Much can also be learnt about a poet's stylistic habits from the judicious use of concordances and glossaries. Yet, in the last resort, nothing is a substitute for wide reading and an informed memory. If you have not noticed that *flouris quhite and reid* (see *Goldyn Targe*, 12) appear again and again ... and *again* in medieval descriptions of spring, no index, glossary or dictionary will ever help you.

I now wish to discuss some possible examples of indebtedness in greater detail. [**93**]

1. Henryson, *Orpheus and Eurydice*, 401–07.

> Quhat art thou lufe? How sall I the dyffyne?
> Bitter and suete, cruel and merciable;
> Plesand to sum, til othir playnt and pyne;
> To sum constant, till othir variabill;
> Hard is thy law, thi bandis vnbrekable;
> Quha seruis the, thouch he be newir sa trewe,
> Perchance sum tyme he sall haue cause to rew.

In the course of an erudite article, 'Neoplatonism and Orphism in Fifteenth-Century Scotland' (*Scottish Studies*, 20 (1976), 68–89), Professor J. MacQueen has argued that these lines have a specific 'source' (85) in the Italian philosopher, Marsilio Ficino. He calls attention to a passage from Ficino's commentary on Plato's *Symposium*, which he quotes in the following translation:

> Do not let the fact that Orpheus has sung about the bitter afflictions of lovers trouble you. Listen carefully, I beg you, to the way in which these troubles are to be borne, and in which these lovers are to be helped. Plato calls Love bitter, not unjustly, because everyone dies who loves. For this reason Orpheus too calls Love γλυκυπτκρον, that is sweet and bitter. Insofar as Love is a voluntary death, as death it is bitter, as voluntary sweet. But anyone who loves, dies.
>
> *De Amore*, II.viii

Now the sole idea common to both passages is that love is simultaneously bitter and sweet. Is this idea such a rarity? It is surely one of the established paradoxes about love, expressed by many medieval poets: Henryson himself in *The Testament of Cresseid*, 234ff.; Douglas in *Eneados*, Prologue IV; and Gower in *Confessio Amantis*, VIII.190–91: 'For al such time of love is lore / And lich unto the bitterswete ...' The question of availability also raises itself. How easily could Henryson have procured this work of Ficino's? According to MacQueen, it was 'published in 1469'. But the textual history of the *Symposium*-commentary is complicated: although it seems to have originated in 1469, it did not assume definitive shape till 1482, and could not have circulated widely until the first printed edition, Florence, 1484.[6] We [**94**]

---

6 Marsile Ficin, *Commentaire sur le Banquet de Platon*, ed. R. Marcel (Paris, 1956), pp. 114ff.

still do not know the precise date of Henryson's *Orpheus* either. In an area of such uncertainty, I cannot accept that this brief passage furnishes convincing proof of Henryson's acquaintance with Ficino.

Rather than seeking a definite source for these lines, it might be better to relate them to a topos, which could be given the title of Marvell's poem, 'The Definition of Love'. Notice Henryson's use of the verb, *dyffyne* (401), and his opening question. Rosemond Tuve has discussed several sixteenth-century English songs, which open similarly.[7] Examples are the poem from *The Phoenix Nest*, sometimes attributed to Raleigh, 'Now what is Love, I praie thee tell?'; Greene's 'Ah, what is love?'; and Lodge's 'I'll teach thee, lovely Phillis, what love is ...' But we can trace the theme much earlier in time, and further afield than Britain. There is, for instance, a definition of love by Mellin de Saint-Gelais, a poem that opens rather like Henryson's: 'Qu'est-ce qu'Amour? Est-ce une deité ... ?'[8] There is Petrarch's sonnet 132, which appears – somewhat altered – as the *Canticus Troili* in *Troilus and Criseyde*, I, 400–20. Perhaps the beginning of the tradition, as so often, can be traced to *Le Roman de la Rose*, to the section where the Lover explicitly asks Reason to 'define' love. Reason delivers a long exposition of its paradoxical nature:

> Here of love discriptioun,
> Love it is an hateful pees ...
> Delit richt ful of hevynesse ...
> Bitter swetnesse and swet errour ...
> *Romaunt*, 4727ff.

Thematically, the ironic attitude to love that Henryson voices in this stanza resembles that of Reason in the *Roman*. Structurally, the affinities with lyric are interesting, since this stanza is an inset song, as was Orpheus's earlier lament for Eurydice, which it is clearly designed to recall. [95]

2.   In volume 8 of *Studies in Scottish Literature* (1970–71), 215–27, R. D. S. Jack has published an article, 'Dunbar and Lydgate', which – among other things – argues that an English poem, *Reson and Sensuallyte*, was the 'basic model' for Dunbar's *Goldyn Targe*. This article has been influential, as we may see from allusions to it in G. Kratzmann's recent book and Kinsley's edition of Dunbar. I do not find it wholly convincing, however, and think it should be challenged before its contentions become an established part of literary history.

What is known of *Reson and Sensuallyte*? It is hardly a favourite, even with medievalists. First, it is not an original work but a translation of a French poem, *Les Echecs Amoureux*. Secondly, Lydgate's authorship is by no means established – it derives, like the title, from the late authority of John Stow, a sixteenth-century antiquary, whose statements are not always trustworthy.[9] If anonymous, this poem would not have had

---

7   Rosemond Tuve, *Elizabethan and Metaphysical Imagery* (Chicago, 1947), p. 302.
8   See further, Frank Kermode, 'Definitions of Love', *Review of English Studies*, 7.26 (1956), 183–87.
9   See the edition, *Lydgate's Reson and Sensuallyte*, ed. E. Sieper, 2 vols, EETS, ES, 84, 89 (Oxford, 1901, 1903); also Derek Pearsall, *John Lydgate* (London, 1970), p. 79.

the prestige of Lydgate's name; nor would the fact that Dunbar mentions Lydgate at the end of *The Goldyn Targe* have any relevance. Thirdly, only one medieval manuscript of *Reson and Sensuallyte* survives, although there seems no doubt that it was composed before Dunbar's time. There is no evidence that it was well known, perhaps because it is incomplete – one hesitates to apply the term 'fragmentary' to a work over 7,000 lines long. This contrasts with the obvious popularity in Scotland of such poems by Lydgate as *The Complaint of the Black Knight*. Such facts do not necessarily rule out Dunbar's knowledge of *Reson and Sensuallyte*, but they raise an initial doubt.

It is clearly impossible here to discuss every aspect of this article. I will single out three important assertions, the first of which is that Dunbar's conception of Nature derives from *Reson and Sensuallyte*. We are told that both poets 'highlight Nature as procreation' [**96**] (p. 223) and depict her as a ruler of creation and intermediary with God. In *Reson and Sensuallyte*, Nature harangues the poet-dreamer, and her appearance – including a remarkable mantle – is described in great detail. In *The Goldyn Targe*, lines 87–90 are devoted to a gown, which – so we are told – Dunbar's Nature hands to Venus; this is held to imply 'that Nature at this point abdicates her control over all animals to Love, thus anticipating the psychomachia' (pp. 223–24).

Before proceeding, fact should be disentangled from fiction. Nowhere in *The Goldyn Targe* does Dunbar use language of a highly philosophical kind to describe Nature. What is more, Dunbar's Nature presents a gown not to Venus but to a personified May. The *significatio* cannot be that Nature abdicates to Love, but is more commonplace: in May, natural processes cause the drab earth to become colourful with flowers. Later, at line 251, this is called Nature's 'anamalyng'. Nature is often associated with Spring as the creator of flowers in medieval French poems – she has been called 'an item in a conventional formula'[10] – and other poets link Nature and Flora, or speak of Nature's 'tapestries'.[11]

To return to the point at issue: was Dunbar's Nature influenced by the portrait in *Reson and Sensuallyte*? Throughout the medieval period, Nature was enormously important, as a philosophical concept and as a personification. Whether as *princeps*, goddess, queen or empress, she appears in poets as varied as Statius and Claudian, Jean de Meun and Charles d'Orléans, Holland and Douglas. It seems lacking in rigour to single out one source for Dunbar's Nature without mentioning this complex background or referring to the abundant scholarly discussion, above all, without mentioning that key document, Alain de Lille's *Complaint of Nature*. This twelfth-century work is the undoubted source for the portrait of Nature in *Reson* [**97**] *and Sensuallyte*; when Chaucer and Spenser mention the dress of Nature, they too refer us to the striking description in Alain.[12] Indeed the curious modern reader still cannot do better than follow Spenser's advice: 'Go seek he out that Alane where he may be sought' (*Mutabilitie Cantos*, vii.9). Nature makes such a fleeting appearance

---

[10] E. C. Knowlton, 'Nature in Old French', *Modern Philology*, 20.3 (1922), 309–29 (310); see also his 'Nature in Middle English', *Journal of English and Germanic Philology*, 20.2 (1921), 186–207.

[11] Lydgate, *Black Knight*, 50–52; Douglas, *Palice of Honour*, 20; *Eneados*, XII.Prol.102; Lyndsay, *Monarche*, 179–80.

[12] *Alan of Lille: The Plaint of Nature*, trans. and commentary James J. Sheridan (Toronto, 1980), Prose I, pp. 85ff.

in *The Goldyn Targe* that I doubt whether one can identify a 'source'. But if one had to choose, *The Complaint of Nature* has this in its favour that it seems to have enjoyed something of a vogue in the Middle Ages: over one hundred manuscripts survive, half of which belong to the fifteenth century.[13]

In the opening section of *The Goldyn Targe* (50–53), there is a brilliant piece of metonymy: the dreamer sees not a ship but

> A saill als quhite as blossum upon spray,
> Wyth merse of gold brycht as the stern of day,
> Quhilk tendit to the land full lustily,
> As falcoune swift desyrouse of hir pray.

This is vivid on its own, but even more striking in context: after the static opening, it is dynamic, packed with the natural imagery paradoxically missing from the description of real-life nature. Above all, the falcon simile contains an explicit threat: this ship has the beauty of a warship. It is proposed [by Jack] that the idea of the ship may have originated in Lydgate (p. 224); we are referred to the passage in *Reson and Sensuallyte* where the poet, marvelling at the world's beauty, sees tidal rivers: 'Somme so myghty and so large / To bere a gret ship or a barge' (943–44). This is *all*. The poet proceeds to speak of many other things, but there is no further mention of the ship; it is simply an attribute of the rivers, implicitly a merchant ship, unvisualized, unallegorical, playing no further part in the poem. Is the very idea of a ship such a rarity in medieval poetry that we can be impressed by this argument? Is it not a case of 'there is ships in both'? [**98**]

Dunbar devotes several stanzas (lines 55–90) to the disembarkation of one hundred ladies, or goddesses. We are told that it is 'incontestable … that the idea of the ship, followed by the list of goddesses originates from a reading of Lydgate' (p. 224). R. J. Lyall, in an important study of *The Goldyn Targe*, accepts this proposition, although he disputes other points: he speaks of Dunbar's allegory being indebted to Lydgate's, and says that 'classical gaffes and a number of other details are easily accounted for if Dunbar was following the catalogue of goddesses in Lydgate's poem, but not always reading accurately'.[14] What then does this catalogue contain? At line 1021, Lydgate's dreamer sees approach *three* 'ladyes of gret apparaille'; but it should be noted that they have no connection with the ship, mentioned some eighty lines earlier. Approximately six hundred lines are devoted to describing Pallas, Juno and Venus, together with their guide, Mercury. The dreamer is clearly re-enacting the Judgment of Paris, and he makes the same choice. This then is Lydgate's list – by the standards of the Lord High Executioner it does not seem much of a list! Pallas, Juno and Venus do indeed appear in Dunbar, but they are not exactly rare figures. What then of the so-called errors, which are held to arise from a misreading of *Reson and Sensuallyte* – the inclusion of Apollo among otherwise female deities, and the doubling of Pallas and Minerva? I am reluctant to attribute stupidity to the razor-sharp Dunbar. But in any case there seems a flaw in the logic. Imagine that

---

[13] G. Raynaud de Lage, *Alain de Lille: Poète du XIIe Siècle* (Montreal and Paris, 1951), p. 34.
[14] R. J. Lyall, 'Moral Allegory in Dunbar's *Goldyn Targe*', *Studies in Scottish Literature*, II.I (1973), 47–65 (49).

Dunbar told us that 2+2 = 5, whereas Lydgate told us 2+2 = 4. Should we therefore conclude that Dunbar made a mistake in his sums because – and only because – he was copying from Lydgate and misread 4 as 5? The proposition is absurd. In *Reson and Sensuallyte*, we are told that Pallas was sometimes given the name of Minerva, but the same information is found in other late medieval authors. As for Apollo, I find no mention of the name in this [**99**] passage of *Reson and Sensuallyte*, although there is a reference to Phoebus. If we consider that Dunbar got his mythology wrong, there is no need to hold Lydgate responsible. (There are indeed puzzles in this stanza, but it is possible to devise other solutions for them.)

As a corrective to undue preoccupation with Chaucer and his influence, 'Dunbar and Lydgate' is undoubtedly valuable; but the case for Dunbar's knowledge of *Reson and Sensuallyte* remains non-proven.

3.　　I wish now to turn to a sonnet by William Drummond:

> Now while the Night her sable vaile hath spred,
> And silently her restie coach doth rolle,
> Rowsing with her from Tethis azure bed
> Those starrie Nymphes which dance about the pole;
> While Cynthia, in purest cipres cled,
> The Latmian shepheard in a trance descries,
> And whiles lookes pale from hight of all the skies,
> Whiles dyes her beauties in a bashfull red;
> While Sleepe (in triumph) closed hath all eyes,
> And birds and beastes a silence sweet doe keepe,
> And Proteus monstrous people in the deepe
> The winds and waues (husht vp) to rest entise,
> I wake, muse, weepe, and who my heart hath slaine
> See still before me to augment my paine.
>
> Sonnet 8, ed. Kastner, I, 7

Drummond's editor, L. E. Kastner, and the scholar Ruth Wallerstein,[15] thought that the poem originated in Petrarch, but this view has been challenged by R. D. S. Jack in his 'Drummond of Hawthornden: The Major Scottish Sources', *Studies in Scottish Literature*, 6.1 (1968), 36–46: 'Kastner is wrong in seeing Drummond's sonnet as an amplification of the octet in Petrarch's "Or che 'l cielo [sic] e la terra e 'l vento tace". It is clearly a close rendering of one of Fowler's best sonnets ...' (39)[16]

I find this conclusion debatable, and should like to re-examine the evidence: [**100**]

> The day is done, the Sunn doth ells declyne,
> Night now approaches and the Moone appeares,

---

[15] [*Poetical Works of William Drummond of Hawthornden with 'A Cypresse Grove'*, ed. L. E. Kastner, 2 vols, STS, 2nd ser. 3, 4 (Edinburgh, 1913), I, p. 7]; Ruth Wallerstein, 'The Style of Drummond of Hawthornden in Its Relation to His Translations', *PMLA*, 48.4 (1933), 1090–1107.

[16] See also Jack, *Italian Influence*, p. 115.

> The tuinkling starrs in the firmament dois schyne,
> Decoring with the pooles there circled spheres;
> The birds to nests, wyld beasts to denns reteirs,
> The mouing leafes vnmoued now repose,
> Dew dropps dois fall, the portraicts of my teares,
> The wawes within the seas theme calmly close.
> To all things Nature ordour dois impose,
> Bot not to Love that proudlye dothe me thrall,
> Quha all the dayes and night, but chainge or choyse,
> Steirs vp the coales of fyre vnto my fall,
> And sawes his breirs and thornes within my hart,
> The fruits quhairoff ar doole, greiff, grones and smart.
>
> Fowler, The Tarantula of Love, sonnet 22

> Or che 'l ciel e la terra e 'l vento tace
> e le fere e gli augelli il sonno affrena,
> Notte il carro stellato in giro mena,
> e nel suo letto il mar senz'onda giace,
> vegghio, penso, ardo, piango; e chi mi sface
> sempre m'e inanzi per mia dolce pena.
>
> Petrarch, sonnet, In vita, 164, 1–6

How can one possibly call the Drummond sonnet 'a close rendering' of Fowler's? The resemblances are highly general in kind, and demonstrate that both poets were familiar with a stock sonnet theme: that night brings peace and quiet to all but the sleepless lover. The theme can be traced back to the sleepless misery of Dido in Virgil's *Aeneid* (IV.522–28). Indeed, it is the differences between Fowler and Drummond that strike me most forcibly: Drummond's decorative use of myth and personification has no parallel in Fowler; and where in Fowler is the tormenting vision of his mistress that forms the climax to Drummond's poem? Petrarch's sonnet was well known – there is a translation of it by the Earl of Surrey – and if we look at its first six lines, we find more convincing resemblances to Drummond, for example:

1. The suspended syntax of 'Now while the Night …' recalls Petrarch's opening line.

2. There is a similar use of personification: Night rolls her coach in Drummond; in Petrarch, she drives a *carro* [101] *stellato*.

3. Perhaps most persuasive is Drummond's final couplet, with its rather awkward and unidiomatic translation of Petrarch's lines 5–6.

I do not for a moment deny Drummond's acquaintance with Fowler's poetry or the possibility that he may have been influenced by him; what I cannot accept is that this sonnet provides proof of such a relationship.

4.

> Into that Park did properlie appeir,
> Richt trimlie trottand into trowpis and twais,   100
> The wilde quhite cullourit ky and falow deir,
> With brawland bowkis, bendand ouir the brais,
> The flingand fownis, followand dune dais:
> Sa curage causit beistis mak besines,
> His Maiestie muifand to merines.   105
>
> Bot to behald it was ane perfite joy,
> And as ane eirdlie plesand paradice:
> To heir and se, thair at the Kingis conuoy,
> The merle and maweis changeing notes nice,
> The kiddis skippand with rais throw the rice   110
> Quhair birdis blyithlie on the branches sang,
> With sic ane reird, quhill all the rokkis rang.
>
> Swa, schortlie, throw sic heuinlie harmoneis,
> Become richt coy, heiring the fowlis sing,
> Baith Eolus and Neptune, god of seis,   115
> Behalding fast the cumming of that King,
> Quhilk was sa welcum vnto euerie thing.
> Quhat misteris mair? The goldspinkis war sa glaid,
> Culd thai haif spokin, doutles thai had said:
> Welcum maist maikles mirrour and A per se   120
> With euerie princelie prerogatiue possest;
> Welcum worschip, vertew and honestie …

This passage comes from a short poem, called *The Promine*.[17] It was printed in 1580 (by Charteris), and the title page says that it was 'directit' to James VI 'be P. H. familiar seruitour to his Maiestie'. P. H. is generally taken to be Patrick Hume of Polwart, Montgomerie's antagonist in *The Flyting*, and elder brother of the slightly better-known Alexander Hume. The poem celebrates the king's 'first passing to the feildis' on 12 [**102**] June 1579, when James (born 19 June 1566) was a boy of nearly thirteen. To modern taste, the poem seems a piece of gross flattery, but in that turbulent period the occasion it celebrates has more significance than we might realize. For his own safety, the young king had spent most of his life in Stirling Castle; but now, according to the contemporary memoir attributed to David Moysie,

> Vpoune the tuelt day of Junij at fyve houris in the morning, the king past furth at the yet in the nether bailye, and returnit at sevin houris from the perk to the castle … this was the first tyme the king come furthe to the

---

[17] For a text of *The Promine*, see *The Poems of Alexander Hume*, ed. Alexander Lawson, STS, 1st ser. 48 (Edinburgh, 1902), Appendix F, pp. 204–05.

feildis accumpanied only with his owin domestickis. [The last phrase has been glossed as 'without the protection of an armed guard'.][18]

Most readers will be struck by the poem's florid style, which recalls Lyndsay at his most aureate. Indeed, in *The Flyting* (112–13), Montgomerie makes precisely such a charge against Polwart: 'Thy scrows obscure are borrowed fra some buike, / Fra Lindesaye thou tooke; thourt Chaucers cuike.' It is Gavin Douglas, however, to whom this piece is most strikingly indebted. It is largely a rechauffée of phrases and lines from *Eneados*, Prologue XII – rewriting Montgomerie, one might call Polwart 'Douglas's cuike'.

Some illustrations may be given. In Polwart, we are told that the sun at dawn 'Spred furth his purpour springis aureat' (65); in Prologue XII, the sun 'Sched purpour sprangis with gold and asur ment' (22). In Polwart, the dew distils 'on vapouris sweit as sence' (70); Douglas too has 'Mysty vapour vpspryngand, sweit as sens' (44) – it should be noted, however, that 'sweet as incense' is semi-proverbial. Sometimes Polwart goes further. Douglas has a grandiloquent couplet about the scents of flowers rising 'By myghty Phebus operations, / In sappy subtell exhalations' (139–40). Polwart takes this over, but inserts a line of his own in order to adapt it to rhyme royal (72–74): [**103**]

> Quhill throw his michtie operatiounis,
> Furth of fresch fludes, bet with buriall bemis,
> Rais sappie, subtil exhalatiounis.

A similar process may be observed in lines 103 and 110, quoted above. Altering the rhyme, these split up a single couplet from Douglas (181–82):

> The ȝong fownys followand the dun days,
> Kyddis skippand throw ronnys efter rays.

Polwart's lines 116–17 take over, almost verbatim, another couplet from Douglas (273–74):

> And to behald the cummyng of this kyng,
> That was sa welcum tyll all warldly thyng.

I cannot note here all the small phrases for which one may find parallels in Prologue XII.[19] I will simply mention the way in which Polwart's birds salute the king with their repeated 'Welcum' (120ff.). This too derives from Douglas's account of the dawn chorus (XII.Prol.252–66). But there are interesting differences. Douglas, with

---

18 David Moysie, *Memoirs of the Affairs of Scotland*, [ed. James Dennistoun], Bannatyne Club (Edinburgh, 1830), p. 22; see also E. Stair-Kerr, *Stirling Castle* (Stirling, 1928), pp. 92–93.

19 Some smaller parallels may be noted: 'Natures tapestreis' (84); cf. XII.Prol.102; 'dewie perllis round' (85); cf. XII.Prol.134; 'freklit flouris' (89); cf. XII.Prol.112; 'changeing notes nice' (109); cf. XII.Prol.238.

characteristic fouth, says 'Welcome' fourteen times; Polwart tones this down to five. Again, Polwart – with his 'Culd thai haif spokin' – is far more self-conscious about his talking birds than Douglas.

As far as I know, the relationship between these poems has not been pointed out before. It seems to have a twofold interest. First, although Polwart is negligible as a poet, he clearly understood the drift of Douglas's Prologue and shows some wit in what he did with it. His poem is, in effect, an inversion of Douglas's: Douglas celebrates the sun as if it were a monarch in triumph, but Polwart celebrates an actual king as if he were the sun. This is perhaps one reason why his piece does not work as well as Douglas's: hyperbole seems less acceptable when addressed to a *roi-soleil* than to the sun itself. Secondly, it makes a tiny contribution to the map of Scottish literary history, giving higher definition to a [**104**] rather shadowy area. Even in the second half of the sixteenth century, Douglas was still being read and imitated.

I have ended back in Stirling and with James VI. This is appropriate, since the source of my title will be clear. James's *Reulis and Cautelis* was published when he was only eighteen, and one of his biographers calls it – unkindly but not unfairly – 'a schoolboy's essay, expounding with amusing gravity the most obvious matters'.[20] There is a risk then that such a title will rebound upon my head. But sometimes the most obvious matters need to be emphatically re-stated, even to a learned audience. It may be that this paper has seemed at times negative, censorious, and over-critical. If so, may I quote in my defence this medieval aphorism:

An error not repressed is half sustained!
(Whiting, E 145).

Editorial Notes

a This essay, presented in 1981 at the Third International Conference on Scottish Language and Literature (Medieval and Renaissance), University of Stirling, was first published in *Proceedings of the Third International Conference*, ed. Roderick J. Lyall and Felicity Riddy (Stirling/Glasgow, 1981), pp. 85–105. It is reprinted here with the kind permission of the Department of Scottish Literature, University of Glasgow.
b For his full discussion (but not the exact remark), see Kenneth Muir, *The Sources of Shakespeare's Plays* (London, 1977), especially 'Introduction', pp. 1–13.
c *Poems of Alexander Montgomerie: Supplementary Volume*, ed. George Stevenson, STS, 1st ser. 59 (Edinburgh, 1910).
d See further, Ruth McQuillan, 'MacDiarmid's Other Dictionary', *Lines Review*, 66 (1978), 5–14.

[20] D. H. Willson, *King James VI and I* (London, 1956; rpt 1963), p. 60.

3

Elrich Fantasyis in Dunbar and Other Poets

The term *elrich* (or *eldritch*) has been applied by several critics to a type or tradition of comic poetry.[a] Referring specifically to medieval Scottish poetry, C. S. Lewis used phrases like 'eldritch material' and 'eldritch humour', and spoke of the 'eldritch audacity which likes to play with ideas that would ordinarily excite fear or reverence'.[1] A few years later, Muriel Bradbrook tried to place *Dr Faustus* within an 'eldritch' tradition that she defined, in part, as 'horrific jesting'.[2] What does *elrich* mean? Etymology offers no help, since the word appears from nowhere in a way that is appropriately mysterious; the first recorded occurrences are in Dunbar and Douglas. But a word's meaning consists in its use: throughout the sixteenth century, Scottish writers applied *elrich* to 'browneis' and 'bogillis', to Pluto and to the Cyclops and the 'weird sisteris', to angels and also to elves (with whom some etymological link has been posited), to the fairy queen and to the desolate places inhabited by ghosts and demons. In the measured words of *The Scottish National Dictionary*, it is used 'to denote some connection with the supernatural'; modern glosses like 'uncanny', 'weird' or 'spooky' perhaps give an idea of its connotations. The word usually carries some implications of fear, as in Douglas's splendid line on the owl: 'Vgsum to heir was hir wild elrich screke' (*Eneados*, VII.Prol.108); the witches in *Tam O'Shanter* utter a similarly 'eldritch screech'. Disapproving critics of Virgil, according to Douglas, found Book VI of the *Aeneid* pervaded by the elrich:

> 'All is bot gaistis and elrich fantasyis,
> Of browneis and of bogillis ful this buke:
> Owt on thir wandrand speritis, wow!' thou cryis;
> 'It semys a man war mangit, tharon list luke,
> Lyke dremys or dotage in the monys cruke,
> Vayn superstitionys aganyst our richt beleve.'
> *Eneados*, VI.Prol.17–22

It was far from easy, in the sixteenth century, to distinguish true Christian belief from superstition or delusive *fantasyis*, the figments of the imagination that sometimes resulted from dreams or lunacy.

---

[1] C. S. Lewis, *English Literature in the Sixteenth Century Excluding Drama* (Oxford, 1954), pp. 71, 72–73.
[2] Muriel Bradbrook, 'Marlowe's *Doctor Faustus* and the Eldritch Tradition', in *The Artist and Society in Shakespeare's England* (London, 1982), pp. 79–86.

I find the phrase 'elrich fantasyis' a useful label for a small group of humorous poems, preserved chiefly in the Bannatyne Manu[163]script, that have won praise from a few critics but are for the most part ignored. Two are attributed to poets of whom we know virtually nothing but their names – Lichtoun's *Dreme* and Rowll's *Cursing*. But most are anonymous – *Fergus Gaist*, *The Crying of Ane Play*, *Kind Kittok*, *The Gyre Carling*, *King Berdok*, *The First Helandman*, and *Colkelbie Sow*.[3] Little is known definitely about the composition date of these poems. It is probable that they belong to the last decades of the fifteenth or the early decades of the sixteenth century. They are metrically and linguistically inventive, the work of educated poets, some perhaps, like Dunbar, clerics. They seem popular in appeal, but not in origin. They have some resemblance to another group in the Bannatyne: the 'ballatis of unpossibiliteis', sometimes known as lying-poems. But they should be distinguished from the better-known comic poems, such as *The Freiris of Berwick* and *The Wife of Auchtermuchty*, which belong to a basically realistic mode: despite much comic exaggeration, these deal with everyday life in a factual, rational way. In the fantasies, however, although the setting is usually close to home – often in Fife or the Lothians – our sense of place is rapidly shattered. We are disoriented when familiar names, such as Cramond, Haddington, North Berwick, are strangely coupled with remote or imaginary ones. Kittok finds an ale-house just outside the gates of heaven. We are transported to a dreamworld, to an underworld (in *The Cursing*), always to an otherworld. In Lichtoun's *Dreme*, the poet dreams that he is 'tane' by the 'king of farye' (6), and lost for seven years (56). Kittok's adventures start when she comes to 'ane elriche well' (8). Such magic wells are often found in folk-tales, and, according to Juliette Wood, seem to function in Scottish and Irish tradition 'as the extreme limit of the known world'.[4] These poems are peopled with strange creatures: dwarfs and giants, elves, fairies, etins and demons. In one poem, God and St Peter come to earth and take a walk in Argyle; in another, the gyre carling, an ogress, marries Mahomet; and in a third, the offspring of Fergus's ghost and 'the Spenȝie fle' are Orpheus and queen 'Elpha' (*Fergus*, 87, 93). Each of these poems narrates a series of bizarre events, or 'farleis' (*Dreme*, 46); *Fergus Gaist* is introduced as a 'verry grit mervell' (2). They bring together ingredients from many sources: Celtic, Germanic and classical mythology, Arthurian romance, preachers' tales, and a repertory of popular stories, which are mostly lost but to which there exist tantalizing references

---

3 Some of these poems are also extant in prints and in the Maitland Folio. As a group, they are most easily consulted in *The Bannatyne Manuscript*, ed. W. Tod Ritchie, 4 vols, STS, 2nd ser. 22–23, 26; 3rd ser. 5 (1928–34). For bibliographical information, see the facsimile edition, *The Bannatyne Manuscript: National Library of Scotland Advocates' MS 1.1.6*, introd. Denton Fox and William A. Ringler (London, 1980), nos 165, 168, 176, 182, 197, 1977, 208, 230 and 401. See also *Colkelbie Sow* and *The Talis of the Fyve Bestes*, ed. Gregory Kratzmann (New York, 1983); Earl Guy, 'Some Comic and Burlesque Poems in Two Sixteenth-Century Manuscript Anthologies' (PhD dissertation, Edinburgh, 1952) [and, for editions of seven, *'Duncane Laideus Testament' and Other Comic Poems in Older Scots*, ed. Janet Hadley Williams, STS, 5th ser. 15 (Edinburgh, 2016)].
4 'Lakes and Wells: Mediation between the Worlds in Scottish Folklore', in *Scottish Language and Literature, Medieval and Renaissance*, ed. Dietrich Strauss and Horst Drescher, Scottish Studies, 4 (Frankfurt, 1986), pp. 523–32 (526).

in *Colkelbie Sow* and *The Complaynt of Scotland*. But these poets should not lose the credit for a vivid imagination. Enoch and Ely are discovered in paradise:

> Sittand on ȝule evin in ane fresche grene schaw
> Rostand straberries at ane fyre of snaw.
> Lichtoun, *Dreme*, 41–42

King Berdok lodges in summer in 'ane bowkaill stok', but in winter in 'a cokkill schell' (6, 8). Kittok overtakes a newt riding on a snail:

> Scho cryd ourtane fallow haill haill
> And raid ane inch behind the taill.
> *Kind Kittok*, 11–12

[**164**] Other poets give us not this miniature world, but a Scotland created by giants' farts and pisses. Yet *The Crying* swings from such gross Rabelaisian comedy to the romantic image of a giant standing on tiptoe, in order to

> tak the starnis doun with his hand
> And sett thame in a gold garland
> Aboif his wyvis hair.
> *Crying*, 38–40

Most of these poems are included in Bannatyne's 'mirrie ballatis', and are undoubtedly humorous. Unlike some great ballads or *Sir Gawain and the Green Knight*, they do not draw us far into an enchanted world, and invite us to suspend our powers of disbelief. *The Dreme* voices the common-sense view: this 'fantasie' may spring from the consumption of too much ale. Although they are not strictly 'ballatis of vnpossibiliteis', a genre that seems to have developed from the ancient topos of *adynata* or *impossibilia*, their comic method is similar: to pile up impossibilities, absurd juxtapositions, bizarre incongruities. In the *adynaton*, however, absurdity is purposeful, and in its late medieval form anti-feminist: only when Aberdeen and Ayr are both one town, or with historical irony 'Inglische tungis translaitit are in grew [Greek]', will women in general or 'Scho quhome I luve' in particular ever be true and constant.[5] But these fantasies seem to delight in nonsense for its own sake. One is reminded of nursery rhymes, or, fleetingly, of Edward Lear. But we should not forget that there exist medieval parallels: the marginal grotesques and 'droleries' in Gothic manuscripts, for instance, or humorous English poems, such as *The Land of Cockaygne*, a group of fantastic carols, and a tale of 'marvels' that includes a church service entirely conducted by fish, in which the salmon sings the

5 See *Bannatyne Manuscript*, ed. Ritchie, IV, pp. 42–43, lines 3, 13 and refrain. There has been copious discussion of the figure *adynaton* – see articles by H. V. Canter, 'The Figure AΔynaton in Greek and Latin Poetry', *American Journal of Philology*, 51.2 (1930), 32–41, and Galen O. Rowe, 'The Adynaton as a Stylistic Device', *American Journal of Philology*, 86.4 (1965), 387–96.

high mass, and the herring is his clerk.[6] There is no doubt that some of these comic poems contain elements of parody or burlesque. *The Cursing* is a spoof-cursing of those who stole five fat geese, 'With caponis henis and vthir fowlis' (14). *Fergus* is essentially a mock-conjuration of a troublesome ghost, 'with paternoster patter patter' (20). *The Gyre Carling* certainly makes comic use of romance themes: its hero, who is strangely besotted with the monstrous ogress, bleeds not blood but 'ane quart / Off milk pottage' (10–11), and besieges her tower with an army of moles – presumably they are good at tunnelling. *The First Helandman* makes a blasphemous allusion to Genesis, obscenely mimicking the creation of Adam the first man, from the dust of the earth. But such burlesque is mostly intermittent. With the exception of *Kittok* and *The First Helandman*, which are short and neat, these poems ramble and drift in an inconsequential way. Most of their readers will recall vivid lines or images, but I suspect that I am not alone in finding it difficult to remember which poem they come from. In the words of *Colkebie Sow*, they pile 'caisis upoun caisis' (54), and we may well feel that their authors intended 'to bourd' but 'left it in a blondir' (46). What is also striking is their pervasive geniality: the humour is remarkably good-tempered. This is true not only of *Kittok* but even of *The First Helandman*; both play jocularly rather than caustically with stereotypes – [165]woman as a drunkard, the Highlander as an incorrigible thief.

In the past, several of these were attributed to Dunbar and even included in editions of his poems. But there is no early evidence that he wrote any of them – suggestions to this effect are sheer wishful thinking. Occasional similarities of phrase and rhyme-scheme are susceptible of several explanations; and any discussion of influence is impeded by the difficulty of dating all these poems, Dunbar's included. Nonetheless, I am sure that Dunbar was acquainted with some of these comic poems, or with others like them. A few were definitely circulating in Dunbar's lifetime – *Kittok*, for instance, appeared in an early print (*c.* 1509), along with *The Tua Mariit Wemen and the Wedo*. What is more, he seems to have known some version of *Colkelbie Sow*: he refers to the 'Golk of Maryland', heroine of *King Berdok*; and he mentions two poets by the name of 'Roull', one of whom is the presumed author of *The Cursing*.[7] Dunbar shared the same imaginative heritage as these poets, and wrote for a similar audience; he was equally at home in the comic mode of elrich fantasy.

But Dunbar differs from most of them in two important respects. He is a dynamic poet, and his poems do not drift but drive onward, vigorously and purposefully – towards some climax, some disaster, some epigrammatic 'point'. Whatever the absurdity, Dunbar is in control: the elrich is harnessed and put to some purpose, though this is not always or primarily a moral one. But there is an even more striking

---

6 See further Lilian M. C. Randall, *Images in the Margins of Gothic Manuscripts* (Berkeley, CA, 1966); *The Land of Cokaygne*, in *Early Middle English Verse and Prose*, ed. J. A. W. Bennett and G. V. Smithers (Oxford, 1968; rev. ed. 1977), pp. 136–44; *The Early English Carols*, ed. Richard Leighton Greene (Oxford, 1935; 2nd edn 1977), nos 471–74; and the poem beginning 'Herkyn to my tale that I schall to yow schew', in *Reliquiae Antiquae*, ed. Thomas Wright and J. O. Halliwell (London, 1845), I, pp. 1–86.

7 See *The Poems of William Dunbar*, ed. James Kinsley (Oxford, 1979), nos 44 ['Schir, ȝe haue mony servitouris', 66]; 13 ['In secreit place this hindir nycht', 51]; and 62 ['I that in heill wes and gladnes', 77–78].

difference. Dunbar's characteristic tone is not genial, but dark and sinister; we are told that God laughed 'his hairt sair' (21) at Kittok's exploits, as also at the Highlander (*First Helandman*, 11), but in Dunbar's poems the only laughter (apart from the poet's) is that of devils (*Fasternis Eve in in Hell* (K 52), 29 and *Renunce thy God* (K 56), 39). It is not faerie that predominates in his comic poems, but diablerie. (In this respect, the closest parallels are found in Rowll's *Cursing* and Montgomerie's *Flyting*.) C. S. Lewis noted how often in Dunbar 'the comic overlaps with the demoniac and the terrifying'.[8] There is a striking ambivalence in his response to the devil: the superficially flippant and irreverent tone of some poems co-exists with a sombre and more fearful response. At the opening of *The Flyting*, Dunbar threatens Kennedy with appalling consequences and vows to 'rais the Feynd with flytting' (23):

> The erd sould trymbill, the firmament sould schaik,
> And all the air in vennaum suddane stink,
> And all the divillis of hell for redour quaik,
> To heir quhat I suld wryt with pen and ynk ...
> (K 23), 9–12

This is mock-apocalyptic, a vaunt far out of proportion to the ostensible subject. It is comic yet has an intensity that derives from the very solemnity with which hell, damnation and the devil were normally spoken of – not only by others but by Dunbar himself. No reader is disposed to laugh at the menacing figure of the devil in Dunbar's poem on the Resurrection – dragon, cruel serpent, and 'auld kene tegir with his teith on char' [*Surrexit Dominus de sepulchro*], (K 4) 11.

Dunbar's ambivalence had deep and complex roots. He and his contemporaries combined an intense interest in the world of evil [**166**] spirits with great uncertainty about their nature and mode of operation. At every level, learned and popular, they were supplied with abundant but conflicting information. When Robert Burton questioned 'how far the power of spirits and devils doth extend', he drew much of his material from medieval philosophers and theologians.[9] At a more popular level, the imagination was fed in a variety of ways, visually and verbally: in wall-paintings, sculptured capitals, or the woodcuts in prints of the *Ars Moriendi* that showed fiends waiting to seize the soul of a dying man; in sermons, in saints' lives, such as *The Golden Legend*, and dramatic representations of the Fall of Lucifer or the Harrowing of Hell. It is tantalizing to read only the title of the 'ludum de Bellyale' that took place in Aberdeen in 1471.[10] Devils were incorporeal, yet could assume many forms. By the late medieval period, a demonic iconography had evolved that is still familiar. Dunbar was not alone in speaking of 'devillis als blak as pik' [*Renunce thy God*], (K 56), 81 – in their true ugliness, devils were characterized by blackness and deformity. They were depicted with horns and hooves, and sometimes with feathers and wings – we should recall this when reading of the flying abbot of Tungland, and the birds' belief that he may be 'the hornit howle' (*Ane Ballat of the Fenʒeit Freir of Tungland*

---

8   *English Literature*, p. 94.
9   Robert Burton, *The Anatomy of Melancholy* (London, 1932), ['A Digression of the Nature of Spirits, Bad Angels, or Devils, and How They Cause Melancholy'], I.2.1.2. = I, pp. 180ff.
10   Anna Jean Mill, *Mediaeval Plays in Scotland* (Edinburgh, 1927), p. 117.

(K 54), 74). Devils could swell in size to giants and shrink small enough to sit under a lettuce leaf. Devils could assume the shape of animals: Henryson gives the name 'Bawsie Broun' to a dog (*Fables*, 546), but Dunbar gives it to a fiend (*Fasternis Evin* (K 52), 30). This produces a curiously double effect. It might seem reductive, yet it also instils suspicion of everyday creatures, as the special sense of 'familiar' indicates – devils might lurk in the shape of family pets.

The multitudinousness of devils was stressed, along with their ubiquity. Picturesque similes were sought in an effort to convey this. One medieval preacher said that they 'flye above in the eyer as thyke as motis in the sonne'; the analogy recurs in Chaucer and Rowll. Burton quoted learned authors to the same effect: '[T]he air is not so full of flies in summer as it is at all times of invisible devils.'[11] It is within this tradition that Dunbar writes of devils '[s]olistand … as beis thik' (*Renunce thy God* (K 56), 82). The world of devils bordered closely on that of ghosts and fairies, and also oddly paralleled that of the angelic hierarchies. Some believed that there existed nine orders of bad spirits, the first of which comprised the false gods of the Gentiles.[12] Douglas thus equated Pluto with Satan, 'Prynce in that dolorus den of wo and pane' (*Eneados*, VI.Prol.151). Dunbar, however, in *The Goldyn Targe* (K 10), 125, calls Pluto an 'elrich incubus'. This seems to fuse god, demon and fairy, recalling Pluto's rape of Proserpina as well as his medieval identification with the king of faerie. Although most devils were nameless, some acquired names and distinctive personalities. Rowll speaks of 'Devetinus the devill that maid the dyce' (98); his *Cursing* provides a useful compendium of the devil-lore likely to have been familiar to Dunbar. The 'Sanct Girnega' of *The Turnament* (K 52B), 164 thus appears as a devil in *The Cursing* (95), and may have survived in the Scottish children's rhyme concerning 'Girnigo Gibbie, the cat's guid minnie' (see *SND*, *Girnigo*, *n.* and *adj.*). Perhaps the most famous medieval devil was Tutivillus, who appears as a character [**167**] in the Towneley Judgement play and the morality *Mankind*. He is often depicted with a sack or in the act of writing, sometimes recording evil words, sometimes recording female gossip.[13] Kennedy includes Tutivillus among the clan of devilish relations he devises for Dunbar at the end of *The Flyting* (K 23), 513; all designed to lead to the taunt 'Tu es dyabolus' (544), and the final line that consigns Dunbar to hell.

Plenty of medieval jokes exist about the devils and hell. There is an excellent French tale of a minstrel who was carried to hell. One day, he was left in charge of the lost souls and gambled them away in a game of dice with St Peter. Lucifer was so enraged that he threw the minstrel out – and consequently to heaven – and commanded his subordinate devils to bring no more minstrels and gamblers to hell. The tale ends: 'Now cheer up, all you minstrels, rogues, lechers and gamblers, for the one who lost those souls at dice has set you all free!' This is a specimen of a

11 See G. R. Owst, *Literature and Pulpit in Medieval England* (Oxford, 1933; 2nd edn, 1961), p. 112; *The Wife of Bath's Tale* (*Canterbury Tales*, III (D), 868), ironically applied to friars; *Bannatyne Manuscript*, ed. Tod Ritchie, II, p. 280; *Anatomy of Melancholy*, I, pp. 188 and 183.

12 *Anatomy of Melancholy*, I, p. 187. But see discussion in Aquinas, *Summa Theologica*, trans. the Fathers of the English Dominican Province (London, 1922), I.cix, 'The Ordering of the Bad Angels'.

13 The fullest study is Margaret Jennings, 'Tutivillus: The Literary Career of the Recording Demon', *Studies in Philology*, 74 (1977), 1–95.

recurrent folk-joke: why are there no members of a given group (for example, job or nationality) in hell? Why no weavers? Because the devils find their noise intolerable. Welshmen are excluded from heaven for a similar reason.[14] Dunbar alludes to stories of this kind, I think, at the end of *The Dance of the Sevin Deadly Sins*: he intends a double insult in keeping minstrels out of hell and in consigning highland entertainers to its deepest abyss. Some saints' lives show a reluctant admiration for the devil as a clever trickster, rather like the fox in the beast fables. Devils are sometimes subtle and wily; at other times, they dwindle into imps or the 'deblats' who attended upon the St Nicholas bishop; or they degenerate into the clowns and buffoons who bluster and make coarse jokes in medieval drama. Medieval devils were by turns sinister and ridiculous, figures of fear and figures of fun. Jean Frappier sought deep psychological explanations for this pervasive late medieval mockery: it was an unavowed means of escape from a very real and otherwise almost unbearable fear, a defensive weapon against 'le terrorisme du Diable'. He drew a parallel with the behaviour of 'gens qui ont peur, la nuit, au coin d'un bois, et veulent se rassurer, cherchent a rendre leur crainte irréelle en plaisantant, en prenant un petit ton guilleret, en se racontant des histoires droles'.[15] Perhaps we should not seek one single explanation for such varied phenomena, nor even find them astonishing. Black comedy and a perverse delight in playing with fire are not confined to the Middle Ages. Nor is it only children who enjoy what the Opies call 'ghoulism' and 'spookies'.[b] The latent horror is what contributes a comic 'frisson' to many a joke.

Some of Dunbar's most potent comic imagery involves ghosts and evil spirits. At the end of *The Dance*, the Highlanders are summoned:

> Thae tarmegantis with tag and tatter
> Full lowd in Ersche begowth to clatter
> And rowp lyk revin and ruke.
> *Fasternis Evin in Hell* (K 52A), 115–17

To gloss *tarmegantis* as 'blustering bullies' [as Kinsley did] is not wholly adequate. The Scots may not have been aware that *Termagant* was originally a name given to a god of the Saracens in the romances, but [**168**] they clearly knew its diabolic associations – both Henryson and Kennedy use the word as a name for devils. I would also like to revive an old discarded suggestion that Dunbar is making a punning reference to the ptarmigan, whose earliest recorded spellings (at the end of the sixteenth century) coincide with *termagant*. The habitat of the bird is confined, appropriately, to the highlands; and Dunbar's phrase, 'clatter / And rowp lyk revin and ruke' (116–17), is not dissimilar to a modern naturalist's account of the ptarmigan's cry as a 'hoarse croak, with a crackling note'.[16] Dunbar wickedly depicts Highlanders as

---

[14] See *Medieval Comic Tales*, trans. Peter Rickard et al. (Cambridge, 1972), pp. 19–25; Stith Thompson, *Motif-Index of Folk Literature*, 6 vols (Helsinki, 1955), X.251.1; *Medieval Comic Tales* (from a Jestbook of 1526), pp. 55–56.

[15] 'Châtiments infernaux et peur du diable', in *Histoire, Mythe et Symboles* (Geneva, 1976), pp. 129–36.

[16] See the useful discussions of both words in *OED*; also R. S. R. Fitter, *Pocket Guide to British Birds* (London, 1952), p. 73.

half-devils, half-birds. Even more effective is a passage in *The Flyting* (K 23), 161–72, which portrays Kennedy as a Lazarus, returned from the grave as a grisly *memento mori*. Dunbar pretends to exorcise him – 'I conjure the, thow hungert heland gaist' (168) – and ends by comparing Kennedy to 'the spreit of Gy' (172), the central figure in a popular ghost story, known all over Western Europe. The tale was highly didactic, purporting to give information about purgatory and the afterlife. Normally the ghost is invisible, manifesting itself only by speech and an uncanny sound, like that of a broom sweeping the pavement. But Dunbar alludes to the ghost's appearance, which suggests that he may have seen some acted version. Lyndsay, after all, amused the young James V by dressing up as the 'greislie gaist of gye' (*Dreme*, 16).[17]

In *The Tua Mariit Wemen and the Wedo*, the Widow calls her last husband an 'evill spreit' (K 14), 397, but earlier in the poem is an even more striking passage, in which the First Wife recalls her husband's love-making:

> Bot quhen that glowrand gaist grippis me about
> Than think I hiddowus Mahowne hes me in armes.
> Thair ma na sanyne me save fra that auld sathane,
> For thocht I croce me all cleine fra the croun doun
> He wil my corse all beclip and clap me to his breist.
> …
> The luf blenkis of that bogill fra his blerde ene
> As Belȝebub had one me blent abasit my spreit.
> (K 14), 100–04, 111–12

This husband is a shape-shifter: first a ghost, then different manifestations of the devil, lastly a 'bogill' who resembles Beelzebub. Dunbar suggests both the husband's ugliness and the wife's fear and repulsion. She speaks as if she were trying to ward off the embraces of an incubus. The 'ugsome' and the comic are deftly combined in this elrich passage.

Five of Dunbar's poems are pervaded by diablerie: *Renunce thy God, How Dunbar wes Desyrd to be ane Freir, The Ballat of the Abbot of Tungland, The Antechrist,* and *Fasternis Evin in Hell*. All are bad dreams, or nightmares. A dream is an excellent frame for comic fantasy: the constraints of the waking world are absent, yet not totally abolished – they lurk on the margins of the dream. At the same time, a dream's status is ambiguous – dreams provoke questions about their source, significance and truth, voiced by many medieval poets including Dunbar: [**169**]

> Than thocht I thus, This is ane felloun phary,
> Or ellis my witt rycht woundrouslie dois varie;
> This seimes to me ane guidlie companie
> And gif it be ane feindlie fantasie
> Defend me, Ihesu and his moder Marie!
> *Ane Dreme* (K 51), 11–15

---

[17] There are at least three versions of the story in English, as well as in other languages; it was clearly well known in Scotland (see also *Crying of ane Play*, 14).

Many dreams had religious significance (such as Dunbar's concerning Christ's Passion), but others might indeed be 'feindlie fantasie' or diabolic illusion. Innocent III warned that dreams caused many to go astray, and Aquinas said that although a demon could not directly sway a man's reason, he could incline the inferior faculties, such as imagination or the corporeal senses.[18] But other dreams might be sheer nonsense: this common-sense attitude is voiced by Douglas, somewhat ironically, at the end of Prologue VIII: 'Thys was bot faynt [feigned] fantasy ... / Nevir word of verite' (175–76). Despite sharing a similar framework, these poems have Dunbar's characteristic variety. The prominence of the dreamer differs considerably: in *How Dunbar wes Desyrd to be ane Freir* (K 55), he is at the centre of the poem; in *Renunce thy God* (K 56), he is marginal, simply the ironic recorder of what he sees and hears. Our awareness of the poem as a dream also varies. It is strongly felt in *Fasternis Evin*, to which the solemn word *trance* is twice applied, at beginning and end. In *The Antechrist* (K 53), phrases like 'ane dremyng and a fantesy' (10) and 'my dreme it wes so nyce' (41) direct us more explicitly than do some other poems to ponder how reliable and trustworthy this dream may be. But in *Renunce thy God*, although the opening lines of both versions imply that it is a dream, the dreamer almost fades from our consciousness, and when the poem ends he is still apparently asleep. This is unusual since most of Dunbar's dream poems have abrupt, even explosive, endings. But there are so many problems about this poem's text that we should perhaps beware of seeking deep significance in this failure to wake up.

Criticism of *Renunce thy God* has been scanty, and usually depreciative. It tends to be regarded as a piece of social satire, criticizing the corrupt practices of the crafts and the false claims they make for the quality of their wares. This is linked with an even more important and unifying theme: the misuse of oaths and asseverations. Blasphemous references to God and the devil had long been of concern to medieval moralists, and devotional writers were particularly appalled by casual references to parts of God's body, regarding them as a kind of second Crucifixion. Preachers long before Dunbar singled out the marketplace as the special haunt of swearers. They also, in an effort to frighten swearers, told stories of terrible divine or diabolic retribution. One, quoted by G. R. Owst, concerns a man whose favourite oath was 'the devel me adrenche' – it is no surprise to learn that he later fell in a ditch and was drowned.[19]

The figure of the devil is at the heart of Dunbar's poem. He is shown moving from one person to another, tempting and winning them to himself. The very refrain consists of his words, which shockingly invert the baptismal renunciation of the devil and all his works: 'Renunce thy God, and cum to me'. The theme is very ancient. In the book of Job (1: 7), Satan goes 'to and fro in the earth'; and [170] in the New Testament, Christians are warned that 'the devil, as a roaring lion, walketh about, seeking whom he may devour' (I Peter: 5, 8). In this poem, the devil does indeed

---

[18] *De Miseria Condicionis Humanae*, ed. Robert E. Lewis (Athens, GA, 1978), pp. 132–33 (i, 23); *Summa Theologica*, I.cxi.

[19] For Scottish legislation against swearing, see J. W. Baxter, *William Dunbar* (Edinburgh, 1952), p. III; on medieval attitudes, see Rosemary Woolf, *The English Religious Lyric in the Middle Ages* (Oxford, 1968), pp. 395–400; and Owst, *Literature and Pulpit*, pp. 414f. and 424–25.

walk about among men, seeking his prey; but he is no roaring lion, nor a heroic figure like Milton's Satan preparing for his onslaught on mankind. This is an intimate and familiar devil, passing 'throw the mercat' (4) and 'Rownand to Robene and to Dik' (84). The devil is said to be tempting men, but he appears rather to be listening gleefully as one after another damns himself: 'The Feind ressaif me gif I le' (23) or 'I gif me to the Feynd all fre' (28). The poem touches on the long-persisting fear that a moment's thoughtless oath might damn one forever. So in Webster's *White Devil* (V.i.72–73), Lodovico envisages poisoning his victim's tennis racket – 'That while he had been bandying at tennis / He might have sworn himself to hell.' Almost every stanza divides into two sections, containing the words first of some human, then of the devil. But although two voices are heard it is not strictly a dialogue – the devil comments in mocking asides on what has just been said:

> Ane tail3our said, In all this toun
> Be thair ane better weilmaid goun
> I gif me to the Feynd all fre;
> Gramercy tel3our, said Mahoun,
> Renunce thy God and cum to me.
>
> (K 56), 26–30

Much of the pleasure of reading this poem derives from its execution of small variations upon a fixed pattern. We wonder what craft will be next, which oath will be uttered, and what will be the devil's riposte.

Renunce thy God exists in two very different versions, one containing thirteen stanzas, the other seventeen. There has been much controversy about the relationship between these two texts, which I have no space to summarize here. What I would suggest, however, is that the two texts are so different that they should be given the status of independent poems, as is usual with carols and ballads; attempting to prove the superiority or priority of one to the other seems a fruitless task. Both poems are attributed to Dunbar, but it is likely that neither is wholly as he wrote it. His poem was perhaps so popular that it passed rapidly into the public domain and was then reshaped in a way common with popular poetry. It would be particularly easy to add or omit stanzas in a work of this catalogue structure. The poem combines two folk-tale motifs: the rash or heedless oath – 'The Feind ressaif me gif I le' – and the devil's visit to earth. (Chaucer's *Friar's Tale* also combines them, though in a more complex manner.) Long after Dunbar's time, the second motif was treated in vulgar ballads in a manner that recalls this poem:

> A common seventeenth-century broadside, one which also made its way into the droleries, was a satirical tale of the devil's ascent to earth and his encounter with a series of persons, usually the representatives of various occupations.[20]

[171] Four of the Romantic poets, like Dunbar, seized on the satirical possibilities of the theme. Coleridge and Southey collaborated fairly light-heartedly on a doggerel ballad – 'In ding-dong chime of sing-song rhyme' – which, like Dunbar's poem, exists

---

[20] Albert B. Friedman, *The Ballad Revival* (Chicago, IL, 1961), p. 268.

in two versions. The first, *The Devil's Thoughts*, is included in Coleridge's Works; the second is usually attributed to Southey, *The Devil's Walk*. Shelley gave the latter title to one of his juvenilia, printed in a broadside in 1812; and Byron too treated the theme in an 'unfinished rhapsody', which he called *The Devil's Drive* (1814). In an excursion through contemporary England, the devil found that they had better manners in hell than in the House of Lords.

How Dunbar wes Desyrd to be ane Freir (K 55) also treats of an encounter between man and devil. This amusing poem owes much to the traditions of anti-mendicant satire, though I do not see such satire as its primary object. I wish here to comment only on the poem's ending. The dreamer confesses

> Als lang as I did beir the freiris style
> In me, God wait, wes mony wrink and wyle;
> In me wes falset with every wicht to flatter
> Quhilk mycht be flemit with na haly watter –
> I wes ay reddy all men to begyle.
> This freir that did Sanct Francis thair appeir,
> Ane fieind he wes in liknes of ane freir;
> He vaneist away with stynk and fyrie smowk;
> With him me thocht all the hous end he towk,
> And I awoik as wy that wes in weir.
>
> (K 55), 41–50

Discomfited devils traditionally left ruin in their wake: one very similarly 'bare awey an ende of the house' in a sermon discussed by Owst. Still closer to Dunbar in time and place are Hector Boece's stories of defeated demons, circumstantially dated (in 1486) and located in Aberdeenshire or Mar: one flew off, accompanied with venomous odour and 'crak of fyre and reyk'; another flew away, 'berand the bed and ruf of the house'.[21] But why does Dunbar's devil vanish? Was it the dreamer's mention of God's name – a motif of many a folk-tale? Was it his reference to holy water, ritually used to exorcize evil spirits? Neither is sufficient. It seems that the dreamer's self-incriminating confession forces the devil to show himself in his true form. This passage is the culmination of a wit-combat, and the poem as a whole has a pattern similar to that of the medieval riddle-poem, *Diabolus et Virgo*, or the much later *The Fause Knight upon the Road*. What is effective against the devil in such pieces are bold argument and getting the last word.[22]

Two of these poems concern a picturesque figure at James IV's court, John Damian. One has an unusually long title in Bannatyne whose doggerel clumsiness would seem to rule out Dunbar's authorship: 'Ane ballat of the fenʒeit freir of tungland / and how he fell in the myre fleand to turkiland' ([ed. Ritchie, I, p. 311)]. Damian was not a friar but in 1504 became abbot of Tongland, a house of Premonstratensian Canons. I have therefore adopted the title for the poem in Asloan's original [172] contents-list: 'A ballat of the abbot of tungland'. Yet within

---

[21] *Literature and Pulpit*, p. 112; *The Chronicles of Scotland*, trans. John Bellenden, ed. R. W. Chambers et al., 2 vols, STS, 3rd Series 10, 15 (Edinburgh, 1938–41), I, pp. 346–48.
[22] For parallels: Thompson, *Motif-Index*, G 303.3.1.8; G 303.16.8; G 303.16.9; G 303.17.2.5.

the poem itself there is no such precise identification: the protagonist remains nameless throughout. This lack of a name does not seem accidental but corresponds to his lack of a fixed identity: the unnamed 'he' slips through roles, or rather disguises, as easily as he passes through different countries. He is successively an outlaw, 'a religious man' (10), a 'leiche' (17), a 'prelat' (49), a 'new maid channoun' (53) and an alchemist. This shape-shifting, like his vagrancy, is in keeping with his mysterious and diabolic origin: he is 'of Sathanis seid' (4) and comes from Tartary, the land of the Tartars, erroneously believed to be linked with 'Tartarus', hell. But there is an interesting correlation also with the varying references to Damian in *The Treasurer's Accounts*, as 'the Franch leich', or 'Maister John' or 'new maid abbot of tungland'. Dunbar had no need to name names: he dropped hints, which (to judge from the titles given to the poem) his audience picked up readily. Yet the very absence of a name and of a location for that abbot's adventure more specific than 'Scotland' increase the potential for comic invention. We shall never know the precise relation of this tale to reality – far too much trust has been laid on John Leslie's late and suspiciously varied accounts of the incident. What seems certain is that Dunbar here, as so often, is blending fact with fantasy.

I have space to comment on only one striking aspect of the poem, its affinity with myth and folk-tale. Stories from many countries testify to the significance of flight as something superhuman, practised only by birds, spirits and demons. Men who try to fly almost invariably come to disaster. Geoffrey of Monmouth tells how Bladud, father of King Lear, broke his neck in such an attempt. Ranulph Higden tells a similar story of a monk of Malmesbury, who attached feathers to his hands and feet, but fell after a short flight and was lame ever afterwards.[23] In Stith Thompson's classification of folk-tale motifs, the attempt to fly is placed under the heading, 'Overweening ambition is punished' (L 421). Occasionally an unsuccessful flight is treated tragically, as in Virgil's handling of the legend of Daedalus and Icarus, a story alluded to by both Dunbar and Higden. But mockery and derision are more common. There are several jests and facetiae about tricksters who announce to gullible crowds that they are going to fly. One is associated with the name of Scoggin:

> On a time Scoggin made the Frenchman believe that he would fly into England, and did get him many goose-wings and tied them about his arms and legs, and went upon a high tower, and spread his arms abroad as though he would fly, and came down again and said that all his feathers were not fit about him and that he would fly on the morrow … On the morrow Scoggin got upon the tower and did shake his feathers, saying 'Go home, fools, go home. Trow you that I will break my neck for your pleasure?' …
> There was a Frenchman had indignation at Scoggin, and he said, 'To-morrow you shall see me fly to Paris.' And he got him wings, and went upon the tower, and spread his wings abroad, and would have flown, and fell down

---

[23] *The History of the Kings of Britain*, trans. Lewis Thorpe (London, 1966), i.10; Ranulph Higden, *Polychronicon*, ed. Churchill Babington and J. Rawson Lumby, Rolls Series (London, 1865–86), vi.28 (VII, p. 222).

into the moat [**173**] under the tower … Scoggin did take him by the hand, and said, 'Sir, you be welcome from Paris, I think you have been in a great rain.'[24]

This attempt to fly does not illustrate human daring and inventiveness, but folly and stupidity. Dunbar's poem is far funnier (and his protagonist more depraved), yet embedded in it is a similarly sensible, literally 'down to earth' view of man's capacities, which (with hindsight) we may find limited and lacking imagination. Yet we should recall that Samuel Johnson displayed equal scepticism in his handling of the theme. In chapter 6 of *Rasselas*, 'A Dissertation on the Art of Flying', the Artist 'was every day more certain that he should leave vultures and eagles behind him', but he ended, like Dunbar's abbot, in a lake, and 'the prince drew him to land, half dead with terror and vexation'.

In Dunbar's poem, there is one striking motif that is not present in these other versions: it is the birds who are responsible for the flight's failure. They take revenge for the invasion of their element, and expel the intruder. The abbot's attempt to assume their powers is seen as his culminating attempt to go beyond man's earthbound limits – 'The hevin he micht not bruke' (72). Drawing attention to his lack of identity, the birds marvel as to what he is – 'All fowill ferleit quhat he sowld be' (63). The flying abbot is as much a hybrid as the minotaur, neither man nor bird; he assumes the plumage, or 'fedrem', of birds as earlier he had adopted the habit of a 'religious man'. There is a poetic justice, as critics have noted, in the way the punishment inflicted by the birds fits the abbot's crimes. The surgeon who shed blood is now struck 'with buffettis quhill he bled' (78); and the man who 'full clenely carvit' (21) his victims is himself horribly mutilated. In this passage, Dunbar also presents us with powerful illustrations of *impossibilia*, or 'the World Upside Down' topos. One disturbance of natural order is countered by another, or by a reversal of what is assumed to be the normal relationship between birds and men. Birds attacking men are shown in some representations of the 'World Upside Down', along with an ox cutting up a butcher or a fish eating a fisherman.[25] The poem derives much power from our response to such a reversal, the basic human fear of the sharp beaks of birds.

The Antechrist (K 53) seems to have been inspired by the same incident as *The Abbot of Tungland*, and they are regularly treated as companion pieces, although the only manuscript to contain both poems does not place them together. *The Antechrist* is dominated by Dame Fortune's speech to the dreamer, which occupies the six central stanzas. Her speech is a prediction, not a sermon, and contains in miniature several characteristic features of the medieval prophecy. A future event is said to depend upon the fulfilment of certain seemingly impossible 'taikinis' (20), or signs. The dreamer's troubles will be 'at ane end' (19) (ominously ambiguous) only when an abbot flies:

---

[24] See John Wardroper, *Jest upon Jest: A Selection from the Jestbooks and Collections of Merry Tales Published from the Reign of Richard III to George III* (London, 1970), p. 93.

[25] See further, David Kunzle, 'World Upside Down: The Iconography of a European Broadsheet Type', in *The Reversible World*, ed. Barbara Babcock (Ithaca, NY, 1978), pp. 39–94.

He sall ascend as ane horreble grephoun;
Him meit sall in the air ane scho dragoun;
Thir terrible monsteris sall togidder thrist
And in the cludis gett the Antechrist ...

(K 53), 26–29 [**174**]

Such bizarre events and such mysteriously symbolic creatures were the stuff of medieval prophecy, particularly of that type associated with Merlin and Thomas of Ercildoun, and first given currency by Geoffrey of Monmouth.[26] Shakespeare's Glendower was likewise reported to speak

Of the dreamer Merlin and his prophecies,
And of a dragon and a finless fish,
A clip-winged griffin and a moulten raven ...

I Henry IV, III.i.143–45

Although Hotspur termed it 'skimble-skamble stuff', such prophecy was taken very seriously, not just by ignorant peasants but by kings and their counsellors, throughout England and Scotland, well into the seventeenth century. Fortune's words are characteristic of the genre in their riddling and cryptic tone. What is more, her prophecy is apocalyptic, ending with a vision of Doomsday:

And syne thay sall discend with reik and fyre
And preiche in erth the Antechrystis impyre;
Be than it salbe neir this warldis end.

(K 53), 36–38

In his flight, the abbot meets an elrich company of witches, magicians and evil spirits. They include Merlin, reputed son of a devil; 'Mahoun', regarded as pagan god and devil, and thought to have flown on a winged horse to Jerusalem; and Simon Magus, who in the New Testament was condemned for his traffic in holy things, and according to later legend made an attempt to fly to heaven, aided by devils, but was dashed to the ground at the prayer of St Peter. Dunbar clearly hints at the parallels between the abbot and all these nefarious beings.

But it is the Antichrist who is the key figure in this poem. John Jewel, a sixteenth-century Protestant, provides some idea of the enormous popular interest in the Antichrist, and the amazing prophecies and 'fond tales' that circulated about what one Scottish writer called his [Antichrist's] 'curst procreacoun, werst lyf and most dampnable end':

Some say he should be a Jew of the tribe of Dan; some that he should be born in Babylon ... some that Mahomet is Antichrist ... some that he should be born

---

26 See R. Taylor, *The Political Prophecy in England* (New York, 1911); and Madeleine Hope Dodds, 'Political Prophecies in the Reign of Henry VIII', *Modern Language Review*, 11.3 (1916), 276–84.

of a friar and a nun; some that he should continue but three years and a half
... and then should flee up into heaven, and fall down and break his neck.[27]

This attempt at flight was a central part of the Antichrist legend and regarded as a
blasphemous imitation of Christ: climbing the Mount of Olives, he tries to ascend
into heaven, and is killed, as was Simon Magus. Such beliefs were partly founded
upon Christ's own words concerning the false Christs who would appear before his
second coming and the end of the world (Matt. 24). Antichrist was a pseudo-Christ,
who would appear in human form at a climactic point in history, leading the forces
of evil: [**175**] he 'heads a body made up of pagans, unbelievers, false Christians,
and all evil ecclesiastics'. Writing of the Last Judgement, a Scottish contemporary
of Dunbar says:

> Gret taikin is the antechrist drawis neir,
> Fast flokis his furiouris, graithand his luging;
> His pursiphantis, propheitis, and precheouris can appeir.[28]
> *Contemplacioun of Synnaris*, 713–15

The abbot of this dream is clearly one of these 'evil ecclesiastics', and a harbinger of
Antichrist, ready to preach his *impyre*, or reign; and in his own attempt to fly, he joins
Simon Magus as a diabolic type, or pre-figuration, of Antichrist himself.

Yet despite the apocalyptic tone, we do not take this prophecy seriously. What
hangs upon its fulfilment is hardly momentous – neither the end of the world nor
the fate of a great kingdom, merely the bestowal of a benefice. We should recall
that serious prophecies were often intended to exert pressure upon a king and his
counsellors. This poem is, in part, a circuitous petition. It is a spoof-prophecy,
rendered comic by the trivial nature of the subject-matter. It might be compared
to the Enigma, or 'prophetical riddle', at the end of *Gargantua*, on which the Monk
commented:

> it is the style of the Prophet Merlin: make upon it as many grave allegories
> and glosses as you will ... for my part, I can conceive no other meaning in it,
> but a description of a set at tennis in dark and obscure termes.[29]

At the time of Rabelais, according to M. A. Screech, there was a taste for such
'amusing enigmas, which seem to be dealing with great matters, but which turn
out to be merely hidden ways of alluding to trivial, ordinary or obscene things'.[30]

---

[27] I owe this quotation to the useful study by R. K. Emmerson, *Antichrist in the Middle Ages*
(Seattle, WA, 1981), p. 8. See also *The Sex Werkdayis and Agis*, in *The Asloan Manuscript*,
ed. W. A. Craigie, 2 vols, STS, 2nd ser. 14, 16 (1923–25), I, p. 330.

[28] See Emmerson, *Antichrist*, p. 20; and *Contemplacioun of Synnaris*, 713–15, in *Devotional
Pieces in Verse and Prose*, ed. J. A. W. Bennett, STS, 3rd ser. 33 (Edinburgh, 1955), p. 112
[BL, MS Arundel 285].

[29] *Gargantua and Pantagruel*, trans. Sir Thomas Urquhart (London, 1921), I, p. 180.

[30] M. A. Screech, *Rabelais* (London, 1979), p. 195.

The mock-prophecy was closely akin to the mock-prognostication, for which there was also a vogue in the fifteenth and sixteenth centuries, especially in France. The most famous example of the kind was Rabelais' *Pantagrueline Prognostication* (1533), but it had many precursors. The genre became popular in England, although the earliest surviving example is dated 1544, and in Scotland also in the later sixteenth century there was a market for 'Merry Prognostications'.[31] At the end of the poem, the dreamer awakes and rejoices when he learns that an abbot is indeed preparing to fly:

> Full weill I wist to me wald nevir cum thrift
> Quhill that twa monis wer sene up in the lift,
> Or quhill ane abbot flew aboif the mone.
> *The Antechrist* (K 53), 48–50

But this ending is highly ambiguous. The presence of several moons in the sky is more commonly a portent of disaster than of 'thrift' [good fortune]. When five moons are reported to have been seen, in *King John* (IV.ii.182), 'Old men and beldames … Do prophesy upon it dangerously.' Fortune is an unreliable goddess – in another of Dunbar's poems, she is called a whore (K 63 ['Quhom to sall I complene my wo', 57–58]). This dream is delusive, and the prophecy cheating. Dunbar's audience would know that whatever the abbot achieved, he did not fly above the moon. If the dreamer feels 'confort', he deludes himself and he is still without a benefice. This poem makes fun of the poet himself as well as the abbot.

I have had space to discuss only a few features of these elrich [**176**] poems, and virtually omitted the most famous of all, *Fasternis Evin in Hell* ['Off Februar the fyiftene nycht']. In recent years, we have heard much of Dunbar the moralist and writer of 'serious comedy'. Although I would not deny that some of these poems have very serious implications, I think it important to re-assert the comic and popular aspects of Dunbar's genius. Several of the anonymous poems I mentioned earlier end in a convivial way that recalls minstrel poetry: 'Drynk with my guddame quhen ʒe gang by' (*Kittok*, 38); or 'skynk first to me the can' (*Crying of Ane Playe*, 136); or 'Gar fill the cop' (Lichtoun's *Dreme*, 89). We know sadly little of how Dunbar's poems reached their first audience, but it is worth recalling Maitland's comment on one usually known as *The Amendis to the Telʒouris and Soutaris* (K 53C): 'Quod Dunbar quhone he drank to the Dekynnis for amendis to the bodeis of their craftis.' Several of the anonymous poems end flippantly, but none can match Dunbar's throw-away ending to *Fasternis Evin* (228): 'Now trow this, gif ʒe list.'

31 Cf. *Rabelais*, pp. 195–200; F. P. Wilson, 'Some English Mock-Prognostications', *The Library*, 4.1 (1938), 6–43; an example is mentioned in Robert Gourlaw's will: *The Bannatyne Miscellany*, II, ed. David Laing (Edinburgh 1836), p. 214; see also M. A. Bald, 'Vernacular Books Imported into Scotland', *Scottish Historical Review*, 23 (1926), 258.

Editorial Notes

a This essay, presented at the Fifth International Conference on Scottish Language and Literature (Medieval and Renaissance), University of Aberdeen, 1987, was first published in *Bryght Lanternis: Essays on the Language and Literature of Medieval and Renaissance Scotland*, ed. J. Derrick McClure and Michael R. G. Spiller (Aberdeen, 1989), pp. 162–78. It is reprinted with the kind permission of Dr Nigel Bawcutt. The current Aberdeen University Press, not being a continuation of the original Press, holds no rights over its publications, and has no objection or permission restrictions on the use of this essay.

b See Iona and Peter Opie, *The Lore and Language of Schoolchildren* (London, 1959), pp. 32–35: 'Ghoulism'; pp. 35–37: 'Spookies'.

4

'Mankit and Mutillait':
The Text of John Rolland's *The Court of Venus*

John Rolland is a neglected but far from negligible poet, who, like several other early Scottish poets, was a notary public.[a] Although little definite is known of his life, he is recorded as practising in Melrose and Dalkeith, and legal documents bearing his name date from 1551 to 1580.[1] Rolland's most popular work was *The Seuin Seages* (composed *c.* 1560); the earliest extant edition was printed by John Ross for Henry Charteris in 1578 (*STC*, 21254), and there were at least five subsequent editions or reprints between that date and 1635.[2] *The Court of Venus*, by contrast, survives in a single edition, also printed by John Ross (and probably for Henry Charteris), dated 1575 (*STC*, 21258). According to the title page, the work was 'Newlie Compylit be Johne Rolland in Dalkeith', but, despite this statement, there is evidence that *The Court of Venus* was composed earlier than 1575 and pre-dated *The Seuin Seages*. In his 'Prologue' to *The Seuin Seages*, Rolland implies that *The Court of Venus* was written during the lifetime of four poets: Sir David Lyndsay (d. 1555), Bishop Andrew Durie (d. 1558), John Bellenden (d. ?1548) and William Stewart (d. ?1548). If true, this would suggest that *The Court of Venus* – or a first version of it – was composed some time before 1548, and that Ross's 'newlie compylit' perhaps derives from the title page of an earlier edition. But the passage in the 'Prologue' sounds more like jocular fiction about Rolland's literary allegiances than a statement of fact, and the precise date of *The Court of Venus* remains uncertain.[3]

One might well wonder what prompted the printing of Rolland's two poems in 1575 and 1578. Literary critics pay little attention to the early years of James VI's reign and usually regard the 1570s as a decade dominated by the polemical verse of Robert Sempill. But during this period older Scottish literature experienced a remarkable revival, for which the chief credit lies with the energetic bookseller and printer Henry [12] Charteris. From 1568 onwards, he commissioned from a number of different printers, and at his own 'expensis', an impressive series of publications that included not only *The Seuin Seages* and probably *The Court of Venus* but several of what are

---

[1]   On the scanty details of Rolland's life, see John Rolland, *The Seuin Seages*, ed. George F. Black, STS, 3rd ser. 3 (Edinburgh, 1932), 'Introduction', pp. xi–xvi, and John Durkan, *Protocol Book of John Foular 1528–1534*, SRS, n.s. 10 (Edinburgh, 1985), p. xix.

[2]   See C. B. L. Barr, 'Early Scottish Editions of "The seven sages of Rome" ', *Bibliotheck*, 5 (1967–70), 62–72, and S. Couper, 'Time, Sex and Authority in John Rolland's *Seuin Seages*', *Forum for Modern Language Studies*, 38 (2002), 435–48.

[3]   *Seuin Seages*, ed. Black, pp. 1–3.

now regarded as the classics of early Scottish poetry: Sir David Lyndsay's *Warkis* (1568), Robert Henryson's *Fables* (1570), Hary's *Wallace* (1570), Barbour's *Bruce* (1571) and Douglas's *The Palice of Honour* (1578).[4] Charteris was a learned, patriotic and highly articulate man, and in various prefaces and 'Adhortatiounis' (most importantly, to Lyndsay's *Warkis*, the *Bruce* and the edition of the *Wallace* printed in 1594) he stressed the literary and historical value of these works. Speaking of Lyndsay, for instance, he proclaimed his intention

> that na thing of sa Nobill ane wrytar suld perische, throw negligence or sleuthfulnes of this present age, bot suld be reseruit to ye fruite of all posteriteis following.
>
> 'Vnto the Godlie and Christiane Reidar', *Warkis* (1568), [p. 8][5]

Sir Walter Scott attributed to George Bannatyne the 'plan of saving the literature of a whole nation'.[6] But it is arguable that this tribute might have been more fittingly paid to Henry Charteris. Charteris expressed a strong personal liking for several of these old poems – his favourite term of commendation was 'plesand and delectabill'. But he was also a shrewd and wealthy businessman, and it seems most unlikely that he would have commissioned these works unless he saw a potential market for them.

The Court of Venus is a long and learned work on the theme of love: divided into a 'Prologue' and four books, it contains nearly four thousand lines.[7] It is an ambitious poem that testifies to the strong and persistent Scottish interest in allegorical poetry throughout the sixteenth century. Indeed it stands almost at the midpoint of that tradition, looking back to Lyndsay's *Dreme*, Dunbar's *Goldyn Targe* and Douglas's *Palice of Honour* (to which it is indebted, stylistically and structurally), but also forward to three significant poems composed later in James VI's reign – John Stewart of Baldynneis' *Ane Schersing out of Trew Felicitie* (*c.* 1584), Alexander Montgomerie's *The Cherrie and the Slae* (first printed in 1597) and Elizabeth Melville's *Ane Godlie Dreame* (printed in 1603). Some motifs characteristic of the tradition that might be mentioned are the quest for intellectual enlightenment or true 'felicitie', the anxious or bemused protagonist who requires assistance from a divine or supernatural guide, debates between personified abstractions, and lavish set pieces of description, such as the allegorical palace or castle. The [13] elaborate nine-line stanza of Rolland's

4   On the career of Henry Charteris, see R. Dickson and J. P. Edmond, *Annals of Scottish Printing: From the Beginning of the Art in 1507 to the Beginning of the Seventeenth Century* (Cambridge, 1890), pp. 348–76. On his commissions, see the chapters on John Scot, Robert Lekpreuik and John Ross. On his support for vernacular poetry, see A. J. Mann, *The Scottish Book Trade, 1500–1720: Print Commerce and Print Control in Early Modern Scotland* (East Linton, 2000), p. 110 and 65n. See also Joseph Marshall, 'Charteris, Henry (d. 1599), Printer and Bookseller (2004; rev. 2006)', *ODNB Online*: https://doi.org/10.1093/ref:odnb/5176.

5   Reprinted in *The Works of Sir David Lindsay*, ed. Douglas Hamer, 4 vols, STS, 3rd ser. 1, 2, 6, 8 (Edinburgh, 1931–36), I, p. 403.

6   See 'Memoir of George Bannatyne', in *Memorials of George Bannatyne*, [ed. David Laing], Bannatyne Club (Edinburgh, 1829), pp. 3–23 (11).

7   See *Ane Treatise callit The Court of Venus deuidit into four buikis, newly compylit be Iohne Rolland in Dalkeith, 1575*, ed. Walter Gregor, STS, 1st ser. 3 (Edinburgh, 1884).

Court of Venus is employed also in *The Goldyn Targe*, *The Palice of Honour* and (with a slight variation of form) in *Ane Schersing out of Trew Felicitie*. There are other small resemblances to Rolland's poem that may be more than accidental: the unspecified bush, under which Rolland's narrator conceals himself (Bk I, ll. 42, 56), reappears in the 1597 text of *The Cherrie and the Slae*, l. 7;[8] and the boggy journey of Rolland's Desperance 'Throw mos and myre' (Bk II, l. 388) is paralleled in *Ane Godlie Dreame*, l. 165.[9] Of more significance is the debate between Esperance and Desperance in Book II of *The Court of Venus*, which may perhaps have influenced the more fluid and informal arguments between Hope and Despair and other personifications in *The Cherrie and the Slae*.

Few twentieth-century critics examined *The Court of Venus* closely, and most of these were dismissive, terming it 'conventional and unoriginal', 'dull' and 'old-fashioned'. According to J. H. Millar, 'the most that can be said for it is that it offers some tolerably attractive material for the legal antiquary'.[10] C. S. Lewis, however, devoted several pages of *The Allegory of Love* to a subtle and sympathetic reading of the poem and spoke of the 'peculiarly Scottish and medieval blend of gallantry, satire, fantasy and pedantry'.[11] More recently, R. J. Lyall has published a major re-evaluation of *The Court of Venus*. He finds in the poem 'a much greater cultural significance than has been realized, placing [Rolland] in the vanguard of those who transmitted the materials, and to a degree, the values, of continental Christian humanism, into Scotland'. He argues that *The Court of Venus* was in its time

> a remarkable, if aesthetically top-heavy, synthesis of classical and biblical scholarship, and can be related to debates which were taking place among humanist poets in France towards the end of the second quarter of the century, and thus forms part of the same cultural process as the emergence of a scholarly circle at St Leonard's College in St Andrews and the work of the expatriate Florens Wilson.[12]

My object in this article is not to engage in criticism of *The Court of Venus*, although it seems to me the poem has many merits, but rather to indicate how most literary

---

8 *Alexander Montgomerie: Poems*, ed. David Parkinson, 2 vols, STS, 4th ser. 28–29 (Edinburgh, 2000), I, pp. 178–254.

9 For *Ane Godlie Dreame*, see *The Poems of Alexander Hume*, ed. Alexander Lawson, STS, 1st ser. 48 (Edinburgh, 1902), Appendix D, pp. 184–97.

10 J. H. Millar, *A Literary History of Scotland* (London, 1903), p. 201. See also Agnes Mure Mackenzie, 'The Renaissance Poets: (1) Scots and English', in *Scottish Poetry: A Critical Survey*, ed. James Kinsley (London, 1955), pp. 33–97; 293, 26n; Gregory Kratzmann, 'Sixteenth-Century Secular Poetry', in *The History of Scottish Literature: Volume One; Origins to 1640*, ed. R. D. S. Jack (Aberdeen, 1988), pp. 105–24 (121); and William Calin, 'The *dit amoureux*, Alain Chartier, and the *Belle Dame sans mercy* Cycle in Scotland: John Rolland's *The Court of Venus*', in *Chartier in Europe*, ed. Emma Cayley and Ashby Kinch (Cambridge, 2008), pp. 149–64.

11 C. S. Lewis, *The Allegory of Love* (Oxford, 1936), p. 292.

12 R. J. Lyall, 'Christian Humanism in John Rolland's *Court of Venus*', in *Challenging Humanism: Essays in Honour of Dominic Baker-Smith*, ed. T. Hoenselaars and Arthur F. Kinney (Newark, NJ, 2005), pp. 108–25 (108).

judgements upon it have been based on a highly imperfect text. *The Court of Venus* is a poem with a most unfortunate history. It is not known how many copies of the 1575 edition were printed, although it is perhaps worth noting, for the purposes of comparison, that after John Ross's death in 1580 an inventory of his goods recorded 'tua hundreth Sevin Seigis vnbund'.[13] Today, however, only a single complete copy survives, in possession of the British Library, [14] (C.34.e.46). It is printed on poor-quality paper, has many broken and imperfectly inked letters, and other typographical errors, and, worst of all, is now in such a damaged state that there are many incomplete lines, especially in the 'Prologue' and first two books. This is bad enough, but, towards the end of the nineteenth century, Rolland's poem suffered a further blow, from someone who was attempting to make it more accessible to modern readers. The reverend Walter Gregor (1825–97), minister of Pitsligo, is remembered today as a distinguished folklorist, author of *Notes on the Folklore of the North-East of Scotland* (1881), and one of the founders of the Scottish Text Society. Nonetheless, his edition of *The Court of Venus* (1884), which was one of the first works to be published by the Society, is deeply flawed and does Rolland and his poem a grave disservice.

Gregor says of his edition that 'the text now issued is an exact reprint of the original'.[14] This statement, alas, could not be further from the truth. The text contains literally hundreds of errors; some are of minor significance, but others cause gross distortions of Rolland's sense, style and metre. Gregor does not claim to have examined the poem himself, but states: 'It was copied by Miss Marx, whose name is a guarantee for accuracy. The proofs were revised by her.'[15] Eleanor Marx (1855–98) was the daughter of Karl Marx; a fascinating but tragic figure, she is remembered chiefly for her energetic activities on behalf of the Socialist movement and the liaison with Edward Aveling, which ultimately led her to commit suicide.[16] She was one of the many clever young women befriended by F. J. Furnivall, and from 1877 onwards she worked regularly in the British Museum, on behalf of the Philological, the Chaucer, and the Shakespearean Societies.[17] A German friend, Eduard Bernstein, describes her in 1880 as '"devilling", that is, taking excerpts or doing research for a pittance to save well-to-do people who wanted to write books the trouble of looking things up for themselves'.[18] Eleanor Marx had many talents, but she was not a scholar. She was probably recommended to Walter Gregor by Furnivall in the same 'lighthearted' way that he invited Alfred W. Pollard to edit a volume for the Wyclif Society: Pollard reports that 'at the time I had never read a page of Mediaeval Latin, nor looked at a manuscript except through a glass case'.[19] Furnivall certainly introduced Eleanor to James Murray, who was later scornful of her activities on behalf of the *Oxford English Dictionary*: according to him, she 'claimed to have spent 110 hours collecting 144 words', but the work she produced 'was of no

---

13 *The Bannatyne Miscellany*, II, ed. David Laing, Bannatyne Club (Edinburgh, 1836), p. 205.
14 *Court of Venus*, ed. Gregor, p. xxxi.
15 *Court of Venus*, ed. Gregor, p. xxxi.
16 See Yvonne Kapp, *Eleanor Marx*, 2 vols (London, 1972–76).
17 Kapp, *Eleanor Marx*, I, p. 187.
18 Kapp, *Eleanor Marx*, I, p. 206.
19 John James Monro et al., *Frederick James Furnivall: A Volume of Personal Record* (London, 1911), p. 147.

use as all the words were from modern dictionaries and glossaries and none were new'.[20] Eleanor [15] herself regarded much of what she did as 'dull Museum drudgery'; the phrase occurs in a letter written to her sister in March 1882, two years before the publication of *The Court of Venus*.[21] It seems that Gregor placed far too great a trust in her 'accuracy', and never thought it advisable to travel from Aberdeenshire to London in order to check her copy against the original.

One of the few readers of the poem to have noticed the deficiencies of this work was the great lexicographer William Craigie. In 1898, at the beginning of his scholarly career, he published a brief article, in which he voiced scathing criticism of the edition. He recognized that

> the copyist employed by the editor is probably responsible for a large number of blunders in the text, many of which are obvious to anyone who reads the book with attention, and yet are passed over in silence or incorrectly explained. Others are of a more subtle kind, and not to be corrected without reference to the original edition.[22]

Craigie's comments on the 'blunders in the text' are fully justified, yet it is characteristic of the period that he, too, like Gregor, failed to examine the text for himself. It was then not uncommon for Scottish Text Society editors to work with transcripts made by other persons, whose contribution might later be acknowledged only in a brief note at the end of the Preface or Introduction. Thus A. F. Mitchell, editor of *The Gude and Godlie Ballatis*, thanked the Rev. Dr Blair, 'who transcribed the old volume for me'.[23] William Craigie himself said that his edition of Bellenden's translation of Livy was based on an 'exact transcript … made … by the Rev. Walter Macleod',[24] that the Maitland Folio was printed from 'a careful transcript by Mr A. Rogers of the University Library, Cambridge',[25] and that the Asloan Manuscript was 'a long task carefully executed by Miss I. B. Hutchen'.[26] Isabella Hutchen, Craigie's sister-in-law, was in fact a skilled and competent reader of manuscripts, who did much valuable work for *DOST*.[27]

---

20 K. M. Elisabeth Murray, *Caught in the Web of Words: James Murray and the Oxford English Dictionary* (Oxford, 1979), p. 212.

21 Chushichi Tsuzuki, *The Life of Eleanor Marx 1855–1898: A Socialist Tragedy* (Oxford, 1967), p. 66.

22 W. A. Craigie, 'Rolland's "Court of Venus"', *The Modern Quarterly of Language and Literature*, I.1 (1898), 9–16 (9–10).

23 *A Compendious Book of Godly and Spiritual Songs Commonly Known as 'The Gude and Godlie Ballatis'*, ed. A. F. Mitchell, STS, 1st ser. 39 (Edinburgh, 1897), pp. lxxvii–lxxviii.

24 *Livy's History of Rome: The First Five Books; Translated into Scots by John Bellenden 1533*, ed. W. A. Craigie, 2 vols, STS, 1st ser. 47, 51 (Edinburgh, 1901–03), I, Introduction, p. xiv.

25 *The Maitland Folio Manuscript*, ed. W. A. Craigie, 2 vols, STS, 2nd ser. 7, 20 (Edinburgh, 1919–27), I, Preface, p. vi.

26 *The Asloan Manuscript*, ed. W. A. Craigie, 2 vols, STS, 2nd ser. 14, 16 (Edinburgh, 1923–25), I, Preface, p. x. See also *The New Testament in Scots*, ed. T. G. Law, 3 vols, STS, 1st ser. 46, 49, 52 (Edinburgh, 1901–05), I, p. xxxiv.

27 On Isabella Hutchen, see the tributes in *DOST*, I, p. viii, XII, p. x.

Craigie's suspicions, in the case of *The Court of Venus*, were awakened by his intimate knowledge of the Scots language and experience as a lexicographer, but he still deputed the job of checking the original to someone else:

> All the passages which seemed in any way suspicious have been collated for me by Mr Walter Robinson, with the result that many of them turn out to be correct in the original: it seems probable that a thorough collation of the whole text would yield more results of this kind.[28]

[**16**] Craigie's intelligence led him to spot many misreadings, which are collected and discussed with some acerbity in the rest of his short article. But it is unfortunately true that 'thorough collation of the whole text' has yielded many more instances. A list of these mistranscriptions is provided in an Appendix to this article, but it may be helpful to analyse and illustrate some different categories of error, most quite elementary, yet often profoundly damaging to the sense.

The long form of the letter *s* is often misunderstood and confused with the letter *f*. This produces the ghost word *feindill* ('Prologue', l. 31), which Gregor explains variously as 'cruel' or 'ill-natured', instead of the correct *seindill*, 'seldom'. There are repeated instances of *fair* instead of *sair* (Bk I, l. 663 and *passim*); *defait* (Bk III, ll. 592, 650), instead of *desait*, 'deceit', and *thrift* (Bk IV, l. 360) instead of *thrist*, literally 'thirst'. The reverse error is less common, but two instances are *sickill* (Bk I, l. 557), which should read *fickill*, and *saw* (Bk III, l. 427), which should read *faw*, 'fall'. A similarly elementary error is the confusion of the letters *t* and *r*: *thait* ('Prologue', l. 194) for *thair*; *contrait* ('Prologue', l. 222) for *contrair*; *he it is* ('Prologue', l. 273) for *heiris*; and *rimes* (Bk II, l. 707) for *times*. There are also many examples of incorrect word division – *at hir* (Bk III, l. 319) should read *athir*, 'either', and – with particular absurdity – *This be* (Bk IV, l. 419) appears instead of the name *Thisbe*.

Throughout the poem, the spelling of Scots words is repeatedly anglicized. Some common examples are: *care* for *cure*, *scandalous* for *sclanderous*, *well* for *weill*, *sundrie* for *sindrie*, *are* for *ar*, *so* for *sa*, *wrong* for *wrang*, *long* for *lang*, *right* for *richt*, *they* for *thay*, *their* for *thair*, and *she* for *scho*. These do not impair our understanding of the poem, of course, but they certainly affect our sense of its Scottishness. Latin words and phrases too are occasionally mangled. Rolland's original text reads *Finit Prologus* ('Prologue', l. 338a), not *Finis Prologus*; *dilexi* (Bk I, l. 448a), not *delexi*; and *Rhamnusia* (Bk I, l. 913), not *Rhammusia*. In a rubric on the Nine Worthies, we are told that three cities took their name from Alexander the Great. According to Greg, this reads:

> Alexander ... construxit tres vrbes,
> vno nomine vocatas, scilicet alexandria in Ægypto.
> alexandria in Asia propre hostium nili fluuij &
> alexandria in Scithia ...
>
> (Bk II, l. 236a)

---

28 Craigie, 'Rolland's "Court of Venus"', p. 10.

But there is a tilde over the final letter at each occurrence of *alexandria*, indicating the accusative case, *alexandriam*, and *propre* should read *prope*, 'near'. Both Rolland and his printer knew their Latin grammar. [**17**]

Omission of text is a particularly grievous fault in any edition. There are two cases in the 'Prologue' where whole lines are omitted, as the rhyme scheme makes clear. Line 6 should be followed by: 'And that throw heuinlie Constellatiounis.' After line 175, another line has similarly vanished: 'Sum ar Pelouris, and part ar fals pursep[ykis].' It is less easy, however, for modern readers to spot when words have been omitted within the line. These are usually short, colourless grammatical words, yet their omission harms both Rolland's sense and the rhythmical fluency of his verse. In the following examples, the words that have been wrongly omitted are italicized.

That Salomon *sic* wordis said in vane	(Bk I, l. 490)
In latin toung was *ane* most faculent	(Bk III, l. 589)
Prayand to send to thame *зour* auisement	(Bk IV, l. 135)
Venus beheld the bill geuin *be* Thisbe	(Bk IV, l. 145)

Rolland himself twice apologizes for his 'haltand verse' (see 'Prologue', l. 279 and Bk IV, l. 740). But he was less metrically lame than would appear from this edition.[29] There is a double error in another line describing the Sibyls: '[Quh]a ar forsuith forsuith Prophettes ilkane' (Bk II, l. 381). Here the loss of a syllable from *Prophetisses* is compounded by the unwarranted repetition of *forsuith*.

Craigie pointed out many egregious cases of substantive error: *flat* ('Prologue', l. 16) for *fat*; *slow* ('Prologue', l. 222), glossed as 'sloth', for *kow*; *Philistiane* (Bk I, l. 167) for *Phisitiane*; *Lameurie* (Bk I, l. 397), glossed as 'sorcery', for *Lamenrie*, 'sexual love'; *distrust* (Bk II, l. 42), glossed as 'solved', for *discust*; *Flane bellief lawcht* (Bk II, l. 373), for [**18**] *Flane bellie flawcht*. In this last case, Gregor glossed *flane* as 'arrow' and *bellief* as the adverb, 'at once'; but Rolland's *flane bellieflawcht* is an idiomatic Scots phrase, which means 'flayed by pulling the skin off whole over the head'.[30] A few further instances, unnoticed by Craigie, will be mentioned here.

1.   Sa thay him *sasit* on ground quhair he lay stil

(Bk II, l. 360)

The correct reading is *rasit*, 'raised'.

2.   As he had been fra wit *examinat*.

(Bk II, l. 364)

Gregor's Glossary explains this as 'examined, questioned under torture, driven out of his mind … (Prof. Skeat.)'. But the correct reading is *exanimat*, 'deprived of life'.

---

[29] For other instances, see the Appendix following: Bk I, 71, 244, and 681; Bk II, 739; Bk III, 43, 315, 469, 622, 773, 788; Bk IV, 135, 156, 201, 589, 684.

[30] See *The Poems of Robert Henryson*, ed. Denton Fox (Oxford 1981), 'The Paddock and the Mouse', pp. 103–10, l. 2904. For other uses, see *DOST*, *belly-flaucht*, https://www.dsl.ac.uk/entry/dost/belly_flaucht.

3. Sa full thair warkis was of *oporcitie*.

(Bk II, l. 497)

Gregor glosses *oporcitie* as 'difficulty', and *DOST*, unfortunately, records this ghost word under the correct reading, *opacitie*, 'darkness, obscurity of meaning'.

4. *Expand* on hie, ga far about the wall.

(Bk II, l. 859)

Expand is an error for *Cryand*. The reference is to Chastity, personified in the preceding stanza as a watchman, and here crying, or shouting, on the castle wall.

5. Ops, Philyra, *Sicoris*, and Drimo.

(Bk III, l. 60)

This line occurs in a long list of nymphs and famous classical women. The sources of the passage have been usefully discussed by R. J. Lyall, who describes *Sicoris* as a 'clear-cut mistake' on Rolland's part.[31] The mistake, however, is not Rolland's, since the original text reads *Licoris*, who can be identified as *Lycoris*, mistress of the poet Cornelius Gallus.[32] [**19**]

6. Siclike becaus Diomeid wald *forleir*
    The fers Troians quhair that he faucht in weir.

(Bk III, ll. 274–75)

Gregor glosses as 'kill', but the correct reading is *forbeir*, that is, forbear, either 'spare' or 'avoid'. *Forleir*, however, has entered *DOST*, because of this passage, as an unexplained ghost word.

7. For weill I wait his stomake is stormestaid
    Becaus he is put in ane *Merriment*.

(Bk IV, ll. 234–35)

The correct reading is *Merciment*: this is a favourite word of Rolland's, used several times in *The Court of Venus* (cf. Bk IV, ll. 270 and 414). It is a legalism, meaning 'the condition of being subject to a pecuniary penalty at the "mercy" or discretion of a court or judge'. *Merriment* was not a word then common in Scots.

8. But obstakill, *generall* or reuocatioun.

(Bk IV, l. 251)

The correct reading is *ganecall*, also a Scottish legal term, which has much the same sense as 'revocation'. It is less common in Scots, apparently, than *ganecalling*.

---

[31] Lyall, 'Christian Humanism in John Rolland's *Court of Venus*', p. 115.

[32] On Lycoris, see Virgil, *Eclogue* 10 and Ovid, *Amores* 1.15.30.

The defective condition of the British Library copy of *The Court of Venus*, particularly in Books I and II, has already been remarked. Gregor used square brackets to 'mark the lacunae caused by the ravages of time'; he attempted to supply some of these lacunae, but regretfully confessed that 'many of them have baffled me'.[33] Here, too, Craigie was highly critical of Gregor's efforts. Of lines that lack the beginning, he said: 'It does not seem to have occurred to him to ascertain how many letters were missing, so that his insertions might at least answer to the space available.' Concerning cases where the end of the line is defective, Craigie further complained that Gregor 'is also frequently at fault, and either prints it as if complete, or inserts words that will not suit the rimes of the verse'.[34] There is much validity in these criticisms, although not all Gregor's insertions are implausible. But his insensitivity to the metrical requirements of the line is particularly unfortunate, since Rolland seems to have taken pleasure in varying his metre: he employs five-stress couplets in the 'Prologue', a nine-line stanza employing only two rhymes (*aabaabbab*) as his staple narrative form, an eight-line stanza with refrain for the debate between the two [20] lovers in Book II, and a form of tail rhyme for the 'Summons' sent by Venus (see Bk I, ll. 811–74).

Awareness of rhyme patterns, together with sensitivity to Rolland's style and characteristic diction, is indeed a most valuable aid to supplying missing portions of text. Two small illustrations may be given. At Bk I, ll. 100–05, Gregor's text reads:

> His dowblet was of goldin bruid riche
> All set about with the cleir Cristalline.
> And in the breist ane Charbukill sa cl[eir]
> Quhilk did resplend as the sterne M[erceir]
> Cleir Apollo Esperus or Lucine,
> Before the day quhen thay so first a[ppeir].

Gregor's conjectures *cleir* and *appeir* are plausible. But line 100 is incomplete, and should read, more accurately, as 'His dowblet was of goldin buird richt [fine]'. The form *Merceir* seems an unlikely coinage, and fails to provide the required rhyme in *–ine*, which is supplied by Craigie's ingenious conjecture 'sterne M[atutine]'. At Bk II, l. 62, Gregor reads: 'Quhairthrow ȝe can not chaip Indignati[e]'. *Indignatie* is otherwise unknown, and as the stanza pattern requires a rhyme on *–ioun*, the most plausible reading here is *Indignatioun*.

There exist, however, several further clues to restoring sections of *The Court of Venus*, of which neither Gregor nor Craigie were aware. The first is the close similarity between some lines in Rolland's 'Prologue' (ll. 10–31) that describe the different 'complexions' (phlegmatic, sanguine, choleric and melancholy) and a passage on the same subject in an anonymous Scottish poem on physiognomy, which is now extant only in two seventeenth-century manuscripts in the National Library of Scotland (Adv. 34.3.11 and Adv. 34.3.12), but was probably composed in the early sixteenth century. The poem was discovered and first printed by Mrs Joyce Sanderson,[35]

---

33 *Court of Venus*, ed. Gregor, p. xxxi.
34 Craigie, 'Rolland's "Court of Venus"', p. 10.
35 Joyce M. Sanderson, 'A Recently-Discovered Poem in Scots Vernacular: "Complections of Men in Verse"', *Scottish Studies*, 28 (1987), 49–68.

and more recently has been re-edited by Dr Sally Mapstone,[36] who has shown it to be closely related to the physiognomy section in Hay's *Buik of King Alexander the Conquerour*. There is no doubt that Rolland, who mentions a 'buik of Phisnomy' in *The Seuin Seages* (l. 7259), was much interested in physiognomy.

[**21**] A few of the undamaged lines in the 'Prologue' to *The Court of Venus* are virtually identical with their equivalents in the 'Physiognomy'.[37]

> The feird and last, is callit Melancolie.
> (Rolland, 'Prologue', l. 13)

> The feird and the last is called melancholly.
> ('Physiognomy', l. 3)

> [F]or Flewme is fat, slaw, richt slipperie and sweir.
> (Rolland, 'Prologue', l. 16)

> Flewmen is fatt and slaw, sweir and sliparie.
> ('Physiognomy', l. 5)

In the light of these and other correspondences, it is possible to make a few further small improvements to the text. In Gregor, two lines on the sanguine man read:

> [Joyous and] in blythnes ay singand,
> [ ] genes and with delyte lauchand.
> ('Prologue', ll. 20–21)

Rolland seems here to recall and transpose two lines from 'Physiognomy', ll. 8–9:

> Luifand and larg, and lachand with delyte,
> In blythnes ay singand and wys hardy.

The original text in the 'Prologue' possibly read:

> [Wys and hardy] in blythnes ay singand
> [Full of lar]genes and with delyte lauchand.

Again, in the passage describing the choleric man Gregor has these lines:

> [I]n air nobill of valure.
> [do]gmatike: for it is hardie and fre.
> ('Prologue', ll. 23–24)

36 Sally Mapstone, 'The Scots *Buke of Phisnomy* and Sir Gilbert Hay', in *The Renaissance in Scotland: Studies in Literature, Religion, History and Culture Offered to John Durkan*, ed. A. A. MacDonald, Michael Lynch and Ian B. Cowan (Leiden, 1994), pp. 1–44.
37 Sanderson, 'Complections', 62–63.

It seems likely, however, that Rolland's original read: [**22**]

> [And it is far m]air nobill of valure
> [Na Phle]gmatike: for it is hardie and fre.

Compare 'Physiognomy', ll. 12–13:

> A far mair noble is na flewmatik.
> For it is frie, bayth lairg, hardy and stout.

A second aid to filling some lacunae in *The Court of Venus* was brought to my attention by *STC*. This records that fragments of the same edition of the poem exist in the Bodleian Library: they are Douce Collection, Fragments d.12(11). Disappointingly, the fragments are extremely small; they derive from a single unfolded sheet and comprise parts of leaves 26, 27, 32 and 33 (representing signatures Ei, Eii, Evii and Eviii). The fragment of leaf 26 indicates that the original text of Bk II, l. 495 has *In* rather than Gregor's conjecture *On*: '[On] future thingis, and Predestinatioun.' But Gregor's rather conjectural insertions in Bk II, ll. 496–97 and 524–25 are correct. The fragments of leaves 27 and 32 are too small to be of use.

Leaf 33, however, has some value, because it establishes the text of two hitherto defective passages in Book II. The first reads in Gregor:

> [I] tak on me that Preter Ihoms* queir
> [Is] not so riche vmbeset with plesance,
> [For] all that place with burnist gold did glance
> [Circ]umferat with Christall and Sapheir.
> [R]ubie sperkis and diamont most deir.
> [So]urelie drest with sic daliance:
> [In al] this warld I traist it had no peir.
> (*corrected in footnote to Iohnis)
>   (Bk II, ll. 897–903)

The Douce fragment of this passage (33^r) confirms the correctness of Gregor's insertions in lines 897, 898 and 900, but indicates that line 899 began with *As* not *For*. The last three lines, interestingly, have different and better openings:

> With rubie sperkis …
> So demurelie drest …
> That in this warld …

[**23**] The second passage consists of two lines, with defective endings, which Gregor supplied conjecturally as:

> Sine Ladie hoip scho past in wit[h Desperance]
> Till that scho come to Dame Vestai[s Mance].
>   Bk II, ll. 931–32

The Douce fragment (33^v) reveals that the correct endings of these lines are *with licence* and *Vestais presence*. These accord well with the rhymes in the rest of the stanza on *–ence*. Such corrections, though slight, are significant, and make one regret that more does not survive of the fragmentary Douce text.

A third aid to restoring a defective passage occurs in an unexpected location: BL, MS Add. 30371. This is a small miscellany, containing 'A Collection of Ancient and Scotish Poems', that was compiled by an otherwise unknown 'James Bruce, Alderman', probably in 1824. Its texts have been little studied, but seem largely to derive from printed sources, such as Allan Ramsay's *The Ever Green* (1724) and John Pinkerton's *Ancient Scotish Poems* (1786).[38] Item 52 (on fols 87^v–88^r) contains three stanzas from *The Court of Venus* (Bk I, ll. 289–312), together with a title – *Laus Veneris* – that also precedes this passage in the poem, and the colophon 'Quod Jo: Rollande of Dalkeith'. It seems a reasonable hypothesis that this excerpt was copied from a more perfect and now lost copy of the 1575 edition of *The Court of Venus*. The text corresponds closely to those lines that are still complete in the British Library copy, and usefully supplies those that are defective. It much improves the sense of lines 301–04, for instance, revealing (as Gregor's edition does not) that they are an apostrophe to Venus:

> O Venus quene of all quenis the flour
> Adres my spreit that I may say sumthing
> Within this garthe to thy laude & honour
> The to salute & thy sone Cupide King.

The manuscript similarly improves the sense of lines 305–09:

> My spreitis thay feir for dreid my hairt dois quake
> My tong tremblis half in ane ecstasie
> Fra my febill and faint Ingyne to tak
> And to discriue the greit nobilite
> And tendirnes that dois remane in the.

[24] *Tendirnes*, with the sense of 'benevolence', is markedly superior to *clevernes*, Gregor's conjecture at this point.

---

[38] The *Catalogue of Additions to Manuscripts of the British Museum* (London, 1882), p. 74 gives the date as 1724 [as does the entry for Add. MS 30371 in BL, Archives and Manuscripts Catalogue], but although this appears on leaf 5^r, it is not the original date; the number 7 has been written above 8 in a different and blacker ink. Several leaves also have a watermark with the date 1819. The manuscript contains poems by Dunbar that were not published until 1786 in Pinkerton's *Ancient Scotish Poems*; what is more, their texts and titles – one instance is 'Meditation wryttin in Wynter' – clearly derive from Pinkerton. For further discussion: P. Bawcutt, 'The Contents of the Bannatyne Manuscript: New Sources and Analogues', *Journal of the Edinburgh Bibliographical Society*, 3 (2008), 95–132 (110). [See this essay herein.]

'Mankit and mutillait' was George Bannatyne's term for some of the sources that he drew upon when compiling his famous anthology.[39] Sadly that pungent phrase is all too appropriate a description of Gregor's edition of *The Court of Venus*. This article is chiefly designed to warn future readers of its flaws. It also attempts to provide them with some assistance in correcting the oddities and errors of the text, until a new edition of the poem, which is clearly highly desirable, eventually appears. [25]

Editorial Note

[a]   First published in *The Apparelling of Truth: Literature and Literary Culture in the Reign of James VI. A Festschrift for Roderick J. Lyall*, ed. Kevin J. McGinley and Nicola Royan (Newcastle upon Tyne, 2010), pp. 11–29, and reprinted with the kind permission of Cambridge Scholars Publishing.

[39] *Bannatyne Manuscript*, ed. Ritchie, II, p. 1.

APPENDIX

The STS reading is placed to the left, marked off by an angle bracket. The correct reading is placed to the right. Square brackets [-] indicate a lacuna in the text of the original. Letters within the square brackets are conjectural emendations. Round brackets enclose glosses or explanatory comments.

Title page (in type facsimile)

Buikes;> Buikis,
[Impre]ntit> Imprentit

Prologue

1 Philosopher> Philosophour
3 verie> verse
6a *Line omitted*:
    And that throw heuinlie
    Constellatiounis
11 sicklike> siclike
16 flat> fat
20 blythnes> blyithnes
22 calit> crabit
25 Sultell> Subtell
    more> moir
30 Drowpond> Drowpand
    gredie,> gredie
31 feindill> seindill
34 ring and> ringand
54 ȝown> ȝow[-]
55 curagon> curag[-]
70 geuen> geuin
77 well> weill
86 commixt> conmixt
87 haue> haue his
90 his is> he is
108 stairt> stait
115 Sparhawks> Sparhalkis
118 sundrie> sindrie
130 Cajus> Cayus
155 are> ar   common> commoun
173 hedis> he di [e]
175 tratloris> tratlaris   other> vther
175a *Line omitted*:
    Sum ar Pelouris, and part ar fals
    pursep[ykis]
197 wyittis> wyitis
205 incontrait> incontrair

222 contrait … slow … gardans>
    contrair … kow … gar dans
233 dayly> daylie
244 chang[e]> chang[it be]
257 So … many> Sa … man
273 he it is> heiris
276 [-]art of Venus> [Co]urt of Venus
278 Correcte> Correctar,
286 wrong> wrang
300 Reprouvit> Repreuit
338a Finis> Finit

Book I

35 Pausing> Pansing
44 con> con[-] (Rhyme suggests:
    com[pleit]
45 Knowit … I> Knokit … I[-]
    (Rhyme suggests: I [cryde])
65 noo git> not gif
71 be> be my
75 thretie> threttie
90 Bowe> Bowr
100 bruid riche> buird richt [-]
108 Turkes> Turkas
113 body> bodye
119 bordonit> bordorit
124 taffeteis> taffateis
125 ȝe> ye ('the') [26]
129 frok> [-]rk. (Probably: sark)
131 [-]d rache. [id] rache
135 gret> grcit
143 quhairnin…pinid> quhairin …
    puud (error for pund)
147 Cinamone> Cinamome
156 Als> As
159 dowlet> dowblet
160 ȝailow> ȝallow
167 Philistiane> Phisitiane
192 [ȝo]unkeir> [ȝo]ungkeir

200 have> haue
218 rite> rute
223 vencreane> venereane
226 court> couet
241 but> bot
242 waike> waik:
243 as> , als
244 I the> I se the
250 fustrate> frustrate
267 bot> but
302 [Insp]ires> [–]cres (Read: Incres
304 [All the] abute> [–] alute (Read:
   And the salute)
309 remoue> remane
337 saif and> saifand
365 obitant> obstant
369 ahite> alite ('a little')
380 constante> constance,
395 holdis> haldis
397 Lameurie> Lamenrie
402 fen3eirnes> fen3eitnes
435 Intoxitait> Intoxicait
448a delexi> dilexi
486 see> se
487 diuilrie> deuilrie
490 wordis> sic wordis
497 hier> heir
503 by … are> ly … ar
516 Sclandour … drawes> Sclander …
   drawis
537 spekes> speikis
553 aspect> respect
557 sickill> fickill
558 reckes> reckis
562 but> bot
568a scor[-] one> scor[-]on*em*
   (Probably scorpion*em*)
572 right> richt
575 right> richt
589 also> als
598 Scandalous> Sclanderous
613 fierce> feirce
614 griefand> greifand
620 halfwo> half wo
640 Umquhill> Vmquhile
654 Inquerit> Inquirit
663 rich fair> richt sair

681 [Wod, ire]full, angrie, and
   rigerous> [–]full angrie crabit and
   rigorous
684 [And grew m]or> [And w]o*x*
689 soll> sall
712 Als> As
716 thairon> thairin
744 Man> Men
756 licht> sicht
771 an> and
818 greeting> greting
882 copy> copie
898 euir> cuir
913 Rhammusia> Rhamnusia

Book II

22 and hecht> hecht
42 distrust> discust
44 So> Sa
54 follow> fallow
62 Indignati[e]> Indignati[oun]
109 Grammar> Grammer
111 subtialtie> subtilitie
154 *Line is first of next stanza – wrongly
   placed in original*
193 fair> sair
229 vail3eand> vail3eant victorious>
   victorius
234 disconfeitour> discomfeitour
236a alexandria … propre> alexandria*m* (3 instances) … prope
245 Quhairsumeuer> Quhatsumeuer
313 I> It [**27**]
324 cho is> chois
326 kneiling> kneilling
353 vith> with
360 sasit> rasit
364 examinat> exanimat
373 Flane bellief lawcht> Flane
   bellieflawcht
376 let> bet
381 forsuith forsuith Prophettes>
   forsuith Prophetisses
417 dear> deir
418 schow> schaw
441 knais> kneis

497 oporcitie> opacitie
504 three> thre
526 *Line is first of next stanza*
527 citie> cietie
528 Ordainit> Ordanit
557 dwell> duell
588 Te> To
601 hid hing> did hing
631 alone> abone
642 name> nane
651 Ta> To
689 deffine> diffine
691 cristalline> Christalline
696 gladderand> gadderand
697 Than> Thair
700 kiruit> keruit
707 rimes> times
717 soir> sair
724 Ladies> Ladeis
731 or> nor
738 so> sa
739 to> for to
747 wisdome> visdome
748 her> hir
793 his> hir
798 or ... hier> and ... heir
825 couetis> couettis
848 suld> sould
859 Expand> Cryand
860 they> thay
862 hespeciall> hes speciall
884 was> war
897 Ihoms> Ihonis
906 3eet> 3e at
907 so> sa
923 odour> ordour
926 an> ay
928 Eclesiastik> Ecclesiastik
930 Thet> That
943 fair> sair
960 norine> nocine (Error in original
        for nociue, 'harmful')
971 pack> pak
973 but> bot
975 be:> bot
991 schaw> schew
1028 so> sa

Book III

3 Great membris> Creat membres
4 All> As
6 Clark> Clerk
13 Ladies> Ladeis
33 pleasant> plesant
36 and> ane
41 her> hir
43 was> quhilk was
45 sliches> slichts
46 wist ... Euridece> wife ... Erudices
60 Sicoris> Licoris
73 Parsiphae> Pasiphae
80 Harpolice> Harpalice
100 despyre> desyre
101 Thair> Thir
107 Remedio> Remebio (sic)
123 dekep> dekey
140 theis> cheis
157 aducat> aduocat
181 quhill> quhilk
199 but onymair> but ony mair
200 speid full> speidfull
207 this> thir
253 stomachat> stomochat
272 Ladies> Ladeis
274 forleir> forbeir
315 the self point> the self that point
319 at hir> athir ('either') [28]
324 ressoun> to ressoun
325 vererund> verecund
327 pretendant> pretendand
333 conditoun> conditioun
377 Idollis> Ydollis
378 Long> Lang
396 ayin> ay in
400 schaw> schew (Cf. II, l. 991)
423 Desirand> Disirand
426 care ... your> cure ... 30ur
427 saw> faw ('fall')
469 quhilk> the quhilk
490 abhorit> abhorrit
540 Then> Than
589 most> ane most
592 defait> desait (Cf. III, l. 650 below)
621 extirminate> exterminate
622 Empriours> & Empriours

633 liue> luif
636 wil full> wilfull
650 defait> desait
727 Plenit> Plenist
749 women> wemen
773 put> in put
788 richt> quhilkis richt
793 are> ar
865 virginitie> virginite
867 minded> minde &
875 bot> but
889 Protesteand> Protestand
895 detirmine> determine
906 thes> this
919 alhail> alhaill

Book IV

26 alegeance> allegeance
135 auisement> 3our auisement
138 secretlie> secreitlie
142 they> thay
145 Thisbe> be Thisbe
151 she> scho
156 faid> may faid
197 deseis> diseis
201 [–]nan solist be> [–]an solist scho be
227 stomachait> stomochait
235 Merriment> Merciment
246 benouolence> beneuolence
251 generall> ganecall
297 deis> dois
298 3ic> 3ie
300 preiudice> preiudeis
310 Vidimus> *In roman* (Latin
    legalism)
313 resoun> ressoun
360 friend … thrift> freind … thrist
386 knax> knak
419 This be> Thisbe
432 was> vs ('us')
438 mak> make
448 come> cum
456 plesand> plesant
472 So> To
511 no more> no man
512 3ier> 3eir

553 dowt … 3ou> dout … 3ow
556 my> thy
562 Dalience> Daliance
565 euer ilkane> euerilkane
573 richt chief> cheif
580 Sport and> Sport with
589 dub> dub the ('thee')
601 soir> sair
610 but bald> but baid
612 fairnes> sairnes
626 discomfit> discomfist
650 wos> was
680 were> was
684 matilent> in matilent
703 abuilyement> abuil3ement
720 no> na
722 closit> cloisit
725 their> thair
727 come> cum
744 for3it> forgit ('forged, contrived')
745 contrarie> contrairie
748 lufaris> luifaris

5

'Holy Words for Healing': Some Early Scottish Charms and their Ancient Religious Roots

Middle English charms in recent years have received growing attention from folklorists, students of religion and literary historians.[a] Those in verse have been indexed in *A New Index of Middle English Verse*;[1] some are included in anthologies, such as Rossell Hope Robbins's *Secular Lyrics* (1952) and Theodore Silverstein's *Medieval English Lyrics* (1971),[2] and several others are printed in scholarly journals.[3] A subtle and learned article on the topic was published by Douglas Gray in 1974, and Eamon Duffy devoted a substantial section of *The Stripping of the Altars* (1992) to 'Prayers and Spells'.[4] The position of Scotland is quite different: the charms known to survive from the early period are few in number, and so far little studied. The purpose of this essay is to make these Scottish charms better known, and to indicate their religious significance and wider cultural interest. Since they are not easily accessible and their sense has often been misunderstood, a text of each charm is also provided, freshly transcribed and edited from the manuscript.

One simple yet characteristic example is preserved in the Kirk Session Records of Perth. There it is recorded that on 21 May 1632 Laurence Boik and his wife Janet Black were accused of 'charming'. They confessed that 'they would sometime use some holy words for healing of shotts and sores, which words are these, [**128**]

> Thir sairis are risen thro' God's work,
> And must be laid thro' God's help;
> The mother Mary and her dear Son,
> Lay thir sairis that are begun.'[5]

---

1   Julia Boffey and A. S. G. Edwards, *A New Index of Middle English Verse* (London, 2005); henceforth *NIMEV*.

2   *Secular Lyrics of the XIVth and XVth Centuries*, ed. Rossell Hope Robbins (Oxford, 1952); *Medieval English Lyrics*, ed. Theodore Silverstein, York Medieval Texts (London, 1971).

3   See, for instance, Curt Bühler, 'Prayers and Charms in Certain Middle English Rolls', *Speculum*, 39.2 (1964), 270–78.

4   See Douglas Gray, 'Notes on Some Middle English Charms', in *Chaucer and Middle English Studies in Honour of Rossell Hope Robbins*, ed. Beryl Rowland (London, 1974), pp. 56–71; and Eamon Duffy, *The Stripping of the Altars: Traditional Religion in England, c.1400–c.1580* (New Haven, CT, 1992), pp. 207–98.

5   'Extracts from the Kirk Session Records', in *The Chronicle of Perth, a Register of Remarkable Occurrences, Chiefly Connected with that City, from the Year 1210 to 1668*,

73

It is clear that the purpose of these charms was not black magic or the raising of spirits or the devil, but 'healing' – the alleviation of everyday ailments in men and beasts, in a period when both the causes and the cures of disease were mysterious. Many of the charms surviving from England had a similar purpose, being designed to heal wounds, reduce toothache, or staunch bleeding. One such, discussed below, has the title *Medicina pro morbo caduco & le fevre*. It is striking too that Robbins placed the Middle English specimens in the 'practical' section of his anthology, along with other useful verses, such as mnemonics for the length of months.

But it is the 'holy' rather than the medical aspect of charms that is the topic of this article. The words uttered by this Perthshire couple today appear innocuous and highly pious, a plea for God's help against disease. Indeed in many cases the dividing line between a medieval charm and a prayer seems very fine, and it is not surprising that they were sometimes termed 'orisons'. Charms, like prayers, turned for assistance to Jesus, and more particularly his Passion, and also (as in this case) to his mother the Virgin Mary. Often they also invoked the aid of saints. Two Scottish charms that were added at some time in the fourteenth or early fifteenth century to fol. 2^v of the Herdmanston Breviary (NLS, Adv. MS 18.2.13A) were designed to heal a virulent cattle-disease known as 'lung-socht'.[6] The first is largely in Latin:

> Coniuro te morbum qui dicitur lowngsocht per uirtutem quinque wlnerum Ihesu Christi et per preciosum sanguinem eius per quem redempti sumus et per quinque gaudia dulsissime matris sue Marie et per dulsissimum lac quod de uberibus sue suxit vt non habeas [129] plus potestatem inter ista animalia migrare aut amplius nocere contra mandatum regale nostri redemptoris …

The second, entitled 'Carmen pro lonsoucht', opens in Latin but later switches to Scots:

> In nomine patris et filij et spiritus sancti amen. Deus benedicat greges istos sicut benedixit greges in deserto et per uirtutem illorum uerborum quod nocet non nocebit morbo de lonsoucht nec aliquo alio morbo caduco in uirtute et per uirtutem sancte Brigide sicut Deus dedit potestatem ei benedicere omnia animalia in terra. amen.

---

ed. James Maidment, Maitland Club 10 (Edinburgh, 1831), pp. 49–97 (97); also William George Black, *Folk-Medicine: A Chapter in the History of Culture*, Publications of the Folklore Society (London, 1883), p. 74.

6   *DOST*, *lung-*, *lowngsocht*, on the circulation and meaning of this word. The Herdmanston Breviary is thought to have originated in the north of England but came into the possession of the Sinclairs of Herdmanston some time in the fourteenth century. For further information, see *Kalendars of Scottish Saints with Personal Notices of Those of Alba, Laudonia, & Strathclyde, an Attempt to fix the Districts of their Several Missions and the Churches where they were Chiefly had in Remembrance*, ed. A. P. Forbes (Edinburgh, 1872), pp. liii, liv; and Catherine R. Borland, 'Catalogue of Mediaeval Manuscripts in the Library of the Faculty of Advocates at Edinburgh', [4 vols (Unpublished manuscript, Edinburgh, 1906–08), I, fols 101–08. NLS Reference: FR. 198a/1]. For advice and assistance concerning Adv. MS 18.2.13A, I am much indebted to Dr Kenneth Dunn and Miss Elspeth Yeo.

Nov ye sal tak a best and mak a bor [hole] in the horne and that in put this forsaid charm and tak a peny and bow [bend] in the bestis hevyd [head] and gar a voman gan to sant Brid and offer it in hir nam and tak holy vater and cast on tham as thai gan furth fra the charmyng. Non plus, etc.

St Bridget, or St Bride, was particularly popular in Scotland and, as Sir David Lyndsay satirically noted, she was the saint to whom women regularly prayed 'to keip calf and koow'.[7]

Although the medieval Church did not approve of charms and conjurations, nonetheless it seems to have permitted their use. Chaucer's Parson well conveys something of the ambivalence of medieval churchmen on this topic: trenchant disapproval of 'malefice of sorcerie' is combined with a grudging tolerance of 'charmes for woundes or maladie of men or of beestes'. Perhaps, he says, 'if they taken any effect, it may be peraventure that God suffreth it, for folk sholden yeve the moore feith and reverence to his name'.[8] In the sixteenth and seventeenth centuries, however, vehement attacks were made by Protestants, such as Conrad Platz and William Perkins, on charmers and 'blessers'. It was not simply that such charms alluded to beliefs and doctrines that were now regarded by the Reformers as papistical. What was offensive, as Stuart Clark has shown, was the inappropriate and devilish use of 'holy words':

> To claim that holy words in particular had an inherent efficacy was an outright rejection of the second commandment. If success was obtained, if children and livestock in fact recovered, this was by demonic intervention and should not be taken as a gain but as a loss – as a *punishment* for lack of steadfastness in affliction … It was one thing to say [130] the words of blessing over the baptized child as part of a formal ceremony, and quite another to bless adults and cows in the home and in the fields; it was one thing to speak of the 'power' of prayers and sermons, but quite another to attribute to utterances a material efficacy.[9]

It was thus not merely superstitious but demonic, if one attempted to heal cattle by invoking St Bridget or by reciting the *Ave Maria* over them in their byres.

The latter accusation was laid against Agnes Sampson, a midwife, cunning woman and diviner from Haddington, who is known to history as one of the alleged ringleaders of the North Berwick witches, accused of plotting with the devil to murder King James VI on his return from Denmark in 1590.[10] Their subsequent

---

7   The bending of pennies in this way was apparently common in medieval healing rituals. See Ronald C. Finucane, *Miracles and Pilgrims: Popular Beliefs in Medieval England* (London, 1977), p. 94; and *Ane Dialog* in *The Works of Sir David Lindsay*, ed. Douglas Hamer, 4 vols, STS, 3rd ser. 1, 2, 6, 8 (Edinburgh, 1931–36), I, pp. 197–386, lines 2382 and 2386.

8   See *The Riverside Chaucer*, gen. ed. Larry D. Benson (Oxford, 1988), *Canterbury Tales*, ParsT, X (I), 340; X(I), 603–06.

9   Stuart Clark, 'Protestant Demonology: Sin, Superstition, and Society', in *Early Modern European Witchcraft: Centres and Peripheries*, ed. Bengt Ankarloo and Gustav Henningsen (Oxford, 1990), pp. 66–67.

10   See *Witchcraft in Early Modern Scotland: King James VI's Demonology and the North Berwick Witches*, ed. Lawrence Normand and Gareth Roberts (Exeter, 2000), pp. 241–42

trial in Edinburgh in January 1591 is one of the most notorious episodes in Scottish history.[11] Agnes Sampson (also known by other names such as Annie Simpson) was eventually found guilty and sentenced to death. The many detailed charges against her were listed in the *dittay*, or indictment, preserved in the Books of Adjournal that record trials and court decisions of the sixteenth and seventeenth centuries, and now in the National Records of Scotland (NRS, JC 2/2, fols 201–06ᵛ). They contain two particularly interesting verse charms or conjurations that Agnes Sampson is said to have used for healing sick people or animals.[12] Since the witch trials were so sensational – in view of the king's involvement – there was enormous interest in England. The English ambassador, Robert Bowes, in a letter to Lord Burghley (23 February 1591), included an account of them compiled by a Scotsman; this account also contains copies of the two charms (TNA, SP 52/47).[13] [**131**]

The shorter charm, 'All kindis of illis that ewir may be', must have circulated in Edinburgh legal circles, because a third unpublished copy of it is preserved, along with other miscellaneous jottings, by the Clerks of Chancery, on a formerly blank page in the Responds Book, Register of Signatures (NRS, E30/13, fol. 61). Although most of the material in this volume of the Register of Signatures is dated 1580–81, the charm, which is here entitled 'Agnes Samsonis orisoun', was presumably entered much later, at a time when interest in the trial was at its height. The other entries on the page unfortunately do not aid the dating. One, written in the same hand as the charm, is a short untraced prose prophecy, here attributed to 'mr Iohne Capgraith [?Capgrave] Inglisman'; the other, in a different hand, is a verse riddle included in the Bannatyne Manuscript.[14]

Further light on this particular charm is shed by the existence of an earlier English text that appears to be its source. This is preserved in the Register of Missenden Abbey, Buckinghamshire (BL, Sloane MS 747, fol. 57ʳ). The work is a collection of Latin documents relating to the possessions of the abbey, compiled in the reign of Henry VII; the charm and many other miscellaneous items in English are thought to have been added *c.* 1501–06.[15] These are mostly religious and didactic in character; the page on which the charm occurs also contains lists of the ten commandments

---

(item 46).

[11] There is a vast literature on this subject, but for an excellent general introduction, see Julian Goodare, *The Scottish Witch-Hunt in Context* (Manchester, 2002).

[12] These were first printed in Robert Pitcairn, *Ancient Criminal Trials in Scotland ... Compiled from the Original Records and MSS*, 3 vols, Bannatyne Club 42 (Edinburgh, 1833), I, pp. 234–47. A modernized text is also printed in Normand and Roberts, *Witchcraft in Early Modern Scotland*, pp. 231–46. Unfortunately, neither text is wholly accurate.

[13] The letter of Robert Bowes, together with the Scottish report, is printed in *Calendar of the State Papers Relating to Scotland and Mary, Queen of Scots, 1547–1603* [CSP Scot.], X, 1589–93, ed. William Kenneth Boyd and Henry W. Meikle (Edinburgh, 1936), item 526, pp. 462–67. There are some inaccuracies in the transcription.

[14] For more information on the latter, see Priscilla Bawcutt, 'The Contents of the Bannatyne Manuscript: New Sources and Analogues', *Journal of the Edinburgh Bibliographical Society*, 3 (2008), 95–133 (115–16). [See this essay herein.]

[15] For a brief account of the manuscript and its contents, see William A. Ringler, *Bibliography and Index of English Verse in Manuscript, 1501–1558*, prepared and completed by Michael Rudick and S. J. Ringler (London, 1992), p. 33. Ringler classifies the piece (TM 1822) as 'Medical'.

and the seven deadly sins. Although the English charm cannot be precisely dated, it must have been circulating in England in the fifteenth century, and probably reached Scotland at least a century before it was recorded at the trial of Agnes Sampson.

I print here first the Scots version of the charm (based on NRS, JC 2/2, fol. 205), collated with the texts in E (Register of Signatures) and B (Bowes' letter); secondly the English version.

All kindis of illis that ewir may be,
In Crystis name I coniure the.
I coniure the, baith mair and les,
With all the vertewis of the mes.
And rycht sa be the naillis sa   5
That naillit Iesus, and na ma,
And rycht sa be the samin blude
That raikit owre the ruithfull rwid,
Furth of the flesch and of the bane
And in the eird and in the stane,   10
I coniure the, in Godis name.   **[132]**

Textual Notes
1. illis] euill E evils B   3. baith mair] both more B   6. Iesus] deir Iesus B   8. owre] on E over B ruithfull] michtefull E   9. Furth] Out E and of] and in E   10. *Line missing in* B

Medicina pro morbo caduco & le fevre.
In nomine patris et filii et spiritus sancti Amen.

What manere of ivell thou be,
In Goddes name I coungere the.
I counger the with the holy crosse
That Iesus was done on with fors.
I con[g]ure the with nayles thre   5
That Iesus was nayled vpon the tree.
I coungere the with the crowne of thorne
That on Iesus hede was done with skorne.
I coungere the with the precious blode
That Iesus shewyd vpon the rode.   10
I coungere the with woundes five
That Iesus suffred be his lyve.
I coungere [the] with that holy spere
That Longenus to Iesus hert can bere.
I coungere the neuerthelesse   15
With all the vertues of the masse,
And all the holy prayeres of seynt Dorathe.[16]

---

[16] This charm is also published in *Secular Lyrics*, [ed. Robbins], no. 65; and *Lyrics* [ed. Silverstein], no. 103. My readings occasionally differ.

Textual Notes
5. MS conure.   13. the] *Not in* MS.

How significant are the differences between these versions of the charm? The English text is longer, and much more overtly Catholic, invoking the instruments of the Passion with a reverence that resembles the tracts in the famous pre-Reformation Scottish devotional anthology, BL, MS Arundel 285.[17] The Scottish version retains [133] some original rhymes (in lines 1–2, 3–4, 7–8) but is obviously abridged. It omits key references to the Crown of Thorns, the Five Wounds and the Centurion Longinus and his spear, whom it was not uncommon to invoke in charms to staunch bleeding. The omission of St Dorothy is less surprising. Her cult was possibly less popular in medieval Scotland than in England – she does not figure in the fourteenth-century Scottish *Legends of the Saints*, for instance, nor is she mentioned in Sir David Lyndsay's satiric lists of saints idolatrously worshipped in sixteenth-century Scotland.[18] Even in the English text, Dorothy seems indeed something of an afterthought – one wonders if the scribe had a special devotion to that saint. Nonetheless the Scottish charm does keep the unambiguously Catholic appeal to 'the vertewis of the mes'.

Line 5 of the Scottish charm appears corrupt, although it is difficult to supply a satisfactory emendation. There is a clumsy repetition of *sa* within the line, and the phrase *na ma* (6) would imply that a definite number of nails had been mentioned, as in the English text. The devotional tradition of the Crucifixion was as specific concerning the Three Nails as the Five Wounds. In Walter Kennedy's *Passioun of Christ*, Thomas thus says that he would only believe in the risen Christ when 'in his handis and in his feit I see / All the taikynnis of the nalis thre' (1588–89). A graphic illustration of 'The Measure of the Nails', taken from Henry VIII's prayer roll, is provided by Eamon Duffy.[19]

Lines 9–10 of the Scottish charm are peculiarly interesting, since they have no equivalent in the English text. The 'illis' that are here addressed may not be simply conjured away into thin air, but must be transferred to some other location: 'Furth of the flesche and of the bane / And in the eird and in the stane.' In his *Discours des Sorciers* (*c.* 1590), Henry Boguet (*c.* 1550–1619) remarked on cures performed by witches: 'the cure is only effective for a limited time, or else it is necessary for the sickness to be transferred to someone else'.[20] Such a belief might have alarming consequences, as is evident from the remarks of Robert Kirk, writing later in the seventeenth century, concerning charmers in the Highlands:

---

[17] *Devotional Pieces in Verse and Prose from MS Arundel 285 and MS Harleian 6919*, ed. J. A. W. Bennett, STS, 3rd ser. 23 (Edinburgh, 1955). On the background, see A. A. MacDonald, 'Passion Devotion in Late-Medieval Scotland', in *The Broken Body: Passion Devotion in Late-Medieval Culture*, ed. A. A. MacDonald, H. N. B. Ridderbos and R. M. Schlusemann, Mediaevalia Groningana 21 (Groningen, 1998), pp. 109–31.

[18] See Lindsay, ed. Hamer, *Dialog*, I, pp. 268–70, lines 2325–85.

[19] See *The Poems of Walter Kennedy*, ed. Nicole Meier, STS, 5th ser. 6 (Woodbridge, 2008), and Duffy, *Stripping of the Altars*, plate 110.

[20] For this citation, see Henry Boguet, *An Examen of Witches Drawn from Various Trials*, trans. E. Allen Ashwin, ed. A. J. A. M. Summers, 1971 edn (London, 1929), p. 108.

There are words instituted for transferring of the soul or sickness on other Persons, Beasts, Trees, Waters, Hills or Stones, according as the Charmer is pleased to name ... which scares many sober persons among the Tramontanes from going in to see a sick person, [134] til they put a dog in befor them or one that perteans to the house: For where charmers are cherished they transfer the sickness on the first living creature that enters after the charm is pronunced.[21]

The second charm attributed to Agnes Sampson is preserved in two witnesses: the *dittay* (fol. 204[r–v]) and Robert Bowes' letter to Lord Burghley.

I trow in almychtie God that wrocht	
Baith heavin and erth and all of nocht.	
In to his deare sone Chryst Iesu,	
In to that anaplie lord I trow,	
Wes gottin of the haly gaist	5
Borne of the Virgin Marie.	
Stoppit to heavin that all weill[dand]	
And sittis att his faderis rycht hand.	
He baid ws cum, and thair to [deme]	
Baith quick and deid as he thocht [queme].	10
I trow als in the haly gaist,	
In haly kirk my hoip is maist,	
That haly schip quhair hallowaris winnis,	
To ask forgevenes of my sinnis	
And syne to ryis in flesch and bane	15
The lyffe that newir mair hes gane [?]	
Thou sayis, lord, lovit mot ye be,	
That formd and maid mankynd of me,	
Thow coft me on the [h]aly croce,	
And lent me body, saull and voce,	20
And ordanit me to heavinnis bliss,	
Quhairefore I thank the lord of this.	
And all your hallowaris lovit be,	
To pray to thame to pray for me	
And keep me fra that fellon fea	25
And from the syn that saull wald slay.	
Thow lord, for thy bytter passioun,	
To keip me frome syn and wardlie schame	
And endles damnatioun,	
Grant me the joy newir wilbe gane.	
Sweit Iesus Cristus Amen.	30 [135]

21 Robert Kirk, *The Secret Common-Wealth & A Short Treatise of Charms and Spels*, ed. Stewart Sanderson, Mistletoe Series (Cambridge, 1976), p. 109.

Textual Notes
Copy-text JC (the *dittay*); B (Bowes); CSPS (*CSP Scot.* transcript)
1. in] intil B til CSPS   2. Baith] Both B   4. anaplie B aullholie CSPS   5. haly gaist] holie ghost B   7. Stoppit] Steppit B weilldand] *ed. conj.* weill yane JC wene than B went then CSPS   8. faderis] fathers B   9. deme] *ed. conj.* dome JC B   10. queme] *ed. conj.* conuene JC quhome B   16. hes] is B   25. fra] from B   28. and] *not in* B

Most later commentators have been struck by the Christian orthodoxy of this charm. Pitcairn described it as 'a doggerel version of the Apostles' Creed,'[22] and Normand and Roberts called it 'impeccably orthodox'.[23] The charm does indeed contain the main outlines of the Creed, although it oddly omits one important clause concerning Jesus's crucifixion, death and descent into hell. Jesus, in Dunbar's succinct version of the Creed, was 'Off Mary borne, on croce deid and discendit, / The thrid day rais, to the faderis rycht hand ascendit.'[24] There seems no obvious reason for this omission – perhaps it may be attributed to forgetfulness on the part of Agnes, or carelessness on the part of the scribe. Similar metrical versions of the Creed were common in Middle English, usually based on the Latin, but varying considerably in length and metrical form.[25] There also exists an interesting Scottish parallel, copied on a blank page of the Makculloch Manuscript (EUL, Laing III.149, fol. 87ᵛ).[26] This consists of twenty-one lines, arranged in slightly irregular rhyme royal stanzas. There is no close verbal resemblance, however, apart from the opening lines: 'I trow in god the fader almychty / Makar of hewyne and erd and alkyne thing.' [136] The charm was termed a devilish prayer, however, despite its orthodoxy, because of the use to which it was put, which involved the practice of divination, a skill that Agnes Sampson was said to have learned from her father. According to Robert Bowes' informant, Agnes Sampson 'understude be her said prayer gif the patient wald die or leive'; and in the *dittay* itself it is said that if she halted in its recitation over the sick person, she refused to visit him further, because she knew he would die.[27]

The language of sacred texts often preserves ancient words, idioms and formulaic expressions that with the passage of time have dropped out of common use. Charms are no exception to this, their literal sense sometimes being misunderstood by later users, copyists and even scholars. This is particularly evident in this charm, and may be a sign of its antiquity. The word *anaplie* (4), for instance, is likely to baffle many modern readers. Pitcairn commented: '"Anaplie" seems to be written for

---

[22] Pitcairn, *Ancient Criminal Trials*, p. 234.
[23] Normand and Roberts, *Witchcraft in Early Modern Scotland*, p. 208.
[24] 'The Tabill of Confessioun', B 83, lines 60–61, in *The Poems of William Dunbar*, ed. Priscilla Bawcutt, 2 vols, ASLS, 27, 28 (Glasgow, 1998).
[25] *NIMEV* lists sixteen examples. For discussion, see R. H. Bowers, 'Three Middle English Poems on the Apostles' Creed', *PMLA*, 70.1 (1955), 210–22.
[26] The text is printed in *Pieces from the Makculloch and Gray MSS Together with the Chepman and Myllar Prints*, ed. George S. Stevenson, STS, 1st ser. 65 (Edinburgh, 1918), p. 19.
[27] *CSP Scot.*, X, p. 465; Normand and Roberts, *Witchcraft in Early Modern Scotland*, pp. 208 and 233.

aneplie, "aefald", "afald", literally *one-fold*, "sincere, without guile, &c."[28] The editors of *Calendar of the State Papers Relating to Scotland* could make no sense of the word either, and mistranscribed it as *aullholie*. The historical dictionaries, however, show that the word was current throughout the Middle Ages, that it derived from an OE word *anlepiȝ* and that it had such senses as 'only, sole, single, unique'.[29] It is probable that the word was becoming archaic by the end of the fifteenth century, since the latest occurrence in *MED* is dated before 1450. What is also striking is that the word is most commonly used, as here, in vernacular versions of the Creed, of Jesus the 'only' begotten son of God.

Although Normand and Roberts gloss this rare word correctly as 'single, sole, unique', a few everyday words have, unfortunately, defeated them. *Coft* in 'Thow coft me on the haly croce' (19) is not only misprinted as *cost*, but rendered as 'made an exchange for'. Yet *coft* was a common Scots word, and makes good sense as 'bought, redeemed'. It was frequently used in a theological sense of the redemption of man effected by the Crucifixion. Henryson wrote of 'Chryst that deit on tre / And coft our synnis deir' in *The Bludy Serk* (102), and in *The Gude and Godlie Ballatis* a repentant sinner says, 'I was sauld, and thow me bocht, / With thy blude thow hes me coft.'[30] [**137**]

Fellon fea (25) has likewise received bizarre modern interpretations, being transcribed by one scholar as *sell sea*,[31] and explained by Normand and Roberts as 'terrible inheritance', that is, 'original sin'. But, as the rhyme with *slay* suggests, *fea* is a late sixteenth-century spelling for a word more commonly spelt *fa*, 'foe, enemy', and the reference is to man's ancient foe, the devil. The same alliterative formula is found in Richard Holland's *Howlat* (746): 'The fende is our felloune fa.'[32]

Even in the sixteenth century, some words in this text were already posing problems. Both scribes appear to have had difficulty with lines 9–10, which in the unemended text of the *dittay* read:

> He baid ws cum and thair to dome
> Baith quick and deid as he thocht conuene.

The rhyme here is clearly faulty, yet the sense is not obviously improved by B's reading *quhome* instead of *conuene*. As these lines refer to the Last Judgement, *dome* might at first seem highly appropriate. The sense of line 10, however, requires a verb – Christ will come to *judge* the living and the dead – and *deme* seems a better reading than *dome*. The puzzling last word of line 10 is likely to be an error for *queme*, a mostly northern

28 Pitcairn, *Ancient Criminal Trials*, p. 234.

29 For discussion and copious illustration of the usage in Scots and Middle English, see *DOST*, anelape; *MED*, onlepi; and *OED*, anlepi, onlepy, onelepi, lepi.

30 See *The Poems of Robert Henryson*, ed. Denton Fox (Oxford, 1981), p. 161; and *The Gude and Godlie Ballatis*, ed. A. F. Mitchell, STS, 1st ser. 39 (Edinburgh, 1897), p. 220.

31 P. G. Maxwell-Stuart, *Satan's Conspiracy: Magic and Witchcraft in Sixteenth-Century Scotland* (East Linton, 2001), p. 20.

32 For the context, see *The Buke of the Howlat* in *Longer Scottish Poems Volume One 1375–1650*, ed. Priscilla Bawcutt and Felicity Riddy (Edinburgh, 1987), p. 74. This alliterative phrase was often applied to the devil; cf. citations in *DOST*, fa.

and Scottish adjective, with a range of senses, of which the first in *DOST* – 'fit, proper, right' – provides excellent sense.[33] It is interesting that the usage here is remarkably close to that found in several passages in the fourteenth-century Scottish *Legends of the Saints*. These two lines resemble a passage that describes Jesus in heaven, sitting

> of god, his faddyr, one þe rycht hand,
> & sal cum thine, ȝe vndirstand,
> þe quek & ded bath to deme
> on domysday, as hym think queme.[34]

Other instances of this formulaic usage occur elsewhere in references to the Last Judgement in *The Legends of the Saints*, and also in *Cursor Mundi*.[35] It is possible to devise a palaeographical explanation for both misreadings of the word *queme*. The letter *q* was sometimes confused with *quh*, as was *e* with *o*; hence *queme* > *quhome*. In the case of [138] *conuene*, it is likely that the scribe misunderstood a badly written *q* as the common contraction for the prefix *con–*.[36]

There remain other obscurities in the text that cannot be easily solved, such as the sense of *haly schip* (13). Normand and Roberts take it as 'holy ship', whereas *DOST* glosses as 'a holy place'. The line corresponds to that part of the Creed that speaks of the *Communio Sanctorum*, a late clause that has provoked much discussion but is usually interpreted as the fellowship of all holy persons.[37] Also puzzling is the second half of line 7 that in the *dittay* reads 'all weill thane'. The poor rhyme and dislocated syntax are ignored by Normand and Roberts, who explain as 'So that all was then well, that is, after Christ's Ascension'. My emendation is based on the need to provide a rhyme with *hand* (8) and a subject for the verb *stoppit*, 'stepped, ascended'. I take it to be a compound noun: *all-weilldand*, signifying the 'all ruling, the almighty', that is, God. This word can be traced to Old English and was employed in northern Middle English and Scots, usually as a participial adjective.[38] It was regularly applied to God, and occasionally, as here, specifically to the second person of the Trinity.

Other charms were associated with Agnes Sampson's name, long after her execution. George Sinclair, author of *Satan's Invisible World Discovered* (1685), commented on her use of 'Long Scriptural Prayers and Rhyms, containing the main points of Christianity so that she may seem not so much a white Witch as an holy

---

33 The word derives from OE *gecweme*. On its later history and uses, see *DOST*, *queme*; *MED*, *queme*; *OED*, *queme*.

34 *Legends of the Saints in the Scottish Dialect of the Fourteenth Century*, ed. W. M. Metcalf, 3 vols, STS, 1st ser. 13/18; 23/25; 35/37 (Edinburgh, 1888–96), I, p. 155, lines 183–86.

35 *Legends*, ed. Metcalf, II, p. 207, lines 95–96; p. 258, lines 1235–36; citation from *Cursor Mundi*, in *MED*, *queme(e*, 1 (a).

36 For illustrations, see Grant G. Simpson, *Scottish Handwriting 1150–1560* (Aberdeen, 1986), p. 44 and plate 1, ['Some Common Forms of Abbreviation'], item 6. Also *The Sex Werkdays and Agis*, ed. L. A. J. R. Houwen, Mediaevalia Groningana 10 (Groningen, 1990), p. 24.

37 See J. N. D. Kelly, *Early Christian Creeds*, 3rd edn (Harlow, 1972), pp. 388–97.

38 See *DOST*, *all-weldand*; *MED*, *al-welding*.

Woman.'[39] He quotes one 'Nonsensical Rhym' that opens 'White Pater Noster, God was my foster.' A second is termed 'The Black *Pater Noster*':

> Four newks in this house for haly Angels,
> A post in the midst, that's Christ Jesus,
> Lucas, Marcus, Matthew, Joannes,
> God be into this house, and all that belangs us.[40]

The prayer, of which this is a Scottish version, has a very long history. As Iona and Peter Opie noted, 'its beginning lies centuries deep, and it is part of the living traditional matter in most European countries'.[41] In some form, it was known to Chaucer, who alludes in 'The Miller's Tale' to what he terms the white *pater noster*: [**139**]

> Therwith the nyght-spel seyde he anon-rightes
> On foure halves of the hous aboute,
> And on the thresshfold of the dore withoute:
> 'Jhesu Crist and Seinte Benedight,
> Blesse this hous from every wikked wight,
> For nyghtes verye, the white *pater noster*![42]

Thomas Ady, an English contemporary of Sinclair, recorded a version, very similar to that still familiar to English children, in *A Candle in the Dark: Or a Treatise concerning the Nature of Witches and Witchcraft* (1656). His source was 'an old woman in Essex who was living in my time'. She 'had learned many Popish charms, one whereof was this: every night when she lay down to sleep she charmed her Bed, saying: "Matthew, Mark, Luke and John, / The Bed be blest that I lye on". This she claimed to have been taught "by the Church-men of those times"'.[43]

Another long-forgotten Scottish charm occurs in a fifteenth-century chartulary belonging to the Cistercian convent at Coldstream, founded in the twelfth century by Gospatric, Earl of Dunbar (BL, MS Harley 6670). This collection of charters and other muniments was copied by John Lawrence, a notary public, who recorded its completion on 3 April 1434 (fol. 55).[44] The charm is recorded on a blank leaf (now foliated as 56^r), and written in a different hand, probably of the late fifteenth or early sixteenth century. Although laid out as prose, it consists of three rough four-stress

39 Quotations come from George Sinclair, *Satans Invisible World Discovered* (Edinburgh, 1871), p. 22.
40 Sinclair, *Satans Invisible World*, pp. 22–23.
41 *The Oxford Dictionary of Nursery Rhymes*, ed. Iona Opie and Peter Opie (Oxford, 1952), p. 304.
42 *Riverside Chaucer*, gen. ed. Benson, *Canterbury Tales*, MilT, I (A), 3480–85.
43 Thomas Ady, *A Candle in the Dark: Or, a Treatise concerning the Nature of Witches & Witchcraft* (London, 1656), p. 58.
44 See *Chartulary of the Cistercian Priory of Coldstream with Relative Documents*, ed. Revd Charles Rogers, Grampian Club 18 (London, 1879) for further information and transcripts of the charters; also Ian B. Cowan, David E. Easson and Richard N. Hadcock, *Medieval Religious Houses: Scotland. With an Appendix on the Houses in the Isle of Man*, 2nd edn (London, 1976), pp. 145–46.

couplets, followed by a direction to utter the name of the person afflicted, then another couplet and directions for various prayers.

> For blud stanchyn
> Lord, as thow was don on rud,
> Throw thi mychtfulnes stem this blud.
> Fader and son and haly gast
> Stem and stanch this blus in hast.　　　　　　　5
> Suchtfast lord in personis thre
> I nem this nam in nam of the　　　　　　　[140]
> And than say the man or woman name and
> That ilka forbyddyn (?) forbyd I the
> That Ihesu partit land and se.
> And than say v paternosteris and v awe maryas and
> a creid and say this oryson thris and ilk tym wyth v
> paternosteris and v awe maryas and a creid, and gif
> it stanchis nocht quhen it is said thris, than say it ix
> tymis.[45]

Charms designed to stem the flow of blood are very common, and several Middle English examples survive. One, as yet unpublished, has a very similar incipit to this: 'Lord as thow hange vpon the rode.'[46] What appear to be vestiges of a Gaelic charm of this type exist, written in the late fourteenth or early fifteenth century in the Murthly Hours (NLS, MS 21000).[47] The Scots charm is simple, yet characteristic of the genre in its appeal to Christ, who shed his own blood on the cross, to 'Stem and stanch this blud in hast'. The devotional cult of the Holy Blood was then at the height of its popularity. No less traditional is the number symbolism, with the stress on three (explicitly mentioning the persons of the Trinity in line 5), and five (recalling though not mentioning the Five Wounds of Christ). Other charms are sometimes more explicit: 'sey thys Charme fyue times with fyue Paternosters, in the worschep of the fyue woundys'.[48] The sense of the last couplet is obscure, but seems to allude to the well-known legend that the River Jordan stood still on the day that Jesus was baptized. Many charms devised to staunch blood, known as the so-called *Flum Jordan* type, allude to this legend: in Middle English, they commonly began with some version of the line 'Crist was born in Bethlehem' (see *NIMEV* 624, 993, 993.11 and 2451.77).[49]

---

[45] The charm is printed, with some inaccuracies, in *Chartulary*, ed. Rogers, pp. 44–45. It is followed by a note, in a different hand, on *dies mali*, 'unlucky days'.

[46] See *NIMEV* 1946.5 (Manchester, John Rylands Library of the University of Manchester, Latin MS 228, fol. 74).

[47] Cf. the note by Ronald Black, ['Transcription, Translation and Commentary' (Appendix 6, 'Later Additions in Gaelic')], in John Higgitt, *The Murthly Hours: Devotion, Literacy and Luxury in Paris, England and the Gaelic West* (London, 2000), pp. 336–45 (339–40).

[48] Black, *Folk-Medicine*, pp. 76, 79–80.

[49] See the charm printed in *The Oxford Book of Late Medieval Verse and Prose*, ed. Douglas Gray (Oxford, 1989), p. 137; also Gray, 'Charms', p. 62.

Many other charms probably circulated in sixteenth-century Scotland. One such is recalled in a mysterious and haunting couplet recorded in *The Complaynt of Scotland* (printed *c.* 1550):

> Arthour knycht he raid on nycht
> Vitht gyltin spur and candil lycht.[50]

[141] This occurs, written as prose, in the famous pastoral interlude that describes how Scottish shepherds and their wives passed the time with songs, tales and dances. It is sandwiched between the titles of romances well known in Scotland, some Arthurian – for example, 'Lancelot du lac' and 'Gauen [Gawain] and gollogras'.[51] The closest analogy to these two lines, however, is found not in an Arthurian romance but in a charm recorded in the nineteenth century and communicated by a Shetlander to the scholar and journalist Karl Blind, who printed it in 1879:[52]

> Arthur Knight
> He rade a' night
> Wi' open swird
> An' candle light.
> He sought da mare;
> He fan' da mare;
> He bund da mare
> Wi' her ain hair.
> And made da mare
> To swear:
> 'At she should never
> Bide a' night
> Whar ever she heard
> O' Arthur Knight.

The 'mare' in this charm is the nightmare, which was believed to afflict both humans and animals. Another version was recorded by Mrs J. M. E. Saxby from the Shetlands at almost the same time, which differs chiefly in its opening phrase: 'De man o' meicht / he rod a' neicht'.[53]

---

50 *The Complaynt of Scotland, c. 1550*, ed. A. M. Stewart, STS, 4th ser. 11 (Edinburgh, 1979), p. 50. Many titles have long been unidentified; see Priscilla Bawcutt, 'A Song from *The Complaynt of Scotland*: "My Hart is Leiuit on the Land"', *Notes and Queries*, 49.2 (2002), 193–97.

51 On these, see Rhiannon Purdie, 'Medieval Romance in Scotland', in *A Companion to Medieval Scottish Poetry*, ed. Priscilla Bawcutt and Janet Hadley Williams (Cambridge, 2006), pp. 165–77.

52 See Karl Blind, 'Discovery of Odinic Songs in Shetland', *The Nineteenth Century*, 5 (1879), 1106. I am much indebted to Jacqueline Simpson, for communicating to me her discoveries about these charms, later published as Jacqueline Simpson, 'The Nightmare Charm in *King Lear*', in *Charms, Charmers, and Charming: International Research on Verbal Magic*, ed. Jonathan Roper (Basingstoke, 2009), pp. 100–07.

53 See Revd Biot Edmondston and J. M. E. Saxby, *The Home of a Naturalist*, 2nd edn (London, 1889), pp. 186–87. Both of the Shetland versions are cited in *County Folklore: Printed Extracts*

Both these nineteenth-century Scottish charms correspond closely to a medieval English one, later versions of which survive from the sixteenth century. This English charm, however, invoked the protective powers not of 'Arthur knight' or a mysterious unnamed man of might but St George: [**142**]

> Seynt Iorge, our lady kny3th,
> He walked day, he walked ny3th,
> Till that he fownde that fowle wy3th;
> And whan that he here fownde,
> He here bete and he here bownde,
> Till trewly ther here trowthe sche ply3th
> That sche sholde not come be ny3hte,
> With-inne vij rode of londe space
> Ther as Seynt Ieorge I-namyd was.[54]

This, the oldest English version, was particularly associated with the healing of horses: according to the rubric, it was to be written in a bill, and hung either over the stable door or in the horse's mane. A later but similar version was quoted by Thomas Blundevill in *Fower Chiefyst Offices Belongyng to Horsemanshippe* (1566) in a section on horse diseases; rather defensively, he claimed to have included it, in part to make the reader laugh, and said contemptuously that it was 'a fonde folishe charme' invented by 'the false Fryers in tymes paste' to extract money from the gullible.[55]

But what is the sense of 'Arthur Knight' or 'Arthour knycht'? Karl Blind asserted that 'Arthur Knight' was 'a substitution for the Germanic god of storms and battles', that is, Odin, and also claimed that 'in half romantic, half boorish form, an Odinic myth is thus preserved in this Nightmare incantation'.[56] This assertion is wholly unconvincing. But should we then interpret the phrase as signifying King Arthur himself? This too seems mistaken. Grammatically, 'Arthur' in the phrase 'Arthur knight' is best interpreted as an example of the rare uninflected zero-genitive, which in Older Scots was commonly found with nouns of relationship ending in *–r* (examples are 'sister son' and 'brother dochter').[57] Such zero-genitives are said to occur occasionally with personal names, and the fact that *Arthur* ends in *–r* is probably significant. Indeed one can find other instances of this very construction in sixteenth-century Scottish verse: what we today call 'Arthur's Seat' in Edinburgh appears as 'Arthour Sait' in

---

No. 5; Examples of Printed Folklore concerning the Orkney and Shetland Islands, ed. G. F. Black and N. W. Thomas, Publications of the Folk-Lore Society (London, 1903), p. 145.

54 *NIMEV* 2903; see *Secular Lyrics*, ed. Robbins, no. 66

55 Thomas Blundeville, *The Fower Chiefyst Offices Belongyng to Horsemanshippe* (London, 1566), pp. 17–18 [*STC* (2nd edn) 3152]; Iona Opie and Moira Tatem, *A Dictionary of Superstitions* (Oxford, 1990), p. 378.

56 Blind, 'Discovery of Odinic Songs', pp. 1108 and 1113.

57 For discussion of the zero-genitive in Scots, see A. J. Aitken, 'Variation and Variety in Written Middle Scots', in *Edinburgh Studies in English and Scots*, ed. A. J. Aitken, Angus McIntosh and Hermann Pálsson (London, 1971), pp. 177–209 (179 and note 13); Caroline Macafee, in *DOST*, XII, p. cvi; and Anne King, 'The Inflectional Morphology of Older Scots', in *The Edinburgh History of the Scots Language*, ed. Charles Jones (Edinburgh, 1997), pp. 156–181 (165).

Bannatyne's text of [**143**] *The Flyting of Dunbar and Kennedie*, and as 'Arthure Sait' in one of the satirical poems attributed to Robert Sempill.[58]

In the world of Arthurian myth, it was surely more common for one of the knights to ride out in search of adventure than for King Arthur himself. Even so, how does one account for the metamorphosis of St George into 'Arthur's knight'? Jacqueline Simpson has suggested that St George was possibly discarded in Scotland, 'as too English and too Catholic (especially when called "Our Lady's Knight")'.[59] It is true that by the later Middle Ages St George had become the patron saint of England, and the phrase 'Our Lady's Knight' was so often linked with his name in carols and religious lyrics that R. L. Greene called it his 'most hackneyed epithet'.[60] But devotion to this saint was by no means confined to the English. St George was widely popular throughout Europe, and evidence exists for his veneration in late medieval Scotland.[61] There are many parallels between the activities of a military saint, such as St George, and the exploits of the knights of King Arthur. Indeed in the ceremonies of the Order of the Garter, St George was closely associated with the Arthurian world.[62] Dr Simpson's hypothesis is highly plausible, yet it is arguable that simple confusion of protective warriors, rather than nationalistic sentiment or Protestant censorship, might have led to the substitution of 'Arthour knycht' for St George.

'Arthour knycht', with its vivid imagery, is hardly typical of the verse charms discussed in this article, which are examples of the simplest and most elementary kind of poetry. Yet they are not completely lacking in verbal art. The traditional poetic formulae, alliteration, octosyllabic couplets and other simple repetitions – 'I conjure thee … I conjure thee' – would have lifted them out of the language of the everyday, contributed to their incantatory effect, and made them easily memorable.

Editorial Note

[a] First published in *Literature and Religion in Late Medieval and Early Modern Scotland*: *Essays in Honour of Alasdair A. MacDonald*, ed. Luuk Houwen, Mediaevalia Groningana n.s. 18 (Leuven, 2012), pp. 127–43; and reprinted with the kind permission of Peeters Publishers.

[58] See *The Bannatyne Manuscript*, ed. W. Tod Ritchie, 4 vols, STS, 2nd ser. 22, 23, 26; 3rd ser. 4 (Edinburgh, 1928–34), III, p. 55, line 336; *Satirical Poems of the Time of the Reformation*, ed. James Cranstoun, 2 vols, STS, 1st ser. 20/24, 28/30 (Edinburgh, 1891–93), ['The hailsome admonitioun'], I, pp. 165–69, line 118.

[59] Simpson, 'Nightmare Charm', p. 103.

[60] *The Early English Carols*, ed. Richard Leighton Greene, 2nd edn (Oxford, 1977), note to 311.1. For Scottish familiarity with this phrase, see also *Legends of the Saints*, ed. Metcalf, II, p. 176, line 14.

[61] See the valuable study by Steve Boardman, 'The Cult of St George in Scotland', in *Saints' Cults in the Celtic World*, ed. Steve Boardman, John Reuben Davies and Eila Williamson (Woodbridge, 2009), pp. 146–59. Cf. Lindsay, ed. Hamer, *Dialog*, I, p. 267, line 2304; John Higgitt, *'Imageis maid with mennis hand': Saints, Images, Belief and Identity in Later Medieval Scotland*, Whithorn Lecture (Whithorn, 2003), *passim*; and David Ditchburn, *Scotland and Europe: The Medieval Kingdom and Its Contacts with Christendom, c.1215–1545* (East Linton, 2001), pp. 55–56.

[62] Cf. Jonathan Good, *The Cult of Saint George in Medieval England* (Woodbridge, 2009).

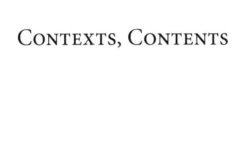

CONTEXTS, CONTENTS

6

Manuscript Miscellanies in Scotland from the Fifteenth to the Seventeenth Century

'Mo sterres, God wot, than a payre.'

(Chaucer, *The Parliament of Fowls*, 595)

My starting-point is a very bright star in the Scottish firmament, the Bannatyne Manuscript.[a] Recently termed, with some hyperbole, 'the most important literary document of early Scottish literature',[1] it has been closely scrutinized by many scholars especially in the last quarter of a century. Yet despite all the undoubted advances in our knowledge, this manuscript poses many unsolved problems, and I am increasingly uneasy about the way conjecture, unverified assumptions and hypotheses, and even downright errors are rapidly assuming the status of fact. Michael Lynch erroneously claims, in *Scotland: A New History*, that the collection contains 'more love poetry than anything else', and that it was 'compiled' in 1565–66.[2] The wide dissemination of such beliefs is ensured by the well-deserved popularity of his important book. Enshrined in the very title of *Poetry of the Stewart Court* is another tenacious yet dubious notion, that the Bannatyne Manuscript is 'a court anthology'. In the tart words of Denton Fox, 'to describe the whole contents of the manuscript as court poetry is to stretch the term out of all reason'.[3] Several preconceptions can be traced ultimately to one great man: Sir Water Scott, who viewed George Bannatyne in the light of his own [190] Romantic beliefs and assumptions and imputed to him the patriotic and antiquarian plan 'of saving the literature of a whole nation'.[4] Another current idea – that 'the collection was destined for the printer' – can likewise be

1 Theo van Heijnsbergen, 'The Interaction between Literature and History in Queen Mary's Edinburgh: The Bannatyne Manuscript and its Prosopographical Context', in *The Renaissance in Scotland: Studies in Literature, Religion, History and Culture Offered to John Durkan*, ed. A. A. MacDonald, M. Lynch and I. B. Cowan (Leiden, 1994), pp. 183–225 (183).

2 Michael Lynch, *Scotland: A New History* (London, 1991; rev. edn, 1992), p. 213.

3 See *Poetry of the Stewart Court*, ed. Joan Hughes and W. S. Ramson (Canberra, 1982); and Fox's review in *Times Literary Supplement*, no. 4200 (30 September 1983), 1065.

4 Walter Scott, 'Memoir of George Bannatyne', cited in *The Bannatyne Manuscript*, ed. W. Tod Ritchie, STS, 3rd ser. 5 (Edinburgh, 1932), I, pp. cxxix–cxxx.

traced ultimately to Scott's speculation that Bannatyne 'designed' the work 'to be sent to the press'.[5]

The Bannatyne Manuscript, above all, is perceived as unique: many distinguished scholars have studied it, but few have questioned this unique status, or made much attempt to view it in the context of other manuscript miscellanies, whether English or Scottish. The one exception is a curious longstanding rivalry with the Maitland Folio (Appendix, no. 6): when John Pinkerton, in the eighteenth century, called the Folio 'the chief treasure of ancient Scottish poetry', he was vigorously attacked by the defenders of the Bannatyne.[6] In this essay, I shall look at a number of Scottish literary miscellanies – a subject inherently interesting in itself, I believe – and then return to the Bannatyne Manuscript, and re-examine it in the light of these other manuscripts. Such a comparison, as I hope to show, is profitable.[7]

Quite a large number of Scottish anthologies survive, and in the past there must have existed many more. Only one Catholic devotional collection is now extant (London, BL, Arundel 285; Appendix, no. 4), and it is inherently unlikely that no others were produced. Yet these manuscripts are, in general, not well known and have been curiously neglected by scholars. In the first half of the twentieth century, excellent transcripts of some [191] were published by the Scottish Text Society (Appendix nos 2, 3 , 4, 5, 6 and 7); yet their apparatuses were sketchy, and few have been followed up by further study. There now exist good facsimiles of the Bannatyne Manuscript and Oxford, Bodleian Arch. Selden. B. 24 (Appendix,

---

5 Scott, 'Memoir', in *Bannatyne Manuscript*, ed. Ritchie, I, pp. cxxix, cxxxii; for later expressions of this view, see I, p. xxxviii; and A. A. MacDonald: 'The Bannatyne Manuscript: A Marian Anthology', *Innes Review*, 37 (1986), 36–47 (41–42); also A. A. MacDonald, 'The Printed Book That Never Was: George Bannatyne's Poetic Anthology (1568)', in *Boeken in de late Middeleeuwen*, ed. J. M. M. Hermans and K. van der Hoek (Groningen, 1994), pp. 101–10 (105). For discussion of other important issues, see Denton Fox, 'Manuscripts and Prints of Scots Poetry in the Sixteenth Century', in *Bards and Makars: Scottish Language and Literature; Medieval and Renaissance*, ed. Adam J. Aitken, Matthew P. McDiarmid and Derick S. Thomson (Glasgow, 1977), pp. 156–71; William Ramson, 'On Bannatyne's Editing', in *Bards and Makars*, pp. 172–83; and Evelyn S. Newlyn, '"The Wryttar to the Reidaris": Editing Practices and Politics in the Bannatyne Manuscript', *Studies in Scottish Literature*, 31 (1999), 14–30.

6 On the background, see *Ancient Scotish Poems*, ed. John Pinkerton, 2 vols (London, 1786), I, p. vii; *Bannatyne Manuscript*, ed. Ritchie, I, p. clxv; and Priscilla Bawcutt, 'The Earliest Texts of Dunbar', in *Regionalism in Late Medieval Manuscripts and Texts*, ed. Felicity Riddy (Cambridge, 1991), pp. 183–98 (196–97).

7 I exclude from consideration copies of single long poems such as Gavin Douglas's *Eneados*, legal and heraldic miscellanies, and works such as the Makculloch Manuscript (EUL, MS Laing III.149), which is essentially a Latin compilation to which vernacular poems were added at a later date. There is, unfortunately, no space to discuss comparable English literary miscellanies, such as the Devonshire Manuscript (BL, Add. MS 17492), the Welles Manuscript (Bodleian, Rawlinson MS C.813), ed. Sharon L. Jansen and Kathleen H. Jordan (Binghamton, NY, 1991), and the Arundel Harington Manuscript [BL, Egerton MS 2711] (owned by the Duke of Norfolk), ed. Ruth Hughey, 2 vols (Columbus, OH, 1961).

no. 1),[8] and useful descriptive studies of the Asloan Manuscript [Edinburgh, NLS, 16500] (Appendix, no. 3) and Arundel 285;[9] nothing comparable exists for any other miscellany. A few manuscripts have been published in part, often modernized, bowdlerized, or with the order of their contents re-arranged. In 1899, for instance, William Walker published *Extracts from the Commonplace Book of Andrew Melville 1621–1640* (Aberdeen University Library, MS 28; Appendix, no. 16); he omitted a bawdy sonnet, and the very first item, a substantial prose piece, at the beginning of which is inscribed in a nineteenth-century hand (probably Walker's): 'An Essay on Women – not complimentary.' Another small verse miscellany (EUL, Laing III.447; Appendix, no. 18) has been printed, but the order of items is totally rearranged, for no obvious reason; what is even more misleading is that it is published in the Scottish Text Society's Montgomerie supplementary volume, although it has only three poems certainly by that poet (*The Cherrie and the Slae*; no. vi; and no. xxx).[10] None of the later manuscripts has been described carefully and systematically; [**192**] information about them is difficult to find, muddled and sometimes quite misleading. When I first came across a reference by Dr Helena Shire to the Melvill Buik of Roundels (Appendix, no. 13), I was intrigued by the title, but wondered why

---

8   *The Bannatyne Manuscript: National Library of Scotland Advocates' MS 1.1.6*, introd. Denton Fox and William Ringler (London, 1980); and *The Works of Geoffrey Chaucer and the 'Kingis Quair': A Facsimile of Bodleian Library MS Arch. Selden. B. 24*, introd. Julia Boffey and A. S. G. Edwards, app. B. C. Barker-Benfield (Cambridge, 1997). See also, J. Boffey, 'Annotation in Some Manuscripts of *Troilus and Criseyde*', *English Manuscript Studies*, 5 (1995), 1–17; A. S. G. Edwards, 'Bodleian Library MS Arch. Selden. B. 24: A "Transitional" Collection', in *The Whole Book: Cultural Perspectives on the Medieval Miscellany*, ed. Stephen G. Nichols and Siegfried Wenzel (Ann Arbor, MI, 1996), pp. 53–67; Julia Boffey and A. S. G. Edwards, 'Bodleian MS Arch. Selden. B. 24 and the "Scotticization" of Middle English Verse', in *Rewriting Chaucer: Culture, Authority and the Idea of the Authentic Text, 1400–1602*, ed. T. A. Prendergast and B. Kline (Columbus, OH, 1999), pp. 166–85; Julia Boffey, 'Bodleian Library, MS Arch. Selden. B. 24 and Definitions of the "Household Book"', in *The English Medieval Book: Studies in Memory of Jeremy Griffiths*, ed. A. S. G. Edwards, Vincent Gillespie and Ralph Hanna (London, 2000), pp. 125–34.

9   On the former manuscript, see *The Buke of the Sevyne Sagis*, ed. Catherine van Buuren (Leiden, 1982), esp. pp. 5–42; also 'John Asloan and His Manuscript', in *Stewart Style 1513–1542: Essays on the Court of James V*, ed. Janet Hadley Williams (East Linton, 1996), pp. 15–51; and I. C. Cunningham, 'The Asloan Manuscript', in *Renaissance in Scotland*, ed. MacDonald, Lynch and Cowan, pp. 107–35. On the latter, see Introduction to *Devotional Pieces in Verse and Prose from MS Arundel 285 and MS Harleian 6919*, ed. J. A. W. Bennett, STS, 3rd ser. 33 (Edinburgh, 1955), pp. i–xxxviii; J. A. W. Bennett, 'Scottish Pre-Reformation Devotion: Some Notes on British Library MS. Arundel 285', in *So Meny People Longages and Tonges*, ed. Michael Benskin and M. L. Samuels (Edinburgh, 1981), pp. 299–308; and A. A. MacDonald, 'Passion Devotion in Late Medieval Scotland', in *The Broken Body: Passion Devotion in Late-Medieval Culture*, ed. A. A. MacDonald, H. N. Ridderbos and R. M. Schlusemann (Groningen, 1998), pp. 109–31.

10 *Poems of Alexander Montgomerie: Supplementary Volume*, ed. George Stevenson, STS, 1st ser. 59 (Edinburgh, 1910). These three poems are included in the new edition of *Alexander Montgomerie: Poems*, ed. David J. Parkinson, 2 vols, STS, 4th ser. 28, 29 (Edinburgh, 2000), [I, pp. 176–274; I, no. 16, pp. 27–28; I, no. 4, pp. 7–9].

she mentioned only two poems and gave no further description of the manuscript's contents. It is symptomatic that W. H. Auden, who also showed some awareness of this work in *An Elizabethan Song Book*, said that 'the only known manuscript' was in Australia. In fact it has been owned by the Library of Congress in Washington since 1945.[11]

There are many different and legitimate ways of approaching a manuscript. We all, editors and critics alike, seek out what we can understand, interpret or find interesting: ballads, perhaps, or works in a specific genre, or new poems by a particular poet – Dunbar, Montgomerie, Ayton. Above all, Scottish scholars have looked for works authentically Scottish. The history of Bodleian Arch. Selden. B. 24 is typical: one item from it has been reprinted again and again, and it has sometimes been called 'the *Kingis Quair* manuscript'; its other, largely Chaucerian, contents have been virtually ignored in Scotland. Today, in somewhat the same patriotic spirit, the seventeenth-century song manuscripts are searched for 'the music of Scotland'; the presence in them of works by English composers is rarely mentioned. I do not wish to be misunderstood. To assemble the lost, scattered or forgotten compositions of Scottish poets and musicians is a worthy enterprise.[12] Nonetheless, silent selectivity, whether inspired by nationalism or some other motive – extracting merely the plums, like little Jack Horner – may lead to distortion and falsification, not only of a manuscript's character but of a society's literary and musical culture.

In recent decades, there has been a remarkable resurgence of interest in manuscripts belonging to the late medieval and early modern period. Some pointers to this are the biennial York Manuscript conference, and the newish journal *English Manuscript Studies 1100–1700*. Two features in this I find particularly significant. The first is a concern with the manuscript as a whole, not just as a quarry from which choice items are selected. An analogy might be drawn with the methods and motives of modern archaeologists: no longer mere treasure-seekers, they analyse the structure and social significance of a site. One keen advocate of modern [**193**] codicology comments: '[t]he methods of compilers and manuscript editors of all kinds, whether professional or amateur, need to be studied, if we are to understand the reception and readership assumed for the literary works contained in their collections'.[13] Yet nothing is ever wholly new. Long ago, M. R. James urged scholars to describe the complete manuscript: we should not neglect 'anything that a manuscript can tell us

---

[11] See Helena Mennie Shire, *Song, Dance and Poetry of the Court of Scotland under King James VI* (Cambridge, 1969), pp. 145, 255; and *An Elizabethan Song Book: Lute Songs, Madrigals and Rounds*, ed. N. Greenberg (Music), W. H. Auden and C. Kallman (Texts) (New York, 1955), p. xxiii. Auden's anthology included seven of the modernized texts from the Roxburghe Club publication (no. 168) of *The Melvill Book of Roundels*, ed. Granville Bantock and H. Orsmond Anderton (London, 1916). Auden was puzzled by the corrupt rhymes in 'O lusty May', for which Bannatyne provides a much better text (fol. 229^v).

[12] Pioneering and valuable contributions to this enterprise are Kenneth Elliott, 'Music of Scotland 1500–1700' (unpublished PhD thesis, Cambridge, 1959) and *Music of Scotland 1500–1700*, ed. Kenneth Elliott and Helena Mennie Shire, Musica Britannica 15 (3rd rev. edn, London, 1975).

[13] See *Manuscripts and Readers in Fifteenth-Century England: The Literary Implications of Manuscript Study*, ed. Derek Pearsall (Cambridge, 1983), p. 1.

as to its place of origin, its scribe, or its owners. Names and scribblings … which to one student suggest nothing, may combine in the memory of another into a coherent piece of history.'[14] The second point (to which I shall return) concerns the relationship of manuscripts and printed books. Scribal activity, both professional and amateur, continued to be important for centuries after the invention of printing: the late date of the Robert Tait Manuscript (Appendix, no. 20) should be noted. Poems were not only preserved, but also transmitted, and, in a sense, published in manuscript. The complex and shifting relationship between the two media of print and manuscript in the sixteenth and seventeenth centuries is presently the subject of intense discussion and debate by such scholars as Harold Love, Mary Hobbs, Henry Woudhuysen and Arthur Marotti.[15] Some modern scholars, however, still tend, almost automatically, to privilege the printed book.

In the Appendix, I list twenty Scottish miscellanies mentioned in this article (bracketed numbers henceforth refer to this list). They are arranged in approximately chronological order, from the late fifteenth century to the last quarter of the seventeenth century. In fact I shall say little of numbers 1–4, or 20, despite their considerable interest. I shall be chiefly concerned with a shorter and more homogeneous period: the 1560s to 1640s. Even so, it is clearly impossible to discuss every aspect of every miscellany. I shall give more prominence to some manuscripts than others, and focus on such questions as who compiled them, what they contain, where their material came from and how they are arranged. [194]

I must stress at the outset the diversity of these manuscripts, in size as in other respects. At one extreme is the Asloan Manuscript (no. 3), which even in its present imperfect condition contains over 300 leaves (230 x 170 mm); at the other is the much smaller Maxwell Manuscript (no. 9), which has only thirty-six leaves (approximately 125 x 100 mm). Time has treated these works very differently. Some, such as the Maitland Quarto (no. 7), are still in a state of remarkably good preservation; others, such as the Maitland Folio (no. 6), are worn and damp-stained. Perhaps in the worst state of all is the fragmentary manuscript in the National Records of Scotland in Edinburgh (RH 13/35; no. 8), which has been 'sadly ravaged by time, damp, and mice'.[16] Later owners of some manuscripts cut out leaves – the stubs of many such

---

14 M. R. James, *The Wanderings and Homes of Manuscripts* (London, 1919), p. 23. For an excellent survey of the late medieval period, see *Book Production and Publishing in Britain 1375–1475*, ed. Jeremy Griffiths and Derek Pearsall (Cambridge, 1989). For an illustration of the value of such 'scribblings', see Priscilla Bawcutt, 'The Boston Public Library Manuscript of John Lydgate's *Siege of Thebes*: Its Scottish Owners and Inscriptions', *Medium Ævum*, 70 (2001), 80–94. [See this essay herein.]

15 See Harold Love, *Scribal Publication in Seventeenth-Century England* (Oxford, 1993); Mary Hobbs, *Early Seventeenth-Century Verse Miscellanies* (Aldershot, 1992); H. R. Woudhuysen, *Sir Philip Sidney and the Circulation of Manuscripts 1558–1640* (Oxford, 1996); and A. F. Marotti, *Manuscript, Print and the English Renaissance Lyric* (Ithaca, NY, 1995). For a bibliographic overview, see Noel J. Kinnamon, 'Recent Studies in Renaissance English Manuscripts', *English Literary Renaissance*, 27 (1997), 281–326. All these works, though primarily concerned with English manuscript culture, contain much that is relevant to Scotland.

16 On this manuscript, see Marion Stewart, 'King Orphius', *Scottish Studies*, 17 (1973), 1–16; also Sally Mapstone, '*The Thre Prestis of Peblis* in the Sixteenth Century', in *A Day*

can be seen in the Robert Edward Manuscript (no. 19); other owners attempted to preserve and embellish them by rebinding, but this too led to damage and the loss of important features vital for explaining a manuscript's make-up.

What can be discovered about the copyists, compilers or owners of these collections? (Sometimes one person was all three.) Predominantly they were young men; educated, but not highly learned; members of the middle classes rather than great noble families – notaries, ministers, schoolteachers and lairds. In some cases (EUL, Laing III.467; no. 18), we know nothing. All that we can say of the compilers of Cambridge University Library, Kk.1.5, no. 6 (no. 2), and BL, Arundel 285 (no. 4), is that, judging by the contents, they were good Catholics; by contrast, the contents of NLS, Adv. 19.3.6 (no. 10) suggest that he (or she) was no less devout, but a Protestant. Other copyists, however, have placed their names not only at the beginning, but throughout the manuscript: 'per manum Iohannis Asloan'; 'be me Maxwell of Southbar 3oungar'; 'the penner Robertus Edwardus'; and 'by me R Taitt' or 'per me R Tatium'. From data such as these, scholars have plausibly identified John Asloan as a notary, active in Edinburgh during the first thirty years of the sixteenth century. The scribe of NRS RH 13/35 seems likely also to have been a notary, called Thomas White, who lived in the Haddington area, and apparently compiled this miscellany for the Cockburns of Ormiston, a family largely sympathetic to the Reformers. John Maxwell, however, was probably a Catholic, and came from a different area of Scotland; he was heir to the estate of Southbar in Renfrewshire, and lived until 1606. A young amateur versifier and translator from Latin, he copied some poems and composed others, largely, as he says, 'for spoirt / me to conforte' ([EUL, Laing III.467], fol. 5ʳ).[17] Robert Edward and Robert Tait were conservative in their tastes, and, although they lived in the seventeenth century, preserved much verse and music from the [**195**] preceding century. Robert Edward (*c.* 1616–96) was a graduate of St Andrews, and minister of Murroes, in Angus; his patron was the Earl of Panmure, in whose family his manuscript was preserved.[18] A little more is known about the career of Robert Tait, a 'doctour', or assistant teacher, in Lauder parish, and a supporter of Episcopalianism and James VII. He was appointed session clerk in Lauder on 7 January 1677, but seems to have been removed from office after the Revolution,

---

Estivall: Essays ... in Honour of Helena Mennie Shire, ed. Alisoun Gardner-Medwin and Janet Hadley Williams (Aberdeen, 1990), pp. 81–95.

17 There is an unpublished transcript of this manuscript among the materials used for the *DOST*. For a description, see Priscilla Bawcutt, 'The Commonplace Book of John Maxwell', in *A Day Estivall*, ed. Gardner-Medwin and Hadley Williams, pp. 59–68. [See this essay herein.]

18 No detailed account of Robert Edward (*sic*) and his manuscript exists. See, however, NLS, *Catalogue of Manuscripts Acquired since 1925*, 7 (Edinburgh, 1989), no. 9450, pp. 160–61; H. Scott, *Fasti Ecclesiae Scoticanae* (Edinburgh, 1866–71; rev. and enlarged edn, 1915–50), 5 (1925), pp. 367–68; Helena M. Shire, 'Robert Edwards' Commonplace Book and Scots Literary Tradition', *Scottish Studies*, 5 (1961), 43–49; and Kenneth Elliott, 'Robert Edwards' Commonplace Book and Scots Musical History', *Scottish Studies*, 5 (1961), 50–56. Dr Shire prints three of the poems in *Poems from Panmure House* (Cambridge, 1960).

because of his anti-Presbyterian views. His manuscript, compiled between 1676 and 1689, contains verse in Scots and Latin, as well as an important repertory of songs.[19]

Several manuscripts are associated with the name of Melvill, and the north-east of Scotland. The Andrew Melvill of Aberdeen University Library, MS 28 (no. 16) was not the famous Reformer, but a teacher at the Aberdeen song school between 1621 and 1640. When Melvill was appointed master in 1637, he was said to be of 'gude lyff and conversatioun', and qualified in the 'airt of musick'. Unfortunately, his manuscript contains no song-settings, although there are copies of printed works on musical theory. Among its contents are rhyming proverbs, moral and religious verse, and, at the end (fols 79^v–80^r) an interesting list of 'the buiks in my pressis', which includes 'Gray Steill' and the 'feables of Easope'.[20] David Melvill was apparently his brother, and a bookseller in Aberdeen. Three manuscripts (nos 11–13) are associated with his name: one is the Buik of Roundels (1612), mentioned earlier; in addition there are a Bassus part-book, compiled c. 1604 (BL, Add. 36484); and a manuscript now in the Fitzwilliam Museum, Cambridge, sometimes known as the Tolquhon Cantus book. Its cover bears the [196] ownership inscription: 'A. F. 1611', usually taken to refer to Alexander Forbes, Master of Tolquhon. Both this and the Bassus part-book long remained in the possession of the Forbes of Tolquhon, Aberdeenshire. Although the copyist of the Cantus manuscript is not named, its hand is said to be identical with that in the Bassus book.[21]

One shamefully neglected cluster of manuscripts is associated with the Maitland family; singly and as a group they call out for further investigation. At their centre is the distinguished figure of Sir Richard Maitland of Lethington (1496–1586), whose long life spanned the reigns of James IV and James VI. A lawyer and landowner, he

[19] The most valuable source of information is W. H. Rubsamen, 'Scottish and English Music of the Renaissance in a Newly Discovered Manuscript', in *Festschrift Heinrich Besseler zum Sechzigsten Geburtstag*, ed. E. Klemm (Leipzig, 1961), pp. 259–84. Unfortunately, some scholarly confusion has occurred because Rubsamen transcribed Tait's monogram, or signature, as 'T. Raitt'. There is no doubt, however, that the name is correctly 'R. Tait(t)'; it agrees closely with Tait's signature in the Lauder kirk session register for 7 January 1677 (NRS, CH. 2/534/1). I am indebted to Dr Tristram Clarke of the NRS [formerly, NAS], who brought this document to my attention, and commented: 'His signature is done with a typical flourish, the initial R overlaying the "T".' Robert Tait appears in a list of schoolmasters teaching Latin in 1690: see 'List of Schoolmasters Teaching Latin, 1690', ed. Donald J. Withrington, in *Miscellany*, 10, SHS, 4th ser. 2 (Edinburgh, 1965), pp. 121–42 (138).

[20] See *Extracts from the Commonplace Book of Andrew Melville 1621–1640*, ed. W. Walker (Aberdeen, 1899); also Helena M. Shire, 'Andro Melvill's Music Library: Aberdeen 1637', *Transactions of the Edinburgh Bibliographical Society*, 4, part 1 (1955–57), 3–12.

[21] On the Melvill Bassus part-book, see A. Hughes-Hughes, *Catalogue of Manuscript Music in the British Museum*, 3 vols (London, 1906–09), II, pp. 144–46; the contents are listed, and English and Italian music sources of the music are identified. See also H. M. Shire and P. M. Giles, 'The Tolquhon Cantus Part Book: A Fine Scots Binding of 1611', *Transactions of the Edinburgh Bibliographical Society*, 3, part 3 (1951–52), 161–65; H. M. Shire, 'The Forbes-Leith Music Books (1611–1779)', *Transactions of the Edinburgh Bibliographical Society*, 3, part 3 (1951–55), 165–68; and H. M. Shire, 'Scottish Song-book, 1611', *Saltire Review*, 1.2 (1954), 46–52.

had varied literary interests: he compiled *Practicks of the Law of Scotland* and also wrote short prose histories of the house of Seton (his mother's family) and of the house of Douglas. His own poems are extant in three manuscripts whose inter-re-lations have never been properly studied: the Maitland Folio (no. 6), the Maitland Quarto (no. 7) and a manuscript in Edinburgh University Library that belonged to the poet William Drummond of Hawthornden.[22] All three collections originated in family piety and were designed in the first place to preserve Sir Richard's poems. This purpose is particularly evident in the Quarto, which begins with a prefatory sonnet in honour of Sir Richard and ends with elegies and epitaphs on him and his wife. Approximately half the poems in it are by Sir Richard, or written in honour of members of the family. Some lines from a charming poem on Lethington, their home, are revealing:

> Quha dois not knaw the Maitland bliud [blood]
> the best in all this land?
> (No. lxviii ['Virgil his village Mantua'], 141–42)[23]

[**197**] The same preoccupation with the family and its continued prosperity is evident in the Folio, which contains poems in what might be called the 'Polonius' genre – good advice to one's sons (nos xiv, xlvii) – and another piece that opens: 'Giff þou desyre þi hous lang stand' (no. cvii).[24] The Folio is particularly important as the single largest repository of poems by Dunbar.[25]

---

[22] See Priscilla Bawcutt, 'The Earliest Texts of Dunbar', in *Regionalism*, ed. Riddy, pp. 190–93; also Sir Richard Maitland, *The History of the House of Seytoun*, Maitland Club (Glasgow, 1829). The recently discovered and unpublished history of the Douglases is among the Hamilton manuscripts at Lennoxlove House, bundle 2098; see also *David Hume of Godscroft's History of the House of Douglas*, ed. David Reid, STS, 4th ser. 25 (Edinburgh, 1996), I, p. xi. and *passim*. Drummond's manuscript of the poems is EUL, De.3.71; see also R. H. MacDonald, *The Library of Drummond of Hawthornden* (Edinburgh, 1971), p. 226, no. 1372; and A. A. MacDonald, 'The Poetry of Sir Richard Maitland of Lethington', *Transactions of the East Lothian Antiquarian and Field Naturalists' Society*, 13 (1972), 7–19. Two recent studies are: Julia Boffey, 'The Maitland Folio Manuscript as a Verse Anthology', in *William Dunbar, 'The Nobill Poyet'*, ed. S. Mapstone (East Linton, 2001), pp. 40–50; and A. A. MacDonald, 'Sir Richard Maitland and William Dunbar: Textual Symbiosis and Poetic Individuality', in *William Dunbar*, ed. Mapstone, pp. 134–49.

[23] *The Maitland Quarto Manuscript*, ed. W. A. Craigie, STS, 2nd ser. 9 (Edinburgh, 1920).

[24] Maitland Folio Manuscript, ed. W. A. Craigie, 2 vols, STS, 2nd ser. 7, 20 (Edinburgh, 1919–27). On this topic, cf. Love, *Scribal Publication*, p. 202. Poem cvii is attributed to Sir Richard Maitland in both the Folio and the Quarto, the first in a later hand, but it should be noted that there exists another very similar early text, attributed to Alexander Barclay, a fifteenth-century laird of Mathers. This was first printed by Robert Barclay in *A Genealogical Account of the Barclays of Urie, Formerly of Mathers* (Aberdeen, 1740), pp. 10–11, where it is said to derive from a manuscript 'Genealogy of the Barons of the Mearns', dated 1578.

[25] See also *The Poems of William Dunbar*, ed. Priscilla Bawcutt, 2 vols, ASLS, 27, 28 (Glasgow, 1998), esp. I, pp. 7–8.

The Reidpeth Manuscript (no. 14) is a partial transcript of the Folio and illustrates the importance of family links and networks at this time, in literature as in politics. Its copyist, John Reidpeth, has not been identified, but something can be said of the man for whom it was apparently compiled: Master Christopher Cockburn, younger son of James Cockburn of Choicelee, and an Edinburgh graduate (1592). The different branches of the Cockburn family were close neighbours of the Maitlands; they intermarried with them and received favours from John Maitland, when he was Chancellor. Christopher Cockburn himself was a servitor (*c.* 1619) to Lord Thirlestane, who was the grandson of Sir Richard Maitland.[26] (Very much later in the seventeenth century Robert Tait compiled part of his manuscript 'at the castle' of Thirlestane.[27])

The Maitland Folio contains a marginal scribble: 'This buke pertenis to helyne m'; Helen is likely to be Sir Richard's daughter, who married another Cockburn, Sir John Cockburn of Clerkington.[28] The Maitland Quarto, however, is even more certainly a woman's book. Inscribed 'Marie Maitland 1586', it was owned by Sir Richard's youngest daughter, who, according to Maurice Lee, 'sacrificed herself for many years to the requirements of' her blind father and only on his death (in March 1586) was 'free to live her own life' (that is, to marry).[29] The Quarto may be Marie's book in the further sense that she was its copyist. Sir William Craigie, because of its attractive italic script, thought it more probably 'written for her by some expert penman'. Yet the most distinguished [198] calligrapher in Scotland at this time was Esther Inglis, and the use of italic was particularly associated with women; some considered the secretary hand too difficult for them.[30] The Quarto is a woman's book in another sense, since it includes several pieces that might appeal to feminine taste: Arbuthnot's 'Contrapoysoun to the Ballat falslie intitulit the properteis of gud

---

[26] For a fuller account, see Bawcutt, 'Earliest Texts', pp. 193–94; also Maurice Lee, *John Maitland of Thirlestane and the Foundation of the Stewart Despotism in Scotland* (Princeton, 1959), pp. 153–54, and 223–24.

[27] See Rubsamen, 'Scottish and English Music', p. 261. [On John Reidpeth, see further: Sally Mapstone, 'Introduction: Older Scots and the Sixteenth Century', in *Older Scots Literature*, ed. S. Mapstone (Edinburgh, 2005), pp. 175–88 (181–82).]

[28] *Maitland Folio Manuscript*, II, p. 5.

[29] Lee, *John Maitland*, p. 96. Rosalind K. Marshall, *Virgins and Viragos: A History of Women in Scotland from 1080 to 1980* (London, 1983), p. 123, says that Marie 'acted as her father's secretary'. Marie married Alexander Lauder of Halton, and their son George was himself a poet.

[30] *Maitland Quarto Manuscript*, pp. v–vi. Cf. also Sarah Dunnigan, 'Scottish Women Writers *c.* 1560– *c.* 1650', in *A History of Scottish Women's Writing*, ed. D. Gifford and D. McMillan (Edinburgh, 1997), pp. 15–43 (29–31). On Esther Inglis, see A. H. Scott-Elliott and Elspeth Yeo, 'Calligraphic Manuscripts of Esther Inglis (1571–1624): A Catalogue', *Papers of the Bibliographical Society of America*, 84 (1990), 11–86; A. Tjan-Bakker, 'Dame Flora's Blossoms: Esther Inglis's Flower-Illustrated Manuscripts', *English Manuscript Studies*, 9 (2000), 49–72; and Georgianna Ziegler, 'Hand-Ma[i]de Books: The Manuscripts of Esther Inglis, Early-Modern Precursors of the Artists' Book', *English Manuscript Studies*, 9 (2000), 73–87; Woudhuysen, *Sir Philip Sidney*, pp. 32, 98–99. See also Love, *Scribal Publication*, p. 99; and G. E. Dawson and L. Kennedy-Skipton, *Elizabethan Handwriting: 1500–1650* (New York, 1966), p. 10.

Wemen' (no. xxxv); and an 'Elagie' on an unhappy marriage, spoken by the wife (no. lxvi).[31] Another poem (no. lxix) is a eulogy of Marie Maitland herself, which opens 'Intill ane morning mirthfullest of May'; this and other lines recall Dunbar's *The Goldyn Targe*. Another (no. lxxxv), explicitly addressed to 'Maistres Marie', urges her to write more poetry, and to join the company of Sappho and 'Olimpia o lampe of Latine land' (6). A remarkable piece (no. xlix), written by one unnamed woman and addressed to another, celebrates female friendship: 'Thair is mair constancie in our sex' (67).[32]

Marie Maitland is interesting in herself, and also as a portent of the future. Several of the seventeenth-century manuscripts that contain songs and music were compiled by young gentlewomen with leisure and a taste for polite accomplishments. Some account books of the Foulis family, who inherited the Bannatyne Manuscript, are revealing in this respect. They record the purchase of 'a pair of virginals' and payments to a tutor 'for learning Meg to play on the violl'.[33] There is space to mention two only of these manuscripts here. The first (no. 17) was made by Lady Margaret Wemyss, daughter of David, second Earl of Wemyss (1610–79). Born in 1630, Margaret lived only to the age of nineteen; she began her 'booke containing some pleasant airs collected out of diverse authors' on 5 June 1643. Later she notes that 'all the lesons behind this are learned of my sisteres book', that is, her elder sister Jean, later Countess of Sutherland. The lute music in this manuscript has attracted particular interest, but it [**199**] also contains twenty-seven love poems without musical settings. These range from an old but very popular poem by Henry Howard, Earl of Surrey, 'Giue cair doe caus men cry, quhy doe I not complain', to modish and witty pieces by Thomas Carew. The Scottish items include poems by Ayton, and Montgomerie's 'What mighty motion so my mind mischiuis'.[34]

My second example is the tantalizing figure of Margaret Robertson. Very little seems to be known of her life, but her father and her husband, Alexander Stewart of Bonskeid, possessed estates in Perthshire, near Blair Atholl. Her family apparently fought on both sides of the Civil War, but she herself raised soldiers for Montrose in 1646. It is unfortunate that the original manuscript of her collection has disappeared, although in the early nineteenth century it was seen and described with great enthusiasm by Colonel David Stewart:

[31] On the French source of this poem, see Priscilla Bawcutt, 'French Connections? From the *Grands Rhétoriqueurs* to Clément Marot', in *The European Sun: Proceedings of the Seventh International Conference on Medieval and Renaissance Scottish Language and Literature*, ed. Graham Caie et al. (East Linton, 2001), pp. 119–28 (127–28).

[32] For further discussion of this poem, see Sarah Dunnigan, 'Feminising the Early Modern Erotic: Female-Voiced Love Lyrics and Mary Queen of Scots', in *Older Scots Literature*, ed. Sally Mapstone (Edinburgh, 2005), pp. 441–66.

[33] *The Account Books of Sir John Foulis of Ravelston 1671–1707*, SHS, 1st ser. 16 (Edinburgh, 1894), pp. 46, 107, 112.

[34] See Matthew Spring, 'The Lady Margaret Wemyss Manuscript', *The Lute*, 27 (1987), 5–29; also D. James Ross, *Musick Fyne* (Edinburgh, 1993), pp. 146–47. Montgomeries's poem is edited in Parkinson, I, no. 12, pp. 21–22.

There is a manuscript volume preserved in the family of Stewart of Urrard, of 260 pages, consisting of poems, songs and short tracts, in the Scotch language, written, as is stated on the first page, by Margaret Robertson, daughter of George Robertson of Fascally, and wife of Alexander Stewart of Bonskeid, dated 1643. It is written in a beautiful hand, and with such correctness, that it might be sent to the press.[35]

Two nineteenth-century transcripts survive (see no. 15); both of these, however, give the date of their original as 1630, not 1643. How accurate they are it is impossible to say.[36] The contents resemble those of the Wemyss Manuscript: love songs in English and Scots, though without musical settings.[37]

Not all these miscellanies are carefully arranged. Some seem to have grown haphazardly over several years and contain what appear to be random entries in no particular order. This is largely true of the Maxwell Manuscript (no. 9) and the Andrew Melvill Manuscript (no. 16), yet even in these there appears some principle of order: in the first case, it is [**200**] thematic (verses on friendship or other topics being grouped together); in the second, there is an alphabetical arrangement of some items. Many collections, however, show signs of care and planning. BL Arundel 285 (no. 4) is laid out neatly, with titles, colophons and other headings in red; it also has 'illustrations and decorated capitals that derive from printed books'.[38] The Maitland Quarto is – in Pinkerton's words – 'exquisitely written' in contrasted styles. Craigie suggested that what he called 'the old Scottish hand' was chosen for Sir Richard's poems, whereas the more modern pieces were in 'a large Italic lettering resembling print'.[39]

David Melvill lavished great care on his manuscripts. The Bassus part-book (no. 11) is very attractive; the use of different inks and scripts makes its layout easy to follow, and each song is numbered. Another of his manuscripts (no. 12) has a splendid contemporary binding, and an elaborate title:

35 Col. David Stewart, *Sketches of the Character, Manners and Present State of the Highlanders of Scotland*, 2 vols (Edinburgh, 1882; 2nd edn, rpt 1977), II, Appendix S, pp. xxxi–xxxii.

36 On Margaret Robertson, see also Priscilla Bawcutt, 'A New Scottish Poem: On the Literary Interest of Timothy Pont's Map 23', *Scottish Literary Journal*, 20.2 (1993), 5–20 (15–18); NLS, Typescript Catalogue of Manuscripts, no. 15937; and MS 2617 (ii) (a photo of the 1646 document). BL Add. 29409 is the second volume of a collection made by the antiquary Peter Buchan and contains only a partial transcript of the Robertson manuscript. Buchan elsewhere, in *Ancient Ballads and Songs of the North of Scotland* (Edinburgh, 1828), I, p. xv, says that the manuscript was lent to him by John Richardson, Esq. of Pitfour Castle, Perthshire.

37 A manuscript of comparable date, also compiled by a young woman, is NLS, 9449: see Evelyn Stell, 'Lady Jean Campbell's Seventeenth-Century Music Book', *Review of Scottish Culture*, 8 (1993), 11–19. The only verse it contains is a repeated pious couplet: 'Doth Adam die, Christ in the live, / Christ shall Eternall life the give'.

38 *Devotional Pieces in Verse and Prose*, ed. Bennett, pp. ii and xxxii–xxxv.

39 [For John Pinkerton's words: *Ancient Scotish Poems* (Edinburgh, 1786), II, p. 467]; *Maitland Quarto*, ed. Craigie, p. vi. [For examples of the hands, see the frontispiece illustrations in *The Maitland Quarto*, ed. Joanna Martin, STS, 5th ser. 13 (2015).]

Ane buik of roundells / Whairin thair is conteined songs and / roundells that
may be sung with / thrie, four, fyue or mo voices / haifing prettie and pleasantt
/ letters sum in Latin and / sum in Inglish quhilks / ar an hundreth in number.
/ Collected and notted by dauid meluill. 1612.

Unfortunately, something went wrong with Melvill's count, and he did not achieve his
century. The manuscript contains ninety-six songs, comprising eighty-eight rounds
and eight part-songs. At the end is a 'table of the wholl songs and roundels within
this buke', indicating 'alsweill the number as the leiff'. Such consideration for the
reader was by no means unusual. Other manuscripts were also user-friendly. The
Asloan Manuscript (no. 3) has at the beginning a contemporary list of the contents
'of the buke follow[and]'. Robert Edward similarly provided for no. 19 a 'table of the
songs goinge before choeinge [showing] there ordur by the alphabetical ordur'. This
particular manuscript even has a running title: 'fyn' on the verso, and 'musik' on the
recto. Items are numbered; explanatory rubrics call attention to different sections;
and there is a list of 'Annotations and significations' of terms (fol. 74^v).

Anyone who examines the seventeenth-century song-books must be struck by
the presence in them of English poets and composers: Dowland, Campion and
Morley, for instance, were obviously popular in Scotland. It is far too simplistic
to attribute the responsibility for this solely to the departure of James VI and his
court to England in 1603. The taste for English verse and music was not a novel
phenomenon that suddenly occurred at the turn of the seventeenth century. These
miscellanies constitute a valuable index of literary taste: one thing they show is that
English poems were attractive to Scottish readers well over a century before James
departed for London. Bodleian Arch. Selden. B. 24 [(no. 1)] is an early witness to
this, but all the sixteenth-century collections contain English material; this ranges
from an extract from *The Polychronicon* (in [**201**] the Asloan Manuscript) to Chaucer,
Lydgate and a mass of anonymous didactic verse.[40] Scholars have been very slow
to recognize the English origin of some poems: the anti-feminist punctuation piece
in the Maitland Folio (no. clxxvi), 'All wemeine ar guid noble and excellent', also
exists in English miscellanies, such as the Devonshire Manuscript and the Arundel
Harington Manuscript. Indeed in several cases the compilers themselves possibly
did not know or were unconcerned, cheerfully scotticizing the texts or giving them
to Scottish authors. One small example is the fourteenth-century poem, 'Earth upon
earth', which is attributed in the Maitland Folio (no. clxiii) to Mersar, and in the
Reidpeth manuscript to Dunbar.[41]

Many items in these Scottish miscellanies were copied from printed books. This
phenomenon is rarely noted, perhaps because it seems like a bizarre reversal of
the natural order. Yet scholars are becoming increasingly aware of how common it
was throughout the fifteenth and sixteenth centuries to copy not only extracts, but

---

[40] For fuller discussion, see Priscilla Bawcutt, 'English Books and Scottish Readers in the
Fifteenth and Sixteenth Centuries', *Review of Scottish Culture*, 14 (2001–02), 1–12.

[41] For English texts of the punctuation poem, see Hughey, I, no. 151; her commentary [2,
208–11] includes the Devonshire Manuscript version [BL, Add. 17492, fol. 18^v]. On the
antiquity and wide distribution of the 'Earth upon Earth' poems, see *The Middle English
Poem Erthe upon Erthe*, ed. H. M. R. Murray, EETS, OS 141 (London, 1911).

sometimes whole books. People who, for a range of reasons, were unable to acquire the printed texts that they needed made their own copies or had them made by professional scribes.[42] Perhaps the most attractive Scottish instance is the illustrated Harleian Manuscript of Henryson's *Fables*, which is thought to be a copy of the Bassandyne print (1571).[43] But there are many other examples: one is the manuscript of John Mirk's *Festial* (based on the Rouen edition of 1499), which belonged to Oliver Sinclair of Roslin and was apparently written by the main scribe of Arch. Selden. B. 24;[44] another is Adam Wallace's copy (*c.* 1600) of two medical works, *The Treasure of Poor Men* and Andrew Boorde's *Dietary of Health*.[45] In miscellanies, this practice both provides clues to the compiler's reading and sometimes assists in dating. Much of John Maxwell's proverbial lore was culled not from popular tradition but from two recently printed books: George Pettie's *A Petite Pallace of Pettie His Pleasure* (1576) and [202] John Lyly's *Euphues* (1578).[46] Evidence for the date of NLS, Adv. 19.3.6 is furnished by its copy of a prose tract printed in London in 1601, entitled *Eight learned personages lately conuerted ... from papistrie to the Churches Reformed* [*STC* 1073]. Other material in this manuscript tallies with an early seventeenth-century dating: it contains extracts from the 1599 print of Alexander Hume's *Hymnes*. David Melvill says that he 'collected' his roundels in 1612, but gives no hint of their source. The Roxburghe Club editors of this manuscript suggested that they derived from 'the floating material of the day'. William Ringler, however, has shown that all but ten – both texts and tunes – were taken from two works by Thomas Ravenscroft, *Pammelia* and *Deuteromelia*, printed in London three years earlier, in 1609. (Only four items in the Buik of Roundels are definitely Scottish.) *Deuteromelia* also supplied a song to the compiler of EUL, Laing III.447 (no. 18): 'Glade am I, glade am I'.[47] It was mentioned earlier that the editor of the Andrew Melvill manuscript (no. 16) omitted the very first item. This too derives from a print, whose title, copied word for word by Melvill, gives some idea of its tone and contents:

---

[42] Cf. J. K. Moore, *Primary Materials Relating to Copy and Print in English Books of the Sixteenth and Seventeenth Centuries*, Occasional Publication 24, Oxford Bibliographical Society (Oxford, 1922), pp. 1–2 ('Manuscripts Copied from Books Printed before 1640'); C. F. Bühler, *The Fifteenth-Century Book* (Philadelphia, PA, 1960), pp. 34–39; and N. F. Blake, 'Manuscript to Print', in *Book Production*, ed. Griffiths and Pearsall, pp. 403–32.

[43] BL, Harley 3865; [and BL, Catalogue of Manuscripts, for digitized images]. See *The Poems of Robert Henryson*, ed. Denton Fox (Oxford, 1981), pp. liii–liv.

[44] Bühler, *Fifteenth-Century Book*, p. 34, comments on the scribe's 'lack of training, learning, or attention'; see also Boffey and Edwards, Introduction to *Works of Geoffrey Chaucer and the 'Kingis Quair'*, p. 10.

[45] EUL, Dc.8.130; see discussion in J. D. Comrie, *History of Scottish Medicine*, 2 vols (London, 2nd edn, 1932), I, pp. 188–89; and Bawcutt, 'English Books', 4.

[46] See Bawcutt, 'Commonplace Book', pp. 61–62.

[47] Ringler's article, 'Sources of the Melvill Book of Roundels', which unfortunately was not published, is among his papers [mssRingler] in the Huntington Library, San Marino, California. See also David Greer, 'Five Variations on "Farewel dear loue"', in *The Well Enchanting Skill: Music, Poetry and Drama in the Culture of the Renaissance*, ed. J. Caldwell, E. Olleson and S. Wollenberg (Oxford, 1990), pp. 213–29 (216, 8n).

> The Arraignment of Lewd, Idle, Froward, and Vnconstant Women ... Pleasant
> for Married men, Profitable for Young men, and hurtful to none.

This work was first printed in London in 1615, but Melvill probably used a reprint published in 1629 by John Wreittoun.[48]

One particular type of print, the broadside ballad, interested several compilers. Andrew Melvill included a pair of religious poems that circulated on the same broadsheet: one on the Nativity, the other on the Passion, beginning respectively, 'Jewry came to Jerusalem' and 'Turn your eyes that are affixed.'[49] NLS, Adv. 19.3.6 contains a pious poem with a title more intriguing than its text: 'Certaine wise sentences of Salomon to the tune of Wigmores galliard'. Here too the source is a broadside, dated in the first quarter of the seventeenth century: 'An excellent ditty, shewing the sage sayings and wise sentences of Solomon. To the tune of Wigmore's Galliard.'[50] The origins of a poem, in another [203] manuscript, EUL, Laing III.447 (no. 18), are particularly interesting. 'Some men for suddane joy do weip' is a religious poem, consisting of 112 lines arranged in quatrains. Although printed in the Montgomerie supplement, the editor wisely denied it to Montgomerie, noting anti-Catholic gibes at 'the hour [whore] of rome', and attributed it instead to Alexander Hume. In fact the poem was written very much earlier: it is a ballad associated with the name of John Carewell, a Protestant martyr executed in the reign of Mary Tudor. First printed in 1564, it became immensely popular – a snatch is quoted by the Fool in *King Lear* – and may indeed have been known to Hume.[51]

Who were the likely readers of these manuscripts? A printed book's readership was potentially large, geographically dispersed, and mostly unknown to author or publisher.[52] A manuscript's readership was likely to be smaller, close at hand, and more intimate. One might roughly analyse its components as the compiler; his (or her) family and friends; and later generations of the family. There is clearly an element of the commonplace book in some of these miscellanies. Along with poems, they record practical information and memorable dates (of battles or children's birthdays). Some

---

[48] See Aldis, 719; *STC* 23540; and W. Beattie, 'Handlist of Works from the Press of John Wreitton', *Transactions of the Edinburgh Bibliographical Society*, II (1946), no. 32. Material copied from prints is found in the Wemyss Manuscript (from English song-books) and the Tait Manuscript (from Ravenscroft, for instance, or one of the three editions of the Forbes *Cantus*, 1662, 1666 and 1682).

[49] For texts and information, including *Dulcina*, the tune to which they were sung, see *The Shirburn Ballads 1585–1616*, ed. Andrew Clark (Oxford, 1907), pp. 59–63.

[50] See *The Roxburghe Ballads*, ed. William Chappell (London, 1874), II, pp. 538–43. Wigmore's Galliard 'started life as a dance tune ... by 1588 the tune was specified for use with solemn verses ... and by around 1675 the tune itself had become known as the Dying Christian's Exhortation': J. Blezzard, *Borrowings in English Church Music 1550–1950* (London, 1990), p. 110.

[51] See *Montgomerie: Supplementary Volume*, ed. Stevenson, pp. 222–26, 363–64; Greer, '*Five Variations*', p. 216, 8n; and *Old English Ballads 1553–1625*, ed. H. E. Rollins (Cambridge, 1920), pp. 47–53.

[52] Cf. Lotte Hellinga, 'Importation of Books Printed on the Continent into England and Scotland before *c.*1520', in *Printing the Written Word: The Social History of Books, c.1450–1520*, ed. S. Hindman (Ithaca, NY, 1991), pp. 205–24.

also have a self-recreational function, well expressed by John Maxwell: 'to exerce my awin ingyne' (fol. 23ᵛ). Others were manifestly intended for the extended family – those related by blood or marriage, those who had been to the same university, or who held the same religious beliefs, or had similar tastes, whether for bawdy jokes, or music. Obvious illustrations of this are seen in the dependence of the Reidpeth Manuscript upon the Maitland Folio, or in the song manuscripts, which were clearly designed for communal use. The layout of the Robert Tait Manuscript shows it was used 'for actual part-singing, or playing across the table'.[53]

Later generations of a family evidently continued to take interest in some of these manuscripts. Indeed they often contributed to them, using scripts and spellings that may be distinguished from those of the first compiler, even if they are not always precisely datable. Additions of this kind may have important implications. Literary historians have sometimes been unaware that the colophon to a poem was not written by its original copyist. There is a poem in the Maitland Folio (no. lxxxviii) that begins: 'Gif bissie branit bodyis ʒow bakbyte'. A conventional attack on slanderers, it belongs to the same genre as two pieces by Dunbar ('Musing allone this hinder nicht', B 33, and 'How sould [204] I rewill me or in quhat wys', B 18). Like another copy of the same poem in the Maitland Quarto (no. xliii), the text in the Folio was originally anonymous. Later, presumably in or after 1595, someone added to the Folio text the following: 'Quod Iohne Maitland … Chancellor of Scotland and died 3 October 1595'.[54] This attribution may perhaps be correct, yet there is surely a question mark over John Maitland's authorship of this poem, as there is over the few other vernacular pieces attributed to him. He seems much better evidenced as a Latin poet.[55]

The Maitland Folio also contains a marginal entry, unmentioned by its editor, placed on p. 318 to the right of Dunbar's 'In to thir dirk and drublie dayis' (no. cxliii). It is short but metrical: 'The Lord is onlye my support / and he that doth me feed'. This sounds like the opening of the twenty-third Psalm, and the wording is indeed identical with a version of that psalm in *The Forme of Prayers*.[56] Such an origin suggests a reader belonging to the Reformers; elsewhere in the Folio there are added verses from the *Gude and Godlie Ballatis*.[57] What is more, the location next to Dunbar's melancholy poem may be no accident, but an interesting example of reader response – a kind of 'contrapoyson', or antidote.

To return to the Bannatyne Manuscript: does it differ from the other Scottish miscellanies as strikingly as is sometimes said? In sheer size, it is undoubtedly

---

53 Rubsamen, 'Scottish and English Music', p. 262.

54 The preceding page in the Maitland Folio contains the late attribution of *King Hart* to Gavin Douglas.

55 For further discussion, see Sally Mapstone, Introduction to *A Palace in the Wild: Essays on Vernacular Culture and Humanism in Late-Medieval and Renaissance Scotland*, ed. L. A. J. R. Houwen, A. A. MacDonald and S. L. Mapstone (Leuven, 2000), pp. xvi–xvii.

56 Probably taken from one of the many Scottish editions of this work; it is present, however, in the Geneva editions of 1556 and 1558: see Ringler, TP 1777.

57 The lower half of p. 185 contains the first thirteen lines of 'Allace that same sweit face', written as prose. See *Maitland Folio Manuscript*, II, p. 4; and *The Gude and Godlie Ballatis*, ed. A. F. Mitchell, STS, 1st ser. 39 (Edinburgh, 1897), pp. 63–66.

impressive; yet it should be noted that the Asloan Manuscript, although incomplete, contains over 300 leaves. The Bannatyne Manuscript is also remarkable for the rich variety of its contents. The notion that it contains more love poetry than anything else can be refuted simply by looking at it, by noting the number of leaves devoted to different sections, and by observing the satirical nature of many of the 'ballatis of luve'. Critics are inclined to disregard the high proportion of space that Bannatyne devotes to moral and religious verse; this is an area, however, where he is closely akin to other compilers, especially John Maxwell and Andrew Melvill. It is also striking how many items supposedly 'unique' to Bannatyne occur in other manuscripts. A good illustration is the advice poem that begins 'Grund the in patience' (fol. 74^r); this is described as 'unique', although I have encountered at [**205**] least six other copies.[58] Explicit didacticism does not please us today, but it clearly appealed to Bannatyne and his contemporaries. Although the Bannatyne Manuscript contains no music, it is now recognized that the 'ballatis of luve' look forward, interestingly, to the seventeenth-century song collections. The Robert Edward Manuscript contains settings (not necessarily texts) of at least seven of these poems.[59] It is curious that one small clue to Bannatyne's inclusion of songs was long disregarded: the popular poem 'O lusty May with Flora queen' (no. 279, fol. 229^v) has been printed in several modern anthologies, yet the musician's *bis*, indicating that a phrase in line 8 is to be repeated, is rarely reproduced.[60]

The Bannatyne Manuscript also resembles other Scottish miscellanies in containing a large yet rarely acknowledged English element: there are poems by Chaucer, Lydgate, Hoccleve, Walton, Heywood and Wyatt, together with various anonymous pieces. Many of these are noted in the Introduction to the Scolar Facsimile, but by no means all; a small instance is no. 107 (fol. 75^v), 'Now quhen ane wreche is sett to he estait', which is a moralizing extract from Lydgate's *Fall of Princes* (IV.3151–70).[61] Among Bannatyne's 'ballettis mirry' is a curious work called 'The nyne ordour of knavis' (no. 223), which – as far as I know – has been totally ignored by all critics, except Denton Fox. In an unpublished note, he shows that it is closely related to a work published in London sometime during the 1560s by John Awdelay, known as 'The xxv Orders of Knaves'. A work in the rogue tradition, it may have had an appeal similar to *Colkelbie Sow*.[62]

---

58 See *Bannatyne Manuscript*, introd. Fox and Ringler, no. 91. Other manuscripts that have copies of 'Grund the in patience' are: Maxwell Manuscript, EUL, Laing III.467, fols 19^r and 23^v; Laing III.447, fols 76^v and 77^v (see Montgomerie, *Supplementary Volume*, p. 213). On the different versions of this poem, see Bawcutt, 'Boston Public Library Manuscript', 86–88. [See this essay herein.]

59 See *Bannatyne Manuscript*, introd. Fox and Ringler, nos 277, 279, 289, 290, 294, 296 and 306.

60 See, for instance, *Scottish Poetry from Barbour to James VI*, ed. M. M. Gray (London, 1935), p. 224, and *Ballatis of Luve*, ed. J. MacQueen (Edinburgh, 1970), p. 53.

61 I owe this information to Professor A. S. G. Edwards.

62 There are problems over the dating of this work (*STC* 993). It is in prose, not verse, but there is an entry in the Stationers' Register 1560–61 for 'a ballett called the Description of Vakabondes'.

Bannatyne famously described his sources as 'copeis awld mankit and mvtillait' (Bd, p. 59),[63] but this phrase should not be interpreted as referring solely to other manuscripts. Much of his material came from prints. Seven of the poems with erroneous attributions to Chaucer derive from Thynne's Chaucer, probably from the edition published *c.* 1545–50.[64] Two poems by John Bellenden (nos 4 and 403) seem to derive from Davidson's edition of Bellenden's translation of Hector Boece.[65] Other printed sources include Douglas's *Eneados* (1553), Heywood's *Epigrams* [206] (apparently from either the 1562 or the 1566 edition), and *The Forme of Prayers* (either 1564 or 1565).[66] Careful comparison with these prints would shed light on Bannatyne's practices as a copyist. Perhaps the most significant of his printed sources is William Baldwin's *Treatise of Morall Philosophye*. This sententious work seems unreadable today, but was immensely popular in its own time – especially among Protestants – and Ringler has demonstrated that Bannatyne used an edition pirated by Palfreyman, which was printed in July 1567. This, it should be noted, supports Bannatyne's own dating of his manuscript of 1568.[67]

Bannatyne's printed sources also included broadside ballads.[68] A particularly interesting instance is no. 246 (fol. 215[v]), one of the 'ballatis of luve', which begins:

> Was nocht gud king Salamon
> Reuisit in sindry wyis.

It is termed a 'unique copy' by Fox and Ringler, although the colophon provides a disregarded clue to its origin: 'Quod ane inglisman'. This poem is, in fact, a lightly scotticized version of a broadside, written by William Elderton, called 'The Pangs of Love and Lovers' Fitts'. Only a single copy of the print now survives, dated 22 March 1560,[69] but the ballad's great popularity is well attested.[70] There is a much extended parodic version in the *Gude and Godlie Ballatis*, which begins:

---

[63] Bannatyne may recall Gavin Douglas's use of a similar phrase (*Eneados*, V.Prol.51), but 'mank(it)' and 'mutilait' formed a popular alliterative pair, used by several other Scottish writers at this time.

[64] *STC* 5071–74.

[65] *STC* 3203.

[66] Dr Sally Mapstone was the first to note the correspondence between the version of the 83rd Psalm in this work and that in Bannatyne (fol. 14[r]); see Mapstone, *Scots and Their Books in the Middle Ages and the Renaissance* (Oxford, 1996), p. 26.

[67] See *Bannatyne Manuscript*, introd. Fox and Ringler, pp. xv–xvi. On Baldwin, see N. A. Gutieriez, *Dictionary of Literary Biography*, vol. 132 (Sixteenth-Century British Nondramatic Writers), ed. D. A. Richardson (Detroit, MI, 1993), pp. 19–26. On Baldwin's popularity in Scotland, see Bawcutt, 'English Books', p. 3.

[68] Items that possibly derive from broadsides are no. 6, entitled 'ane ballat of the creatioun of the warld ... maid to the tone of the bankis of helecon'; and no. 131: 'Sustene, abstene' (cf. *STC* 23446, *c*.1555).

[69] *STC* 7561.

[70] See Hyder E. Rollins, 'William Elderton: Elizabethan Actor and Ballad-Writer', *Studies in Philology*, 17 (1920), 199–245 (201), and Carole R. Livingston, *British Broadside Ballads of the Sixteenth Century* (New York, 1991), no. 56. There is a reprint in *Old Ballads*, ed. J. P. Collier, Percy Society (London, 1840), pp. 25–28. Fuller discussion is found in my

Was not Salomon, the king
To miserie be wemen brocht?'[71]

The tune to which it was sung (which may well have been known to Bannatyne) is found both in the Dublin Virginal Manuscript and the Mulliner Book.[72] Bannatyne's version is very close to the print but contains a final stanza, which ends: [**207**]

Quhy suld nocht I, pur sempill man,
La[d]y, la[d]y,
Lawbour and serwe ʒow the best that I can,
My deir lady.

It is tempting, but rash, to attribute this addition to the punning pen of Robert Sempill.

The fivefold division of Bannatyne's 'ballat buik' is probably its most original feature. There exists no close analogue, as far as I am aware, to its interesting attempt at a generic arrangement of the poems. Nonetheless, the care that was lavished on the manuscript and certain features of its layout are paralleled in other Scottish miscellanies. Like the Asloan Manuscript, the Maitland Quarto, the Buik of Roundels and others, the Bannatyne Manuscript is a handsome 'buik' in its own right, and I am unconvinced by suggestions that it was designed for printing. The table of contents, as I have shown, has parallels in several miscellanies; it does not necessarily constitute proof 'of an editor anticipating a printed form for his collection'.[73] Bannatyne ends with a verse valediction, from 'The wryttar to the redar': 'Heir endis this buik writtin in tyme of pest' (fol. 375[r]). A. A. MacDonald said of this: 'it is scarcely credible that [Bannatyne] wrote such stanzas for his own benefit'.[74] Indeed not – but why must we assume, anachronistically, that the only 'buiks' read by sixteenth-century readers were printed? Why, incidentally, must we also accept the linked proposition that Bannatyne's Protestantism resulted from censorship or 'an eye for the market', not from deep inner conviction? Bannatyne's closing words belong to the double tradition of the scribal colophon and the poet's *envoi*. His manuscript was certainly read by later generations of his family, who during the sixteenth and seventeenth centuries made their own contributions to it, ranging from more epigrams to bawdy love poems.

Bannatyne says that his poems came from 'diuers new and ancient poettis' (fol. 211[r]). Neither these words nor his choice of texts suggests to me the self-conscious antiquarian who regarded older Scottish poetry as an endangered species. To think this is surely critical hindsightism, born of Romantic nostalgia. What the collection

---

[article, 'The Contents of the Bannatyne Manuscript: New Sources and Analogues', *The Journal of the Edinburgh Bibliographical Society*, 3 (2008), 95–133]. [See this essay herein.]

[71] *Gude and Godlie Ballatis*, pp. 213–19.

[72] See Denis Stevens, *The Mulliner Book: A Commentary* (London, 1952), p. 82, and *The Dublin Virginal Manuscript*, ed. J. Ward (Wellesley, MA, 1954), no. 13 (pp. 46–47).

[73] MacDonald, 'Printed Book', p. 109.

[74] MacDonald, 'Printed Book, p. 110.

magnificently displays is Bannatyne's eclecticism and lack of literary nationalism; it demonstrates the remarkable variety of vernacular poetry that was available to him in the 1560s from many sources, 'new and ancient', Scottish and English, manuscript and print. (It is relevant surely, that in the following decade Scottish printers were prepared to publish not only comparatively recent writers, such as Lyndsay and Rolland, but also the 'ancients', such as Barbour, Hary, Henryson and Douglas.) Other Scottish miscellanies likewise illuminate the taste of their compilers and the wider culture to which they belonged. Sometimes their contents merely confirm social or literary trends that are well known; sometimes, however, they correct [208] long-established, yet over-simple views, most strikingly perhaps the notion that seventeenth-century Scotland was 'more prone to religious strife than indulgence in the arts'.[75]

This essay is essentially a brief introduction to a very large subject. Far more material exists than has been mentioned here, especially from the neglected seventeenth century. What seems a desirable goal for the future is to provide a detailed register of these manuscript miscellanies and good analytic descriptions of their contents. To accomplish this well, however, is a task in which literary scholars must co-operate with historians and musicologists.

Editorial Note

[a]   This essay, presented at the Eighth International Conference on Scottish Language and Literature (Medieval and Renaissance), St Hilda's College, Oxford, 1996, was published in the proceedings, *Older Scots Literature*, ed. Sally Mapstone (Edinburgh, 2005), pp. 189–210. It has been reprinted here with the kind permission of Hugh Andrew, Birlinn Ltd. A version also appeared in *English Manuscript Studies, 1100–1700*, 12 (2005), 46–175.

[75] Rubsamen, 'Scottish and English Music', p. 259.

APPENDIX:
Summary List of Scottish Manuscript Miscellanies

The manuscripts are listed in chronological order, in so far as this can be ascertained.

Brief information is supplied on the following: name of the manuscript, where one is in common use today; present location and shelfmark; scribe or compiler (where known), followed by early owner (where known); geographical location; printed editions; and facsimiles. Further information on scholarly discussion of the manuscripts is found in the footnotes. The last column indicates the number of folios in a manuscript, or pages (where it is paginated). The nature of the contents is indicated thus: V (Verse), P (Prose), and M (Music).

1. Oxford, Bodleian, Arch. Selden. B. 24. Henry, Lord Sinclair (owner), Roslin, Midlothian. *The Works of Geoffrey Chaucer and the 'Kingis Quair': A Facsimile of Bodleian Library, Oxford, MS Arch. Selden. B. 24*, introd. J. Boffey and A. S. G. Edwards, app. B. C. Barker-Benfield (Cambridge, 1997).	*c.* 1488–1513	230 fols (V)
2. Cambridge, CUL, Kk.1.5. no. 6. V de F. *Ratis Raving, and Other Early Scots Poems on Morals*, ed. R. Girvan (STS, 1939).	second half fifteenth century	55 fols (V, P)
3. Asloan Manuscript. Edinburgh, NLS, 16500. John Asloan, Edinburgh. *The Asloan Manuscript*, ed. W. A. Craigie, 2 vols (STS, 1923–25).	*c.* 1513–32	304 fols (V, P)
4. London, BL, Arundel 285. [Lord William Howard of Naworth (late six- teenth-century owner).] *Devotional Pieces in Verse and Prose from MS Arun- del 285 and MS Harleian 6919*, ed. J. A. W. Bennett (STS, 1955).	*c.* 1540?	224 fols (V, P) [**209**]
5. Bannatyne Manuscript. Edinburgh, NLS, Adv.1.1.6. George Bannatyne, Edinburgh. *The Bannatyne Manuscript*, ed. W. Tod Ritchie, 4 vols (STS, 1928–34). *The Bannatyne Manuscript: National Library of Scot- land Advocates' MS 1. 1. 6*, introd. D. Fox and W. A. Ringler (London, 1980). [This is a facsimile.]	*c.* 1568	375 fols + 58 pp. (V)
6. Maitland Folio Manuscript. Cambridge, Magdalene College, Pepys Library 2553. Family of Sir Richard Maitland of Lethington. *The Maitland Folio Manuscript*, ed. W. A. Craigie, 2 vols (STS, 1919–27).	*c.* 1570–86	366 pp. (V)

7. Maitland Quarto Manuscript. 1586 140 fols
Cambridge, Magdalene College, Pepys Library 1408. (V)
Marie Maitland, Lethington (owner).
The Maitland Quarto Manuscript, ed. W. A. Craigie
(STS, 1920).
[*The Maitland Quarto: A New Edition*, ed. Joanna M.
Martin (STS, 2015).]

8. Edinburgh, NRS, RH 13/35. *c.* 1582–86 Fragmentary
?Thomas White, Haddington. Family of Cockburn of (V, P)
Ormiston (?owners).
Unpublished.

9. Maxwell Manuscript. 1584–89 36 fols
Edinburgh, EUL, Laing III.467. (V, P)
John Maxwell of Southbar, Renfrewshire.
Unpublished.

10. Edinburgh, NLS, Adv. 19.3.6. first half 76 fols
Unpublished. seventeenth (V, P)
  century

11. Melvill Bassus. *c.* 1604 71 fols
BL, Add. 36484. (V, P)
David Melvill, Aberdeen.
Unpublished.

12. Tolquhon Cantus. 1611 20 fols
Cambridge, Fitzwilliam Museum, Mu 687. (V, M)
David Melvill; A. F. (owner).
Unpublished.

13. Melvill Buik of Roundels. 1612 151 pp. + 27
Washington, Library of Congress, M1490. M535 A5 unnumbered
David Melvill. pp.
The Melvill Book of Roundels, ed. G. Bantock and H. (V, M)
O. Anderton (Roxburghe Club, 1916). [Modernized.] **[210]**

14. Reidpeth Manuscript. 1622–23 69 fols
Cambridge, CUL, Ll.5.10. (V)
John Reidpeth; Christopher Cockburn (owner),
Berwickshire.
Unpublished.

15. Robertson Manuscript. *c.* 1630? 215 fols
a) Edinburgh, NLS, 15937 (nineteenth-century 21 fols
transcript) (V)
b) BL, Add. 29409 (nineteenth-century partial
transcript)
Margaret Robertson, Bonskeid, Perthshire.
Unpublished.

16. Aberdeen, AUL, 28.   *c.* 1637   81 fols
Andrew Melvill, Aberdeen.   (V, P)
Extracts from the Commonplace Book of Andrew Mel-
ville 1621–1640, ed. W. Walker (Aberdeen, 1899).

17. Edinburgh, NLS, Dep. 314, no. 23.   *c.* 1643–44   177 fols
Lady Margaret Wemyss, Fife.   (V, M)
Unpublished.

18. Edinburgh, EUL, Laing III.447.   first half   84 fols
In *Poems of Alexander Montgomerie. Supplementary*   seventeenth   (V)
Volume, ed. G. Stevenson (STS, 1910).   century

19. Robert Edward's Manuscript.   ?1635–70   79 fols
Edinburgh, NLS, 9450   (V, M)
Robert Edward, Murroes parish, Angus.
Unpublished.

20. Tait Manuscript.   1676–89   193 fols
Los Angeles, CA, Williams Andrews Clark Memorial   (V, M)
Library, T135Z B7 24.
Robert Tait, Lauder.
Unpublished.

7

The Contents of the Bannatyne Manuscript:
New Sources and Analogues

The importance of the Bannatyne Manuscript (NLS, Adv. MS 1.1.6) as a repository of early Scottish poetry has long been recognized,[a] ever since the publication of Allan Ramsay's *Ever Green* in 1724.[1] In the second half of the twentieth century, however, there occurred a marked renewal of interest in the manuscript, and a flood of scholarly publications appeared, discussing such topics as George Bannatyne's life and milieu, his intentions in compiling the collection, the structure and dating of the manuscript, and its relation to other Scottish literary miscellanies.[2] But the most valuable contribution to understanding the manuscript was undoubtedly the facsimile, published jointly by the Scolar Press and the National Library of Scotland in 1980.[3] The primary purpose of this was obviously to facilitate examination of the text by scholars, but it is also furnished with an excellent Introduction by Denton Fox and William A. Ringler. One of the most useful sections of that Introduction,

---

[1] For an overview of the early period, see the Introduction to *The Bannatyne Manuscript*, ed. W. Tod Ritchie, 4 vols, STS, 2nd ser. 22–23, 26; 3rd ser. 5 (1928–34); and Priscilla Bawcutt, 'The Earliest Texts of Dunbar', in *Regionalism in Late Medieval Manuscripts and Texts*, ed. F. Riddy (Cambridge, 1991), pp. 183–98 (194–95).

[2] See, in particular, Denton Fox, 'Manuscripts and Prints of Scots Poetry in the Sixteenth Century', in *Bards and Makars*, ed. A. J. Aitken, M. P. McDiarmid and D. S. Thomson (Glasgow, 1977), pp. 156–71; William Ramson, 'Bannatyne's Editing', in *Bards and Makars*, ed. Aitken, McDiarmid and Thomson, pp. 172–82; A. A. MacDonald, 'The Bannatyne Manuscript: A Marian Anthology', *Innes Review*, 37 (1986), 36–47; A. A. MacDonald, 'The Printed Book That Never Was: George Bannatyne's Poetic Anthology (1568)', in *Boeken in de late Middeleeuwen*, ed. J. M. M. Hermans and K. van der Hoek (Groningen, 1994), pp. 101–10; A. A. MacDonald, 'The Cultural Repertory of Middle Scots Lyric Verse', in *Cultural Repertoires: Structure, Function and Dynamics*, ed. G. J. Dorleijn and H. L. J. Vanstiphout (Leuven, 2003), pp. 59–86; Theo van Heijnsbergen, 'The Interaction between Literature and History in Queen Mary's Edinburgh: The Bannatyne Manuscript and Its Prosopographical Context', in *The Renaissance in Scotland: Studies in Literature, Religion, History and Culture*, ed. A. A. MacDonald, M. Lynch and I. B. Cowan (Leiden, 1994), pp. 183–225; Priscilla Bawcutt, 'Scottish Manuscript Miscellanies from the Fifteenth to the Seventeenth Century', *English Manuscript Studies 1100–1700*, 12 (2005), 46–73; also in *Older Scots Literature*, ed. Sally Mapstone (Edinburgh, 2005), pp. 189–210 [see this essay herein].

[3] *The Bannatyne Manuscript: National Library of Scotland Advocates' MS 1.1.6*, introd. Denton Fox and William A. Ringler (London, 1980).

entitled 'Contents of the Manuscript' (pp. xviii–xl), not only lists the many hundreds of items that it contains, but provides highly condensed information, on various topics, such as a poem's usual title, its author (where known), and other witnesses for the text, whether manuscript or printed. Much of this information, at the time of publication, was available nowhere else. This part of the Introduction indeed constitutes a remarkably useful reference-work and is still unrivalled not only as a guide to the contents of the Bannatyne Manuscript but to many other poems circulating in Scotland in the sixteenth century.

The article that follows is designed essentially as a supplement to this section of the Introduction. It consists of a series of notes, following the order of the items provided by Fox and Ringler, and employs their numbering and nomenclature. The 'Main Manuscript' consists of 375 leaves; bound up with it are twenty-nine leaves (paginated 1–58), which are commonly, if slightly misleadingly, termed the 'Draft' or 'Draft Manuscripts' (for detailed analysis, see Introduction, pp. ix–xiv). References will normally be to 'Fox', since his name appears at the end of the 'Contents' section, although he himself acknowledges that much of what he says there is indebted to the researches of Ringler. For ease of consultation, reference will also be given to W. Tod Ritchie's edition of the Bannatyne Manuscript for the Scottish Text Society (see note 1), by volume and page. My object, in a few cases, is to correct factual errors or misleading statements (see Draft, no. 32; Main Manuscript, [**96**] nos 124, 164, 289 and 309). In most cases, however, the purpose is to provide new information concerning the sources of poems, or their authorship, and to note the existence of earlier or later texts. Most of the new material derives from my own reading and research; for the sake of completeness, however, I have included items that depend on the recent discoveries of other scholars.

In some instances, the new texts merely provide additional evidence for the popularity of poems already known to exist in multiple copies (see Draft, no. 26; Main MS, nos 90, 97, 106, 108, 112, 117, 119, 141, 161, 167, 196, 306 and 310). Particular interest, however, attaches to the newly discovered texts of poems that were previously considered 'unique' (see Draft, nos 1, 3, 6 and 46–52; Main MS, nos 7, 37, 40, 83, 91, 94, 101, 107, 174, 201, 212B, 221, 239, 246, 282, 286, 326, 340, 374 and 407). Fox himself readily acknowledged that when he labelled the text of a poem in the Bannatyne manuscript as a 'unique copy', 'this remark ... should be taken only to mean that no other text of the item has yet been noted' (p. xviii). Some of the 'unique' pieces (nos 91 and 101) indeed turn out to have been extremely popular in Scotland. Bannatyne should not in such cases be regarded as the rescuer of forlorn texts, but rather as a collector who shared the taste of his time. Fox showed that several of Bannatyne's poems were extracts from longer works (some examples are nos 98, 106, 117 and 119), and observed that it was 'probable that some of the shorter items, in particular, are excerpts from long poems which are otherwise known' (p. xviii). This has turned out to be true of no. 37 (deriving from *The Contemplacioun of Synnaris*), no. 107 (from Lydgate's *Fall of Princes*), and Draft, nos 46–52 (from William Alexander's *Tragedie of Darius*). It is striking how often poems that failed at first to be recognized have an altered first line (so nos 101, 107 and 340).

The dating of these new texts of poems is clearly desirable, but can rarely be established with precision. Many are found in manuscripts earlier than 1568, the year in which – as George Bannatyne tells us – he completed his own manuscript (see nos

97, 106, 107, 108, 119, 167, 196, 221, 246, 286, 326, 340), but this does not, of course, necessarily indicate that they provided Bannatyne's exemplars. They have a value of a different kind: some have better texts, suggesting that Bannatyne was careless over copying, or that he had a defective exemplar. The case is different with poems in printed form. It is well known that Bannatyne drew many poems from printed books, including Thynne's edition of Chaucer, Davidson's *Boece*, and John Heywood's *Epigrams*. To these, one can now add his use of a 1560 broadside ballad (no. 246), and the 1564 or 1565 print of the Psalms (no. 7). Slightly more conjecturally, a lost work printed by John Scot probably represents the source of Draft, no. 1 and Main MS, no. 3. It sems likely also that Bannatyne (or another member of his family) had read the 1603 edition of Alexander's *Darius* (Draft, nos 46–52).

Many of these texts, in fact, are found in witnesses that postdate the Bannatyne Manuscript. It has long been known that the Maitland Folio (*c.* [**97**] 1570–86) contains poems (many attributed to Dunbar) that are also found in the Bannatyne Manuscript.[4] But there exist smaller and less famous Scottish manuscript miscellanies of a slightly later date that also preserve Bannatyne poems. One such is the Maxwell Manuscript, compiled *c.* 1584–89 by John Maxwell of Southbar in Renfrewshire (see nos 83, 90, 91, 101, 108, 112, 117, 119 and 218).[5] Another is Aberdeen University Library, MS 28, compiled *c.* 1637 by Andrew Melvill, a teacher at the Aberdeen song school (see nos 108, 119, 196 and 282).[6] There is also a small overlap with the poetic anthology made by the Englishman Henry Stanford (begun *c.* 1582), who shared with Bannatyne a taste for the verse adages from Baldwin and Paulfreyman's *Treatise of Morall Philosophye* (1567) (see nos 139, 140, 141, 142, 144 and 161).[7]

Some of these new texts were jotted down in local and public records dating from the sixteenth to the early seventeenth century (see Draft, no. 26, and Main MS, nos 94, 119, 212B, 340). A version of one Bannatyne poem occurs in an early seventeenth-century English broadside (no. 212B), and a few survived to be printed in chapbook texts (nos 183, 201). Others figured in the decorative schemes of Scottish Renaissance country houses (nos 108, 141, 161), and one is inscribed on a fine silver-gilt cup (no. 112). Such wide circulation and such longevity are important testimony to Bannatyne's taste for popular types of verse, whose homely wisdom or bizarre jests appealed not just to the Edinburgh literati or members of the court but

---

4   See *The Maitland Folio Manuscript*, ed. W. A. Craigie, 2 vols, STS, 2nd ser. 7, 20 (Edinburgh, 1919–27); Bawcutt, 'Earliest Texts', pp. 190–93; Julia Boffey, 'The Maitland Folio as a Verse Anthology', in *William Dunbar, 'The Nobill Poyet': Essays in Honour of Priscilla Bawcutt*, ed. Sally Mapstone (East Linton, 2001), pp. 40–50; and Bawcutt, 'Scottish Manuscript Miscellanies', 53–54.

5   This manuscript (EUL, Laing III.467) is unpublished, but see Priscilla Bawcutt, 'The Commonplace Book of John Maxwell', in *A Day Estivall: Essays ... in Honour of Helena Mennie Shire*, ed. A. Gardner-Medwin and J. Hadley Williams (Aberdeen, 1990), pp. 59–68. [See this essay herein.]

6   Selections from this were published in *Extracts from the Commonplace Book of Andrew Melville 1621–1640*, ed. W. Walker (Aberdeen, 1899).

7   See *Henry Stanford's Anthology: An Edition of Cambridge University Library Manuscript Dd. 5.75*, ed. Steven W. May (New York, 1988). Fox records the presence of no. 139 in this MS, but no others.

to people of varying occupations in far flung parts of Scotland – Aberdeen, Dumfries, Selkirk or Lauder.

The new texts also increase awareness of Anglo-Scottish cultural contacts. Few readers familiar with this period will be surprised that some poems may be traced to a definite English source (see nos 107, 239, 246, 286 and 407), or that others have a curious and less easily defined relationship with an English work (see Draft, no. 6, and Main MS, nos 169, 189, 221 and 223). But the literary traffic across the Border was by no means one-way. Two Scottish love poems in the Bannatyne Manuscript also occur in a mid-sixteenth-century English music manuscript (see nos 167 and 326); a proverb-compilation (no. 196) seems to have appealed to English collectors as well as Scottish ones; and a comic poem clearly pleased English taste, although in its passage south it suffered an extraordinary metamorphosis (no. 212B). It should be noted that Bannatyne saw no incongruity in placing a copy of an Elizabethan ballad by William Elderton (no. 246) immediately after Henryson's 'Garmont of Gud Ladeis' (no. 245) in the same way that he placed his own love complaint (no. 284) after 'the Song of Troilus' (no. 283). His selection of poems seems to have been swayed largely by considerations of genre, not nationality. Most of the English poems are scotticized by Bannatyne, as had long been the practice in Scotland, and this has sometimes obscured their origin (see nos 107, 141, 246); even some pieces that were undoubtedly Scottish in authorship but English in orthography have been similarly scotticized in the Bannatyne Manuscript (see Draft, nos 46–52, and Main MS, no. 7). [**98**]

The Draft Manuscript

Draft, no. 1.   'Quhen goldin phebus movit fra the ram'
(Bd, pp. 3–5; Ritchie, I, pp. 3–8).

A second copy of this important religious poem on the Incarnation occurs as item 3 in the Main MS (fols 1ʳ–3ᵛ; Ritchie, II, pp. 3–8). In the Draft, it is attributed to 'ballentyne', and lacks a title; in the Main MS, it is attributed, with greater formality, to 'maister Iohine bellentyne archedene of murray', and entitled 'the benner of peetie'. According to Fox, 'no other texts survive, but the poem was in the Marchmont Library MS of Fordun's *Scotichronicon*; the MS has disappeared, but Laing's collation survives'. In fact the Marchmont manuscript of what is today more commonly called the *Liber Pluscardensis* still exists and is now owned by the Mitchell Library, Glasgow (MS 308876; formerly 7396).[8] Although the original manuscript is dated *c.* 1500, Bellenden's poem was added on the flyleaves (now foliated as v–vi) at a later date.

The Mitchell Library text of this poem is important, because it contributes a scrap of evidence to the history of Scottish printing. It has a long descriptive title: 'Ane ballat of the cuming of crist and of the annunciatioun of our Ladye Compylit be maister Iohne ballenden'; and at the end (fol. viᵛ) is written 'Finis Amen / Imprentit

---

8   On this manuscript, see *Liber Pluscardensis*, ed. Felix J. H. Skene, Historians of Scotland series, 7 (Edinburgh, 1877), I, pp. xiv–xvi; and Neil R. Ker, *Medieval Manuscripts in British Libraries II, Abbotsford–Keele* (Oxford, 1977), pp. 862–63. [MS numbers in the original essay were transposed and are corrected here.]

be Iohne Scot etc'. Beneath this in larger letters and darker ink is 'Imprentit Be me Iohne Scot'. This is an instance of the not uncommon scribal practice of copying part or whole of a printer's colophon, as well as the text.[9] Scot's extant publications are dated between 1552 and 1571, but it is impossible to say when this was printed. Since the poem is comparatively short (176 lines), it may have appeared not as a separate publication but as a 'filler' at the end of a longer work. The Bannatyne MS contains two other poems by Bellenden (nos 4 and 403), both of which were copied from a printed source: Davidson's edition of Bellenden's translation of Hector Bece's *Scotorum Historiae* (*c.* 1540). It seems likely that Bannatyne's text of this poem likewise derives from the lost Scot print, or one closely related to it.

A collation of the Mitchell text with the two copies in Bannatyne establishes that the Mitchell text (M) is closer to the copy in the Bannatyne Draft (Bd) than that in the Main MS (B). (This confirms and supplements the previous conclusions of E. A. Sheppard, based on a transcript made by David Laing (EUL, MS Laing IV.27) while the manuscript was still at Marchmont House.[10]) In some cases, B has a clearly erroneous reading: *schowris* instead of M, Bd *flowris* (line 8). Elsewhere archaic or old-fashioned words are modernized in B: *thrall* in Bd, M is replaced by *thrald* (20, 103); *satyfye* by *satisfie* (64). In the last three lines of the poem (174–76), M differs markedly from both Bannatyne texts. Bd reads:

> Bring ws amang thai happie senatouris
> Quhome thow coftin with thy woundis fyve
> Quhen saull departis in our latter houris.

[**99**] B agrees with Bd, except in reading the grammatically better *thow hes coftin*. M, however, reads:

> Mak me ane of thi happy cietesouris
> Quhome thow redemit with thy woundis fyve
> Quhen saull departis in my latter houris.

This, couched in the first person singular, is a more intimate prayer. *Cietesouris*, it should be noted, is a rare, probably archaic term for 'citizen', which forms a regular part of Bellenden's vocabulary in his translation of Boece.[11] The Mitchell text seems a superior witness for this interesting, yet neglected poem.

---

9 For two instances, see P. Bawcutt, 'English Books and Scottish Readers in the Fifteenth and Sixteenth Centuries', *Review of Scottish Culture*, 14 (2001–02), 1–12 (2). On John Scot, see Robert Dickson and J. P. Edmond, *Annals of Scottish Printing* (Cambridge, 1890), pp. 159–97; and Paul B. Watry, 'Sixteenth-Century Printing Types and Ornaments of Scotland' (unpublished D. Phil. thesis, Oxford, 1992), pp. 23–25.

10 See E. A. Sheppard's Appendix to *The Chronicles of Scotland ... Translated into Scots by John Bellenden*, ed. R. W. Chambers, E. C. Batho and H. W. Husbands, 2 vols, STS, 3rd ser. 10, 15 (Edinburgh, 1938–41), II, pp. 449–51.

11 For instances, see the Glossary to Bellenden, *Chronicles of Scotland*, II, p. 466; cf. also *DOST*, s.v.. *cieteʒour*.

Draft, no. 3.   'O Lord my god sen I am brocht / In grit distres'
                 (Bd, pp. 7–8; Ritchie, I, pp. 10–12).

A second copy occurs in the Main MS, fols 14ᵛ–15ʳ (Ritchie, II, pp. 34–35), which has the title: 'A song of him lying in poynt o[f] deth'. Fox records no other text, but a third exists in an early seventeenth-century verse miscellany (EUL, MS Laing III.447, fol. 38ᵛ). Much of this manuscript was printed in *Poems of Alexander Montgomerie: Supplementary Volume*, ed. G. Stevenson (1910), where this piece is printed as 'Miscellaneous Poems', no. xxxii (pp. 231–32).[12] There are few divergencies of text.

Draft, no. 6.   'O most heich and eternall king'
                 (Bd, pp. 12–13; Ritchie, I, pp. 18–21);
                 also Main MS, no. 20 (B, fols 20ʳ–21ʳ; Ritchie, II, pp. 47–50).

This devout poem is attributed by Bannatyne to 'ro / norvell' (Bd), or 'norvall' (B), who is here termed 'unknown'. Robert Norvell, however, would have been well known in Protestant circles in Edinburgh during the reigns of Mary Queen of Scots and James VI. Norvell, who had served as a soldier in France, was a friend of Knox and a committed Reformer, and in 1561 published a collection of verse, *The Meroure of ane Chr[i]stiane* (*STC* 18688). Several of his poems are translated from Clément Marot.[13] Some doubt hangs over the attribution to Norvell. The poem is not found in *The Meroure*, but its first stanza occurs with a musical setting in an Elizabethan work printed by John Day in 1563: *Tenor of the whole psalmes in four partes* (*STC* 2431; May and Ringler, no. 18711), signatures Tiiiiʳ⁻ᵛ. The piece is there headed 'A Prayer', followed by the initials T. C. The correspondence between the two stanzas is close, with some slight scotticizing of forms by Bannatyne: so 'helppis' for 'helpest', but Bd contains 10 (in B 9) further stanzas not found in the English music book. These may well be English, since they contain no distinctive Scots rhymes or vocabulary. It was not uncommon in music books to set only the first stanza of a well-known song or hymn.

Draft, no. 17.   'With nalis a rud tre nalit to'
                  (Bd, p. 22; Ritchie, I, pp. 36–37).

Fox notes: 'these seven lines are cancelled', but, as A. A. MacDonald has [100] shown, they represent a misplaced section of a religious poem copied earlier: 'Chryst crownit

---

12 For more information, see *Poems of Alexander Montgomerie and Other Pieces from Laing MS. No. 447: Supplementary Volume*, ed. George Stevenson, STS, 1st ser. 59 (Edinburgh, 1910), pp. xxxv–xxxvii; and Bawcutt, 'Scottish Manuscript Miscellanies', pp. 47 and 58.

13 See W. Beattie, 'Some Early Scottish Books', in *The Scottish Tradition*, ed. G. W. S. Barrow (Edinburgh, 1974), pp. 107–20 (118–20); and P. Bawcutt, 'French Connections? From the *Grands Rhétoriqueurs* to Clément Marot', in *The European Sun: Proceedings of the Seventh International Conference on Medieval and Renaissance Scottish Language and Literature*, ed. G. Caie et al. (East Linton, 2001), pp. 119–28 (125–26).

king and conquerour' (Bd, no. 14).[14] It is curious that Bannatyne did not attempt to remedy the error, when he made a second copy of the poem in the Main MS (no. 45).

Draft, no. 26.   'Allone as I went vp and doun'
                   (Bd, pp. 30–31; Ritchie, I, pp. 50–52);
                   Also Main MS, no. 54 (B, fols 46^v–47^r; Ritchie, II, pp. 116–17).

There is a reminiscence of the first four lines of this poem (usually known as *The Abbey Walk* and attributed to Henryson) in some marginal annotations in the Selkirk Protocol Book 1557–75 (NRS, B 68/7/1).[15] Two copies, possibly dated between 1609 and 1611, occur on fols 76^r and 173^r.

>   As I was wandring myne alane
>   Into ane hall now fair to sie
>   Thinkand quhat consolatioun
>   Was best into adversitie.

In the Maitland Folio text of the poem (no. cxxvii), as in Bannatyne, the setting is an 'abbay' not a 'hall'. Another seventeenth-century version, the now lost Forbes print of 1686, apparently had a different second line: 'Into a place was fair to see.'[16] The change in location in these later texts suggests Protestant unease about giving the poem a setting with such papistical associations.

Draft, no. 32   'Walkin allone amangis þir levis grene'
                  (Bd, pp. 39–41; Ritchie I, pp. 64–68;
                  also Main MS, no. 62 (B, fol. 53^r; Ritchie, II, pp. 132–36).

According to Fox, this long religious poem, with a stereotyped *chanson d'aventure* opening, also occurs 'in Public Record Office [now The National Archives], SP 1/246 (mid-sixteenth century), f. 23. with music'. This statement, however, is highly misleading. The manuscript in question is a bassus part-book, dating from the latter part of Henry VIII's reign. The texts of some songs are written in full, but others (as was common) are indicated only by their incipits. Song no. 14 (on fol. 23) consists of no more than two words: 'Walking alone', together with a musical setting.[17] Such an incipit is too brief and too commonplace for one to be certain that it refers to this Scottish poem. A number of poems, both English and Scottish, have very similar opening lines; cf. a brief Scottish love poem, 'Walkin in wo allone / my cair dois

---

[14] See A. A. MacDonald, 'The Middle Scots Expansion of *Iesu, Nostra Redemptio* and a Ghost in the Bannatyne Manuscript', *Neophilologus*, 70 (1986), 472–74.

[15] On this MS and its contents, see Eila Williamson, 'Schoolboy Scribbles on a Burgh Court Book', *Scottish Archives*, 8 (2002), 96–112.

[16] For more information, see *The Poems of Robert Henryson*, ed. Denton Fox (Oxford, 1981), p. 434; and *The Poems and Fables of Robert Henryson*, ed. H. Harvey Wood (Edinburgh, 1933), pp. xxviii–xxix.

[17] See *Addenda* to *Letters and Papers, Foreign and Domestic of the Reign of Henry VIII*, I, part 2 (1932), item 1880; and Denis Stevens, 'A Part-Book in the Public Record Office', *Music Survey*, 2.3 (1950), 161–70 (170).

ay incres' copied in a printed legal work that belonged to Alexander Myln (NLS, Rb m.76, part 2, fol. 1);[18] also 'Walkyng allon of wyt full desolat' (*IMEV* 3860); and 'Walkyng alone Ryght secretly'. (Ringler, TM 1798, considers this latter poem, by John Redford, to be the poem to which the National Archives incipit refers.)

Draft, no. 43.   'The Lord most he / I knaw wilbe / Ane hird to me'
                  (Bd, pp. 51–52; Ritchie, I, pp. 85–86).

This translation of Psalm 23, here attributed to 'montgumry', is commonly included in editions of Alexander Montgomerie's poems.[19] A second text also occurs in *The Mindes Melody* (Edinburgh, 1605; *STC* 18051); the poems in [**101**] this work have usually been attributed to Montgomerie, although all are anonymous. Fox does not note the presence of a third early printed text of the poem in James Melville's *Ane Fruitfull and Comfortable Exhortation anent Death* (Edinburgh 1597; *STC* 17815.5), pp. 111–12, where it is attributed to 'I. M.', that is, James Melville. This complicates the question of authorship considerably. In Melville, the poem is said to be 'to the tune of Solsequium', which perhaps led to the attribution to Montgomerie. In Bannatyne, the poem is copied in 'part of a different and perhaps later compilation' (Fox and Ringler, p. xi).

Draft, no. 44.   'Lyik as the dum solsequium / with cair overcum'
                  (Bd, pp. 52–53; Ritchie, I, pp. 86–87).

According to Fox, one of the later manuscripts that contain this popular poem by Montgomerie is 'the Raitt MS' (see also Main MS, nos 279, 294, 296, 306, 310 and 321). There has been much scholarly confusion as to the name of the man who compiled this late seventeenth-century miscellany, an important repertory of songs, as well as verse in Scots and Latin (Los Angeles, CA, William Andrews Clark Memorial Library, MS T135 Z B724). There is no doubt, however, that the compiler was Robert Tait(t), an assistant teacher and, for a time, session clerk in Lauder.[20]

Draft, nos 46–52.
                  (Bd, pp. 52–43; Ritchie, I, p. 89).

This page contains seven sententious verses, chiefly couplets, added either by Bannatyne very late in his life or by another member of his family. They are here attributed to 'william alexander of menstry', but Fox voices doubt as to Alexander's authorship, saying that they are 'unlike his other prolix works, but they have been accepted by his editors'. It has recently been noted, however, by Dr Sally Mapstone,

---

18 The quatrain is printed in P. Bawcutt, 'Writing about Love in Late Medieval Scotland', in *Writings on Love in the English Middle Ages*, ed. Helen Cooney (New York, 2006), pp. 179–96 (182).
19 See *The Poems of Alexander Montgomerie*, ed. James Cranstoun, STS, 1st ser. 9 (Edinburgh, 1887), pp. 255–56; and *Alexander Montgomerie: Poems*, ed. David J. Parkinson, 2 vols, STS, 4th ser. 28, 29 (Edinburgh, 2000), I, no. 106 (pp. 282–83).
20 For light on Tait's life, see Bawcutt, 'Scottish Manuscript Miscellanies', p. 69, 19n.

that all seven were indeed written by Alexander and derive from *The Tragedie of Darius*, which was first published in 1603, and later appeared, slightly revised, in *The Monarchicke Tragedies* (1604; 1607; 1617), and *Recreations with the Muses* (1637). The verses derive from the Choruses in various parts of this play, in several cases from the epigrammatic concluding lines of a passage.[21] To judge from their wording in the Bannatyne MS, the copyist chose his excerpts from the 1603 text, and lightly scotticized the spelling, introducing *quh*-forms, for instance, not in the original. Interestingly, at about the same time, another Scottish reader copied similar extracts from William Alexander into another manuscript (EUL, MS Dk.7.49). This is a composite volume containing, first, Douglas's *Eneados* and, secondly, poems by Lyndsay, of which the most substantial is *The Monarche* ['ane dialog betuix / experience & ane courtiour', 1ᵛ of second foliation]. At the end of the second section (fol. 146ʳ⁻ᵛ) are copies of two Choruses from Alexander's *Croesus*, the first of which begins 'What can confine mans wandring thought', and the second 'of all the creatures below'. The wording shows that the extracts derive from either the 1604 or the 1607 editions of *The Monarchick Tragedies*. Although the 'moral pointing' of these Choruses was not to the taste of Alexander's twentieth-century editors, it [**102**] clearly pleased his contemporary readers.[22]

Draft, no. 53. 'The seventh of July the suith to say' (Bd, pp. 55–58; Ritchie, I, pp. 90–96).

An eighteenth-century addition, this is written in the hand of William Carmichael, who had been given the manuscript in 1712. Entitled 'The Song of the rid square' (that is, Reidswire), it is a rather pedestrian ballad narrating a well-known Border affray that took place on 7 July 1575.[23] It should be noted that at least two other early texts are extant. One of these is found in NLS, Adv. MS 23.3.24, fol. 107ʳ⁻ᵛ. This MS is a miscellany in the hand of Robert Mylne, son of the antiquary of the same name, which is provisionally dated *c.* 1670–1713.[24] Another copy of 'the Song of the Rid square' also exists in NLS, MS 20800, fols 38–40; according to the NLS typescript catalogue, the ballad was 'formerly enclosed in MS 20779'. This latter manuscript is a miscellaneous collection of papers primarily associated with Sir James Carmichael, first Lord Carmichael (1615–51). It seems likely that the ballad was written by a

21 See 'Older Scots and the Sixteenth Century', in *Older Scots Literature*, ed. Mapstone, pp. 175–88 (178–79); and *The Poetical Works of Sir William Alexander of Stirling*, ed. L. E. Kastner and H. B. Charlton, I: *The Dramatic Works*, STS, 2nd ser. 11 (Edinburgh, 1921), pp. 145, 129, 197, 128, 173, 175 and 174. [See also Sebastiaan Verweij, 'King Darius in the Archives', in *Premodern Scotland: Literature and Governance 1420–1587; Essays for Sally Mapstone*, ed. Joanna Martin and Emily Wingfield (Oxford, 2017), pp. 211–30.]
22 *Poetical Works*, I, pp. 19–21, 36–39; and for editorial comment, p. cxci.
23 On the historical background, see G. M. Fraser, *The Steel Bonnets* (1971; 1990), pp. 310–12; and *David Hume of Godscroft's The History of the House of Angus*, ed. David Reid, 2 vols, STS, 4th ser. 4, 5 (Edinburgh, 2005), I, pp. 237–39.
24 On Adv. MS 23.3.24, see Harriet Harvey Wood's edition of *James Watson's Choice Collection of Comic and Serious Scots Poems*, 2 vols, STS, 4th ser. 10, 20 (Edinburgh, 1977; 1991), II, pp. 129 and 234.

seventeenth-century member of the Carmichaels, who wished to celebrate the part played by their family in battle.

The Main Manuscript

No. 7.   'God for thy grace / thow keip no moir silence'
             (B, fol. 14; Ritchie, II, pp. 33–34).

Bannatyne gives this a title – 'the lxxxiii phaslme [sic] of dauid' – but no author. Fox termed the text 'unique', but Sally Mapstone pointed out that it corresponds to Robert Pont's translation of the eighty-third Psalm, in the Bodleian Library's copy of *The CL Psalmes of Dauid in English metre. With The Forme of Prayers.*[25] The Bodleian copy of this important manual for public worship in the Reformed Church was printed in 1575 (*STC* 16580), but the first edition was published in 1564 (*STC* 16577) and reprinted in 1565 (*STC* 16577a). The psalm's text does not vary in either of these editions, and it seems likely that Bannatyne took his text from one or other of them. Bannatyne follows his original very closely, apart from occasional scotticizations, such as 'thaye' for 'these', and 'sic' for 'such', and one or two careless errors. Pont's 'With subtile slight' thus reads in Bannatyne as 'With subteill flicht' (9). And Pont's 'Further be made, no mention for euer' loses the negative: 'Forther be maid mentioun for evir' (14). It should be noted, in fairness to Bannatyne, that other apparent errors in Ritchie's text are due to mistranscription. 'Considerat' (4) and 'considder' (21) would be more accurately transcribed as 'Confiderat' and 'confidder', and thus correspond closely to Pont's 'Confedred' and 'confeder'.

No. 37.   'O wondit spreit and saule in till exile'
             (B, fols 32^r–33^v; Ritchie, II, pp. 80–83).

Fox termed this anonymous 112-line piece on the Passion 'unique', but A. A. MacDonald has shown that it represents an extract from *The Contemplacioun* [103] *of Synnaris*, a long devotional poem by Friar William of Touris, of which several texts survive and which was extremely popular in the first half of the sixteenth century.[26] Bannatyne's text derives from the fifth 'Passion' section of this work, but is much altered: the original eight-line stanza has been clumsily shortened to rhyme royal, and the order of the stanzas has been re-arranged, a few (chiefly those in honour of the Virgin Mary) being omitted. It is not clear whether Bannatyne or some other versifier was responsible for these changes.

No. 40.   'Thow þat hes bene obedient'
             (B, fol. 34^{r-v}; Ritchie, II, pp. 85–87).

This poem, one of a cluster on the Resurrection, is termed a 'unique copy'. But an earlier text occurs in the important devotional miscellany, BL, Arundel MS 285 (fols

---

[25] See *Scots and Their Books in the Middle Ages and the Renaissance* (Oxford, 1996), p. 26.
[26] 'Catholic Devotion into Protestant Lyric: The Case of the *Contemplacioun of Synnaris*', *Innes Review*, 35 (1984), 58–87.

175^v–176^v). It has a slightly different first line: 'Thow that in prayeris hes bene lent', and retains a few words relating to penance, notably 'confessit' (4) and 'contricioun' (34), not present in Bannatyne's text.[27]

No. 83   'Man of maist fragilitie / full of wo and miserie'
     (B, fols 69^v–70^r; Ritchie, II, pp. 170–72).

This moral poem on death and the vanity of worldly pleasures is striking chiefly for the ingenuity of its rhyme scheme. Each of the six stanzas, with the pattern *aaabaaab*, has the same two rhymes, on –*ie*, and –*es*. The text is here said to be 'unique', but in a later publication Fox noted that it had one line in common with a short moral poem in the Maxwell MS [EUL, Laing III.467] (fol. 6^v).[28] This was 'Be not lefull to lie', which furnishes line 22 of the Bannatyne poem, and was the incipit of the Maxwell poem. Elsewhere in the Maxwell MS (fol. 10^v), however, there is a much more substantial excerpt from the Bannatyne poem, corresponding to the central section (lines 13–24, and 33–40). It is laid out in quatrains, rather than eight-line stanzas:

Gif thow wald leif in cheratie
Fra thrawart companie thow flie
With fwillis and thow follow the   [B has fellow]
Thy fame sall decres.

Be nocht peirte in prewetie
Till ws na Iniquitie
For he that sall thy Iwge be
Seis all expres

From wrangows gwidis absteine the
Be nocht lefwll to lie
For at the last the weretie
Beis knawin mair and les

Be patient in powertie
And intill moist prosperitie   **[104]**
Haif ay god befoir thy ee
And no man expres   [B has *oppres*]

And thocht thow had awthoritie
To nane do thow crewaltie
Thy Iwge seis all sickerlie
Quhilk all sall redres

[27] The text is printed in *Devotional Pieces in Verse and Prose from MS. Arundel 285 and MS. Harleian 6919*, ed. J. A. W. Bennett, STS, 3rd ser. 33 (Edinburgh, 1955), pp. 275–76.
[28] See his '*DOST* and Evidence for Authorship: Some Poems Connected with *Ratis Raving*', in *The Nuttis Schell: Essays on the Scots Language*, ed. C. Macafee and I. Macleod (Aberdeen, 1987), pp. 96–105 (104–05).

Here, deprived of the sombre beginning and end, the poem has a different tone. Maxwell also places it in a different context, among verses on the right use of wealth (one of these is Bannatyne, no. 119).

No. 90.   'Serue thy god meikly / and þe warld besely'
                 (B, fol. 74ʳ; Ritchie, II, p. 181).

Fox notes that versions of this quatrain occur in nine other manuscripts (see *IMEV* 3087; and Whiting, G259). As all these manuscripts are English, it is worth pointing out that Bannatyne does not provide the sole evidence for the Scottish circulation of this class of gnomic poetry, the so-called 'precepts in –*ly*'.[29] The earliest text was copied into the Scottish parliamentary records after an act belonging to the reign of James III and dated 1469; according to William Robertson, the first editor of the suppressed edition of these records, 'in the same hand that writes the rest of the volume'.[30] This text is virtually identical with that in the Bannatyne MS, and, interestingly, is preceded by Bannatyne, no. 91, which here is not treated as a separate item. A later text occurs in the Maxwell MS (fol. 12ʳ) – the chief difference is that it begins with Bannatyne's second line, 'Eit thy meit merelie'.

No. 91.   'Grund the in patience / blind nocht thy conscience'
                 (B, fol. 74ʳ; Ritchie, II, p. 181).

Fox terms this piece 'unique', but this is not the case, since it was a much-copied text in Scotland from the fifteenth to the seventeenth century. There was considerable variation, however, in layout. In Bannatyne, it is laid out as a single quatrain containing long lines, with virgules marking the position of the internal rhymes. The earliest text (*c.* 1469), arranged similarly to that in Bannatyne, is found in the Scottish parliamentary records (see no. 90 above). Another version was copied in an English manuscript of Lydgate's *Siege of Thebes*, which came into Scottish possession at the end of the fifteenth century and contains several Scottish additions.[31] Here the poem is arranged as eight short lines, the first three rhyming lines in each quatrain being linked by a bracket, with the short 'tail' to the right. The Maxwell MS contains two versions. The first of these (fol. 19ʳ) is almost identical with the text in Bannatyne; the second (fol. 23ᵛ), however, is much expanded:

> Grounde the in pacience, my deir sone deir,
> Blinde not thi conscience, for na warldis geir.
> Do thy god rewerence, this I to the leir,

---

29 See *The Commonplace Book of Robert Reynes of Acle: An Edition of Tanner MS 407*, ed. Cameron Louis (New York, 1980), pp. 179–80; 392–96.

30 There are transcripts in *The Parliamentary Records of Scotland*, ed. W. Robertson (Edinburgh, 1804), p. 49, col. 1; and W. P. Reeves, 'Stray Verse', *Modern Language Notes*, 9.4 (1894), 101–03, cols 205–06.

31 Printed and discussed by P. Bawcutt in 'The Boston Public Library Manuscript of John Lydgate's *Siege of Thebes*: Its Scottish Owners and Inscriptions', *Medium Ævum*, 70 (2001), 80–94 (86–87). [See this essay herein.]

Set the with sufficence, with wisdome and feir
Preis the with diligence, baith hyne and heir,   [**105**]
To put away negligence, my deir sone deir.

Maxwell was a versifier, and may have himself composed this version in which each of the long lines is lengthened by tags, but the metrical 'tails' ('thankand him ay' and 'this warld will away') are removed. An early seventeenth-century poetic miscellany (EUL, Laing III.447) also contains two copies (fols 76^v and 77^v), which are verbally close to Bannatyne.[32] I have not been able to locate another late text, said to be contained in the so-called 'Chronicle of Aberdeen', a series of notes inserted in the Aberdeen Register of Baptisms, Marriages and Deaths by Walter Cullen.[33]

No. 94.   'Remembir man on endles hellis vexatioun'
                 (B, fol. 74^v; Ritchie, II, p. 182).

This six-line stanza on mortality, with intricate internal rhyme, is termed 'unique'. Another and later copy, however, occurs in the Aberdeen Register of Baptisms, Marriages and Deaths in the section entitled 'David Robertson sacrister's book 1602–1622', fol. 135^r. This work is in the keeping of the Registrar General for Scotland [now merged as National Records of Scotland] (OPR 168A / 12). The text is identical with that in Bannatyne, apart from a slightly altered first line: 'Memento mas (presumably an error for 'man') on hell's endles wexation', and 'foule' instead of 'vyle' in line 4.

No. 97.   'This warldis Ioy is only bot fantesy'
                 (B, fol. 74^v; Ritchie, II, p. 183).

Fox records that copies of this are present in the Maitland Folio [Cambridge, Magdalene College, Pepys Library 1408] and Reidpeth MS [Cambridge, CUL, Ll.5.10], but does not note the existence of a fourth and earlier text in Bodleian, MS Arch. Selden. B. 24, fol. 138^r.[34] All the texts are closely similar, except that Selden. B. 24 has a slight variation in the incipit: 'This wardly Ioy is onely fantasy', and a few anglicized spellings, such as 'quhich'. The variation between 'warldly' and 'warldis' is not uncommon in such phrases: cf. lines 21 of Dunbar's 'Full oft I mvse and hes in thocht' (B 14), where one witness has 'wardlie guddis' and the other has 'warldis gud'. John Norton-Smith queried whether the author of this piece was John Walton but produced no evidence to support his conjecture.[35] It is interesting that Bannatyne's

---

32 Printed in *Montgomerie: Supplementary Volume*, ed. Stevenson, p. 213.
33 It is printed in *Miscellany of the Spalding Club*, ed. J. Stuart (Aberdeen, 1842), II, p. 60.
34 See *The Works of Geoffrey Chaucer and The Kingis Quair: A Facsimile of Bodleian Library, Oxford, MS Arch. Selden. B. 24*, introd. Julia Boffey and A. S. G. Edwards; app. B. C. Barker-Benfield (Cambridge, 1997), no. 11; for a transcript, see *Religious Lyrics of the Fifteenth Century*, ed. Carleton Brown (Oxford, 1939), p. 260.
35 See *The Quare of Jelusy*, ed. J. Norton-Smith and I. Pravda, Middle English Texts 3 (Heidelberg, 1976), p. 10.

preceding item, also highly moral, is present in Arch. Selden. B. 24. But they do not there occur together.

No. 101.   'Befoir þe tyme is wisdome to prowyd'
                (B, fol. 75^r; Ritchie, II, p. 185).

This poem on time, consisting of two rhyme royal stanzas, has a strongly proverbial flavour. It is here termed 'unique', but was evidently well known in Scotland, since several shorter versions exist elsewhere. The Maxwell MS contains a small cluster of advisory poems concerning the proper use of time (fol. 19^{r-v}). Among those on fol. 19^r is a quatrain, consisting of the first four lines of the piece in Bannatyne, with precisely the same incipit. Overleaf is a slightly altered version, containing five lines:

> Befoir the tyme is wisdome to prowyde
> That into tyme thair be no thing to borrow   **[106]**
> Tyme tint this day can not be funde the morrow
> Thairfoir tak tyme quhill it is oportune
> And not mak duill for it quhen it is done.

Another text of the first stanza is found, with other verses, on the verso of the last leaf (now numbered as 31^v) of NLS, MS Acc. 9268 (formerly TD 313). This is a manuscript of Quintin Kennedy's *Ane Litil Breif Tracteit*, which belonged to John Greenlaw (d. 1566).[36] It has an altered incipit, and lines 6–7 are closer to the Maxwell text than that in Bannatyne:

> Afoir the tyme is wysdowme to prouide
> That owt of tyme thair be na thynge to borrowe
> For quha tynes tyme lattand the tyme our slyde
> Tyme may cum swa to twrne his Ioye In sorowe
> Tynt tyme this nycht cumes not agayne the morrow
> Thairfor tak tyme quhile it is oportwne
> And mak noucht dowle for tyme quhen tyme in downe.

No. 106.   'Rycht as pouerte causis sobirnes'
                (B, fol. 75^v; Ritchie, II, p. 186–87).

Fox indicates that this eight-line stanza is an extract from John Walton's Prologue to his translation of Boethius's *Consolation of Philosophy*, lines 83–90, and states that it is found as a separate stanza in six English manuscripts (see *IMEV* 2820). It should be noted, however, that this stanza also occurs in two earlier Scottish manuscripts, both belonging to the late fifteenth century: Bodleian, Arch. Selden. B. 24, fol. 119^r;[37]

---

36 On the background, see *Quintin Kennedy (1520–1564): Two Eucharistic Tracts*, ed. Cornelis H. Kuipers (Nijmegen, 1964), pp. 106–08.

37 *Facsimile*, introd. Boffey and Edwards, no. 4. The text is printed in *Chaucerian and Other Pieces*, ed. Walter Skeat (Oxford, 1897), no. xxvi.

and BL, Cotton Vitellius E. xi, fol. 4^v. The latter manuscript is a copy of John of Fordun's *Chronica Gentis Scotorum*, and the poem's presence there might seem at first sight slightly incongruous.[38] None of the Scottish scribes knew that Walton was the author of this piece of verse: in Bannatyne, it is anonymous, and in the two other manuscripts it is attributed to Geoffrey Chaucer, illustrating the then common view of Chaucer as a proverbial, sententious poet. It is possible that all the Scottish copies derive, ultimately, from a single exemplar: in line 3, all read 'riches' instead of Walton's 'sekirnesse'. Of the three texts, Bannatyne's is noticeably the weakest, reading 'anseris' (2) instead of the correct 'enforceth', and 'hewes' (6) instead of 'thewes'.

No. 107.   'Now quhen ane wreche is sett to he estait'
                  (B, fol. 75^v; Ritchie, II, p. 187).

Although termed 'unique', this single rhyme royal stanza, with an altered first line, is an extract from John Lydgate's *Fall of Princes*, IV.3151–57, which commonly begins: 'Thus whan a wrech is set in hih estat.'[39] The text illustrates the popularity of the didactic material in the *Fall of Princes*. Bannatyne contains another extract from the same work: 'Dissait dissauis and salbe dissauit' (no. 98). This stanza is thematically grouped with a number of other poems, treating the fall from high to low 'estait', and perils of ambition (see nos 106 and 108). [**107**]

No. 108.   'Bettir it is to suffer fortoun and abyd'
                  (B, fol. 75^v; Ritchie, II, p. 187).

This is a well-known English sententious couplet, which circulated, sometimes separately and sometimes, as here, forming part of a series of metrical proverbs (see *IMEV* 4137; Whiting, F505). It was popular in Scotland, being recorded, for instance, in the Maxwell MS (fol. 12^r), and in an 'ABC of Proverbs' in Aberdeen [University Library], MS 28 (fol. 11^r). It is said to occur in the print of the *Buik of Alexander*, written in a late sixteenth-century hand on the margin of Eviii, and was copied on the beams of the 'Inscribed Chamber' in Delgaty Castle (*c.* 1592).[40]

No. 112.   'He þat thy freind hes bene rycht lang'
                  (B, fol. 76^r; Ritchie, II, p. 189).

Fox notes one other occurrence, in the Maxwell MS (fol. 19^v), of this quatrain on the virtue of loyalty to old friends. But there exist two other versions, whose relation to this piece is obscured by a slightly altered first line. The earlier and more interesting of these is inscribed not in a manuscript but on a handsome silver-gilt cup usually

---

38 See further, Julia Boffey, 'Proverbial Chaucer and the Chaucer Canon', *Huntington Library Quarterly*, 58 (1996), 37–47.

39 First noted by A. S. G. Edwards, 'Selections from Lydgate's *Fall of Princes*: A Checklist', *The Library*, 5th ser., 26 (1971), 337–42 (341); also *NIMEV* 2378.22.

40 See *The Buik of Alexander*, ed. R. L. G. Ritchie, 4 vols, STS, 2nd ser. 12, 17, 21, 25 (Edinburgh, 1921–29), IV, p. xviii; and Michael Bath, *Renaissance Decorative Painting in Scotland* (Edinburgh, 2003), p. 222, 3b.

known as the Methuen (or Methven) Cup, which is now the property of the Los Angeles County Museum of Art (William Randolph Hearst Collection, 49.14. 6a–b).[41] The following inscription is arranged in three bands, two on the cover, and the third on the cup just below the brim:

> Gif that thov hes a frind of lang
> Svppos he sumtim dov the vrang
> Oppres him not bot ay of mein   [have mind of]
> The kandes that afor has bein. MAL   [kindness]
>
> At thi bvrd qvan thov art set
> Think on the puir standis at thi ʒet
> Loue god do lav keip cherati   [law]
> Sva sal al grace abovndand be.

The letters MAL have not been explained, but possibly represent the owner's initials; M might indicate 'maister'. No other text of the second quatrain is known, but there is some similarity to lines in the alliterative poem, *The Awyntyrs of Arthure*: 'Have pite on þe poer … The praier of þe poer may purches þe pes, / Of þase þat ʒellis at thi ʒete, whan þou art set in þi sete'. There are parallels also to a later, undated inscription recorded in Paisley: 'He that has pitie on the puir / Of grace and mercie sal be suir'.[42] A misspelt Latin inscription occurs at the foot of the cup: 'Qvcqvid agas sapienter agas et resspise finem'.[43]

The early history of the cup is obscure. It came to public attention in 1920 when it was sold at Christie's by Lord Methuen, but there is no heraldic or other evidence that it was necessarily owned by a member of the Methuen family in the sixteenth century. The Los Angeles County Museum dates the cup 'around 1550', but Ian Finlay considers that it 'could easily be as early as [108] 1530 or even 1525'. He interpreted what seems to be the maker's mark 'vh' (enclosed in a small shield) as possibly 'the monogram of John Vaich, an Edinburgh goldsmith who became burgess in 1517'.[44] The function of the cup has also been disputed. According to Francis Eeles, 'there is no reason to suppose that it was even intended for anything else than a piece of table plate'; but Norman-Wilcox argued that the presence of the sacred monogram IHS inside the bowl of the cup, together with the inscriptions, rendered it 'appropriate

---

[41] I am grateful to the Museum for sending me information and excellent photos of the Methuen Cup. [Despite the direction 'See Plate I', an image did not appear in the original text; see this volume's cover and frontispiece.]

[42] See *The Awntyrs off Arthure*, ed. Ralph Hanna (Manchester, 1974), lines 173, 178–80. The Paisley inscription is said to have been on the walls of a hospital or almshouse by C. Rogers, *Monuments and Monumental Inscriptions in Scotland*, 2 vols (London, 1872), I, p. 424.

[43] On the ancient maxim *Respice finem*, see Ecclesiasticus, 7.36; Whiting E84, and Whiting, 'Proverbs', part I, p. 162.

[44] See Gregor Norman-Wilcox, 'The Methuen Cup', *Bulletin of the Art Division, Los Angeles County Museum of Art*, 13.3 (1961), 10–15; and Ian Finlay, *Scottish Gold and Silver Work*, rev. and ed. Henry Fotheringham (Stevenage, 1991), pp. 58–60 (60).

to church use, either as a chalice … or a ciborium'.[45] The IHS monogram was a devotional emblem, associated with the cult of the name of Jesus, but its use was not confined to religious objects. It seems to have been a popular motif in the decorative arts of the early sixteenth century, and appears on pendants and brooches, and even on a marchpane mould, together with a pious inscription, 'An harte that is wyse will obstine from sinnes'.[46] A number of English and Scottish cups and mazers that survive from the fifteenth and sixteenth centuries bear inscriptions in Latin or the vernacular; some are convivial, many are pious.[47] The verses on the Methuen cup belong to this latter tradition: they exhort the reader – imagined as sitting at a table ('at thi bvrd') – to practise charity, in the double sense of affection towards friends and generosity to the poor. The reference to 'grace' in the last line may recall the custom of saying grace at the end of meals, followed by communal drinking. The Methuen cup, however, appears too small to have circulated among the company in the manner of a 'grace cup'.[48]

The second copy of the quatrain on friendship is closer to the wording of the Methuen cup than that of Bannatyne:

> Giue thow hes had ane freind rycht lang
> Suppois he sumtyme do the wrang
> Oppres him nocht bot rather him mein
> For kyndnes that befoir hes bein.

This too occurs in an unexpected location, on the margin of a thirteenth-century Latin Bible (NLS, Adv. MS 18.1.2, fol. 159ᵛ). It was copied by Thomas McBurnie, a Dumfries notary, probably early in the seventeenth century.[49] McBurnie asserted his ownership of the Bible with many inscriptions – one example is 'Thomas McBurnie with my hand / The worst wryttar in ony land' (fol. 288ᵛ) – and wrote in it other brief verses, one of which is an analogue to no. 282 (see below). A related piece on this theme of friendship occurs in Aberdeen MS 28, fol. 20r: 'Thy freind that hath bein of long continuance'.

---

45 Francis Eeles, 'The Methven Cup: A Piece of Sixteenth-Century Scottish Plate', *Proceedings of the Society of Antiquaries of Scotland*, 55 (1920–21), 285–89 (288); and Norman-Wilcox, 'Methuen Cup', p. 12.

46 Cf. Joan Evans, *A History of Jewellery 1100–1870* (London, 1953), p. 104 and pl. 66; Peter Brears, *All the King's Cooks: The Tudor Kitchens of Henry VIII at Hampton Court Palace* (London, 1999), p. 74 with accompanying plate; and Alison Hanham, *The Celys and Their World* (Cambridge, 1985), pp. 261–62.

47 For a useful survey, see A. S. G. Edwards, 'Middle English Inscriptional Verse Texts', in *Texts and Their Contexts: Papers from the Early Book Society*, ed. J. Scattergood and J. Boffey (Dublin, 1997), pp. 26–43 (37). For illustration and discussion, see also the catalogue, *Gothic: Art for England 1400–1547*, ed. Richard Marks and P. Williamson (London, 2003), nos 183, 187 and 189.

48 On grace cups, see *Gothic*, p. 311 and nos 187 and 189.

49 On McBurnie, see the NLS typescript catalogue entry for MS Adv. 18.1.2.

No. 117.   'Grit fule is he þat puttis in denger'
                     (B, fol. 76ᵛ; Ritchie, II, p. 190).

This single rhyme royal stanza is anonymous in Bannatyne, but Fox identified it as
an extract from Henryson's *Fables*, 1860–66. Further evidence that this stanza was
circulating independently in the sixteenth century is provided by the poor version
of it in the Maxwell MS, which has a slightly altered first line: 'Ane fwill he is that
puttis in dainger' (fol. 11ᵛ).[50] **[109]**

No. 119.   'Quha wilbe riche haif E to honour ay'
                     (B, fol. 76ᵛ; Ritchie, II, p. 191).

Fox points out that this single rhyme royal stanza, like no. 116, is an extract from a
poem in the *speculum principis* tradition, known variously as *The Harp*, or *De Regimine
Principum*. But it should be noted that this stanza circulated independently, and that
copies exist in four other manuscripts. In approximately chronological order, these are:
(1) a fragmentary leaf found in a Selkirk protocol book, compiled by Ninian Brydin
(Walter Mason Collection WM/26/3);[51] (2) the verso of the last leaf of NLS, MS Acc.
9268 (on this MS, see item 101); (3) the Maxwell MS, fol. 10ᵛ; and (4) Aberdeen MS 28,
fol. 18ᵛ. Versions (1) and (2) belong to the mid-sixteenth century, and possibly antedate
the text in Bannatyne; version (3) belongs to the 1580s; and (4) to the first half of the
seventeenth century. In the witnesses for the complete poem, the text of this stanza is
remarkably stable.[52] In its life as a separate advice poem, however, the text was far less
stable; in line 1, the original 'wald be' is retained by the other manuscripts, but appears
as 'wilbe' in Bannatyne; in line 7, original 'travell' is replaced by 'labour' in Maxwell's
copy; and the stanza shortened to six lines in the Selkirk and Aberdeen copies.

No. 124   'All rychtous thing the quhilk dois now proceid'
                     (B, fol. 79ᵛ; Ritchie, II, pp. 201–02).

This is the only known Scottish text of Lydgate's poem (*IMEV* 199). Fox, however,
states that the large number of other copies includes 'another Scots version in
Bodleian, MS Ashmole 61, f. 5ᵛ'. This is mistaken. The error derives, in the first
place, from MacCracken's edition of the poem in Lydgate's *Minor Poems* (1911–12),
II, pp. 461–64; and, ultimately, from confusion between the 'Rate' who compiled
MS Ashmole 61 and the 'Rate' of the Scottish work known as *Ratis Raving*. Both
are mysterious figures, but the language of MS Ashmole 61 is not Scots, and the
manuscript is thought to have been compiled for a Leicestershire family, *c.* 1500.[53]

---

[50] The full text is printed in Bawcutt, 'Commonplace Book of John Maxwell', p. 63. [See
    this essay herein.]
[51] The text is printed and discussed in Bawcutt, 'A First-Line Index of Early Scottish Verse',
    Studies in Scottish Literature, 26 (1991), 254–70 (259–60).
[52] Texts of these are printed in *The Chepman and Myllar Prints*, introd. W. Beattie (Edinburgh,
    1950), tract V; *Maitland Folio*, ed. Craigie, I, pp. 115–25; also II, pp. 74–91.
[53] See *Ratis Raving and Other Scots Poems on Morals*, ed. R. Girvan, STS, 3rd ser. 11
    (Edinburgh, 1937), pp. xxxii–xxxvi. For work on the English 'Rate', see Lynne S.

No. 140.   'To stryk ane vþir gife þat thow pretend'.
                (B, fol. 85ᵛ; Ritchie, II, p. 220).

A couplet from Baldwin and Paulfreyman; also in the Stanford MS [CUL, Dd. 5.75],
no. 69.

No. 141.   'The freindis quhome proffeit or lucre encres'
                (B, fol. 85ᵛ; Ritchie, II, p. 220).

This quatrain from Baldwin and Paulfreyman occurs in the Stanford MS, no. 163,
and on the ceiling of the 'Painted Chamber' in Delgaty Castle.[54]

No. 142.   'Almes deliuerit to þe Indigent'
                (B, fol. 85ᵛ; Ritchie, II, p, 220).

A couplet from Baldwin and Paulfreyman; also in the Stanford MS, no. 177.

No. 144.   'Better it is for a man to be mvte'
                (B, fol. 85ᵛ; Ritichie, II, p. 220).

A quatrain from Baldwin and Paulfreyman; also in the Stanford MS, no. 178.

No. 161.   'Be mirry and glaid honest and vertewous'
                (B, fol. 97ᵛ; Ritchie, II, p. 259).

[110] A couplet from Baldwin and Paulfreyman; it occurs in the Stanford MS, no.
162; and also, slightly altered, in the 'Inscribed Chamber' in Delgaty Castle.[55]

No. 164.   'Was nevir in scotland hard nor sene'
                (B, fols 99ʳ–101ʳ; Ritchie, II, pp. 262–68).

This is the earliest known copy of *Christis Kirk on the Grene*, which Bannatyne's
colophon attributes to 'King Iames the First'. Among the later manuscripts that
contain the poem, Fox lists BL, MS Add. 30371, which is said to be dated 1724 and
also to contain an attribution to this king. But the date 'January Anno Dom. 1724'
in MS Add. 30371 is not original: the numeral 7 seems a later alteration from 8, and
several of the leaves (13, 21, 38, 64), contain a watermark with the date 1819. The
copyist James Bruce took his text chiefly from anthologies printed in the eighteenth
century. He knew Allan Ramsay's *Ever Green* (1724), since he gives to Dunbar's 'In

---

Blanchfield, 'The Romances of MS Ashmole 61: An Idiosyncratic Scribe', in *Romance in
Medieval England*, ed. Maldwyn Mills, Jennifer Fellows and Carol Meale (Cambridge,
1991), pp. 65–87; also her 'Rate Revisited: The Compilation of the Narrative Works in MS
Ashmole 61', in *Romance Reading on the Book: Essays in Medieval Narrative Presented
to Maldwyn Mills*, ed. Jennifer Fellows et al. (Cardiff, 1996), pp. 208–20.

54 Bath, *Renaissance Decorative Painting*, p. 222, 4b.

55 Bath, *Renaissance Decorative Painting*, p. 222, 8b.

secreit place' (B 25) Ramsay's title 'A Brash Wooing'; and in another poem by Dunbar, 'Sweit rois' (B 71), he incorporates an emendation furnished by James Pinkerton in his edition of *Ancient Scotish Poems* (1786). Bannatyne's attribution of this poem to James I therefore receives no independent support from this late manuscript, and its texts have little value.

No. 167.   'In secreit place this hindir nycht'
            (B, fols 103^v–104^v; Ritchie, II, pp. 275–76).

It has long been known that copies of this erotic dialogue, believed to be by Dunbar (see B 25), are found in two other manuscripts (Maitland Folio, p. 308; Reidpeth, fol. 34^v). A fourth text, however, was recently identified in the Osborn Commonplace Book (Yale University, Beinecke Library, Music, MS 13, fols 50^v–51^r).[56] This is an unpublished mid-sixteenth-century English manuscript, which contains both verse and music. Its text of Dunbar's poem is structurally inferior, but has many interesting lexical variants.

No. 169.   'Quhen he wes 3ung and cled in grene'
            (B, fols 107$^{r–v}$; Ritchie, II, pp. 285–87).

This convivial drinking song is formally a carol: this is implied by internal references to the singing of carols at Yule (36) and the position of the burden, 'Quhy sowld not allane honorit be', before the main text.[57] The poem, which is riddling in tone, celebrates the exploits of its mythical hero 'Allane', and purports to be written by 'allane matsonis suddartis', 'Alan Maltson's soldiers', or heavy drinkers. A second drinking poem, 'Quha hes gud malt and makis ill drynk' (no. 216) is likewise attributed by Bannatyne to 'allanis subdert'. Such joking pseudonymous attributions are not uncommon: other examples in this manuscript are 'Iohine Blyth' (no. 174) and 'Iohine Vponland' (no. 155). Maltson, in fact, was a genuine name: it was recorded as the name of a falconer in the 1490s.[58] But Alan Maltson, as David Laing pointed out long ago, is a precursor of Allane o' Maut and John Barleycorn, celebrated in popular ballads and poems by Burns.[59] There is some evidence, however, that the figure of Alan Maltson was known, very much earlier and [111] outside Scotland. In a late medieval English poem known as *Colyn Blowbol's Testament*, Blowbol appoints 'Aleyn Maltson' as one of his executors (365–66), along with 'Sybour Groutehed' (375).

---

56 For transcript and discussion, see P. Bawcutt, 'New Texts of William Dunbar, Alexander Scott and Other Scottish Poets', *Scottish Studies Review*, 1 (2000), 9–25. It should be noted that – despite Ringler, TM 1363 – this text is not set to music.
57 On carols in Scotland, see P. Bawcutt, 'Dunbar's Christmas Carol', in *Scottish Language and Literature, Medieval and Renaissance*, Scottish Studies, 4, ed. D. Strauss and H. W. Drescher (Frankfurt am Main, 1986), pp. 381–92.
58 *Accounts of the Lord High Treasurer of Scotland*, ed. T. Dickson and J. Balfour Paul (Edinburgh, 1877), I, pp. 306 and 366.
59 See *Popular Ballads and Songs: From Tradition, Manuscripts and Scarce Editions*, ed. Robert Jamieson (Edinburgh, 1806), II, pp. 237ff. and *The Poems and Songs of Robert Burns*, ed. J. Kinsley, 3 vols (Oxford, 1968), I, nos 23: 'John Barleycorn' and 77: 'Scotch Drink'.

Alan Maltson here figures as a boon companion of Blowbol, a term for a habitual drinker, and Grouthead, 'dunce, blockhead'.[60] What is apparently the same name also appears in a curious nonsense ABC, which begins 'A for Alyn Mallson that was armyde in a matt.'[61]

No. 174.   'I mak it kend / he þat will spend'
                       (B, fol. 113ʳ; Ritchie, II, pp. 300–01).

Bannatyne placed this piece among the 'mirrie ballatis', between two of Dunbar's comic poems. It is interesting for its metrical form (here laid out in eleven-line stanzas), use of an internal 'O and I' refrain,[62] and somewhat ambiguous tone. Although termed 'admonitory', and 'moral' by some critics, it is better regarded as one of a cluster of Scottish 'gud cheir' poems.[63] The pseudonymous author 'Iohine Blyth' thus advises 'Mak we gud cheir quhill we art heir' (21) and 'Drink thow to me / and I to the / and lat the cop go round' (32–33). The Bannatyne text is termed 'unique', but another version occurs in NLS, Adv. MS 31.7.22 (fol. iii). This manuscript contains a collection of heraldic material belonging to the first half of the sixteenth century, but the poem appears to have been added by a later hand.[64] The first lines resemble the first four lines of Bannatyne's text:

> He that will spend
> And loiff god lait and air
> God will him mend and grace him send
> Quhen catyffis sall haue cair.

There then follows a passage closely corresponding to lines 9–19 of Bannatyne's text. The effect of this abridgement is doubly reductive: a poem of forty-four lines has been shortened to fifteen, and a simple mortality piece remains, after the 'gude cheir' elements have been jettisoned.

No. 183.   'In Awchtirmwchty thair dwelt ane man'
                       (B, fols 120ᵛ–121ᵛ; Ritchie, II, pp. 320–24)

Fox says of this text: 'Another MS, dated by Laing as "not much later than the year 1600", cannot now be traced, but a copy of it made for Laing in 1821, survives (EUL,

---

[60] *IMEV* 4020. For a text, see *Remains of the Early Popular Poetry of England*, ed. W. Carew Hazlitt (London, 1864), I, pp. 92–109.

[61] Ed. C. F. Bühler in 'A Tudor "Crosse Rowe"', *JEGP*, 58.2 (1959), 248–50. According to Ringler, TM 10 and p. 17, Bühler IA 3420 should be corrected to IA 2856 (13), 270ᵛ–71ᵛ.

[62] Cf. R. L. Greene, 'A Middle English Love Poem and the "O-and-I" Refrain-Phrase', *Medium Ævum*, 30 (1961), 170–75. It does not seem common in Scots use, but cf. Balneves, 'O gallandis all I cry and call' (no. 202).

[63] Cf. *Poetry of the Stewart Court*, ed. Joan Hughes and W. S. Ramson (Canberra, 1982), pp. 107, 122; and P. Bawcutt, *Dunbar the Makar* (Oxford, 1992), pp. 143–44.

[64] For a description of the manuscript, see *The Deidis of Armorie*, ed. L. A. J. R. Houwen, 2 vols, STS, 4th ser. 22, 23 (Aberdeen, 1994), I, pp. lxxviii–lxxxi.

MS Laing IV.28).' (It should be noted that Laing's 'copy' has been published.[65]) Fox's statement might mislead readers into thinking that *The Wife of Auchtermuchty* rapidly fell out of favour in the centuries that followed, when exactly the opposite seems to have been the case. Lord Hailes indeed remarked in 1770: 'This is a favourite poem among the Scots, and has been frequently published';[66] and in 1817 an anonymous writer in *Blackwood's Edinburgh Magazine* likewise stated that 'it has been well preserved both by writing and tradition'. The same writer printed a text, which, he claimed, was based upon the Bannatyne copy, 'collated with another, and apparently, an older copy in the Advocates' Library' – unfortunately he provided no means of locating this older copy.[67] Many other [112] texts of the poem, however, still survive in chapbooks: these small printed books, intended for a popular market, descended from or were closely related to earlier broadsides or broadsheets. They are undated, but were mostly produced from the mid-eighteenth century to the early years of the nineteenth century. The chapbook versions of 'The Goodman of Auchtermuchty; or the Goodwife turned Goodman', are not usually associated with the poem in Bannatyne, yet they clearly derive ultimately from a text closely similar to this, despite modifications of the vocabulary and the addition of extra stanzas. With the opening lines in Bannatyne, for instance, may be compared the first quatrain of one of the Ballads in the Crawford Collection:[68]

> In Auchtermuchty lived a Man,
> If all be true that I heard say
> Who yok'd his Pleugh upon the Plain
> Upon a wet and windy day.

The Goodwife, in stanzas 9–10 of this chapbook, instructs her husband variously:

> See first ye sift and then ye kned [knead] …
> Keep all the Gaislings frae the Gled
> And see the Bairns fyle not the Bed.

Such instructions closely parallel lines 26, 32 and 28 of the Bannatyne text.

The attribution to 'Mofat' appears to be in a slightly later hand; if correct, he might be identified with the 'Schir Iohine Moffett' to whom no. 344 has been attributed. The name was a common one, but Fox's suggestion elsewhere that he might be John Moffat, schoolmaster and notary of Dunfermline, active in the early sixteenth century, seems plausible.[69]

[65] See Janet Templeton, 'Seventeenth-Century Versions of *Christis Kirk on the Grene* and *The Wyf of Awchtirmwchty*', *Studies in Scottish Literature*, 4 (1966–67), 137–43.
[66] Lord Hailes, *Ancient Scottish Poems* (Edinburgh, 1770), p. 316.
[67] *Blackwood's Edinburgh Magazine*, April 1817, pp. 67–68.
[68] NLS, Crawford Ballads, no. 636. For another text, see a chapbook printed by the Robertsons of Glasgow (NLS, L.C.2846, no. 54).
[69] On Moffat, see *Henryson*, ed. Fox (1981), pp. xvi–xvii.

No. 189.   'Be chance bot evin this vþer day'
            (B, fols 127^r–128^r; Ritchie, II, pp. 336–39)

Bannatyne attributes this mocking poem on 'a wenche with chyld' to 'ane Inglisman' (cf. no. 246 below). It is termed 'unique', and no precise source has been found. But there is a curious link with a carol printed in an early English song book, *The Book of XX Songes* (1530; *STC* 22924).[70] This consists of a dialogue between a man and a young woman, and has a burden beginning:

> Bewar my lytyl fynger,
> Syr, I yow desyre!
> Bewar my lytyl fynger …

The woman in the Bannatyne poem likewise complains naively of pain in her little finger, and the refrain rings changes on 'O Lord my littill finger'. Possibly there existed other English erotic poems, now lost, that employed the euphemistic motif of 'the little finger'. Despite its attribution to an Englishman, the language of the piece is largely but not exclusively Scots.

No. 196.   'Mony man makis ryme and lukis to no reason'
            (B, fols 134^v–135^v; Ritchie, III, pp. 8–10).

This work has historical interest as the earliest surviving collection of proverbs written in Scots. At least three other Scottish copies exist: in the Maitland [113] Folio, pp. 139–40; in the Reidpeth MS, fols 31^v–32^v; and (unknown to Fox) in the seventeenth-century Aberdeen MS 28, fols 27^r–29^v. There also exist copies, probably but not certainly pre-dating Bannatyne's text, in two English manuscripts. The first is Bodleian, MS Digby 145, which belonged to Sir Adrian Fortescue (executed in 1539). The greater part of this manuscript consists of texts of *Piers Plowman* and Sir John Fortescue's *Governance of England*, copied by Sir Adrian himself c. 1532; the proverb poem occurs on the last leaves (fols 160^v–161^v). Thomas (Fortescue), Lord Clermont, who printed it in *A History of the Family of Fortescue* (1880), stated that the whole manuscript was written in the same hand, 'the maxims being perhaps more hastily written than the rest'.[71] Most modern scholars, however, consider that the proverb poem is not in Sir Adrian's hand, yet it seems not impossible that it may have been copied for, if not by, him, since there is testimony elsewhere to Sir Adrian's taste for collecting and writing out 'precepts'.[72] The second English text occurs in a manuscript compiled by Richard Cox (1499–1581), tutor to Edward VI and later bishop of Ely until his death in 1581, when the manuscript was presented by his son

---

[70] For the text, see R. Imelmann, 'Zur Kenntnis der vor-Shakespearischen Lyrik: I. Wynkyn de Worde's "Song booke" 1530', *Shakespeare Jahrbuch*, 39 (1903), no. iv, 126–27; also H. M. Nixon, 'The Book of XX Songs', *British Museum Quarterly*, 16 (1951), 33–36.

[71] Thomas (Fortescue), Lord Clermont, *A History of the Family of Fortescue in all its Branches* (London, 1869; 2nd edn, 1880), pp. 263–65 (265).

[72] See Thorlac Turville-Petre, 'Sir Adrian Fortescue and His Copy of *Piers Plowman*', *Yearbook of Langland Studies*, 14 (2000), 29–48 (32–33).

to Corpus Christi College, Cambridge (MS 168). The contents of the manuscript are miscellaneous: they include Latin verses composed by Cox himself, hymns, and two poems by Sir Thomas Wyatt, as well as the proverb poem (fol. 112^{r-v}).[73]

The poem cannot be dated, and is anonymous in all witnesses, except Aberdeen MS 28, which entitles it 'King James the fyft his Pasquill'. There is nothing to support such an attribution; the 1666 print of *Christis Kirk on the Grene* was ascribed, with equal fancifulness, to James V. To label this work as a 'pasquill' also seems inappropriate – it is not a scurrilous lampoon – yet it suggests that contemporary readers found the poem more witty than do modern ones and helps to explain its location among Bannatyne's 'mirrie ballatis', in proximity to humorous poems by Dunbar. At the end, the author modestly disparages his own talents, but the poem has one ingenious feature, its metrical interlacing of items, by which a word at the end of one proverb rhymes with a word in the middle of the next. This helps preserve the work from falling apart into a series of separate couplets and would aid committal to memory.

It is probable, if not wholly certain, that the author was Scottish. There is stronger evidence for the poem's circulation in Scotland than in England. In addition to the four Scottish witnesses, a possible quotation of the first line has been noted in an early printed book, a commentary on Lorenzo Valla by Guido Juvenalis, which had several Scottish owners (NLS, RB.s.1086); but one cannot read very much into this, since the same line occurs independently in the *Carmichaell Proverbs*.[74] There are also pointers to a Scottish (or northern English) origin in what B. J. Whiting called a 'residue of Scottish forms and words' (such as the rhymes *wirk: kirk*) remaining in the English manuscripts.[75] Proverbs are notoriously international, but a few in this poem appear peculiar to Scotland. No other English instance is known to me of the cynical maxim: [**114**] 'Ane king sekand Tresoun / he may fynd land' (2–3). But a closely contemporary Scottish use occurs in Richard Bannatyne's *Memorials*: 'Ane kyng seikand treasone, may fynde lond'.[76] In the English witnesses, the saying seems weakened, and possibly misunderstood: 'A king sekant treason shall fynde it in his lond'. Precisely how the work reached England is not known, but there are various possible channels of transmission. Sir Adrian's great-uncle Sir John Fortescue spent the years 1461–63 as an exile in Scotland. The links between Richard Cox and Scotland are even stronger, ranging from his contacts with Scottish Reformers in

73 For an inventory of Richard Cox's books and a useful short biography, see *Private Libraries in Renaissance England*, ed. R. J. Fehrenbach and E. S. Leedham-Green (Binghamton, NY, 1992), I, pp. 3–9.
74 Cf. Theo van Heijnsbergen, 'Paradigms Lost: Perceptions of the Cultural History of Sixteenth-Century Scotland', in *Schooling and Society: The Ordering and Reordering of Knowledge in the Western Middle Ages*, ed. A. A. MacDonald and M. W. Twomey (Leuven, 2004), pp. 197–211 (206). Cf. *The James Carmichaell Collection of Proverbs in Scots*, ed. M. L. Anderson (Edinburgh, 1957), no. 1169.
75 See Whiting, 'Proverbs': part I, 123–25.
76 Richard Bannatyne, *Memorials of Transactions in Scotland*, ed. R. Pitcairn, Bannatyne Club, 51 (Edinburgh, 1836), p. 9; also *Hume of Godscroft's House of Angus*, I, p. 522.

1555–58, which he spent in exile in Frankfurt, to his custody – on apparently cordial terms – of John Leslie in May to September 1571.[77]

This is not the place for detailed textual comparison. But one set of variants interestingly reflects the religious pressures of the times. Lines 53–55 of the Bannatyne text run: 'be blyth at þi meit / Devoit in distres for littill mair or les / Mak thow na debait …' Fortescue's version has 'devout at thy masse' (p. 264), instead of 'Devoit in distres'; it gives a good contrast with 'blyth at thi meit' and seems likely to be the original reading. All the Scottish witnesses attempt to find substitutes for the dangerous term 'mass': 'sad at thy prayeris' (Maitland Folio and Reidpeth MSS); 'patient in distres' (Aberdeen MS, fol. 28^v).

No. 201   'Robeyns Iok come to wow our Iynny'
                 (B, fols 137^r–138^r; Ritchie, III, pp. 15–18).

This comic description of a peasant betrothal, with a detailed account of the girl's tocher, is said to be a 'unique copy'. This is misleading. Although no other sixteenth-century text is known to survive, there exists a version in *Watson's Choice Collection* (1711), where it has the title 'The Country Wedding'. Watson's text derives, ultimately, from the poem of which Bannatyne has preserved a copy. This may be seen in the opening stanza:

> *Rob's Jock* came to woo our *Jennie*
> On a Feast Day when he was fow …

But the version in Watson is much expanded – containing 128 lines, as opposed to Bannatyne's eighty – and altered in other small respects. Between them, in the words of Harriet Harvey Wood, 'yawns a vast gulf which must be filled hypothetically by a succession of progressively adulterated versions (many, no doubt, broadside) now no longer surviving'.[78] Bannatyne's text may be regarded as one of the first examples of the comic genre of 'Jock and Jenny' ballads, which became particularly popular in England in the seventeenth and eighteenth centuries.

Dr Harvey Wood lists a number of broadside versions of such poems that might have influenced Watson's text. She does not, however, mention one particularly interesting and early example, extant in Bodleian, MS Ashmole 48 (*c.* 1557–65), which begins: 'Our Jockye sale have our Jenny, hope I'.[79] This contains several stanzas almost identical to descriptions of rustic feasting in [**115**] Watson's text. Compare the following passages:

---

77 On Fortescue, cf. Priscilla Bawcutt, 'Crossing the Border: Scottish Poetry and English Readers in the Sixteenth Century', in *The Rose and the Thistle: Essays on the Culture of Late Medieval and Renaissance Scotland*, ed. S. Mapstone and J. Wood (East Linton, 1998), pp. 59–76 (73 and 60n); on Cox, see 'Diary of the Bishop of Ross', in *Bannatyne Miscellany*, III, ed. D. Laing (1855), pp. 115–56.

78 See *Watson's Choice Collection*, ed. Harvey Wood, I, part III, pp. 46–51; II, p. 209.

79 For this poem, see *Songs and Ballads, with Other Short Poems, chiefly of the Reign of Philip and Mary*, ed. T. Wright (London, 1860), no. xxxvi (pp. 119–24).

What sal we set them beforne,
    To Jocky thus dyde the crye;
Gyve them some [read sowe] sardar and sodden corne,
    Tyll thear ballys stande awrye.   [bellies]

Of swynes flesshe ther was great plenttie,
    Whilk ys a pleasant meate;
And garlyk, a sawce that ys full deyntye
    For any that sall it eate.
                (ed. Wright, p. 122)

What Meat shall we set them beforn,
To *Jock* Service loud can they cry,
Serve them with Sowce and sodden Corn,
Till a' their Wyms do stand awray   [wames, bellies]
Of Swine's Flesh there was great Plenty,
Whilk was a very pleasant Meat,
And Garlick was a sawce right dainty
To ony Man that pleas'd to eat.
            ('The Country Wedding', 57–64,
        Watson, ed. Wood, I, part III, p. 48)

Bodleian, MS Ashmole 48 is a miscellany of great interest to ballad scholars. Many of its texts have been copied from broadsides, and this particular piece may well have circulated in print. It is probably Scottish, since it contains Scottish words and spellings, and is attributed to a 'John Wallys' (or Wallace).[80] Its relationship to the Bannatyne poem is generic, providing not a source or derivative text but a closely contemporary analogue.

No. 212B.   'Betuix twa foxis / A crawing cok'
                (B, fol. 144ᵛ; Ritchie, III, p. 37)

This ten-line passage of rough couplets is lineated by Ritchie as if it formed part of the preceding item, a quatrain for which there is a heading: 'The sowtar Inveyand aganis the telȝeour sayis'. Both direct invective against tailors, and both relate to an earlier poem in the manuscript, William Stewart's 'Flytting' between the Tailor and the Sowtar (see nos 203–05; B, fols 139ᵛ–141ʳ; Ritchie, III, pp. 22–26). Fox prefers to treat them as two separate items, and terms both 'unique'. Item 212A belongs to the flyting tradition, being placed in the mouth of a sowtar. Item 212B, entitled 'An Vder', is a kind of simple riddle, and has a very different form. The first four lines depict in turn a cock between two foxes, a maiden between two friars, a mouse between two cats and a louse between two tailors. These are followed by the question: 'quhilk of thais four is grittest in denger?', and a four-line 'Anser'.

---

[80] On this topic, see M. Chestnutt, 'Minstrel Poetry in an English Manuscript of the Sixteenth Century: Richard Sheale and MS Ashmole 48', in *The Entertainer in Medieval and Traditional Culture*, ed. F. G. Andersen, T. Pettit and Reinhold Schröder (Odense, 1997), pp. 73–100 (84–85).

Bannatyne's copy, in fact, is not 'unique'. A closely similar text was copied into the Register of Signatures, around 1581, by one of the clerks in chancery (NRS, Register of Signatures, E 30/13, fol. 61).[81] Although there are some [**116**] slight differences of wording, the pattern is the same: two quatrains linked by the question 'Quhilk of the four ar in greitest danger'; the victims and aggressors are the same, and the tailors occupy the climactic line: 'Bot tailyeouris are tirantis in killing of lyce'.

There also exists a third version of this piece. This is an English broadside, printed in 1623 (*STC* 11211.5).[82] It consists of two horizontal compartments, each of which contains two pictures: these are labelled, 'A Clyent, betweene two Lawyers'; 'A Maide, betweene two Friers'; 'A Goose, betweene two Foxes'; and 'A Rat, betweene two Cats'. Each image is accompanied by captions and six lines of explanatory verse. The structural resemblance to the Bannatyne piece is unmistakable, and placed in the centre is a box containing the familiar question: 'Which of these fower, that here you see, / In greatest daunger you thinke to be'. But there are many interesting differences, of which the most striking is the substitution of lawyers preying upon a poor client for the tailors and a louse. The pictorial element is attractive, and the satire is extremely detailed. The church is said to be but a 'cloke' for lechery and vice; and the Rat complains: 'My smallest faults must punisht be, / When greater theeues are let goe free'. The Scottish piece is a small joke or flyting, with roots in ancient satirical traditions. It possibly reached England through oral circulation, and there was much elaborated, in part through the new developments in printing technology.

No. 218.   'It þat I gife I haif / It þat I len I craif'
                (B, fol. 147ʳ; Ritchie, III, p. 43).

The first two of these rhyming maxims seem to have circulated widely in England and Scotland (see Fox's note; also *IMEV* 1460.5). An expanded version is found in the Maxwell Manuscript (fol. 9ᵛ), and illustrates the freedom with which such traditional verses might be expanded or altered:

> It that I spend on my self I haife it
> It that I len to fals men I crawe it
> It that I gif for my sawll that I finde
> It that I leife to fals execwtowris cwmes behinde.

The lines can be traced to a medieval Latin source, 'Quod expendi habui, Quo donavi habeo'.[83]

---

[81] For a transcript, see M. H. B. Sanderson, *Mary Stewart's People* (Edinburgh, 1987), p. 89.
[82] See Robert Lemon, *Catalogue of a Collection of Broadsides in the Possession of the Society of Antiquaries* ([London], 1866), no. 208. On the background, see Tessa Watt, *Cheap Print and Popular Piety, 1550–1640* (Cambridge, 1991), pp. 146–47. [Figure 27 (p. 117 of the original essay), the 1623 broadside (*STC* 11211.5; Lemon 208), has not been reprinted here.]
[83] See Bawcutt, *Dunbar the Makar*, p. 144.

No. 221.   'I 3eid the gait wes nevir gane'
                           (B, fol. 155^v–156^r; Ritchie, III, pp. 66–67).

This poem of impossibilities (cf. no. 340 below) is termed 'unique'. S. M. Horrall, however, has shown that it closely resembles a thirteenth-century English poem entered on an imperfect copy of Priscian's Commentaries (Westminster Abbey, MS 34/3, fol. 36^v).[84] Although the Scottish poem – at forty-eight lines – is twice the length of the English one, it employs the same stanza and often the same rhymes. It contains numerous similarities of topoi and wording, and, what is more, has essentially the same purpose. The English poem concludes: 'Lemman whan the song is soth / Of loue thou ssalt be trewe.' The Bannatyne poet turns this into an anti-feminist generalization about all women (47–48): [118]

>   Quhen all thir tailis ar trew in deid
>   All wemen will be trew.

No. 223.   'Troll trottes on befoir and takis no heid'
                           (B, fols 157^v–159^r; Ritchie, III, pp. 70–74).

Consisting of ninety-eight lines in irregular couplets, this anonymous work is prefaced by a doggerel title, beginning: 'The nyne ordour of knavis / Thair vse and thair feir.' It is divided into nine sections, each headed by the name of the knave (that is, both servant and rogue) whom it describes. The work belongs to the popular satirical genre of rogue literature; 'ane discriptioun of peder coffeis' (no. 229), is another poem of a similar type, which has been attributed to Lyndsay.[85] This particular text, which is here termed 'unique', has been virtually ignored by scholars, but in an unpublished note (in my possession) Fox has suggested that it is related to an English prose work, published in London by John Awdely (also known as John Samson) under the title *The .xxv. Orders of Knaves*, either on its own, or together with *The Fraternitye of Vacabondes*. The textual history of this publication is difficult to establish: the print of c. 1561 (*STC* 995.5) is defective; and only the title page of the 1565 print (*STC* 993) survives. The earliest complete text, dated 1575 (*STC* 994), was published by Edward Viles and F. J. Furnivall (EETS, ES 9, 1869). There may, in addition, have been a version in verse, which no longer survives.[86] The resemblances between the texts in Bannatyne and Awdely 1575 extend far beyond title and general theme to include names of several knaves, and striking details in their characterization. Bannatyne's 'Troll hasart of the trace' (25) thus corresponds to Awdely's 'Troll hazard of trace'; and Banantyne's 'Troll of the tre trace' (39) corresponds to Awdely's 'Troll hazard of tritrace'. Bannatyne's sixth knave is curiously called 'Chaist luter':

---

[84] S. M. Horrall, 'A Poem of Impossibilities from Westminster Abbey MS 34/3', *Notes and Queries*, 230.4 (1985), 453–55; also Bawcutt, 'Index of Early Scottish Verse', 256–57.

[85] See Janet Hadley Williams, '"Peder coffeis": Ascription and Authorship', in *Rhetoric, Royalty, and Reality: Essays on the Literary Culture of Medieval and Early Modern Scotland*, ed. Alasdair A. MacDonald and Kees Dekker (Leuven, 2005), pp. 121–36.

[86] An entry in the Stationers' Register 1560–61 mentions 'a ballett called the Description of Vakabondes'.

Chaist luter gois to bed and syne rubbis his tais
he will nocht rys to the pott Bot pischis amang the strais.
(65–66)

Chaist luter represents a corruption – either committed by Bannatyne or found
in his exemplar – of Awdely's *Chafe Litter*, that is, 'Rub-bedstraw'. This knave is so
slothful that 'he wyll plucke vp the Fetherbed or Matrice, and pysse in the bedstraw'.
According to Bannatyne, 'With the butis he will fyle the bed and all the array' (77),
just as in Awdely, he 'maketh cleane his shooes with the couerlet or curtaines'. The
precise relationship between these two works is far from clear. The surviving Awdely
text of 1575 is clearly too late to be Bannatyne's source, and in any case it lacks
many piquant details found in the Scottish work, including the final figure of the
'Fathir Abbott'. The most likely hypothesis seems to be that some version of Awdely's
work (either in prose or verse) had reached Scotland in the early 1560s and became
sufficiently popular to provoke a creative rewriting by a Scottish writer. This might
possibly have been Bannatyne himself.

No. 239.   'Lyke as the littill emmet haith hir gall'
                  (B, fol. 211ᵛ; Ritchie, III, pp. 241–42).

[119] This sonnet, a later addition to the manuscript, is termed 'unique'. Another
copy, however, occurs among the additional material in the so-called Tibbermuir
Manuscript; this is the supplementary section added in 1612 by James Murray of
Tibbermuir to a Scottish manuscript of Lydgate's *Troy Book* (CUL, MS Kk.5.30).[87] This
copy of the poem occurs on fol. 78ʳ⁻ᵛ, among a group of sonnets, and is written in
a different hand from that of James Murray. It is a free re-working of a very popular
poem attributed to the Elizabethan poet Sir Edward Dyer: 'The lowest trees have
tops, the ant her gall.' The Scottish poet's theme is summed up in his final line: 'So
luve is luve in peure men as in kingis'. This closely echoes the line that ends Dyer's
first stanza: 'And love is love in beggars and in kings'. Dyer's poem, which was set to
music by Dowland (1603), was well known in Scotland at a later date.[88]

No. 246.   'Was nocht gud king Salamon'
                  (B, fol. 215ᵛ–216ʳ; Ritchie, III, pp. 254–56).

This is termed a 'unique' copy, although the colophon provides a disregarded clue to
its origin: 'quod ane inglisman'. The Englishman was William Elderton, and the poem
is a lightly scotticized version of his 'The Panges of Loue and Louers Fittes'. Numerous
quotations, imitations and allusions by later writers testify to this broadside ballad's

---

[87] For further information, see *A Catalogue of the MSS. Preserved in the Library of the
University of Cambridge*, vol. 5 (Cambridge, 1867), pp. 600–03; also Priscilla. Bawcutt,
'*Sir Lamwell* in Scotland', in *The Scots and Medieval Arthurian Legend*, ed. Rhiannon
Purdie and Nicola Royan (Cambridge, 2005), pp. 83–94.
[88] For an edition of Dyer's poem, see Steven May, *The Elizabethan Courtier Poets: The
Poems and Their Contexts* (Columbia, MO, 1991), pp. 307–09. The text and music occur
in Forbes, *Cantus* (1662), no. 27.

popularity in Elizabethan England. Yet only a single copy now survives, printed in London and dated 22 March 1559/60 (*STC* 7561); according to Carole Livingston, the typographical errors and good condition of the sheet 'proclaim that this sheet was a printer's proof, and was never offered for sale'.[89] Bannatyne, in most respects, follows the print very closely indeed, although this is unfortunately obscured by some errors in Ritchie's transcript. Line 11, for instance, should read 'Quhat sturdie stormes indurit he'; Ritchie omits *he*. In line 38, the text should read *Eiphis* (corresponding to Elderton's *Iphis*), not *Kiphis*; and in line 47 the text should read *schop* (= *schape*), not *chop*. Bannatyne's version contains a final stanza not in the extant print, which may possibly have been added in Scotland. Bannatyne may well have known the tune to which this ballad was sung, and which is found, among some cittern and gittern pieces, in the mid-sixteenth-century Mulliner Book (BL, Add. MS 30513, fol. 123^{r-v}). A better version of this tune is recorded in the Dallis Lute Book (Dublin, Trinity College, MS [410, formerly] D.3.30), and it also appears in continental collections as the almain 'Guerre guerre gay'.[90]

The contemporary popularity of Elderton's ballad in Scotland is further illustrated by one of the most ingenious spiritual parodies in *The Gude and Godlie Ballatis* (1567).[91] This, entitled 'Ane Dissuasioun from Vaine Lust', opens:

> Was not Salomon, the King
> To miserie be wemen brocht?
> Quhilk wisdome out of frame did bring,
> Till he maist wickitly had wrought.

[120] The first nine stanzas correspond closely both to Elderton and Bannatyne in the choice and sequence of famous lovers – for example, Solomon, Paris, Troilus, Leander, Pyramus – but clearly controvert their sense. The Bannatyne text, following its source, concludes that love is to be commended:

> Gif bewty breidis sic blisfulnes
> In amoring [= enamouring] of god and man ...

At the same point in *The Gude and Godlie Ballatis*, however, one reads:

> Thus beutie bredis bitternes,
> And bringis baill to mony men ...

[89] See Hyder E. Rollins, 'William Elderton: Elizabethan Actor and Ballad-Writer', *Studies in Philology*, 17 (1920), 199–245; and Carole R. Livingston, *British Broadside Ballads of the Sixteenth Century: A Catalogue of the Extant Sheets and an Essay* (New York, 1991), pp. 184–85.

[90] On this, see Claude M. Simpson, *The British Broadside Ballad and Its Music* (New Brunswick, NJ, 1966), pp. 410–12; also Dennis Stevens, *The Mulliner Book: A Commentary* (London, 1952), p. 82.

[91] *A Compendious Book of Godly and Spiritual Songs Commonly Known as 'The Gude and Godlie Ballatis'*, ed. A. F. Mitchell, STS, 1st ser. 39 (Edinburgh, 1897), pp. 213–19. A. A. MacDonald informs me that this poem is not in the 1565 edition.

What is more, in order to hammer home the point, the godly version adds fourteen extra stanzas, which illustrate lust's iniquity. Elderton's ballad employed a striking eight-line stanza, with two refrains: 'Ladie, ladie' and 'My dear ladie', which inspired many imitations. The godly ballad has the same metrical shape, but substitutes lugubrious refrains: 'Allace, allace' and 'As come to pas.' The same stanza is also employed in 'Knaw 3e not God omnipotent', a poem attacking the Mass, which immediately precedes this one in *The Gude and Godlie Ballatis*. It seems likely, as Rollins suggests, that it too shows the influence of Elderton's ballad.[92]

No 282.   'Gif 3e wald lufe and luvit be'
                 (B, fol. 230^{r-v}; Ritchie, III, p. 303).

This counsel on success in love has a refrain 'Be secreit, trew and pacient'. In the past, it was attributed to Dunbar by some editors, largely because of a generic resemblance to a poem of his giving advice to a lover (B 7) that has a similar refrain: 'Be secreit, trew, incressing of 3our name.'[93] The Bannatyne text is termed 'unique' but appears to have been known at a later date. A version of the first stanza has an incongruous location in a thirteenth-century Bible (NLS, Adv. MS 18.1.2, fol. 177^v), where it was copied in the early seventeenth century by Thomas McBurnie (on this manuscript, see no. 112 above):

> Gif thow walld luif or luifeit be
> Keip in thy mynd thir things thre
> And euer in thi mynd imprent
> Be secreit trew and pacient.

Later in the seventeenth century the same four lines were copied in Aberdeen Manuscript 28, fol. 13^v. A fourth, more moralized version is also recorded on fol. 212 of NLS, MS 15937. This manuscript is a nineteenth-century transcript of an anthology of English and Scottish verse, compiled *c.* 1630 by Margaret Robertson, 'Relict' of Alexander Stewart of Bonskeid; the present whereabouts of the original are not known.[94] Here the last two lines read:

> Be secreitt true and pacient
> To father and mother obedent [sic].

It is debatable whether these short texts are extracts from the longer poem known to Bannatyne, or whether his text represents an expansion of the quatrain. [**121**]

No. 286.   'Lait lait on sleip as I wes laid'
                 (B, fol. 231^v; Ritchie, III, pp. 308–09).

---

92 *Gude and Godlie Ballatis*, pp. 209–12; Rollins, 'William Elderton', 201, 5n.

93 See J. W. Baxter, *William Dunbar: A Biographical Study* (Edinburgh, 1952), p. 226.

94 See NLS typescript Catalogue of MSS, no. 15937; and Bawcutt, 'Scottish Manuscript Miscellanies', 54.

This poem is incomplete, because folios 232–33 of the manuscript are missing, but the thirty-five lines extant indicate its metrical shape, and show that it belongs to the genre of the erotic dream (for another instance, see no. 400).[95] Although here termed 'unique', it is closely related to a short poem in an English poetic miscellany (Bodleian, MS Rawlinson C. 813) compiled between *c.* 1520 and 1535. This miscellany, published under the title *The Welles Anthology*, contains other examples of the genre (nos 36 and 46).[96] The English poem (no. 37) has a very similar opening line: 'Late on a nyght as I lay slepyng'. There are other verbal similarities between the two poems, including the maiden's 'mantill of lusty blew' (Bannatyne, lines 10, 18; Rawlinson, line 14), and virtually identical refrains:

> But when I waked she was awey (Rawlinson)
> Bot quhen I walknyt scho wes away (Bannatyne)

Bannatyne's text, despite its lack of a conclusion, is an expansion or elaborated version of the English poem: it has a more complex stanza and uses dialogue. (Fox noted that another of Bannatyne's love poems (no. 268) closely resembles *The Welles Anthology*, no. 43: 'Fare well now my lady gaye' (52ᵛ)).

No. 289.   'Lanterne of lufe and lady fair of hew'
            (B, fol. 235ʳ; Ritchie, III, pp. 312–13).

This love poem has been said to resemble *Welles Anthology*, no. 41: 'O lusty lyllye, the lantorne of all gentylnes'. But, apart from two shared and conventional images of the lantern and daisy, there is little similarity. On Bannatyne's attribution to 'Steill', Fox remarks: 'Perhaps George Steill, one of James V's courtiers', but this is an unsubstantiated speculation.[97] Steill was not an uncommon Scottish name. Bannatyne does not give him a Christian name, nor is the George Steill who figures in the records and is mentioned by David Lyndsay called a poet. A stronger candidate might perhaps be the 'dene dauid Steill', to whom a poem in the Maitland Folio is attributed: 'The Ring of the Roy Robert' (no. xli). This historical poem belongs to a very different genre, but nonetheless its author was a poet named 'Steill'.

No. 300.   'My hairt repois the and the rest'
            (B, fol. 239ʳ; Ritchie, III, pp. 325–26).

---

95 Cf. P. J. Frankis, 'The Erotic Dream in Middle English Lyrics', *Neuphilologische Mitteilungen*, 57 (1956), 228–37.

96 *The Welles Anthology*, ed. Sharon L. Jansen and K. J. Jordan (Binghamton, NY, 1991), nos 36, 37 and 46. For criticism of this edition, and further information, see Edward Wilson in *Review of English Studies*, 44.174 (1993), 246–48, and Wilson, *Review of English Studies*, 41.161 (1990), 12–44.

97 Fox's note derives from Helena M. Shire, *Song, Dance and Poetry of the Court of Scotland under King James VI* (Cambridge, 1969), pp. 4 and 281; and *Ballattis of Luve*, ed. J. MacQueen (Edinburgh, 1970), pp. xxxiv–xxxv.

Fox notes that a copy of this love poem is found, 'in part', on a single damaged leaf in Edinburgh University Library (MS Laing II.656). Since this text has never been published, a little more information seems desirable. The top of the leaf is missing, and the poem therefore lacks the first two lines, but has the same number of stanzas in the same order as the Bannatyne text. Although verbally close, some readings appear superior. Lines 7–8 in Bannatyne puzzlingly read: 'bot the publict superlatyve / To tell this taill.' MS Laing II.656 is far more lucid: 'bot be that perle superlative / I tell this tail.' MS Laing II.656 also contains on the other side of the leaf another love poem, similarly [**122**] lacking the first two lines, and beginning: '...or quha suld pres to suffer pyne'. This second poem was printed by David Laing in his *Early Scottish Metrical Tales* (1889), with a substitute opening invented by Charles Sharpe: 'Quhen we to Ladies lufe inclyne / Our guerdon still growis less and less'. In his Preface, Laing gives an interesting but unfortunately brief account of how he found this piece 'in a mutilated state, with various other fragments in verse and prose, pasted together in the boards of an old book of little value'.[98] These may have been the fragments of the lost 'ballat buke'.

No. 306.   'How suld my febill body fure'
             (B, fol. 244ᵛ; Ritchie, III, pp. 340–41).

Fox provides copious evidence of the popularity of this love poem by Alexander Scott. A further illustration of its long-lasting attractiveness to readers is the copy in the Robertson Manuscript (NLS, MS 15937, fols 196–98; on this MS, see no. 282 above). Another small indication of its currency is provided by the quotation of its first line on the flyleaf of the Boston Public Library MS of *The Siege of Thebes*.[99]

No. 309.   'Pansing in hairt with spreit opprest / This hindir nycht bygon'
             (B, fol. 245ʳ⁻ᵛ; Ritchie, III, pp. 343–44).

A love complaint, with a striking refrain 'Cauld cauld culis the lufe that kendillis our het [hot]', this is sandwiched between two poems attributed to Alexander Scott. In tone, it resembles many poems by Scott but is attributed to 'Fethe', a poet and musician of whom little definite is known, despite much speculation. Fox repeats Helena Shire's suggestion that this is the 'text indicated by the title or incipit "Pansing in spreit" of the bass part in the Melvill Bassus Part-Book of 1604'.[100] The remark would seem to imply that no text accompanies the music in the bassus part-book (BL, MS Add. 36484). But this is not the case. Song no. 63, which occupies the lower half of folio 31ᵛ, is cramped and difficult to read, but it consists of the following text:

> Pansing in spreit the frailtie
> vaingloir dissait penuretie

---

[98] *Early Scottish Metrical Tales*, ed. David Laing (Edinburgh, 1889), pp. 42 and 39.

[99] Cf. Bawcutt, 'Boston Public Library Manuscript', 86.

[100] Shire, *Song, Dance and Poetry*, p. 37, 2n. On this MS, see also Bawcutt, 'Scottish Manuscript Miscellanies', p. 52, 21n, and plate 3 [image of BL, Add. MS 36484, fol. 5ʳ: musical setting and text, 'O lustie may with flora quene'].

the paine the vo [woe] the messerie
withoutin fail withoutin fail withoutin fail*
doeth freit my proud nauchtie pretence
contending with sufficience
wirking my god daylie offence
Into this waill [vale] Into this waill Into this waill.
*[ii *indicates repetition*]

It will be evident that these words have no resemblance, either in metre or gloomy penitential tone, to the love song here attributed to 'Fethe'.

No. 310.   'Depairte depairte depairte allace I most depairte'
                 (B, fols 245^v–246^r; Ritchie, III, pp. 344–45).

A late and rather poor copy of this popular love poem by Alexander Scott is found in the Robertson Manuscript (NLS, MS 15937, fols 54–56; on this MS, see also nos 282 and 374). Several lines are missing from this text, together with the reference to the Master of Erskine found in Bannatyne's colophon. [**123**]

No. 326.   'Returne the hairt hamewart again'
                 (B, fols 252^v–253^r; Ritchie, IV, pp. 8–9).

This text of a love song attributed to Alexander Scott is termed 'unique'. Another copy, however, occurs in the Osborn Commonplace Book [Yale University, Beinecke Library, Music MS 13], fols 45^v–46^r (on this manuscript, see no. 167). The text is of considerable interest, since it contains two stanzas not present in the Bannatyne MS.[101]

No. 340.   'Thocht all the wod vnder the hevin that growis'
                 (B, fol. 258^v; Ritchie, IV, p. 23).

This eight-line poem of impossibilities is included in the 'Schort Epegrammis Aganis Women'. It is termed 'unique', but another copy occurs in the first volume of the Aberdeen Sasine Register, preserved in the Aberdeen Town House. The volume contains records dated between June 1484 and January 1501, but this entry cannot be dated precisely since it is a later addition to a blank space on p. 172:

And al the wode in to the warlde at growis
wer trusty pennis convenient to write
and al the sey vnder the hevin at flowis
were changite in Ink and wer so infinite
and al the w[arl]d wer plesand paper quhite
and al the men wer writeris and tuk lif
thai coud nocht writ the dissaitfull dispite
and wikytnes contenit in ane wiffe.

[101] The text is printed and discussed in Bawcutt, 'New Texts', 11–14. It has no musical setting, despite Ringler, TM 1363.

The Aberdeen text accompanies four lines of medieval Latin verse, of which it is a translation. These begin: 'Si totum membrana celum, calamus nemus omne'. Bannatyne's next item, no. 341, an extract from *The Remedy of Love*, also derives ultimately from this well-known medieval Latin text.[102] The Aberdeen text has an attribution, now almost illegible; Shire and Fenton suggest: 'quod Louerty' (p. 53).

No. 374.   'Quha lykis to luve / or that law pruve'
                  (B, fols 285^v–286^r; Ritchie, IV, pp. 94–95).

Attributed to 'Scott', this is one of a group of poems expressing 'the contempt of blyndit luve'. It is termed by Fox a 'unique copy', but another rather poor version of the poem, which opens: 'Quha list to leive or that law proue', exists in the Robertson Manuscript (NLS, MS 15937, fols 136–38; on this MS, see no. 282 above).[103] The text differs considerably from that in the Bannatyne Manuscript. Bannatyne's fourth stanza, for instance, opens:

> This is the quhy / and caus that I
> Complene so peteously in plane
> I lufe the wy / will nocht apply
> Nor grant to gife me grace agane

In NLS, MS 15937, however, this reads:

> This is quhy, and caus that I
> Compleane so petiouslye in paine
> I loue the may: will not apply   [124]
> To grant to if me grace againe

Scott's diction was that of other sixteenth-century poets: *quhy* is a noun ('reason, cause'); *in plane* is a filler, intended to rhyme with *pane* used later in the stanza; *wy* means 'person, creature'; and *gife* is the verb 'give'. But clumsy modernization or sheer incomprehension of his language (whether by Margaret Robertson or the nineteenth-century copyist of her MS) has produced readings that wreck the delicate rhythm and intricate rhyme-scheme of this poem, as well as its sense and syntax.

---

[102] This item was printed, in part, by Helena M. Shire and Alexander Fenton in 'The Sweepings of Parnassus: Four Poems Transcribed from the Record Books of the Burgh Sasines of Aberdeen', *Aberdeen University Review*, 36.12 (1955), 52–53. For the Latin original, see Hans Walther, *Proverbia sententiaeque latinitatis medii aevi* (Göttingen, 1963–69), no. 29305. On the genre, see I. Linn, 'If All the Sky Were Parchment', *PMLA*, 53 (1938), 951–70.

[103] I am much indebted to Theo van Heijnsbergen for knowledge of this text. See his 'Amphibious Lyric: Literature, Music and Dry Land in Early-Modern Verse', in *Notis Musycall: Essays on Music and Scottish Culture in Honour of Kenneth Elliott*, ed. Gordon Munro et al. (Glasgow, 2005), pp. 165–80.

No. 400.   'Once slumbring as I lay within my bed'
(B, fol. 356$^\text{v}$; Ritchie, IV, p. 279).

This poem, a later addition to the manuscript, belongs to the genre of the unfulfilled erotic dream and seems to have been popular in the seventeenth century. Fox notes one other copy, in Bodleian, MS Eng. poet. f. 25, fol. 12$^\text{v}$ (Crum O1145); this is a notebook containing university exercises by Edward Natley. It supplies several better readings (for example, 'all alone' instead of B's 'al along' in line 3), and after line 11, where B has a gap, it furnishes three missing lines:

> And kiss'd me sweetly, bid me be kind hearted,
> And so got vp, with that for feare I quaked
> And trembling lay, cry'd out and so I waked.

Other complete texts exist in an English seventeenth-century miscellany, probably also of university origin (Huntington Library, MS HM 116, p. 30), and a mid-seventeenth-century Scottish miscellany (EUL, Laing MS III.436), p. 58. All have the title 'A Maidens dream'.

Nos 405–407, which occur on fol. 374$^\text{v}$ (Ritchie, IV, p. 330), are all late additions to the manuscript, and written in the same hand, probably in the mid-seventeenth century. They are short witty pieces, and all derive from English sources.

No. 406.   'Why sould we so mutche despyse' has a title: 'Meditatiouns on Tobacco'.

This piece represents a moralized contribution to the seventeenth-century vogue for writing poems in praise or dispraise of tobacco. Fox notes, somewhat vaguely, the existence of other copies in the Bodleian Library: 'Crum W2401, W2419. Also in three MSS'. Since these and other texts are all English, it seems worth noting that another Scottish copy of this piece exists in an unexpected location: this is Adam Abell's 'Roit' or 'Quheill of Tyme' (NLS, MS 1746), a still unpublished historical work composed in the early sixteenth century, which has various late additions.[104] One of these, on fol. xvii, contains a text of the poem that closely resembles that in the Bannatyne Manuscript, although – like most of the English versions – it has two extra stanzas.[105]

---

[104] On NLS, MS 1746 and its compiler, see Alasdair M. Stewart, 'Adam Abell's "Roit or Quheill of Tyme"', *Aberdeen University Review*, 44 (1972), 386–93.

[105] For a transcript of the poem, see Alasdair M. Stewart, 'Think and Drink Tobacco', *Aberdeen University Review*, 47 (1977–78), 261–64.

No. 407.   'Iff thow canst not leive chast'.

This short anti-feminist piece on marriage consists of fourteen couplets, each ending in a Latin tag. Fox terms it 'unique', but another copy occurs in *The Marrow of Complements* (London, 1654), p. 177.[106] The compiler of this [**125**] miscellany containing jokes, 'amorous discurses and complemental Entertainments' is unknown, but the Preface is signed 'Philomusus'. It seems very likely that this miscellany was the source not only of item 407 but also of item 405, an eight-line squib on tobacco, 'Mutche meat doeth Gluttony Procure'. A copy of the latter occurs on p. 176 of *The Marrow of Complements*, directly facing the copy of 'Iff thow canst not leive chast' printed on p. 177. The titles for these pieces in Bannatyne – 'A Songe in Praise of Tobacco' and 'A Songe' – also accompany them in *The Marrow of Complements*.

Those who have studied the contents of the Bannatyne Manuscript in the past have, quite understandably, paid most attention to poems associated with the famous names of Robert Henryson, William Dunbar, Gavin Douglas, Alexander Scott and David Lyndsay. This article, however, has largely been concerned with poems neglected by the critics: many are anonymous, others are attributed to obscure or completely forgotten poets, and few have high literary merit. Nonetheless investigation of this material is rewarding. It increases our awareness of the remarkable eclecticism of George Bannatyne's literary tastes, and it also tells us more about his cultural environment, revealing the quantity and diversity of vernacular verse circulating in Scotland during the sixteenth and early seventeenth centuries. What is also apparent is the frequency of re-writing in this period. In the course of transmission (possibly oral, in some cases), texts were often shortened or lengthened, or the order of lines and stanzas re-arranged; the wording too might be modernized, scotticized or modified so as to be in accord with Protestant beliefs and dogma. Such radical textual revision, of course, is not wholly absent from the works of Henryson, Dunbar or Douglas, but it seems particularly characteristic of verse that is short, popular and anonymous.

Editorial Notes

[a] First published in *The Journal of the Edinburgh Bibliographical Society*, 3 (2008), 95–133; and reprinted by kind permission of the Edinburgh Bibliographical Society. Abbreviations listed on pp. 125–26 of the original essay may be found within the list at the front of this volume.

[106] I was made aware of this work by May and Ringler, no. 11422.

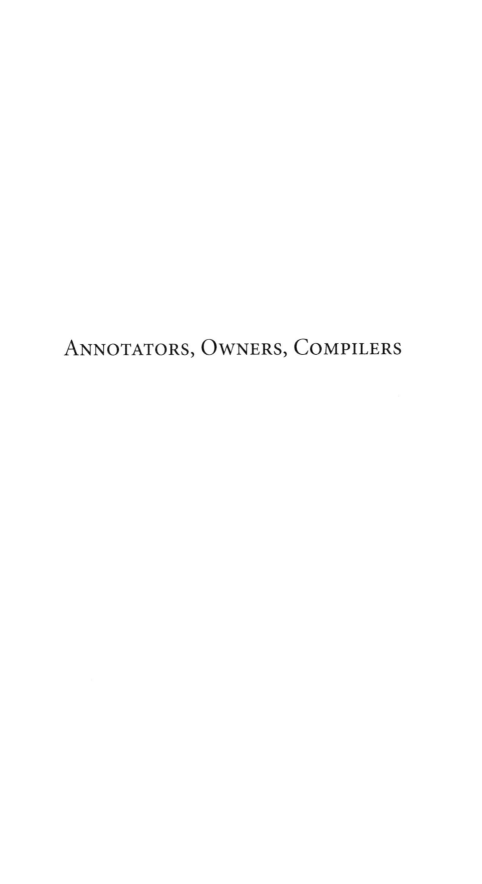

ANNOTATORS, OWNERS, COMPILERS

8

The 'Library' of Gavin Douglas

To the well informed, my title may appear paradoxical.[a] No catalogue of Gavin Douglas's library exists, and there is no mention of books in his will despite several bequests of horses, mules and silver plate.[1] Books belonging to Douglas's friends and colleagues are still to be seen – three law books of Patrick Panter, Robert Cockburn's Livy and Alexander Mylne's Bible[2] – but, as far as I know, not a single book survives from Douglas's collection. My title is a piece of shorthand for what might be regarded as not an 'imaginary museum', but an 'imaginary library' – those books, whether printed or manuscript, whether in Latin or the vernaculars, that came together in Douglas's mind, the books he read and found significant. Some he may have possessed, some borrowed – one trusts that none were stolen!

No-one can doubt that Douglas was a book-lover. He was speaking for himself as well as for others when he noted that 'the clerk reiosys hys bukis our to seyn' (*Eneados*, V.Prol.5).[3] He was not perhaps as zealous a collector as Richard of Bury, whose bedroom (it is said) was piled so high with books that one could hardly step anywhere without treading on them. But Douglas's enthusiasm emerges in his brief portrait of Henry, Lord Sinclair – '[f]ader of bukis' (I.Prol.85) – and his high-pitched comparison of Sinclair to Ptolemy, who 'had sa gret plesour and delyte of bukis that he gadderit togidder in ane librar xxxvi thousand volummys' (I.Prol.100n).

We know a great deal of Douglas's reading and literary tastes. Most of the evidence obviously derives from his own poetry. *The Palice of Honour* and Prologues to the *Eneados* abound in references to books and authors; sometimes there are brief echoes; sometimes long quotations; sometimes the source is concealed, sometimes openly acknowledged. No other early Scottish poet has such a range of allusion. This is supplemented by evidence from other sources, of which perhaps the most valuable is the series of marginal notes that accompany Prologue I and the first seven chapters of *Eneados* I. There can be no doubt that Douglas composed this commentary, although I do not think it is in his own hand. There are other witnesses

---

[1]   Douglas's will is printed in *The Poetical Works of Gavin Douglas*, ed. John Small, 4 vols (Edinburgh, 1874), I, pp. cxix–cxxv.

[2]   For the details, see John Durkan and Anthony Ross, *Early Scottish Libraries* (Glasgow, 1961), [pp. 169, 134–35; and 32–33].

[3]   Quotations from the *Eneados* are taken from *Virgil's 'Aeneid' Translated into Scottish Verse by Gavin Douglas*, ed. D. F. C. Coldwell, 4 vols, STS, 3rd ser. 30, 25, 27, 28 (Edinburgh, 1957–64). Quotations from *The Palice of Honour* are from the Edinburgh text, printed in *The Shorter Poems of Gavin Douglas*, ed. Priscilla Bawcutt, STS, [2nd edn; 5th ser. 2 (Edinburgh, 2003)].

to Douglas's literary interests – one example is the *Dialogus* [*de Materia Theologo Tractanda*] prefixed to John Major's Commentary on the first book of Peter Lombard's [**108**] *Sentences* of which more will be said later. Polydore Vergil's anecdote about meeting the poet in the last year of his life (1521–22) gives what seems to me an authentic picture of Douglas – engaged in controversy, debating with Polydore over the legendary founding of Scotland by Gathelus and Scota. What is particularly interesting here is his lively awareness of new books – the version of Scottish history that he 'vehementlie requiered' Polydore 'in no wise follow' was John Major's History of Britain, very recently published in Paris (April 1521).[4]

Douglas's allusions are sometimes vague. He invokes authority in the time-honoured way, 'the psalmyst says' (*Eneados*, XI.Prol. 29) or 'as Virgill dois report' (*Palice of Honour*, 283). But where appropriate – as in the marginal Comment – he can be quite specific:

> I refer to Iohn Bocas in the Genealogy of gentille Goddis, onto the nynt buyk thereof, and first c. of the sammyn.
>
> (*Eneados*, I.i.82n)

In much the same way but on a very different occasion – speaking before the Lords of Council on 28 February 1519 – Douglas quotes chapter and verse from the *Regiam Majestatem* to prove that since his nephew, Angus, is husband to the Queen Margaret,

> he is lord of hir persoun, doury, and all uthir gudis pertenyng to hir hienes, and maye dispone tharupoun at his plesour, according to all lawis, and in speciall the lawis of this realme here be me schewin and producit …[5]

Douglas is usually accurate in his references, and when he quotes is often so close to his source as to give the impression not of relying on memory but of having the book open in front of him. This procedure may sound less characteristic of the poet than of the scholar or even the pedant. Yet such precision is very welcome in an age that bristles with question marks; 'a period about which', as Durkan and Ross observe, 'so many unchecked assumptions can still be made'.[6] It has been argued, for instance, that Robert Henryson read Caxton's *Fables* and Boccaccio's *Genealogy of the Gods*. Yet I do not find the evidence so far produced on either point convincing – it remains a possibility rather than a certainty. But there can be no doubt that Douglas read both Caxton and Boccaccio, and, what is more, not only that he read them but about *how* he read them.

This last point is important. It is the liveliness of Douglas's response to books that keeps the subject alive for us. He does more than silently transfer huge chunks of his reading into his own work, though this does occur. He tells us what he likes and dislikes; commands us to read some authors (for example, Boccaccio); to read some

---

4   *Polydore Vergil's English History*, ed. Sir Henry Ellis, Camden Society, 36 (London, 1846), I, pp. 105–06.

5   *Acts of the Lords of Council in Public Affairs, 1501–1554*, ed. R. K. Hannay (Edinburgh, 1932), p. 137.

6   Durkan and Ross, *Libraries*, p. 5.

books more than once (his own!); and to cast others (such as Caxton) contemptuously to the floor. Douglas conveys his varied response to his reading: reverence for Virgil and his 'maist excellent buke' (I.Prol.80); respectful disagreement with Chaucer; scorn for Caxton's 'febil proys' (V.Prol.51) – the epithet is only too just. [109] Douglas enjoys not only talking but arguing about books. This controversial streak is apparent in the Prologues as well as in Polydore Vergil's anecdote. Whereas Dunbar makes poetry out of a headache, Douglas makes it out of a book review. Dunbar flytes with Walter Kennedie; Douglas, despite his disclaimer to the contrary, flytes with 'Inglis bukis' (I.Prol.272), and poor dead Caxton cannot answer back.

Gavin Douglas was a churchman. He graduated at St Andrews in 1494 and belonged to that educated, Latin-speaking community of 'clerks' that transcended national frontiers. At his trial in 1515, he testified that he had 'passit his tyme in Scotland, Ingland, France and Rome'. For most of his life, he had a successful if litigious career in the Scottish church – parson of Linton and canon of Dunbar, provost of St Giles, and lastly, bishop of Dunkeld.

With such a background, we might well expect Douglas's writings to abound in references to the theological works that filled the shelves of other Scottish bishops or that he studied the writings of his close contemporary, John Ireland. But this is not so at all. There are no references to scholastic writers in Douglas's poetry and few references to the Fathers of the Church, apart from St Gregory and St Jerome. The striking exception to this is St Augustine, to whom Douglas alludes on several occasions and for whom he clearly held a special reverence. There can be no doubt that Douglas had some knowledge of theology, in view of his education and his friendship with the most distinguished Scottish theologian of his day, John Major. It might be argued that his failure to mention such writings springs simply from a sense of relevance. What have Aquinas or Pierre d'Ailly to do with a secular poem like *The Palice of Honour*? But *The Palice of Honour* is not an exclusively secular work – the repeated parallelism between pagan and Scriptural exemplars (for example Aristotle and Solomon, Iphigenia and Jephtha's daughter) is far from accidental. At a key point in the poem there is a quotation from St Paul to the Corinthians: '3e bene all borne the sonnis of Ire, I ges' (1387). Indeed Douglas's poetry has many echoes from the Bible: the Prologues contain allusions to St Paul, the Psalms and the Book of Proverbs; and in *The Palice of Honour* he shows a familiarity – remarkable to modern ignoramuses – with many of the lesser-known stories of the Old Testament.

What I suggest is not that Douglas lacked interest in theology but that he felt a distaste for certain aspects of its study in the late medieval period. Support for this view comes from a work already mentioned – the *Dialogus* (1510), an imaginary conversation between Douglas and a theologian called David Cranston concerning the subject matter of theology.[b] Although the *Dialogus* is anonymous, I think it may well be the literary counterpart to arguments in which Douglas had recently participated – whether in Paris or Edinburgh. The role adopted by Cranston – a defence of [110] scholasticism – tallies closely with what we know of him in real life. I think therefore that the speeches attributed to Douglas similarly reflect his real-life opinions. In the *Dialogus*, he expresses antagonism towards scholastic philosophy and the undue prominence of Aristotle in the speculations of the schoolmen. He allies himself with Lorenzo Valla in attacking the sterility of modern theology and advocates a return to the Biblical and patristic sources of Christianity.

But there is not enough evidence to speak with great exactitude of Douglas's theological views. If he had lived another ten years, we might have read his pungent opinions of Luther or Erasmus; as it is, there is a curious historical irony in his observation, only five years before Luther published his theses at Wittenberg, that 'blissit be God, the faith is now mair ferm!' (I.Prol.218).

A useful clue to Douglas's literary preferences is provided by the list of writers in the Court of the Muses (*Palice of Honour*, 895–924):

> Thair saw I weill in Poetrie ygroundit
> The greit Homeir, quhilk in Greik langage said
> Maist eloquentlie, in quhome all wit yboundit.
>
> Thair was the greit Latine Virgilius,
> The famous Father Poeit, Ouidius,
> Dictes, Dares and eik the trew Lucane,
> Thair was Plautus, Poggius and Persius,
> Thair was Terence, Donate and Seruius,
> Francis Petrache, Flaccus Valeriane,
> Thair was Esope, Cato and Allane,
> Thair was Gaulteir and Boetius,
> Thair was also the greit Quintiliane.
>
> Thair was the Satir Poet, Iuuenall,
> Thair was the mixt and subtell Martiall.
> Of Thebes Brute thair was the Poet Stace,
> Thair was Faustus and Laurence of the vale,
> Pomponius, quhais fame of lait, sans faill,
> Is blawin wide throw euerie Realm and place.
> Thair was the Morall, wise Poet, Horace,
> With mony vther Clerk of greit auaill,
> Thair was Brunell, Claudius and Bocchas.
>
> Sa greit ane preis of pepill drew vs neir,
> The hundreth part thair names ar not heir.
> 3it saw I thair of Brutus' Albyon
> Geffray Chauceir, as A per se sans peir
> In his vulgare, and morall Iohne Goweir.
> Lydgait, the Monk, raid musing him allone.
> Of this Natioun I knew also anone
> Greit Kennedie and Dunbar 3it vndeid,
> And Quintine with ane Huttock on his heid.   **[111]**

If we read this passage with modern expectations, we may be perplexed by the grouping, or the apparent absence of grouping. Prose-writers and poets, ancients, medievals and moderns, all are jumbled together. This is the Court of the Muses: although Douglas gives great prominence to poets (who are clearly for him the most distinguished exemplars of the 'eloquence' that the Muses confer), nonetheless grammarians and rhetoricians are also servants of the Muses and present in the court.

Douglas's arrangement of names tells us that he still does not make any clear-cut distinction between classical, medieval and humanistic authors. Yet the list is not completely without categories, and these seem important to him since he labels them clearly. They are by language: Greek, Latin, which he elsewhere calls 'maste perfite langage fyne' (I.Prol.382), the 'vulgare' or vernacular of Albion, or Britain, and the language '[o]f this Natioun' (*Palice*, 922) – to Douglas, this means Scots not Gaelic.

It is no accident that Homer comes first in the procession – he has a symbolic position of lonely eminence in 'eloquence' and 'wit'. But I find it difficult to believe that Douglas had more than a smattering of Greek, despite his assertion that Lord Sinclair asked him to 'translait Virgill or Homeir' (I.Prol.88). If indeed he had produced a version of Homer, I suspect it would have been made from a copy of Valla's translation. Douglas has no mention of other Greek poets or dramatists. For him, Greek was still primarily the medium not for poetry or drama but for philosophy, and this he would read in medieval or humanistic translations. Douglas's years at St Andrews perhaps made him over-familiar with Aristotle; according to the *Acta* of the Arts Faculty of St Andrews (1471), '[i]n the second year the students were to begin to take down the logic of Aristotle in their own hand; in the third year they were to proceed in the same fashion to Physics and Natural Philosophy; and in the fourth year they had to write out at least the first seven books of Metaphysics'.[7] Douglas knew something of the thought of Plato, but both his references are, significantly, at second-hand: the one derived from Landino (I.iii.100n), and the other from St Augustine, who 'repreuys the opynion of Plato, that haldis God the sawll of the warld' (*Eneados*, I.v.2n). Douglas also shows interest in the doctrine of metempsychosis, 'that quent philosophy' associated with the name of Pythagoras (I.Prol.185; VI.Prol.130).

I lack space to discuss how closely he was acquainted with the great Latin prose writers. All I can note is that both in the Comment and *The Palice of Honour* Douglas shows an interest in Roman history; he also refers admiringly to several Latin historians, notably Caesar and the 'mylky flud of eloquens, gret Tytys Lyuius' (*Eneados*, I.v.28n). Of the Latin poets listed here, I can comment only on a few. According to an English writer of the late sixteenth century, [**112**]

> *Martial* is muche mislikt and lothde,
>   Of modest mynded men
> For leude lascivious wanton woorkes ...[8]

Perhaps the Scots were less 'modest mynded' than the English, for Douglas was clearly interested in Martial, whom he here calls 'mixt and subtell'. Later in *The Palice of Honour*, Martial re-appears as 'Cuik till roist, seith, farce and fry' (1231). Here he refers to the satirical subject-matter of many of the Epigrams – we may compare modern colloquial senses of 'roast' or 'grill' – and neatly combines this with an allusion to Martial's medieval nickname, *Coquus*. Douglas applies duller

---

7   *Acta Facultatis Artium Universitatis Sanctiandree 1413–1588*, ed. Annie I. Dunlop, SHS, 3rd ser. 54 (Edinburgh, 1964), I, p. lxxxiv.

8   Timothy Kendall, 'To the Reader', *Flovvers of Epigrammes ovt of sundrie the moste singular authours* (London, 1577), STC 14927.

epithets to Horace – 'morall, wise' – and I have noted only one other allusion, to the *Art of Poetry*, in *Eneados*, I.Prol.400ff. A well-known line [*Nec fonte labra prolui caballino*] from the Prologue to Persius's *Satires* lies behind Douglas's later allusion to the Muses' 'Caballine Fontane' and his own failure to drink from it (*Palice of Honour*, 1134, 1143). But such famous lines were sometimes passed from one poet to another, and we cannot necessarily deduce that Douglas had a close familiarity with Persius. Something of the same ambiguity hangs over the allusions to Statius – here, for instance, and later in *The Palice of Honour* (1583–84):

> Thair saw I how, as Statius dois tell,
> Amphiorax the Bischop sank to hell.

It seems likely that Douglas knew the *Thebaid* at first hand – it was continuously popular in the Middle Ages – yet both these allusions are phrased in language that recalls Chaucer more strongly than Statius himself.

I think Douglas genuinely admired Lucan, who was highly regarded in medieval times not only as a poet but as historian and philosopher. He calls the *Pharsalia* a 'gret volum' and seems to place Lucan in the same category as the historians Caesar and Suetonius (*Eneados*, I.v.102n). On one occasion, he quotes a line of Lucan's in Latin (I.v.2n); on another, he echoes one of Lucan's pithy, proverbial-sounding phrases: 'Na thing is done, quhil ocht remanys ado' (VII.Prol.152).

There can be no doubt, however, that the Latin poets who meant most to Douglas were Ovid and Virgil. He proclaims his admiration for Ovid in *The Palice of Honour*: he is the 'father' poet, the great authority – 'as men in Ouide reidis' (1199; 1847) – and a master of style, 'digest and eloquent' (1190). Douglas refers by name to several of Ovid's works – the *Metamorphoses*, the *Art of Love*, and the '[f]acund Epistillis' of Phyllis and Penelope and other *Heroides* (*Palice*, 809–16).

How did Douglas read Ovid? To Chaucer, he was pre-eminently the poet of love:

> That hath ysowen wonder wide
> The grete god of Loves name.
> (*House of Fame*, 1488)

This is not the aspect of Ovid that Douglas celebrates. In *The House of* [113] *Fame*, Chaucer had made Ovid 'Venus' clerk'; but in Douglas's poem Ovid appears as 'Clerk … of Register' (*Palice*, 1187) not to Venus but to Calliope, muse of heroic poetry. At the Muses' picnic on Helicon, Calliope commands Ovid to sing the feats of heroes, such as Hercules and Perseus. Many of the heroes whose names fill *The Palice of Honour* owed the persistence of their fame to the art of Ovid. His poetry was a treasure-house of myth and heroic legend; this was his great importance to Douglas as indeed to many other poets.

Ovid was a great story-teller; to Douglas he was also a great stylist. He tells us this not only by praising him directly but by imitating some of his most splendid descriptive passages. Ovid's account of the sun god and his palace (in *Metamorphoses*, I and II) supplied many details in *The Palice of Honour* and *Eneados*, Prologue XII, such as the steeds of the sun or the sea nymphs combing their hair. Douglas was not alone in his liking for this part of the *Metamorphoses*. Other poets imitated the Ovidian phrase, *Materiam superabat opus* (*Met.*II.5), which Douglas translated:

> The warkmanship exceding mony fold
> The precious mater, thocht it was fynest gold.
> (*Palice of Honour*, 1862–63)

He clearly admired Ovid's 'purple passages', the elaborate set-pieces of rich description. But I would argue that he had some awareness of Ovid's psychological subtlety, and that this coloured the more imaginative parts of *The Palice of Honour*. After Venus threatens to punish the poet for his blasphemy, he anxiously fingers his face, fearing not death but metamorphosis [*Palice*, 742–44].

In the *Conclusio* to the *Eneados*, Douglas boldly asserts the immortality that this work of art will confer on its maker, '[t]hrow owt the ile yclepit Albyon' (11). He has here paraphrased the conclusion to the *Metamorphoses* (XV.871–79) and appended it to a translation not of Ovid but of Virgil. This may seem jarring to purists; to Virgil-worshippers, it may seem irreverent. Why did Douglas do it? I think a chain of reading and associations lie behind this passage. The *Eneados* ends not with Virgil's Book XII but with Maphaeus Vegius's 'Supplementum' or Book XIII; this ends with a section describing the apotheosis of Aeneas, which is closely modelled on the description of the deification of Julius Caesar in *Metamorphosis* XV, and this immediately precedes the Ovidian passage that Douglas translated. I think Douglas was aware of Vegius's imitation of Ovid and devised his own *Conclusio* in the same spirit.

There is nothing surprising about his admiration for Virgil. Virgil was still being studied, as he had been for centuries, by poets and 'clerkis', by children and (as Douglas notes) by 'masteris of grammar sculys, / … techand on ʒour benkis and stulys' (*Directioun*, 47–48). The *Eneados* makes it clear [**114**] that Douglas knew the *Aeneid* itself. He did not translate at second-hand; nor, like the earl of Surrey, did he merely render a couple of the best-loved books. Douglas knew the original and in its entirety. This having been said, I wish to stress that he did not read Virgil in isolation, one poet confronting the bare text of another. He lacked the scholarly aids that we have today, splendid editions, dictionaries and concordances. Nonetheless a surprising amount of Virgilian criticism and commentary had accumulated by the time that Douglas made his translation. He read Virgil in a context of other writers and other books.

Douglas was clearly acquainted with the scholarly tradition in which the text of Virgil was embedded: he knew and quoted from Macrobius's *Saturnalia*; in Prologue IV, he remarks how St Augustine was moved to tears by the fate of Dido; he was also familiar with some recent humanistic writers, such as Boccaccio and Cristoforo Landino. But most important of all to Douglas were the commentaries of two writers: the fourth-century Servius and Jodocus Badius Ascensius (Josse Bade), Douglas's own contemporary. Servius was one the earliest and greatest of Virgilian commentators, and many of his notes and readings are still quoted with respect by modern editors of Virgil. But why did Douglas so often use Ascensius, when his commentary seems clearly inferior to that of Servius? There are many reasons – the sheer convenience and availability of Ascensius's editions of Virgil (elsewhere I have argued that Douglas used the Paris edition of 1501);[9] the many links then existing between Scottish scholars and Ascensius's press; the fact that Ascensius's Latin was of the kind that must have been used by Douglas himself on ecclesiastical business; and lastly, the similarity of purpose between Ascensius and Douglas, both seeking to bring the poet they revered to a wider and less learned audience.

Douglas read Servius and Ascensius attentively: their commentaries affected his understanding of Virgil and frequently coloured the diction and phrasing of his translation. Here, I can give but two illustrations of how wide-ranging and unexpected their influence can be – neither, I think, has been noted before.

1. In his Comment Douglas says of the famous first simile in *Aeneid* I:

> Noyte Virgill in this comparison and symilytud, for therin and in syk lyke baris he the palm of lawd … It is to be consydderit alsso that our all this wark, he comparis batell tyll spayt or dyluge of watyr, or than to suddan fyr, and to nocht ellis.
>
> (*Eneados*, I.iii.92n)

This interest in iterative imagery may strike us as curiously modern, but Douglas has taken the observation from Servius, from the commentary not on Book I (where we might expect it) but on Book XII.534: *bellum semper incendio et fluminibus comparat.* [115]

2. In Book V, Douglas has a striking description of a chariot race:

> nevir sa thyk, with mony lasch and dusch,
> The cartaris smate thar horssis fast in teyn,
> With renȝeys slakkyt, and swete drepand bedeyn.
> (*Eneados*, V.iii.82–84)

The last line is an expansion of Virgil's *undantia lora* – one of those vivid lines that critics select when they wish to talk of Douglas's rusticity. But he was straining to catch Virgil's sense, not to make him homely. He is following a characteristic double interpretation of *undantia* offered by Ascensius: *aut spumis abundantia, sed melius effusa, idest laxa*, that is, 'either foaming with sweat, or better, spread out, loose'.

Douglas was also acquainted with the wider literary context of the *Aeneid*, in which Virgil was but one of many tellers of the tale of Troy. He knew of Dares Phryggyus and Dictys Cretensis, and speaks twice, each time respectfully, of Raoul Lefèvre and his fifteenth-century bestseller, the *Recueil des Histoires de Troie*. Douglas was less respectful to other popular writers, such as Caxton and Guido delle Colonne. He reacted violently against Caxton's version of the *Aeneid*, published in 1490:

9 'Gavin Douglas and the Text of Virgil', *Transactions of the Edinburgh Bibliographical Society*, 4, part 6 (1973), 213–31; [reprinted in *The 'Eneados': Gavin Douglas's Translation of Virgil's 'Aeneid'*, ed. Priscilla Bawcutt with Ian Cunningham, STS, 5th ser. 17 (Edinburgh, 2020), I, Appendix, pp. 41–58].

Thocht Wilȝame Caxtoun, of Inglis natioun,
In proys hes prent ane buke of Inglys gros,
Clepand it Virgill in Eneados,
Quhilk that he says of Franch he dyd translait,
It has na thing ado tharwith, God wait,
Ne na mair lyke than the devill and Sanct Austyne …
(Eneados, I.Prol.138ff.)

Defenders of Caxton may suspect a nationalistic bias in Douglas. They may point to the fact that Caxton was a rival, and that Caxton did his best to forestall critics by admitting that he did not translate directly from Virgil. But Douglas is not content with vague abuse. His criticisms of Caxton are detailed and substantially accurate – they range from trivialities like misspellings to major omissions like the similes. Furthermore, they are based on principle: Douglas is conscious of the translator's duty to preserve as far as possible the structure and proportions of his original. In this respect, Caxton's most glaring falsification of the *Aeneid* lies in his treatment of the Dido story – Douglas does not much exaggerate when he says that it occupies virtually half of Caxton's *Eneydos* (twenty-four out of sixty-five chapters).

He eagerly participated in other controversies then current about Virgil. One of these concerned the character of Aeneas: at the end of the *Eneados* (*Directioun*, 132–33), Douglas proclaims that henceforth let no one consider Aeneas as 'traytour of Troy / Bot as a worthy conquerour and kyng'. [116] Here he rebuts one of the major charges against Aeneas, that together with Antenor he betrayed Troy to the Greeks. This belief had a long history – indeed it is pre-Virgilian – but it owed its wide currency in the late medieval period to Guido delle Colonne and his immensely popular *History of the Destruction of Troy*. Elsewhere Douglas directly challenges Guido on this very point (*Eneados*, I.v.28n):

> Becaus ther is mension of Anthenor, quham mony, followand Gwydo De Columnis, haldis tratour, sum thing of him will I speyk, thocht it may suffis for his purgation that Virgill heir hayth namit him …

His long discussion ends with an exhortation to

> wey the excellent awtorite of Virgill and Tytus Lyuius wyth ȝour pevach and corrupt Gwido.

'Pevach and corrupt Gwido'! – the scorn is far removed from the respectful references in the Asloan manuscript to the 'clerk' Guido. In such passages, Douglas challenged the cherished beliefs of many fellow Scots, both in criticizing Guido and in attempting to remove the label 'traitors of Troy' from Aeneas and Antenor. When Kennedie wished to hurl an insult at Dunbar, he said sarcastically that Aeneas and Antenor were 'his trew kynnismen' (*Flyting*, 539). This belief also furnished the Scots with splendid ammunition against Englishmen; for the English, unlike the Scots, boasted

161

of their descent from the Trojan Brutus, and therefore (by implication) from these same 'tresonable tratouris of troye'.[10]

Douglas defends Aeneas against other charges, notably that he was a traitor in love. His criticism of Chaucer in portraying Aeneas as 'fals' and 'forsworn' is well known and will not be discussed here. Douglas indeed held a highly idealized conception of Aeneas. In I.Prol.330–32, he says that in Aeneas Virgil 'blazons'

> All wirschip, manhed and nobilite,
> With euery bonte belangand a gentill wycht,
> Ane prynce, ane conquerour, or a val3eand knycht.

This is far removed from the presentation of Aeneas in *The House of Fame* and *Legend of Dido*. Yet it has many parallels in the humanistic writers known to Douglas: Cristoforo Landino called Aeneas an 'example to all mankind regardless of rank'; Maphaeus Vegius said Aeneas represented 'man endowed with every virtue'; and Ascensius called him *speculum atque exemplum perfecti viri*.[11] Douglas's idealization of Aeneas was not completely original; what seems to have been new was the expression of such ideas in the vernacular.

It was not simply as a translator that Douglas felt the impact of Virgil. He admired Virgil's artistry and revered him as a model for vernacular poets; on several occasions, he adopted striking phrases or imitated other [117] features of his style. Two illustrations show how varied and how pervasive was Virgil's influence.

At the end of Book XII, Douglas has eight lines listing his 'pryncipall warkis'. In structure, this piece is modelled on four lines of Latin verse that list Virgil's major poems – *Ille ego qui quondam gracili modulatus auena*, and so on. Their authenticity is now questioned, but Douglas almost certainly thought them Virgil's. Douglas here imitated Virgil in another way. He ends by quoting from himself:

> And syne off his hie Honour the Palyce wrait:
> 'Quhen paill Aurora, with face lamentabill,
> Hir russet mantill bordowrit all with sabill, etc'.
>   [*Mensioun of the Pryncipall Warkis*, 6–8]

In the same way, Virgil had half-quoted the opening line of his first Eclogue at the close of the *Georgics* (IV.563–66). The verbal resemblances to this passage of the *Georgics* show that here Douglas was definitely 'followand the flowr of poetry' (*Mensioun*, 1).

His interest in the *Georgics* is evident in several Prologues. Prologue VII has slight echoes of weather-portents in *Georgics* I; Prologue XII contains several passages imitating *Georgics* II, which celebrate the rebirth of nature in spring; and some

---

10 The phrase occurs in *The Asloan Manuscript*, ed. W. A. Craigie, 2 vols, STS, 2nd ser. 14, 16 (Edinburgh 1923–25), I, p. 197 ['Part of þe Ynglis cronikle', fol. 99ʳ, lines 16–17].

11 See Landino's Prohemium to his *Interpretationes in P. Vergilium* (Florence, 1487), fol. 1ᵛ; *De Educatione Liberorum*, trans. Anna Cox Brinton in *Maphaeus Vegius and His Thirteenth Book of the Aeneid* (Stanford, 1930), p. 27; and Ascensius's dedication of his Virgil to Louis of Flanders.

stanzas in Prologue IV derive from the account of *saeuus amor* and its power over man and beast in *Georgics* III. Such admiration for the *Georgics* was a comparatively new phenomenon. Scholars consider that they were not nearly as well known as the *Aeneid* in the Middle Ages – there is no definite proof that Chaucer had read them. Douglas thus seems to have been sensitive to a shift in literary taste first observed among Italian and French poets.[12]

Among the followers of the Muses, Douglas names six Italians: in roughly chronological order, they are Petrarch, Boccaccio, Poggio Bracciolini, Lorenzo Valla, Pomponio Leto and Fausto Andrelini. To these, one may add the fifteenth-century scholar, Cristoforo Landino, whom Douglas mentions in the *Eneados*. These writers were all humanists. They served the Muses variously, sometimes by composing verse of their own, sometimes by interpreting it to others as teachers, scholars and editors. What was their personal significance to Douglas?

Petrarch is here because he was famous throughout Europe as one of the first poets since antiquity to receive the laurel crown, symbolizing his inheritance of the great traditions of the past. Douglas may have read some of his poetry – resemblances are still being suggested between the *Trionfi* and *The Palice of Honour*, though I myself fail to detect any clear and unmistakeable trace of Petrarch's influence.

Douglas undoubtedly had a great admiration for Valla, whom he calls elsewhere 'the worthy clerk hecht Lawrens of the Vaill' (*Eneados*, I.Prol.127). He seems to have known Valla's two most famous and influential works, the *Dialecticae Disputationes* and the *Elegantiae Linguae Latinae*. The [118] *Dialogus* [of John Mair] suggests that Douglas adhered to Valla's side in the contemporary disputes concerning logic and theology; and Douglas's disparaging comment on 'bastard Latyn' (*Eneados*, I.Prol.117) suggests that he may have felt something of Valla's contempt for medieval Latin.

Poggio is best known today for his zeal in recovering lost manuscripts of the classics. To his contemporaries, he was equally famous for his polemical writings, especially his scurrilous *Invectives* against Valla and Filelfo. It is this aspect of Poggio that Douglas heavily emphasizes:

> And Poggius stude with mony girne and grone
> On Laurence Valla spittand and cryand fy!
> (*Palice of Honour*, 1232–33)

If I may digress for a moment, it is noteworthy that of Cicero's many writings the only one that Douglas mentions is the *In Catilinam*. This is the 'buik' that Cicero hurled at Catiline as he was trying to climb sneakily into the Palace of Honour through a window (*Palice*, 1772–73). Douglas clearly had a taste for 'invective orations', the category in which grammarians placed this work of Cicero's – he had some talent at a flyting himself! I suspect that it was this aspect of Fausto Andrelini that appealed to him. Andrelini wrote *Invectives*, directed at Girolamo Balbi, a fellow-teacher at the university of Paris, and was a copious writer, highly acclaimed in his own day. Douglas was probably aware that he had recently received a laurel crown in Rome for his *Livia, seu Amores*. The Scots poet also refers to the 'fame' of Andrelini's former

---

[12] L. P. Wilkinson, *The Georgics of Virgil: A Critical Survey* (Cambridge, 1969), pp. 288ff.

teacher, Pomponio Leto, best known as the founder of the Roman Academy, though Douglas may have found him interesting for his commentaries on Virgil.

Douglas was sufficiently up-to-date to have read Cristoforo Landino, one of the most admired Italian scholars. Landino was closely connected with the Medici court, a member of the Florentine Academy, and a commentator on Dante, Horace and Virgil. In the Comment to the *Eneados*, Douglas shows his familiarity with two quite separate works. The first is Landino's commentary on the *Aeneid*, which from 1487 onwards was published in many editions of Virgil, though not in those of Ascensius. Douglas also knew Landino's famous *Quaestiones Camaldulenses*, a debate as to the merits of the active and contemplative lives. He had read Books 3 and 4, which present a remarkable and systematic Neoplatonic allegorization of the first six books of the *Aeneid*. In a note (*Eneados*, I.iii.100n), he summarizes some of Landino's ideas briefly but reasonably accurately. Douglas thus had some knowledge of one at least of the Florentine Neoplatonists, but, as far as I know, he reveals no acquaintance with the still more famous Ficino or Pico della Mirandola.

There is no doubt that of the Italians the most important to Douglas was Boccaccio; less for his poetry, however, than for his scholarly works written in Latin. Douglas himself directs his readers to one specific work, [**119**] 'Go reid Bochas in the Genolygy of Goddis' (*Directioun*, 68), and to one particular section, '[h]ys twa last bukis' (69). Books 14 and 15 of the *Genealogy of the Gods* constituted a virtual 'Defence of Poetry', and were famous and influential until well into the sixteenth century. Douglas here invoked them to justify his translation of a pagan poet. What little Douglas says of his theory of poetry is also in harmony with Boccaccio's. Poetry is a veiled or cloudy truth (*Eneados*, I.Prol.193–94):

> And vnder the clowdis of dyrk poecy
> Hyd lyis thar mony notabill history.

Poets' fables must be distinguished from falsehood: 'All is nocht fals, traste weill, in cace thai feyn' (I.Prol.198). The Comment to the *Eneados* shows how attentively Douglas had read the earlier books of the *Genealogy*; they supplied him with a much-needed handbook of the mythology and the geography of the ancient world. They also furnished intricate explanations of the 'sentence' or truth that lay beneath the literal surface of myths. I can here give only one illustration of how closely Douglas sometimes followed Boccaccio. In his note on Aeolus (*Eneados*, I.ii.3), Douglas tells us that he was 'an naturall man' who learnt to foretell the direction from which the winds would blow, and hence was termed king of the winds. But Aeolus also signifies reason, whose office is to tame 'the windis of peruersit appetyte' (*Eneados*, I.ii.12n). Douglas here follows Boccaccio in combining a euhemeristic explanation of myth with a moral or allegorical one; neither seems to have felt any inconsistency in doing so.

If we follow Douglas's advice and 'reid Bochas', one reward may be a greater understanding of details in his original poetry. Much as I admired the wintry Prologue VII, I long failed to understand two lines in its astrological opening (33–34):

> And lusty Hebe, Iunoys douchtir gay,
> Stude spulȝeit of hir office and array.

Hebe was Jove's cupbearer – she slipped in the presence of the gods and revealed her nakedness; because of this she was disgraced and succeeded by Ganymede. But what has this to do with the month of December? In the *Genealogy* (Book IX, chapter 2), Boccaccio explains the myth symbolically: Hebe signifies youth and the renewal of living things that occurs in spring; her nakedness and loss of 'array' is linked with autumn and the fall of leaves; Ganymede who took over her 'office' is identified with the sign of Aquarius, into which the sun moves in January. Douglas clearly had this symbolic interpretation of the myth in mind. His image of Hebe, 'spulȝeit of hir office and array', foreshadows the wintry landscape that follows (*Eneados*, VII.Prol.63ff.):

> The grond stud barrant, widderit, dosk or gray
> …
> Woddis, forrestis, with nakyt bewis blowt,
> Stude stripyt of thar weid in euery howt.   [**120**]

With the last stanza, we turn to poets writing in the vernacular. Chaucer, Gower and Lydgate were the best known and most esteemed poets who had written in English. Today we may be more conscious of the disparity between them in poetic achievement, but in Douglas's time the reasons for grouping these poets together were very powerful: the connection between them of a personal kind; their links with the respective courts of Richard II, Henry IV and Henry V; and the similarities also in their subject matter, language and style. To Douglas, this trio symbolized the courtly and rhetorical tradition in English poetry.

Douglas refers to Gower's *Confessio Amantis* in *Eneados*, IV.Prol.213, and there is a curious detail in *The Palice of Honour* (588) which suggests that Gower's version of the Narcissus legend (*Confessio Amantis*, I, 2340–42) was the one most familiar to him. Douglas has no other allusions to Lydgate, however, and although there are many affinities of style and diction, I can trace few precise debts. I am sure that he was familiar with two sections from Lydgate's vast output: the courtly allegories, such as *The Temple of Glas*; and the works treating of classical antiquity, such as the *Troy Book* (a version of Guido).

Douglas had the good sense to regard Chaucer as pre-eminent among these poets: 'as A per se sans peir' (*Palice*, 919). His praise of Chaucer in Prologue I is as hyperbolical as his earlier eulogy of Virgil. Such praise is far from mere lip-service; his admiration for Chaucer often takes the form of imitation. It has long been known that *The Palice of Honour* is modelled in part on Chaucer's *House of Fame* and the other dream poems; but in addition to this almost every Prologue and even part of the translation show some sign of Chaucer's influence. Douglas criticizes Chaucer for perverting Virgil in *The Legend of Dido*, putting it down to an excessive sympathy with women, 'For he was evir (God wait) all womanis frend' (I.Prol.449). Yet the phrasing of Douglas's own translation of *Aeneid* IV shows how attentively he had studied that same *Legend of Dido*. Douglas shared the critical taste of his contemporaries: like Dunbar, he praises Chaucer not for his humour nor his genius as a story-teller but for his style and diction ('eloquens', I.Prol.341); the poems of Chaucer that he most often echoes or alludes to are the courtly and chivalric ones, *The Knight's Tale*, *The Parliament of Fowls*, *The Complaint of Mars*, and *Troilus*. The contents of *The Kingis Quair* manuscript suggest that Lord Henry Sinclair similarly most admired poems like these. I shall say no more, however, of Chaucer's importance to Douglas – not because I wish in any way to undervalue it, but because the subject has been amply discussed by recent scholars;[13] and because I wish here to illustrate the extent and variety of Douglas's reading rather than his undoubted indebtedness to a single author.

Douglas separates the poets '[o]f this Natioun' (*Palice*, 922) from those of Albion. Yet he mentions only three Scottish poets, whereas Dunbar in [**121**] *Lament for the Makaris* ['I that heill wes'] names twenty-one. This does not mean that Douglas lacked interest in his compatriots. The number is symbolic – there are three Scottish poets to parallel the English trio; and in each case the brevity of the list implies the smallness of literary achievement in the vernacular compared to the multitude of those who wrote in Latin. The list is a selection then, but what a selection! To us it is as surprising as the English group is predictable; surprising, both for the inclusions and for the omissions. Who is the strangely hatted Quintin? And where is Henryson?

I can give only tentative answers to these questions. If Douglas wished to have a Scottish equivalent to the English trio – poets who were well known to his audience and between whom there was some kind of literary affiliation, then these three possibly fitted the bill at the time he was writing. Dunbar and Walter Kennedie are linked even today because of their famous *Flyting*; and in the same work Quintin is mentioned several times (for example, 3, 34) as Kennedie's 'second' and as a fellow-poet. The dating of the *Flyting* is difficult but if, as John Baxter suggested,[14] the preliminary sections were composed in 1500, then at the very time to which *The Palice of Honour* is commonly assigned these three poets would be prominent, indeed notorious, in Edinburgh literary circles. The *Flyting* shows them in a raffish guise, but it is clear that they all had pretensions to write a more exalted kind of poetry – to be 'of rethory the rose' (*Flyting*, B 65, 500).

It is almost certain that Douglas knew Dunbar in person. Both lived for some time in Edinburgh and had links with James IV. Both were writing within the first decade of the sixteenth century. Yet there is little affinity between them as poets, and I can find no definite evidence that Douglas was influenced by his slightly older contemporary. *The Palice of Honour* can be compared to *The Goldyn Targe*, but I am more impressed by how differently the two poets use allegory and the dream form. I would suggest that to Douglas Dunbar was important because he showed the rich and varied potentialities of the Scots tongue; he was less a model to be imitated than a brilliant rival with whom to vie – in poetry and perhaps in ecclesiastical preferment.

Why is Henryson missing from the court of the Muses? One possibility is that in the late 1490s Douglas had not yet read him. There is evidence that Douglas knew his three main works, but it is all to be found in the *Eneados* (c. 1512–13) – by this time, one at least of Henryson's poems, *Orpheus*, had been printed – and maybe others too. What is this evidence? There is a direct and unambiguous allusion to 'Mastir Robert Hendirson in New Orpheus' in Douglas's Commentary on the opening lines

13 See Denton Fox, 'The Scottish Chaucerians', in *Chaucer and Chaucerians: Critical Studies in Middle English Literature*, ed. D. S. Brewer (London, 1966), pp. 164–200; and Priscilla Bawcutt, 'Gavin Douglas and Chaucer', *Review of English Studies*, 21.84 (1970), 401–21.

14 John W. Baxter, *William Dunbar: A Biographical Study* (Edinburgh, 1952), pp. 80–81.

of his *Eneados* (I.i.13n). There are also several echoes of *The Testament of Cresseid* in Douglas's Prologues – here it is striking that what Douglas seems to have found most memorable were the splendid planet-portraits, [**122**] especially those of Saturn, Diana and Phoebus. Douglas also knew the *Moral Fables*. He shows particular interest in the fable of the *Lion and the Mouse*, or rather in its Prologue. He echoes, almost verbatim, one line from this, 'The prymeros and the purpour viola' (1336) in his own flower catalogue in Prologue XII (122). What is more, the subject of Henryson's prologue, a dream interview with Aesop, is recalled in Douglas's Prologue XIII. In this, Douglas, like Aesop, takes a stroll in June, falls asleep under a tree (always risky!) and has a vision of an elderly poet, Maphaeus Vegius, who wears on his head a laurel crown, 'Lyke to sum poet of the ald fasson' (88). A similar phrase had been used by Henryson both in his Prologue (1353) and in *The Testament of Cresseid* (245).

Douglas liked aspects of Henryson that today we are inclined to disregard or not to value very highly. The passage from *Orpheus* that he mentions concerns the Muses; its mixture of myth and learned etymology resembles much that Douglas found in Boccaccio's *Genealogy*, and quoted in his Comment. Henryson's didacticism was clearly congenial to him. In Prologue XII, Douglas take over phrases from Henryson and intermingles them with echoes from Chaucer, Ovid and Virgil. These also tell us something important about Douglas's response to Henryson; he may have appreciated his humour and narrative gifts, but it was his descriptive passages that he imitated. To Douglas, Henryson was no simple rustic fabulist but a vernacular master of the high style.

There remains one important body of vernacular poetry hardly mentioned by Douglas yet clearly significant to him. He was acquainted with many of the anonymous tales and legends so popular at this time: he mentions John the Reeve, for instance, and Robin Hood. Douglas also alludes to heroes of two alliterative poems, one Scots, *Rauf Coil3ear*, and the other English, *Piers Plowman*. It seems likely that he also knew Holland's *Buke of the Howlat*. Yet he is tantalizingly silent about alliterative techniques: he neither praises the 'lel letteres loken' like the *Gawain*-poet, nor disparages its 'rum-ram-ruf' effect like Chaucer's Parson (*ParsT*, Prol.43). The best evidence for Douglas's familiarity with alliterative poetry comes indeed from his own practice, particularly from Prologues VII and VIII and passages from the *Eneados*.

Prologue VIII is Douglas's one piece of strict, alliterative verse. Metrically, this Prologue shares several features with the two Scottish poems I have just mentioned – it has a long and complicated stanza, excessive alliteration in the long lines, and an occasional lack of alliteration in the short lines. The alliterative tradition preserved its vitality much longer in Scotland than in England. Yet the ranting, abusive tone of this Prologue suggests that Douglas was aware of the decline in the status of alliterative verse, which was to become increasingly apparent in the sixteenth century. I think he might have agreed with James VI in labelling [**123**] the stanzaic form at least as 'tumbling verse', most suited for 'flytings or invectives'.

Prologue VII, the 'winter' Prologue, is less systematic and, I think, more subtle in its use of alliteration. It shows that Douglas was aware of the sheer variety of alliterative verse, at least in the past. In describing the wider aspects of nature, storms and mountainous scenery, alliterative poets such as the authors of *Sir Gawain and the Green Knight* or the *Morte Arthure* had much greater sensitivity and a wider range of vocabulary than did the courtly poets associated with Chaucer. In Prologue VII, Douglas writes in the tradition of these talented but anonymous poets.

The *Eneados* itself provides further evidence that Douglas was familiar with alliterative poetry. When he translated the more heroic passages of the *Aeneid*, the vernacular tradition that he drew upon was that of the romances, and more particularly the alliterative romances. These possessed a well-established style for describing warfare or other violent activity that was peculiar neither to Scotland nor to England but belonged to 'Albyon', indeed it had its roots in Old English poetry. In the *Eneados*, one can detect several traces of this style. The most obvious is a heavy and emphatic alliterative patterning, in which the alliteration coincides with stressed syllables:

> Of giltyn geir dyd glytter bank and bus (IX.i.63)
> Thar bustuus bowys keynly do thai bend (IX.xi.3)

The vocabulary of such passages is marked by a preference for items from a special 'heroic' diction. Some of these go back to Old English – 'byrne', for instance, or the synonyms for 'man' such as 'bern', 'kemp', 'freik'. Others, like the verbs 'frush' and 'dush', are of more recent origin, yet seem to be equally specialized and marked off from the vocabulary of prose. In phrasing and syntax, these passages have characteristics that are common in alliterative verse, if not peculiar to it. The most obvious is Douglas's fondness for balanced, formulaic phrases – 'blude and brane', 'bonys and brawns', 'stith and stuyr'. He also has a liking for parataxis (*Eneados*, I.iv.91–92):

> Hynt of the hydis, maid the bowkis bair,
> Rent furth the entralis, sum in tailȝeis schare.

Critics speak of the vigour of Douglas's translation, and this effect is often related to his use of alliteration.

In diction and syntax, there are some striking resemblances between Douglas's *Eneados* and Hary's *Wallace*, although neither is technically an alliterative poem. I doubt whether it could be proved conclusively that Douglas read the *Wallace*, but I think the probability is high, much higher than for the *Trionfi*. There is other evidence that Douglas was interested in the history of his own country, and the *Wallace* was a recently composed poem, popular and easily available in the printed edition of 1508. Like the [124] *Aeneid*, it celebrated not only the extremes of patriotism and valour but the pity and the horror of war. Apart from Barbour's *Bruce*, it was the nearest thing to a national epic that Douglas could encounter in his own tongue.

I will anticipate some at least of my critics by noting a few pitfalls in a study of this kind. The mere mention of an author's name (for example, Homer) does not necessarily mean that he was of deep significance to Douglas, or indeed that Douglas had ever read him closely. In much the same way many of us have books on our shelves – the works of Hegel perhaps, or *Teach Yourself Serbo-Croat* – that do not indicate proficiency in a subject but unfulfilled aspirations, to widen our knowledge or simply a long-distant holiday. But this proposition has a converse: the omission of an author's name can be equally misleading. Douglas never mentions Catullus, yet in his dedication of the *Eneados* to Lord Sinclair (I.Prol.101–02) there is an apparent echo of Catullus, which extends the range of his reading in an unexpected direction.

There is a further caveat that concerns what may be termed 'second-hand quotations'. In his commentary, Douglas likes to give an impression of wide-ranging learning. In a single note (*Eneados*, I.v.2n), he assembles allusions to St Augustine, Lucan, Boccaccio and Servius. In a discussion of the word 'Triton' (I.iii.85n), he tells how 'Plynyus in his Naturall History rehersis that Triton is a veray monstre of the sey'. A little later, Douglas has a note on Jupiter's prophecy of 'perpetual empyre' (I.v.87) for the Romans:

> Sanct Augustyn in his volum clepit De Verbis Domini, in the xxix sermond, mokkis at this word, sayand: 'Ȝit is not the end, and the empyr is translat to the Almanys. Bot Virgill was crafty', sais he, 'that wald not on his awyn byhalf rehers thir wordis, bot maid Iupiter pronunce thaim – and as he is a half fenȝeit god, swa is his prophecy.'
>
> (*Eneados*, I.v.85n)

(The *De Verbis Domini* is not now attributed to Augustine.) In each case, it is clear that Douglas did not cull an apt quotation from his abundant reading, but took them from intermediary sources, works that we know he used and used repeatedly. Coldwell pointed out that the Pliny quotation comes from Boccaccio's *Genealogy* (VII.7). But it has not been noted before that the Augustine quotation also comes from a favourite work of Douglas's, Ascensius's commentary on the *Aeneid* (discussing I.278–79). We should not, however, be contemptuous of Douglas in this matter – many modern scholars have been similarly guilty.

Other limitations to this survey have been imposed partly by lack of space, partly by the sheer abundance of material. I have by no means discussed every author whom Douglas mentions –there are over seventy of them, incidentally. Much more could be said of Douglas's reading in French. He mentions the French romance of *Paris and Vienne* (*Palice of Honour*, 576) and twice alludes to the *Recueil des Histoires de Troie*, but both of these were available in English and printed by Caxton. I think he [125] knew some of Nicholas Oresme's translations from Aristotle; I am doubtful that he ever used the translation of the *Aeneid* made by Octavien de Saint Gelais. As for Douglas's possible knowledge of Gaelic, I am not equipped to discuss this – he does once refer to 'Greit Gowmakmorne and Fyn Makcoull, and how / Thay suld be Goddis in Ireland, as thay say' (*Palice of Honour*, 1715–16).

Although Douglas was not a humanist in the strict sense of the word, he clearly shared some of the humanistic values. He seems, like Erasmus, to have felt an antipathy to certain aspects of scholasticism, and an enthusiasm for ancient poetry, history and rhetoric. He proclaimed his admiration for Lorenzo Valla, whose name was a rallying cry to the humanists. Yet if we compare Douglas with his contemporaries, I do not think we can call him exceptionally learned or exceptionally adventurous in his literary tastes. But he had read widely and intelligently, and brought a critical mind to his reading. My study tends to confirm, and sometimes to supplement the evidence provided by Durkan and Ross's valuable *Early Scottish Libraries*. From this, we learn that the chaplain William Ramsay possessed a copy of Guido (Strasbourg, 1494), or that John Vaus possessed a copy of Boccaccio's *Genealogy* (Paris, 1511); from Douglas we learn what he thought of these authors. Durkan and Ross note how few copies of printed books in the vernacular survive; but Douglas makes us aware that one bishop at least read Caxton and Chaucer and Henryson side by side with Ovid and Virgil. An investigation of this kind may also lead to a re-assessment of Douglas as a poet. I have argued elsewhere that only when we take into account the nature of his edition of Virgil can we fairly judge his skill and accuracy as a translator. Greater familiarity with the books that Douglas read can sometimes clear up puzzles in his original poetry, and make sense of apparent nonsense. The very number of Douglas's echoes and allusions makes me think that more will turn up in the future. Despite the fame of his translation of Virgil, the learned and Latin context of his poetry has been insufficiently recognized; oddly enough, the importance to him of alliterative poetry has also been neglected. Once we are aware of the range of his reading, the label 'Scottish Chaucerian' has to be dismissed as an over-simplification.

Editorial Notes

[a] First published in *Bards and Makars: Scottish Language and Literature; Medieval and Renaissance*, ed. Adam J. Aitken, Matthew P. McDiarmid and Derick S. Thomson (Glasgow, 1977), pp. 107–26. It is reprinted with kind permission in accordance with the University of Glasgow Press Ltd Publication Scheme.

[b] See further, Alexander Broadie, 'John Mair's *Dialogus de Materia Theologo Tractanda*: Introduction, Text and Translation', in *Christian Humanism: Essays in Honour of Arjo Vanderjagt*, ed. Alasdair A. MacDonald, Z. R. W. M. von Martels and Jan Veenstra (Leiden, 2009), pp. 419–30.

9

The Commonplace Book of John Maxwell

Most readers of early Scottish poetry are acquainted with the names of George Bannatyne and Sir Richard Maitland; far fewer, I imagine, are familiar with that of John Maxwell.[a] The small collection of verse and prose that he assembled between 1584 and 1589 cannot compare, either in size or richness, with the Bannatyne Manuscript and the Maitland Folio. It does not feature in the standard histories of Scottish literature; only observant users of *A Dictionary of the Older Scottish Tongue* will have noticed occasional citations from Maxwell and the presence of his manuscript in the 'Revised Register of Titles of Works Quoted' (vol. XII). Yet this small work of only thirty-six leaves deserves to be rescued from obscurity. It is a precious Scottish example of a commonplace book, in the sense of that term used by medievalists – a collection of highly miscellaneous material assembled for the interest, instruction and amusement of its compiler. Many such compilations survive from late medieval and early modern England: one of the more famous is Oxford, Balliol College MS 354, which belonged to Richard Hill of London in the early sixteenth century; another that has recently been published in its entirety is the fifteenth-century commonplace book of Robert Reynes (Bodleian, Tanner MS 407).[1] Probably many similar collections were put together in Scotland during the same period, but few now survive. The Maxwell manuscript thus has scarcity value; and it also provides interesting testimony of a minor Scottish poet's literary tastes as well as specimens of his own writing.

The Maxwell manuscript is now in the possession of Edinburgh University Library (MS Laing III.467). Its early history is obscure, but at the beginning of the nineteenth century it was owned by William Motherwell, the poet and ballad collector. In 1828, he published an article in *The Paisley Magazine* (I, no. 8, 379–86), called 'Renfrewshire Poets: John Maxwell Younger of Southbar'; in the next issue (437–46), he printed a portion of the manuscript, containing 'Sum Reasownes and Prowerbes'. Later in the century, the manuscript was owned in turn by several Scottish book-collectors, James Dennistoun, Adam Sim of Coulter and the great David Laing; on Laing's death, it passed to Edinburgh University. Two distinguished American scholars, M. P. Tilley and B. J. Whiting, displayed particular interest in the proverb collection; unfortunately neither knew of the whereabouts of the manuscript, and therefore

---

1   See *Songs, Carols and Other Miscellaneous Poems from Balliol MS 354*, ed. Roman Dyboski, EETS, ES 101 (London, 1907); and *The Commonplace Book of Robert Reynes of Acle*, ed. Cameron Louis, Garland Medieval Texts, no. 1 (New York, 1980). [The Bodleian Library has digitized both Balliol College MS 354 and MS Tanner 407.]

depended solely on Motherwell's transcript. Equally unfortunately their labours seem to have been unknown to the only scholar who devoted much attention to the [60] manuscript in recent years, M. L. Anderson. He made a transcript of the text for *DOST*, and provided it with a brief Introduction, notes and glossary. This exists in typescript, but has never been published. All students of early Scottish literature are indebted to Professor Anderson – he made transcripts of other Scots manuscripts and also edited *The James Carmichaell Collection of Proverbs in Scots* (Edinburgh, 1957). But his edition of this manuscript, valuable though it is, is weakened by his uncritical assumption that almost all the verses in it were 'the original products of Maxwell's brain' ([Anderson transcript], p. 11).[2]

Although there are variations in style, the manuscript seems to be written in one hand, that of Maxwell himself. He was proud of his name, which, along with dates ranging from 1584 to 1589, occurs repeatedly in a variety of spellings – 'Iohne Maxwall' (fol. 1^r), 'Iohne Maxwell' (fol. 21^v), 'Iohne Maxwald' (fol. 6^r) and the Latinized 'Iohannes Maxwaldus' (fol. 16^v). He devises puzzles and verses to tell 'the authouris name': in one place, its last syllable rhymes with *tald* and *wald* (fol. 8^r); in another with *tell* and *sell* (fol. 30^r). He also proudly announces: 'This wers he pennit of his awin hand' (fol. 30^r).

Very little is known of Maxwell. The most precise information is provided by the inscription: 'be me Maxwell of Southbar 3ounger' (fol. 21^r); the Latin version runs *per me Ioannem Maxweldum Iuniorem de Southbarr* (fol. 20^v). This title shows that Maxwell was heir to the estate of Southbar in Renfrewshire. Anderson has assembled a number of contemporary references to the branch of the Maxwell family in the last decades of the sixteenth century; he also identifies the compiler of the manuscript with the John Maxwell *Iuniore de Southbar*, who was a bailie of Renfrewshire in 1603 and who died in 1606. There exists one small piece of external evidence to suggest that Maxwell had some reputation as a poet. This is the dedicatory sonnet by an unidentified 'A. S.' to William Mure of Rowallan, which contains the following lines: 'Sprang thou from Maxwell and Montgomeries muse / To let our poets perisch in the west?'[3]

This coupling of Maxwell and Montgomerie is interesting. The manuscript contains a copy of Montgomerie's 'Can goldin Titan schyning brycht at morne' (fol. 21^r), a complimentary sonnet prefixed to James VI's *Essayes of A Prentise in the Divine Art of Poesie* (1584). The two poets were the same generation and both came from the south-west of Scotland, but whether they were closely acquainted we do not know. Anderson suggests that Maxwell was 'on the side of the Reformers' ([transcript], p. 6), but there is no conclusive evidence for this. The manuscript contains little that is overtly Catholic, but there is a prayer to Mary, *Mater dei memento mei* (fol. 26^v). It is perhaps significant, however, that his copy of the Beatitudes (fol. 7^v) exactly follows the wording of the Geneva Bible (Matt. 5, 3–12). [61]

There still remains much to be discovered about Maxwell's life and career; my chief concern, however, is with the contents of his manuscript. These are highly

---

2   References to Anderson are to his edition, available in the *DOST* office. My citations from the text are taken from the manuscript [EUL, Laing III.467]. The foliation is modern.

3   Anderson quotes in full this and another sonnet by 'A. S.' (from EUL, Laing III.454) in an Appendix to his Introduction. See also *The Works of Sir William Mure of Rowallan*, ed. William Tough, 2 vols, STS, 1st ser. 40, 41 (Edinburgh, 1898), I, p. xi.

miscellaneous, in a manner typical of commonplace books. Some items are in Scots, some in Latin; some in prose, some in verse; there are exercises in penmanship (fol. 6^r), puzzles or riddles (fol. 1^r); a list of classical gods and goddesses (fol. 22^v); historical memorabilia (fol. 25^r); and short satirical squibs on contemporaries, such as the Earl of Glencairn, 'bayth fals and gredie, et nunquam leill' (fol. 25^r). But the part of the manuscript that most interested Motherwell and later scholars was a group of 232 'reasownes and prowerbes' (fols 30^v–36^v). Motherwell printed this not only in *The Paisley Magazine* but in the Preface he supplied to Andrew Henderson's *Scottish Proverbs* (Edinburgh, 1832), pp. xxxiv–xliv. Anderson placed a similarly high value on this section, calling it 'the earliest known collection by a Scot' ([transcript], p. 1). What Motherwell and Anderson failed to realize, however, was that Maxwell culled the bulk of these sayings from two English works then immensely popular, George Pettie's *A Petite Pallace of Pettie his Pleasure* (1576) and John Lyly's *Euphues* (1578). [It is interesting that copies of the former were in the stock of two Edinburgh printer-booksellers, Thomas Bassandyne (*d.* 1577) and Robert Gourlaw (*d.* 1585).][4] The evidence for this is conclusively set out in M. P. Tilley's *Elizabethan Proverb Lore in Lyly's Euphues and in Pettie's Pallace* (New York, 1926), especially on pages 46 and 357–82, and needs no repetition.[5]

One brief illustration of Maxwell's method may suffice. A famous passage in *Euphues* reads:

> althoughe yron the more it is vsed the brighter it is, yet siluer with much wearing dost wast to nothing, though the Cammocke the more it is bowed the better it serueth, yet the bow the more it is bent & occupied, the weaker it waxeth, though the Camomill, the more it is trodden and pressed downe, the more it spreadeth, yet the violet the oftner it is handled and touched, the sooner it withereth and decayeth.[6]

Maxwell deconstructs this into a set of self-contained aphorisms (fols 36^{r-v}):

> Yrne the more it is wsed the brychter it is.
> Siluer with muche wearing doith waist to no thing.
> The cammocke the more it is bowed the better it
> serueth.
> The bow the more it is bent & occupyed the weaker
> it waxeth.

---

4   See *The Bannatyne Miscellany*, II, ed. David Laing, Bannatyne Club (Edinburgh, 1836), pp. 200, 210 and 214.

5   For further information about early Scottish proverb collections, see B. J. Whiting, 'Proverbs and Proverbial Collections from Scottish Writings before 1600' (Parts I and II), *Medieval Studies*, 11 (1949), 123–205, especially the Introduction, 123–25 [and *Medieval Studies*, 13 (1951), 87–164]; and Coleman O. Parsons, 'Scottish Proverb Books', *Studies in Scottish Literature*, 8.3 (1971), 194–205.

6   *The Complete Works of John Lyly*, ed. R. Warwick Bond, 3 vols (Oxford, 1902), I, pp. 195–96.

> The Camomill the more it is troden & pressed downe
> the more it spreadeth.
> The wiolet the ofter it is handeled and twiched the
> sooner it withereth & decayeth.

Lyly's mannered prose was parodied by Shakespeare (in I *Henry IV*, II.iv), but much admired by other Elizabethan writers. Maxwell was one of the first to display an interest in what we now call euphuism – particularly in its [62] sententious subject-matter – and to link together Pettie and Lyly. Tilley found his response highly significant: 'The association of the proverbial contents of the two books in the mind of a contemporary poet may, I believe, be accepted as evidence of the literary importance of this element in Lyly's day' (p. 6).

Maxwell was clearly interested in proverbial wisdom from all sources, and in various languages. B. J. Whiting has demonstrated that another small group of proverbs, numbers 171–80 (fol. 35^v), which interrupts the larger collections from Pettie and Lyly, derives from a Scottish work, John Rolland's *The Sevin Seages* (Edinburgh, 1578).[7] Most of these come not from the narrative of *The Sevin Seages*, but from the appended *Moralitates* – a part of the text unlikely to be read so attentively today. There is one proverb in this collection – 'All erdlie plesure finisseth with wo' (no. 170) – for which neither Tilley nor Whiting could find a definite source. Such a commonplace is perhaps untraceable. But the collection is in other respects so literary that it seems likely to have originated in Maxwell's reading. The closest parallel known to me is Gavin Douglas's 'All erdly glaidnes fynisith with wo' (*Eneados*, II.Prol.21). The manuscript also contains a collection of Latin proverbs and 'reasownes', arranged according to the alphabetical order of their first words (fols 12^v–16^v). Despite the heading *a Salam*, 'from Solomon', these are not all scriptural in origin – item D6 (fol. 13^v), for instance, is the last line of Horace's Ode IV.12: *Dulce est desipere in loco*. After the Latin proverbs comes the rubric (fol. 16^v),

> Her followis the expositiowne and declaratioune of the foir said lateine
> prowerbis in Inglis, liuelie interpreted according as thay ar written ...

The style of this strongly suggests a printed source (as yet unidentified); the vernacular translation unfortunately is incomplete, breaking off at the letter C (fol. 18^v).

Several adages or contentious sayings are attributed to well-known classical authors, such as Seneca (fols 3^v and 11^v) and Ovid (fols 9^v and 26^v). Ennius is credited with *Amicus certus in re incerta cernitur* (fol. 19^v). This had become proverbial, but it is indeed said to be by Ennius in Cicero's *De Amicitia* (17, 64). 'Propertius sayth' introduces reflections on the 'warld of gold' (fol. 26^v) –

> For gold thow salbe lowed and set aloft,
> For gold thow sall ane verteows man be thocht
> For gold is lowe & honowr also gotten,
> For gold is fayth, and for gold the lawes ar broken.

---

7   See B. J. Whiting, 'John Maxwell's *Sum Reasownes and Prowerbes*', *Modern Language Notes*, 63 (1948), 534–36.

This is a free rendering of Propertius, III, 13, 48–50. Perhaps the most interesting piece of Latin origin is the short, unattributed dialogue between two 'huiris' (fol. 9ʳ). In it, Syra exhorts Philotis to be ruthless to men – 'quha so ewer thow finde, thow mot spolȝe him, mank him & rywe him'. Anderson queried [**63**] whether this was 'an attempt at drama' [transcript, note 55]. It is, in fact, a translation of the first eight lines of Terence's *Hecyra*, or 'The Mother-in-Law'. One regrets the brevity of this particular piece.

Maxwell includes many short pieces of verse in his manuscript. Of these, Motherwell said:

> I do not consider them as all emanating from his own 'ingyne', but as being in some measure a mere register of certain popular rhymes which were current in his own day, or perhaps transcribed by him from some then known collection of homely truths. Many of them are familiar to us yet, and are traditionally preserved among children. Others seem very foolish and trivial; but it is worth while to be able to fix even the antiquity of such prattlings.[8]

Anderson objected to this assessment [transcript], pp. 10–11, yet to me it seems both perceptive and accurate. The manuscript provides better evidence for Maxwell the collector than for Maxwell the poet. The boundary between metrical proverbs and sententious verses is not easy to define: Maxwell liked both. Several short pieces are extracts from larger compositions. 'Quha wald be riche haif ee to honowr ay' (fol. 10ᵛ), for instance, is a seven-line stanza from the anonymous *De Regimine Principum*. This stanza seems to have been popular: other copies exist in the Bannatyne Manuscript (no. 119) and in a manuscript of Quintin Kennedy's *Ane Litil Breif Tracteit*.[9] Another interesting example is (fol. 11ᵛ):

> Ane fwill he is that puttis in dainger
> His lyfe, his honowr, for ane thing of nocht.
> Ane fwill he is that will nocht glaidlie cownsall heir
> In tyme quhen it awaill mocht.
> Ane fwill he is that na thing hes in thocht
> Of thing that efter quhat may him befall
> Nor of his end hes no memoriall.

This is a very corrupt version of a stanza from Henryson's *The Preaching of the Swallow* (*Fables*, 1860–66); another copy of the stanza occurs in Bannatyne (no. 117).

The manuscript contains other short pieces that also occur in Bannatyne's 'Ballatis of moralitie'. Denton Fox noted that 'He that thi frende hes bene rycht lange' (fol. 19ᵛ) represents Bannatyne, no. 112. But there are several other unnoticed instances:

---

8 *Paisley Magazine*, I, 381.
9 For poems from the Bannatyne Manuscript, I employ the numbering used in the Scolar Press facsimile, *The Bannatyne Manuscript: National Library of Scotland Advocates' MS 1.1.6*, with an Introduction by Denton Fox and William A. Ringler ([London], 1980). The manuscript of the *Tracteit* has been inserted within a print of Kennedy's *Compendius Tractiue*; it is on deposit at the National Library of Scotland (T.D. 313).

'Befoir the tyme is wisdome to prowyde' (fol. 19^r) corresponds to Bannatyne, no. 101; and 'Grounde the in pacience' (fol. 19^r) corresponds to Bannatyne, no. 91. This latter also appears twice in a manuscript (EUL, Laing III.447) containing pieces often attributed, probably erroneously, to Montgomerie.[10] 'Eit thy meit merelie' (fol. 12^r) is a version of Bannatyne, no. 90. The [64] commonplace books of Richard Hill and Robert Reynes both include variants of this very popular set of 'rhymed precepts in -*ly*'; Whiting gives it proverbial status.[11] Another quatrain closely corresponds to Chaucer, *Wife of Bath's Prologue*, 655–58, which is treated by Whiting as proverbial (fol. 22^r):[12]

> Quho so biggeth his hous all of swalowis [sic = salowis]
> And pricketh his blind hors ouer the falowis
> And sufferth his wyfe to seik halowis
> Is wordie to be hangeth on the galowis.

Another piece can be traced back to the fifteenth century at least: this is the epigram on the paradoxes of the Incarnation, 'Belief is ane wonder that men tell can' (fol. 22^r), that was well known in both England and Scotland.[13]

The Maxwell manuscript contains many other 'popular rhymes'; some, but not all, of these I have identified. There is space to discuss but one further example (fol. 20^r):

> In my defence god me defende
> And bring my saull to ane guid ende,
> Out of this warld quhen that I wende
> Sum succour to my saull to sende.

Several other versions of this quatrain are known: one occurs on folio 21^V of this manuscript; others are found on folio 45^r of the Gray manuscript (NLS, Adv. MS 34.7.3) and folios 150^r and 177^V of a Latin Bible thought to have belonged to St Giles kirk (NLS, Adv. MS 18.1.2). Yet another is said to be inscribed on the inside of the vellum cover of a book that once belonged to Colin Campbell, third Earl of Argyll – Guido delle Colonne's *Historia Troiana* (Strasbourg, 1494):

> In my defens god me defend
> And bring my soull to ane gud end
> In tyme of velth think on our distres
> He that this vret god send him grece.
> Per me Andrew Mallis [?][14]

---

10 I owe this information to Anderson's note on the poem [item 93, p. 5].

11 For fuller information, see *NIMEV* 3087; Whiting G259; and *Commonplace Book of Robert Reynes*, ed. Louis, pp. 392–96.

12 Whiting H618.

13 See further, Bawcutt, 'Dunbar and an Epigram', *Scottish Literary Journal*, 13.2 (1986), 16–19.

14 On the *Historia Troiana*, see J. Durkan and A. Ross, *Early Scottish Libraries* (Glasgow, 1961), p. 136; the book's present location is unknown, but the quatrain is printed in Albi

No versions of the quatrain are so far known from England.[15] The one fixed element in these verses seems to me to be the first line, which also occurs independently, sometimes as a motto linked with the royal arms of Scotland;[16] the rest of the quatrain varies both in wording and in metrical shape. Sometimes the same rhyme is preserved throughout; sometimes the verse divides into two couplets. It is not therefore surprising that the first couple also occurs independently, 'liberally sprinkled on flyleaves, margins and blank sheets of Scottish manuscripts from the sixteenth to the eighteenth century'.[17] The form of the verse may vary slightly – in a way characteristic of popular and oral transmission – yet its function is constant. It is a formula whose recital or [**65**] inscription may preserve the individual (such as John Maxwell or Andrew Mallis?) from adversity, a mixture of prayer and good-luck charm. Its literary merit may not be high, but it has great human interest.

Maxwell called himself an 'authour', but it is difficult to be sure precisely which of the many verses he 'pennit' he also composed. I think it most likely that he was himself responsible for the various short pieces with a distinctive metrical shape that he himself called 'rowndales' (fol. 5^r) and that we today usually term triolets – quatrains characterized by a triple repetition of the initial phrase (fol. 20^v):

> I die for lwife of sweit Susanna,
> But rest or rwife I die for lowe.
> I wald remove & ȝit I canna,
> I die for lowe of sweit Susanna.

This delightful love song – it sounds singable, although not accompanied by music – is followed by another roundel (fol. 20^v):

> O Sara sueit, the lord mot blis the,
> Wis & discreit, o Sara Sweit,
> Eit thow thy meit and I sall kis the,
> O Sara sweit, the lord mot blis the.

One wonders if this was addressed to a child.

Dunbar seems the first Scottish poet to have used this form, in *The Dregy* [*Dumbaris Dirige to the King* (B 84)], and Montgomerie also employs it effectively in the first round of his *Flyting* with Polwart: 'Polwart, ye peip like a Mouse amongst thornes.'[18] Polwart, using the same term as Maxwell, disparages Montgomerie's verse as 'ragged roundels'.[19] Maxwell also uses the form for invective (fol. 20^r):

Rosenthal, *Sale Catalogue*, 5 (Oxford, 1944), p. 11. I owe this information to Denton Fox.

[15] *NIMEV* 1509, has only Scottish examples.

[16] See Priscilla Bawcutt, 'Dunbar's Use of the Symbolic Lion and Thistle', *Cosmos*, 2 (1986), 83 97 (90–91).

[17] My quotation comes from a private communication by Marion Stewart, Archivist, Dumfries Archives Centre.

[18] *Alexander Montgomerie: Poems*, ed. David J. Parkinson, 2 vols, STS, 4th ser. 28, 29 (Edinburgh, 2000), I, p. 175, line 1.

[19] *Montgomerie: Poems*, ed. Parkinson, I, p. 155, line 9.

Lytill foull aipe, quhy sayis thow sa?
Iis brek thy skaipe, lytill foull aipe,   [scalp]
Thowis nebbit lyk ane quhaipe & schankit lyk a ka, [curlew]
Lytill foull aipe, quhy sayis thow sa?

Elsewhere he seems to voice the sarcastic complaint of someone who has been robbed of his sword and cloak (fol. 6ʳ):

I had ane sword & clewk first quhen I come in,
With ȝowr leif honest foik, I had a sword & a clewk,
& now I stand lyk a goik & deill afurth can win,
I had a sword & a clewk first quhen I come in.

Maxwell seems to have found the form congenial – Anderson lists thirty-eight instances in the manuscript ([transcript], p. 6) – and puts it to a variety of uses, chiefly light, [66] humorous or satirical. He explicitly says that he devised 'Thir rowndales schoirte' for his own 'spoirte' – 'Me to comforte quhen I was fainte' (fol. 5ʳ). In another snatch of verse, he speaks of writing, in order 'to exerce my awin ingyne' (23ᵛ).

The notion of sport and 'play' is certainly strong in the following (fol. 5ᵛ):

Schiris we ar cum heir, the trewth for to tell,
Na man for to deir, schiris we ar cum heir,
Nor ȝit for to weir ocht amang our sell,
Schiris we are cum heir the trewth for to tell.

Send it is for play that we ar cum heir,
Guid schiris I ȝow pray, send it is for play,
Let na man affray, as it war for weir,
Send it is for play that we ar cum heir.

Schiris, play all fair, for that is best,
Nocht ower sair, schiris, play all fair,
Ilk man his skair, & syne tak rest,
Schiris, play all fair, for that is best.

This is ritualized 'play', and the tone is communal and public. It would be interesting to know the occasion for which these verses were written; Motherwell said that they sounded 'very like some rymes that are sung by children in their games' (p. 382).

The Maxwell manuscript has interest for historians of the Scots language, but its evidence needs to be treated with circumspection. The proverbs extracted from Pettie and Lyly preserve the inflections and vocabulary of their source; the spelling alone is given a light Scottish dress. The 'Inglis' rendering of the other group of proverbs is full of 'inkhorn' terms – 'amicitie' (fol. 17ᵛ) or 'ignominie' (18ᵛ) – which derive from their Latin source. At the other extreme, linguistically, are the 'rowndales': these, despite their ingenious metrical patterning, seem closest to the Scots vernacular. The flyting, 'Lytill foull aipe', for instance, preserves the Scots pronunciation of *sa* in its rhyme with *ka*; it also employs the distinctive 'cuttit' form, *Iis*, rather than *I sall*,

178

that James VI recommended for flyting.[20] Perhaps one of the most interesting items, linguistically, occurs in another snatch of verse (fol. 5^r):

> Gwide schiris, I ȝow praa,
> Tak dewchane dorus or ȝe gaa.

Dewchane dorus represents Gaelic *deoch an dorus*, 'drink at the door', or 'stirrup cup'. The phrase is familiar in later Scots usage, but it is not recorded in [**67**] *DOST*. This occurrence in the Maxwell manuscript seems to anticipate those recorded in dictionaries, such as *The Scottish National Dictionary* and *The Concise Scots Dictionary*, by at least a century.

This brief study of John Maxwell and his manuscript is designed to be introductory rather than definitive. It must be conceded that the manuscript contains no long-lost poetic masterpieces; we may also regret that it included no ballads or indeed any narrative poems. Bannatyne's anthology is far more wide-ranging. Maxwell's taste was primarily for short pieces of writing. As a poet, he seems to have made a speciality of writing roundels; and as a collector he selected proverbs, axioms and short pieces on a variety of topics. The manuscript reveals some interesting contrasts in Maxwell's reading: Terence, Pettie and Lyly jostle with Rolland and Montgomerie; Latin with English and Scots; recently printed books with poems that had been in popular circulation for a couple of centuries. The manuscript thus has importance of a wide cultural kind, as Motherwell recognized. It would be far-fetched to depict Maxwell as a sixteenth-century forerunner of the Opies;[b] yet he was interested not only in some of the most modish books of his time but also in 'traditionally preserved' rhymes and fragments of verse. To sophisticated readers, many of the latter may appear trite, or 'foolish and trivial', yet they provide fascinating clues to the everyday beliefs, values and preoccupations not only of Maxwell but of many other people living in late sixteenth-century Scotland.[21]

Editorial Note

[a] First published in *A Day Estivall: Essays on the Music, Poetry and History of Scotland and England & Poems Previously Unpublished in Honour of Helena Mennie Shire*, ed. Alisoun Gardner-Medwin and Janet Hadley Williams (Aberdeen, 1990), pp. 59–68, and reprinted with the kind permission of Dr Nigel Bawcutt. The current Aberdeen University Press, not being a continuation of the original Press, holds no rights over its publications, and has no objection or permission restrictions on the use of this essay.
[b] See the *ODNB* articles by Gillian Avery, 'Opie, Peter Mason (1918–1982)', and Neil Philip, 'Opie [*née* Archibald], Iona Margaret Balfour (1923–2017)'.

---

[20] *Reulis and Cautelis*, published in *Poems of King James VI*, ed. James Craigie, 2 vols, STS, 3rd ser. 22, 26 (Edinburgh, 1955–58), I, pp. 75–76.

[21] I am very grateful to Dr John Durkan for making me aware of this manuscript.

10

The Boston Public Library Manuscript of John Lydgate's *Siege of Thebes*: Its Scottish Owners and Inscriptions

John Lydgate's *Siege of Thebes* has received increasing attention in recent years:[a] scholars have debated its date of composition (probably 1421), its conception as an additional 'Canterbury Tale' and, above all, its structure and precise significance.[1] The poem was certainly popular with medieval readers, surviving in at least twenty-nine manuscripts. The copy now in the possession of Boston Public Library (MS f. med. 94) was, like several others, unknown to the editors of the poem for the Early English Text Society.[2] This manuscript has a particular interest, in that its scribe has recently been identified, in important articles by Professor A. S. G. Edwards and Dr A. I. Doyle, as Stephen Dodesham (d. *c.* 1482), who in later life was a Carthusian monk, first at Witham in Somerset, and then at Sheen, near London.[3] Most of the manuscripts copied by Dodesham were religious and

---

[1] See, in particular, Robert W. Ayers, 'Medieval History, Moral Purpose, and the Structure of Lydgate's *Siege of Thebes*', *PMLA*, 73 (1958), pp. 463–74; A. C. Spearing, 'Lydgate's Canterbury Tale: *The Siege of Thebes* and Fifteenth-Century Chaucerianism', in *Fifteenth-Century Studies: Recent Essays*, ed. Robert F. Yeager (Hamden, CT, 1984), pp. 333–64; and James Simpson, '"Dysemol daies and fatal houres": Lydgate's *Destruction of Thebes* and Chaucer's *Knight's Tale*', in *The Long Fifteenth Century: Essays for Douglas Gray*, ed. Helen Cooper and Sally Mapstone (Oxford, 1997), pp. 15–33. There is a useful overview in A. S. G. Edwards, 'Lydgate Scholarship: Progress and Prospects', in *Fifteenth-Century Studies*, ed. Yeager, pp. 29–47 (32–34).

[2] *Lydgate's Siege of Thebes*, ed. Axel Erdmann and E. Ekwall, EETS, ES 108, 125 (1911, 1930; repr. 1996). Simpson's preference for the title *Destruction of Thebes* (see '"Dysemol daies"', p. 15) is supported by several colophons, including that of the Boston copy: 'Explicit Destruccio Ciuitatis Thebanorum'. Lydgate himself, however, speaks of both 'the siege and destruccioun / Of worthy Thebees the myghty Royal toun' (lines 185–86). This couplet is the undoubted source of many colophons; the scribes often slightly varied the wording but had, of necessity, to retain the rhyme word 'destruction'.

[3] See A. S. G. Edwards, 'Beinecke MS 661 and Early Fifteenth-Century English Manuscript Production', *Beinecke Studies in Early Manuscripts: Supplement to Yale University Library Gazette*, 66 (1991), pp. 181–96; and A. I. Doyle, 'Stephen Dodesham of Witham and Sheen', in *Of the Making of Books: Medieval Manuscripts, Their Scribes and Readers; Essays Presented to M. B. Parkes*, ed. P. R. Robinson and R. Zim (Aldershot, 1997), pp. 94–115 (101). For further information, see also C. U. Faye and W. H. Bond, *Supplement to*

devotional, and it seems likely that this and two other copies of *The Siege of Thebes* also made by Dodesham (Beinecke Library, MS 661, and Cambridge University Library, Add. MS 3137) belong to the earlier part of his career, as a lay scribe, before he entered the Carthusian order. On the evidence of the decoration, Professor Edwards conjecturally places the Boston manuscript in the 1430s, Dr Doyle more cautiously dates it *c.* 1430–60.

This article, however, is concerned not with the origin and production of the Boston manuscript but with its later history. Various entries, such as owners' names and short pieces of verse, provide valuable, if scrappy, evidence concerning Lydgate's reception in Scotland, and the literary interests of certain Scottish families in the fifteenth and sixteenth centuries. Nearly twenty years ago, Professor Edwards called for a more systematic study of Lydgate manuscripts and their early owners, yet this aspect of the manuscript has been curiously neglected.[4] *The Siege of Thebes* was certainly known to Gavin Douglas, and there is evidence that it and other poems of Lydgate were popular in Scotland.[5] The Boston text of the poem lacks marginal annotation, but this does not necessarily imply that it was read inattentively. The additional entries occur (as is common enough) on the blank leaves at the beginning and end of the manuscript (now foliated, in a modern hand, as 1, 2, 74, 75 and 76). They are written in a number of different hands, and in several languages – Latin, French and Scots – and, as these leaves are dirty [81] and badly worn, are often extremely difficult to decipher (see item no. 5 below, p. 94). The manuscript contains only one date (1592), but the other entries, which were evidently made at various times, cannot be dated so precisely.

The first owner, who was almost certainly English, probably commissioned the work from Dodesham some time in the mid-fifteenth century. The earliest entries occur on fol. 76ʳ: 'Te deum laudamus te dominum confitemur' (repeated) and

---

the *Census of Medieval and Renaissance Manuscripts in the United States and Canada* (New York, 1962), pp. 209–10.

4 Cf. A. S. G. Edwards, 'Lydgate Manuscripts: Some Directions for Future Research', in *Manuscripts and Readers in Fifteenth-Century England*, ed. Derek Pearsall (Cambridge, 1983), pp. 15–26. See, however, Edwards' 'Bellenden's *Proheme of the History and Croniklis of Scotland*: A Note', *Bibliotheck*, 6 (1972), 89–90; the brief mention by R. J. Lyall in 'Books and Book Owners in Fifteenth-Century Scotland', in *Book Production and Publishing in Britain 1375–1475*, ed. Jeremy Griffiths and Derek Pearsall (Cambridge, 1989), pp. 239–56 (240); and William A. Ringler, *Bibliography and Index of English Verse in Manuscript 1501–1558*, completed by Michael Rudick and S. J. Ringler (London, 1992).

5 See *The Palice of Honour*, 1577–93 in *Shorter Poems of Gavin Douglas*, ed. P. Bawcutt, STS, 1967; rev. edn, 5th ser. 2 (Edinburgh, 2013), which is indebted to *The Siege of Thebes*, 4408ff. Sir David Lyndsay was acquainted with the Thebes story, probably through Lydgate's poem: cf. *The Dreme*, I, 42, and *Ane Dialog*, I, 3832 (*The Works*, ed. D. Hamer, 4 vols, STS, 3rd ser. 1, 2, 6, 8 (Edinburgh, 1931–36). David Wedderburne, a book-loving merchant, possessed a copy of 'the sege of thebes', and recorded its loan to a friend in 1596: *The Compt Buik of David Wedderburne, Merchant of Dundee 1587–1630*, ed. A. H. Millar, SHS, 28 (Edinburgh, 1898), p. 89. On Lydgate's wider popularity in Scotland, see Bawcutt, 'A First-Line Index of Early Scottish Verse', *Studies in Scottish Literature*, 26 (1991), 254–70 (257–58).

Pour dieu Remembres Vous de moy
Remembres Vous de moy pour dieu.

This second inscription, which is written down the outer margin at right angles to the first, is in the same 'neat fifteenth-century secretary hand' that Dr Doyle considers English rather than Scots.[6] He notes also that a piece of verse in Scots (no. 6 below) appears to be later and to be written over the first word of the second inscription. This French inscription might perhaps imply that the manuscript is a gift from one person to another, but, if so, it is impossible to identify the *moy* and *vous*.

By the last decade of the fifteenth century, the manuscript was undoubtedly in Scotland. Some inscriptions on fol. 75[V] show that it was then in the possession of the Lyle family, who owned estates in Renfrewshire. Some of these, unfortunately, are mere scribbles, such as 'Sum scriptyr talis' and 'Ioanne', and many words are now almost illegible. Nonetheless one Latin entry contains the names 'Robertus lyle' and 'Mareota Lylle'; and a little below this is written:

> Memorandum that Robert lylle borruyt a buk
> fra maryown lylle lade off huston
> … Robert lylles hed & xxxv.

There were several Robert Lyles in the fifteenth century. Sir Robert Lyle and his son George were present in England between 1425 and 1427, serving as hostages for James I after he returned to Scotland. But their ownership of this manuscript is ruled out by its dating post-1430. Sir Robert's son, also Robert, was created first Lord Lyle in 1452, and died *c.* 1470. His son, Robert, second Lord Lyle, was a prominent figure in the reigns of James III and James IV. Twice disgraced and once accused of treason, he each time regained the favour of the king and recovered his forfeited estates. More pertinent here is the fact that he frequently visited England in the 1480s and early 1490s. He was a member of the embassy that treated, unsuccessfully, for the marriage of Prince James to Anne de la Pole in 1484, and he also took part in later embassies to conclude truces in 1488 and 1490.[7] It is not implausible that on one such visit to England he obtained this manuscript of *The Siege of Thebes*. Only a little earlier, another Scottish nobleman, Thomas Boyd, Earl of Arran, was sufficiently interested in the poem to borrow it from Anne Paston. John Paston III, in a letter dated 5 June 1472, praised Arran highly: [82]

---

6   Personal communication (April 1990). I am grateful to Dr Doyle for lending me a microfilm of the manuscript. I am much indebted also to the Keeper of Rare Books and Manuscripts in Boston Public Library for allowing me to examine this manuscript in May 1998.

7   Information about the Lyle family may be found in *The Scots Peerage*, ed. Sir J. Balfour Paul, 9 vols (Edinburgh, 1904–14), V, pp. 552–58; *The Complete Peerage of England, Scotland, Ireland, Great Britain, and the United Kingdom*, ed. George E. Cockayne, rev. the Hon. Vicary Gibbs, H. A. Doubleday, Duncan Warrand and Lord Howard de Walden (London, 1910–59), VIII, pp. 291–96; and William Lyle, *'De Insula', or the Lyles of Renfrewshire* (Glasgow, 1936). On the career of Robert, second Lord Lyle, see Norman Macdougall, *James III: A Political Study* (Edinburgh, 1982), [pp. 151, 185, 213–14, 236–37, 242, 238–50], and Norman Macdougall, *James IV* (Edinburgh, 1989), especially pp. 67–76, 80–81.

he is on the lyghtest, delyuerst, best spokyn, fayirest archer, deuowghtest, most perfyght and trewest to hys lady of all the knyghtys … He hath a book of my syster Annys of the Sege of Thebes. When he hath doon wyth it he promysyd to delyuer it yow.[8]

Whatever the nature and the fate of the Paston copy of *The Siege of Thebes*, it should not be identified with the Boston manuscript. The Earl of Arran was an exile in London, and he never returned to Scotland.[9]

The second Lord Lyle is known to have owned other English books. On 3 July 1483, in an action for 'wrangful spoliacioun' against James, Earl of Buchan, heard before the Lords Auditors of Causes and Complaints, he listed three of them, along with items of clothing and chests of gold coins. The stolen books were described as: 'thre inglis bukis, ane of the philosophouris sawis, ane vther of genetris, the thrid of medecyn, the price of the thre bukis ten poundis'.[10] The Lords Auditors decreed that the goods be returned to Lord Lyle, but it is not known whether he definitely regained his books. There is a muddled tradition, dating from the nineteenth century, that all three of them were Caxton prints.[11] It is quite possible that the first book was a copy of Anthony Woodville, Earl Rivers's *The Dicts or Sayings of the Philosophers*, first published by Caxton in 1477; the second may have been an unidentified treatise on 'gentrice', that is, courtesy or chivalry;[12] and the third was presumably one of the many medical works in English compiled in the later Middle Ages.[13] In this account, however, we are told the subjects of the books, not their specific titles, and

8 *Paston Letters and Papers of the Fifteenth Century*, ed. Norman Davis, 2 vols, EETS, Supplementary Ser. (Oxford, 1971–76), I, pp. 574–75. See also G. A. Lester, 'The Books of a Fifteenth-Century English Gentleman, Sir John Paston', *Neuphilologische Mitteilungen*, 88 (1987–88), 200–17.

9 On the downfall and exile of Thomas Boyd, Earl of Arran, see Macdougall, *James III*, pp. 72ff.

10 *The Acts of the Lords Auditors of Causes and Complaints*, ed. T. Thomson (Edinburgh, 1839), p. 112*. Scribal contractions, retained in this edition, are here expanded, and punctuation has been added.

11 See, for instance, Gregory Kratzmann, *Anglo-Scottish Literary Relations 1430–1550* (Cambridge, 1980), p. 6; and Lyle, '*De Insula*', p. 160. The ultimate source appears to be the antiquary C. A. [Andrew Crawfurd], whose 'Lord Lyle v. the Earl of Buchan, 1483' was published in the *Scottish Journal* (1847–48), 165–66, and reprinted in *Loyal Reformers' Gazette* (1850–55), I, 159–60: 'Northern Notes and Queries'. On the complicated bibliographical history of Crawfurd's publications, see Emily B. Lyle, 'The Printed Writings of Andrew Crawfurd', *Bibliotheck*, 7 (1975), 141–58 (154–56).

12 The sense of 'genetris' is debatable. Dr Doyle and Professor Hanna have suggested that it might be an error for 'Generides', the name of the fifteenth-century romance.

13 On the background, see Linda Ehrsam Voigts, 'Scientific and Medical Books', in *Book Production*, ed. Griffiths and Pearsall, pp. 345–402. One such work is the verse 'Dietary' commonly attributed to Lydgate. Three Scottish copies exist: one accompanies a text of Barbour's *Bruce* in St John's College, Cambridge, MS 191; the others are in the Makculloch MS (EUL, Laing III.149) and the Bannatyne MS (NLS, Adv. 1.1.6).

it seems doubtful that any can be positively identified.[14] All three might well have been manuscripts rather than printed books.

Mariota, or Marion, Lyle, Lady of Houston (also in Renfrewshire), was the daughter of the second Lord Lyle; she was married to Peter Houston, probably her cousin and certainly a relative of her mother Margaret Houston. Little is known of Mariota, unfortunately, and her precise lifespan is uncertain, but she was named as the youngest of Lord Lyle's daughters in a document dated 14 December 1471 and had become the wife of Peter Houston by 6 May 1495.[15] The Robert Lyle whose name, in the Boston manuscript, is twice linked, somewhat casually, with Mariota's seems less likely to be her father than her brother, who became third Lord Lyle. (Precisely when he became Lord Lyle seems unknown; his father was dead by 1499, and he himself had died before 11 March 1502.) The wording of the third line of the memorandum is not fully legible, and its sense is not clear to me. The first two lines suggest, however, that the 'buk' that Robert borrowed was not the Boston manuscript, in which it is entered, but another. The entry is made by, or on behalf of, Mariota herself; it is the owner, not the borrower, who is most likely to make such a memorandum. The inference must be that Mariota owned both this manuscript and another unspecified 'buk'. Robert, third Lord Lyle, seems to have inherited the litigious spirit of his father. On 14 January 1499, he took action against Margaret his mother, and Peter Houston (husband of Mariota?), for withholding goods that he should [83] rightfully have inherited from his dead father. Among these, interestingly, were 'a buke of storeis', priced at ten pounds, and a 'buke of law', priced at forty shillings.[16] For the Lyles, books were evidently valued possessions.

During the first half of the sixteenth century, the fortunes of the Lyle family, which had been high in the fifteenth century, plunged inextricably downwards. John, fourth Lord Lyle, sold one estate after another, to Sir James Hamilton of Fymont, Patrick Maxwell of Newark, Sir John Campbell, the Earl of Argyll, and other noblemen,

---

[14] Crawfurd, in his notes to the text (probably taken from the *Acts*, ed. Thomson), suggests that the first book is *The Dicts or Sayings*; explains 'genetris' (glossed as 'chivalry') as a reference to 'the Book of the Order of Chivalry and Knighthood'; and identifies *medecyn* with *The Curial*, which he mistakenly understands to mean 'healing'. Caxton's editions of *The Book of the Ordre of Chyvalry* and *The Curial*, in any case, are assigned to 1484, and thus are too late in date.

[15] See *Calendar of the Laing Charters AD 854–1837 Belonging to the University of Edinburgh*, ed. Revd John Anderson (Edinburgh, 1899), no. 164; also *The Register of the Great Seal of Scotland*, 2 (1424–1513), ed. J. Balfour Paul (Edinburgh, 1882), charter no. 2252; and *Scots Peerage*, V, p. 554. Her death might be established by the mention of *testamenti quondam Mariote Howstoun*, dated December 1507, *Liber Protocollorum M. Cuthberti Simonis*, ed. Joseph Bain and Revd Charles Rogers, 2 vols, Grampian Club (London, 1875), no. 283 [I, pp. 401–02]; but this may be another woman.

[16] *The Acts of the Lords of Council in Civil Causes*, ed. G. Neilson, A. B. Calderwood and H. Paton, 3 vols (Edinburgh, 1839–1993), II, p. 297. For a similar combination of utility and imaginative pleasure in book-owning, cf. Sir James Douglas of Dalkeith's bequest to his son, in 1390, of 'all my books, both of the statutes of the Scots realm and of romances' (Hector L. MacQueen, *Common Law and Feudal Society in Medieval Scotland* (Edinburgh, 1993), p. 94); Latin original in *Bannatyne Miscellany*, II, ed. D. Laing, Bannatyne Club (Edinburgh, 1836), p. 107.

chiefly from the west of Scotland. 'History does not record the causes whereby Lord Lyle was obliged to part with so many of his possessions, but at his death, which must have taken place after 20 July 1551, few, if any, of his lands can have been in his possession'.[17] It was presumably during this period that the Boston manuscript, along with other possessions, passed to new owners. There are two very slight clues as to these owners, which occur, along with a number of pious phrases, on fol. 1[r]. The first, in a small neat hand, at the foot of the page but upside down, is 'liber donald'. 'Donald' is more probably a Highlander's than a Lowlander's name, but he seems otherwise unlikely to be identified. A second entry, in a larger hand, and darker ink, is written to the right of the piece of verse that occupies the centre of the page:

Ihone Swyntoun / With my hand finis.

The Swintons were an East Border family, whose chief house was at Swinton, twelve miles from Berwick upon Tweed and four from Norham. The name John recurs in the family – one earlier John Swinton spent seven years in the service of John of Gaunt, before returning to Scotland and dying at the Battle of Humbleton Hill in 1402 – and it will probably be impossible to identify this sixteenth-century member of the family, who had the manuscript in his hands, though not definitely in his possession.[18]

The case of Duncan Campbell, seventh laird of Glenorchy (c. 1552–1631), is very different; his ownership of the manuscript is irrefutable, and has extremely interesting implications. On the blank space beneath the last words of the poem (fol. 74[r]) is the date 1592, and beneath that, in a large and flamboyant hand, occurs:

This Bwik pertenis to ane Richt honorabill
    Sir Duncane Campbell of
    Glennorquhay Knycht.

Duncan, who was knighted in May 1590, was a substantial landowner in Perthshire, who acquired many other estates during his lifetime, sometimes by nefarious and unscrupulous means.[19] Most of his properties lay in a Gaelic-speaking area of the Highlands; an earlier member of the family wrote Gaelic poems, preserved in the Book of the Dean of Lismore [NLS, MS Adv. 72.1.37], and at his death Duncan was mourned in a Gaelic elegy by Neil MacEwan.[20] Duncan himself, however, was bilingual in Scots and Gaelic, as were many Highlanders, and clearly knew some Latin. In 1598, Master William Bowie, a notary and one of [84] his servitors, wrote

---

[17] *Scots Peerage*, V, p. 556. Lyle, '*De Insula*', p. 100, comments that 'he managed to make most of his lands disappear from Lyle ownership'.

[18] On the family, see A. C. Swinton, *The Swintons of that Ilk and Their Cadets* (Edinburgh, 1883); also G. S. C. Swinton, 'John of Swinton, a Border Fighter of the Middle Ages', *Scottish Historical Review*, 16 (1919), 261–79.

[19] For fuller information, see Revd William A. Gillies, *In Famed Breadalbane* (Perth, 1938), pp. 135–42; and *Scots Peerage*, II: 'Campbells, Earls of Breadalbane'.

[20] Duncan, second laird of Glenorchy, died at Flodden in 1513; on his poems, see W. Gillies, 'The Gaelic Poems of Sir Duncan Campbell of Glenorchy', *Scottish Gaelic Studies*, 13.1 (1978), 18–45; 13.2 (1981), 263–88; and 14.1 (1983), 52–82.

at Duncan's command an account of the first seven lairds of Glenorchy, now known as the Black Book of Taymouth [NRS, GD 112/78/2]. It contains prefatory verses in Latin and Scots.[21]

Duncan evidently had an interest in medieval vernacular romances, particularly those whose subject was the matter of antiquity. He possessed not only this manuscript of *The Siege of Thebes*, but both surviving copies of Sir Gilbert Hay's Alexander romance, *The Buik of King Alexander the Conquerour*. The earliest of these, dated *c.* 1530 (BL, Add. MS 40732), contains an ownership inscription (dated 1579), whose phrasing resembles that in the Boston manuscript. The later copy of the Alexander romance (NRS, MS GD 112/71/9) has on the first flyleaf: 'Ex libris domini Duncani Campbell de Glenwrquhay miles.'[22] In addition to these works, Duncan also possessed the romance of *Florimond of Albany*, which is inscribed: 'Duncan campbell of glenvurquhay with my hand the / blakest laird in all this land' (fol. 1ʳ).[23]

One should not too readily assume that Duncan acquired the Boston manuscript only in 1592: the date might be explained in other ways, perhaps indicating the time when he first became aware of the poem, or finished reading it. He was by no means the first member of his family to appreciate poetry or possess books, and he possibly inherited the manuscript. Colin Campbell, third laird of Glenorchy, owned a fifteenth-century Psalter (BL, MS Egerton 2899); and John Campbell, the fifth laird, is the possible owner of another fifteenth-century manuscript (NRS, MS GD 112/71/1 (1)), which contains part of a chronicle and Earl Rivers' translation of *The Cordial*, copied from Caxton's print of 1479.[24] Duncan's own mother, Catherine Ruthven, owned a printed copy of Sleidan's *Chronicle* (1560), whose location is unfortunately now unknown.[25] The Boston copy of *The Siege of Thebes*, together with other early books and manuscripts, remained for several centuries in the possession of Duncan's descendants, at Taymouth Castle, Perthshire.[26] It was valued at £63, and listed as no. 2300 (next to one of the copies of *King Alexander the Conquerour*), in a manuscript

---

[21] See *Black Book of Taymouth*, [ed. Cosmo Innes], Bannatyne Club (Edinburgh, 1855).

[22] For fuller information, see *The Buik of King Alexander the Conquerour*, ed. John Cartwright, 2 vols [II and III], STS, 4th ser. 16, 18 (Edinburgh and Aberdeen, 1986–90), II, pp. vii–xvii.

[23] NRS, MS GD 112/22/2. The text of this poem, unfortunately without introduction or editorial apparatus, was printed by J. Derrick McClure, *Scottish Literary Journal*, *Supplement* 10 (1979), 1–10. [See the edition in *Shorter Scottish Medieval Romances*, ed. Rhiannon Purdie, STS, 5th ser. 11 (Woodbridge, 2013), pp. 87–103.]

[24] John Campbell, however, is a common Scottish name. For brief discussions of this manuscript, see Lyall, 'Books and Book Owners', p. 242; and N. Blake, 'Manuscript to Print', pp. 420–21, in *Book Production*, ed. Griffiths and Pearsall.

[25] According to Innes, *Black Book of Taymouth*, p. vi, it contains the inscription: 'This buke pertenis to Catherine Ruthven lady of Glenurquhay'.

[26] During the eighteenth century, Thomas Pennant visited Taymouth Castle, and made a transcript of *Duncan Laideus Testament*, a poem found in the NRS copy of *King Alexander the Conquerour* [NRS GD 112/71/9]. See Thomas Warton, *History of English Poetry* (London, 1778; rev. Hazlitt, 1871), III, 251–55 [and the edition in *'Duncane Laideus Testament' and Other Comic Poems in Older Scots*, ed. Janet Hadley Williams, STS, 5th ser. 15 (Edinburgh, 2016), pp. 105–21].

inventory of books and manuscripts belonging to the Marquess of Breadalbane, made in 1863. The dispersal of the library took place, by stages, in the twentieth century.[27]

In addition to the ownership inscriptions and other entries, the Boston manuscript also contains six pieces of verse, which are printed below. With the exception of no. 4, none has previously been transcribed. All are very short; one indeed consists of a single line, and two are brief extracts from works by John Gower and John Bellenden. Each piece seems to have been written by a different hand; all are in versions of sixteenth-century secretary script, differing in size, colour of ink, degree of carefulness and choice of letter-forms. All are in Scots, but a few have distinctive orthographical features or peculiarities that are not found in the other pieces.[28] No. 1, for instance, is characterized by the use of /v/ for /w/: so 'vyrtis', 'writes'; 'vith', 'with'; and 'vecht', 'wight'. No. 5 has /e/, where the standard Scots spelling would have been /i/: so 'kenge', 'king', and 'theng', 'thing'. It is tempting, but [**85**] probably impossible, to associate the hands in which these verses are written with some of the inscriptions; the specimens are too short. Just possibly perhaps Duncan Campbell himself wrote no. 2, which is unusual in its bold, large script.

No. 1

fol. 1[r]

Sum festynnys fast for fifti ȝer
That <l>estis nocht for ten
This fundment makis for euermor
In vane vyrtis his pene
As it var endles eritagis   5
That other man meycht kene
Bot oft it gays fra hym and his
Tyll other kynd of men
Vith ane thousand bot and hunder
Quhar is Vavane the vecht   10
Arthovr Scharlis and Allexander
That mekyll vas of meycht.

[27] See the 'Inventory and Valuation of Books of the Most Noble Marquess of Breadalbane, Made by Messrs Christie, Manson and Woods' (NRS, MS GD 112/22/56). The Glenorchy Psalter was sold at Sotheby's sale, 5–7 February 1912, lot 702; also listed in the same sale-catalogue is a copy of Sleidan's *Chronicle* (1560), likely to have been the copy that belonged to Duncan Campbell's mother. *The Siege of Thebes* was sold by Sotheby's, 16 June 1941 (from the library at Newton Park, Bristol); and purchased by L. and P. Robinson, who in 1947 sold it to Boston Public Library (see Edwards, 'Beinecke MS 661', p. 192).

[28] On such 'substandard' spellings, see A. J. Aitken, 'Variation and Variety in Written Middle Scots', in *Edinburgh Studies in English and Scots*, ed. A. J. Aitken, Angus McIntosh and Hermann Pálsson (London, 1971), pp. 177–209.

Textual Notes and Glosses

1. Sum] 'one person'   festynnys] 'fastens', apparently in the sense 'confirms, ratifies (of bond or agreement)', or else 'draws up a contract'. See *OED*, 'fasten', senses 1b and 5, although these are usually transitive   fifti] MS has l^{ti}

2 <l>] hole in MS   ten] MS has the numeral X

3 fundment] 'foundation'

4 vyrtis … pene] 'writes … pen'

5 eritagis] 'heritable estates, properties'

7 gays] the tail of *y* is very faint; *gans* is also possible in the sense 'goes'. See *DOST*, 'gane', v. 2

9 thousand] MS has the numeral M   bot and] 'as well, in addition'. The line literally means 'with a thousand and also a hundred', and presumably qualifies the following lines. All human beings must die, thousands of unnamed men, as well as the heroes of romance and antiquitiy   hunder] MS has the numeral c. The rhyme requires this Scots form of 'hundred'

10 Vavane…vecht] 'Gawain…strong'

11 Arthur, Charlemagne, and Alexander the Great

No other text is known of this piece, which moralizes rather clumsily on the short duration of legal agreements, and the fleeting nature of worldly possessions. It contrasts interestingly with the more common advice given to Scottish landowners – which chimed with their own beliefs and practices – that they should keep what properties they already possessed, and strive to acquire more. William Bowie, in a prefatory piece of verse addressed to Duncan Campbell of Glenorchy and his posterity, put it succinctly: [86]

> Vill thow thy honour, hows, and rent to stand,
> Conques, or keip thingis conquest to thy hand.[29]

A similar theme appears in some verses attributed to Sir Richard Maitland, which begin:

> Gif thou desyre thi hous lang stand,
> And thi successioun brouk thi land …[30]

Whoever was the author or copyist of this piece of verse, it seems an apposite comment on a family in decline, such as the Lyles, who saw their estates rapidly dispersed in the sixteenth century. The first eight lines form a metrical unit, with alternating lines of eight and six syllables, the shorter lines all rhyming on –*en*. The last four lines, a brief illustration of the *Ubi sunt* theme, seem clumsily tacked on to the preceding piece, and have a different rhyme scheme in the short lines.

---

[29] See *Black Book of Taymouth*, p. [5]; and [in the manuscript, NRS, GD 112/78/2, fol. 3^v].

[30] *The Maitland Folio Manuscript*, ed. W. A. Craigie, 2 vols, STS 2nd ser. 7, 20 (Edinburgh, 1919–27), I, p. 326.

No. 2

Above this poem, on fol. 1ʳ, is a single line of verse. It is now very faded, but reads: 'How suld my febill boye fo<u?>r.' This represents the first line of a love complaint by Alexander Scott, a poet who flourished in the middle of the sixteenth century. The chief repository of his poems is the Bannatyne Manuscript (1568), and the Bannatyne text of this poem (fol. 244ᵛ) opens:

> How suld my febill body fure
> The dowble dolour I indure?

The line copied into the Boston manuscript is no more than a hasty scribble: 'boye' is clearly an error for the correct *body*; and 'four', or 'fure', means 'bear, suffer'.[31] The entry's main interest is that it is an early indication of this poem's popularity, which continued well into the seventeenth century.[32]

No. 3

fol. 1ᵛ

> Grounde the in paciens
> Blynd nocht thi consciens
> Do thi god Reuerens
>   Thankand him ay
>
> Prese the with diligens   5
> To put away necligens
> Cese with sufficiens
>   This ward will a<way>
>
> Se on na way to le
> To the purale be fre   10   [87]
> And kepe ay cherite
>   god for to plese
>
> Thou wate nocht quhen to de
> quhill thou art here prouid the
> That thi saule may be   15
>   Broucht in to ese.

---

[31] This word, which should not be confused with the preterite of *fare*, 'go, proceed', was more common in Scots in such senses as 'convey, transport by sea' (*DOST*, 'fur', v.).

[32] For the complete poem, see *The Bannatyne Manuscript*, ed. W. Tod Ritchie, 4 vols, STS, 2nd ser. 22, 23, 26; 3rd ser. 5 (Edinburgh, 1928–24), III, pp. 340–41; also the comments of D. Fox and W. A. Ringler on poem no. 306 in *The Bannatyne Manuscript* (London, 1980), p. xxxv.

Glosses
8 ward] 'world'
9 le] 'tell lies'
10 purale] 'poor people'   fre] 'generous'
11 cherite] 'charity'
13 de] 'die'

Another copy of the first two quatrains of this piece exists in the Bannatyne manuscript, no. 91 (fol. 74ʳ). Bannatyne's layout, however, differs strikingly: the eight lines are compressed into four long lines, with virgules marking the position of the rhymes. In the Boston manuscript, the first three rhyming lines in each quatrain are linked in a bracket, and the short 'tail' is placed to their right. Such an arrangement was fairly common, especially where space was limited. Fox and Ringler termed the Bannatyne text 'unique',[33] but this is not the case. There are several other copies of this rather banal advice poem, all in Scottish manuscripts dating from the fifteenth to the seventeenth century. Probably the earliest text is that copied into the Scottish parliamentary records after an Act dated 1469.[34] The Maxwell Commonplace Book, compiled by John Maxwell between 1584 and 1589, contains two versions (fols 19ʳ and 23ᵛ);[35] and an early seventeenth-century poetic miscellany also contains two copies.[36] The version of the poem in the Boston manuscript has two quatrains at the end, not found elsewhere, which are a possibly scribal improvisation on the common theme that almsgiving to the poor will 'provide' for the soul's welfare after death.[37]

Beneath this piece of verse, in the same hand, are the following Latin maxims, and a slightly garbled piece of Greek:

Felix quem faciunt aliena pericula cautum
Est fortunatus / felix / dives quod beatus
Τελως τω θεω Χαρης

Above the verse, a different hand has written 'In nomine patris', and repeated the opening line. The first Latin sentence is an extremely popular proverb, quoted by Henryson (*Fables*, 1033), and many other medieval authors.[38] The Greek – roughly

33 Fox and Ringler, *Bannatyne Manuscript*, no. 91, p. xxiv.
34 See W. P. Reeves, 'Stray Verse', *Modern Language Notes*, 9.4 (1894) cols 205–06; also J. T. T. B[rown], *Scots Lore*, 1 (1895), pp. 169–70. Both derive from *The Parliamentary Records of Scotland*, ed. W. Robertson (Edinburgh, 1804), p. 49, col. 1.
35 EUL, MS Laing III.467; on this unpublished manuscript, see Bawcutt, 'The Commonplace Book of John Maxwell', in *A Day Estivall*, ed. A. Gardner-Medwin and J. Hadley Williams (Aberdeen, 1990), pp. 59–68. [See this essay herein.]
36 Edinburgh University Library, MS Laing III.447, fols 76ᵛ and 77ᵛ. One of these texts is printed in *The Poems of Alexander Montgomerie: Supplementary Volume*, ed. George. Stevenson, STS, 1st ser. 59 (1910), p. 213.
37 See, for instance, *The Poems of William Dunbar*, ed. Priscilla Bawcutt, 2 vols, ASLS 27, 28 (Glasgow, 1998), I, B 31: 'Man, sen thy lyf is ay in weir'; and *The Awntyrs off Arthure*, ed. Ralph Hanna (Manchester, 1974), lines 172–82.
38 See Hans Walther, *Proverbia sententiaeque Latinitatis Medii Aevi* (Göttingen, 1963–67), no. 8952; the note to *Fables*, 1033, *The Poems of Robert Henryson*, ed. Denton Fox

'The end, by the grace of God' – corresponds to the more common *Finis*. This use of Τελως in a vernacular manuscript is interesting, and suggests some aspiration to learning. The Greek word seems to have been first adopted into Latin manuscripts in 1415 by the Florentine [88] scholar Sozomeno da Pistoia, and was characteristic of humanist works, both manuscript and printed, throughout the fifteenth and sixteenth centuries.[39]

No. 4

fol. 2ʳ

Amang the oist of greikis as we hard
Twa knychtis war Achillis and Tesete
The ane moist vail3eand the other moist cowart
Bettir is to be sayis Iuuenale poete
Thersetis sone havand Achillis spreitt   5
With manlie force his purpos to fulfill
Than to be lord of everie land and streite
And syne moist cowart cummyn of Achill

This eight-line stanza is an extract from John Bellenden's 'Proheme of the history', one of the prologues to his translation of Hector Boece's *Scotorum historia* (1527). Bellenden began the translation in 1530, and presented it to James V in 1533. The work exists in a printed edition, undated but usually assigned to *c.* 1536–40, and in a number of manuscripts, whose relation to the print is very complicated.[40] Although the 'Proheme' was lengthened and revised, this passage is substantially the same in the print (where it is stanza 10) and the manuscript versions (where it is stanza 9).[41] The Boston copyist makes no mention of Bellenden's authorship, however, and it is possible that he was not aware of the author. Like many other self-contained and sententious passages from longer works, this stanza seems to have circulated separately and been regarded as an independent poem. A second copy of the stanza exists, made by one of the sixteenth-century owners of a fifteenth-century manuscript of Porphyry's *Isagoge*, now in Aberdeen University Library (MS 223, fol. 58ᵛ).[42]

(Oxford, 1981); and Whiting, W391.

39 I am grateful to Professor Nigel Palmer for directing me to Dieter Wuttke, 'Telos als Explicit', in *Das Verhältnis der Humanisten zum Buch*, ed. Fritz Krafft and D. Wuttke (Boppard, 1997), pp. 47–62.

40 See Nicola Royan, 'The Relationship between the *Scotorum Historia* of Hector Boece and John Bellenden's *Chronicles of Scotland*', in *The Rose and the Thistle: Essays on the Culture of Late Medieval and Renaissance Scotland*, ed. Sally Mapstone and Juliette Wood (East Linton, 1998), pp. 136–57.

41 There is a text of Bellenden's 'Proheme of the History' in the Bannatyne Manuscript, copied from the print, but this stanza is now missing, owing to the loss of fols 368–69. See Fox and Ringler, *Bannatyne Manuscript*, no. 403, p. xxxix.

42 For a transcript of the Aberdeen copy, see *Bannatyne Manuscript*, ed. Ritchie, I, p. x. On the history of the manuscript, see Leslie Macfarlane, 'William Elphinstone's Library Revisited', in *The Renaissance in Scotland: Studies in Literature, Religion, History and*

Professor A. S. G. Edwards, who was the first to identify and print the stanza from the Boston manuscript, was puzzled by its popularity and that of Bellenden's 'Proheme'.[43] But meditations of the nature of true nobility, interlinked with other topics, such as the greatness of ancient heroes or kings, and the degeneracy of their modern descendants, were particularly common in Scottish writers of the fifteenth and sixteenth centuries. The theme figures, for instance, at the beginning of Hary's *Wallace*, and in the first twenty-eight lines of Henryson's *Orpheus and Eurydice*. The theologian John Major discusses the subject several times and quotes the very verses from Juvenal that are here freely paraphrased by Bellenden:

> Malo pater tibi sit Thersites, dummodo tu sis
> Aeacidae similis Vulcaniaque arma capessas,
> quam te Thersitae similem producat Achilles.
> (*Satire* VIII.269–71)[44]

Juvenal's lines, which come as the climax of his poem, have epigrammatic force, something to which Bellenden perhaps aspired but cannot match. [**89**]

No. 5

fol. 74ᵛ

> The kengis qwosteown wos thys
> of thengis qwhylk that strangast is
> The wyn the woman or the kenge
> And that thay sowld apon this theng
> of thar anssowr awyssyt be   5
> he gaf tham dayis fowle thre
> And hatht behot tham by hys fath
> Qwhoso best resson sait
> he sal resaf ane wordi med
> apon this theng thay tokyn hed   10
> And stwdiit in dwspwtassiown
> that thay by diuers opownown
> of argomentis qwhat thay …

Glosses
6 fowle] 'fully'
9 wordi] 'worthy'

Culture, ed. A. A. MacDonald, Michael Lynch and Ian B. Cowan (Leiden, 1994), pp. 66–81 (70–71).

43 See 'Bellenden's *Proheme*'.

44 See John Major [Mair], *A History of Greater Britain*, trans. A. Constable, SHS (Edinburgh, 1892), p. 46 (I.vii); and pp. 397–400 (an extract from *In quartum sententiarum*). Juvenal's lines were well known in the Middle Ages. Gower refers to them twice, although misattributing them to Horace: see *Confessio Amantis*, VII.3581–85; and *Mirour de l'Omme*, 23371ff.

This represents a text of Gower, *Confessio Amantis*, VII.1811–23.[45] Questions and debates of this type were popular in the late Middle Ages, and Gower's tale of the so-called 'Three Questions' in Book I of the *Confessio Amantis* circulated separately in a few manuscripts. But his tale of the debate between a king's three counsellors concerning the relative power of wine, woman, or a king does not seem to have been much excerpted elsewhere (as far as I know).[46] It is curious that this extract is so short (thirteen lines out of 202); it merely poses the opening question, and does not proceed to the tale's conclusion that *veritas super omnia vincit* – truth is an important part of 'every kinges regiment'. One can only conjecture: that the copyist was interrupted, or realized there was insufficient space, or perhaps designed it as an aide-mémoire to an interesting topic. He might well have been prompted by the reading of *The Siege of Thebes*, with its reference to the biblical source of Gower's story in I Esdras iii and iv (see lines 1728ff.). Whatever the reason, this excerpt indicates that Gower was being read carefully in Scotland, and gives substance to the various passing allusions to 'moral Gower' by poets such as Douglas and Dunbar.[47] It is noteworthy also that the passage comes from Book VII, largely concerned with the education of a king, and that an earlier Scot, John Ireland, singled out for mention a passage preceding this section of *Confessio Amantis*, on the symbolism of jewels in a royal crown (VII.819–47).[48] Scottish interest in Gower was less 'perfunctory' than has been asserted.[49]

Above this verse extract, and in the same hand, is a single line:

In daj nomine amen per hoc presens pwbilicwm.

This pen trial represents the first words of a common formula, regularly [**90**] employed at the beginning of a notarial instrument: 'In dei [*or* domini] nomine, amen. Per hoc presens publicum instrumentum cunctis pateat evidenter ...' (In the name of God, Amen. Let it be known plainly to all men by this present public instrument ...).[50] It is regrettable therefore that in the *Bibliography and Index of English Verse in Manuscript 1501–1558* this has been mistranscribed 'In Day now amang That presumss qwilichis', as if it were the first line of a poem written in garbled Scots.[51]

[45] I am much indebted to Dr Sally Mapstone for identifying the source of this passage.
[46] See the discussion of the manuscripts in *The Complete Works of John Gower*, 4 vols (Oxford, 1899–1902; repr. 1968), II, pp. cxxxviii–clxvii (clxv–clxvi).
[47] Douglas, *Palice of Honour*, 920; and *Poems of Dunbar* (B 59): *The Goldyn Targe*, 262.
[48] See John Ireland, *The Meroure of Wysdome*, ed. Craig McDonald, STS, 4th ser. 19 (Aberdeen, 1990), III, p. 160: 'And of the precius stanis of the crovne ryall spekis mony clerkis and wis gower in his buk twichis the significacioun of the sammyn mater'.
[49] Cf. Derek Pearsall, 'The Gower Tradition', in *Gower's 'Confessio Amantis': Responses and Reassessments*, ed. A. J. Minnis (Cambridge, 1983), pp. 179–97 (189).
[50] For an example, see Grant G. Simpson, *Scottish Handwriting 1150–1650* (Aberdeen, 1977), plate 11.
[51] Ringler, *Bibliography and Index*, TM 760.

No. 6

fol. 76r

> Now lat ws all go loif the lord
> both grit and small now lat ws all
> quhen we war thrall he ws restord
> now lat ws all go loif the lord.

No other text of this piece is known to me. Medieval works commonly concluded with a prayer, and Lydgate himself ended *The Siege of Thebes* with a prayer for peace and heavenly bliss (see lines 4709–16). An earlier owner had followed this with 'Te deum laudamus', and so on (see above), and the short Scottish poem seems designed as a vernacular equivalent of the 'Te deum' immediately above it. ('Loif' here is likely to mean 'praise', not 'love'.) The poem has the metrical shape of a triolet, best known from its use in Dunbar's *Dirige*.[52] It may have been intended for singing, and has some stylistic affinity with *The Gude and Godlie Ballatis*.[53]

Almost a century ago, M. R. James urged scholars to make their descriptions of manuscripts as complete as possible: 'Names and scribblings on flyleaves, which to one student suggest nothing, may combine in the memory of another into a coherent piece of history and show him the home of the book at a particular date, and by consequence unveil a whole section of the story of its wanderings'.[54] The Boston manuscript of *The Siege of Thebes* illustrates the wisdom of his advice. The history of this much-travelled manuscript is not as 'coherent' as one would like, and there still remain gaps in it that may never be fully explained. But the names and scribbled verses that it contains do indeed combine fruitfully with evidence from other sources, historical and literary. Not only do they illustrate the persistent Scottish interest in Lydgate, they yield small, yet precious, glimpses of other literary tastes – here somewhat conservative, highly moral and pious – of both Lowlanders and Highlanders in the fifteenth and sixteenth centuries.

Editorial Note

[a] First published in *Medium Ævum*, 70.1 (2001), pp. 80–94, and reprinted with the kind permission of The Society for the Study of Medieval Languages and Literature.

[52] See *Poems of Dunbar*, I, B 84. On the many instances of the form in the Maxwell Commonplace Book, see Bawcutt, 'Commonplace Book', p. 65–66. [See this essay herein.]
[53] Cf. 'Now lat vs sing with joy and myrth', in *The Gude and Godlie Ballatis*, ed. A. F. Mitchell, STS, 1st ser. 39 (Edinburgh, 1897), p. 75. [See also Alasdair A. MacDonald, ed., *The Gude and Godlie Ballatis*, STS, 5th ser. 14 (Woodbridge, 2015), pp. 144–45.]
[54] M. R. James, *The Wanderings and Homes of Manuscripts* (London, 1910), p. 23.

11

Lord William Howard of Naworth (1563–1640): Antiquary, Book Collector and Owner of the Scottish Devotional Manuscript British Library, Arundel 285

Lord William Howard of Naworth belonged to one of the most famous noble families in England.[a] He is the direct ancestor of the modern Earls of Carlisle of Castle Howard, in Yorkshire. His father was the fourth Duke of Norfolk, his grandfather was the poet Henry Howard, Earl of Surrey, and a slightly more distant ancestor was the second Duke of Norfolk, who commanded the English forces at the battle of Flodden. At times, one feels that Lord William was related to half the earls in England, including his nephew, the great connoisseur second Earl of Arundel, to whom he was particularly close. Lord William, however, is far less famous than these other eminent and sometimes ill-fated members of the Howard family. Yet the more I know of him, the more interesting I find his life, his personality and, above all, his activities as an antiquary and collector of manuscripts and printed books. This paper will focus on three topics – Lord William's [159] life, his activities as a collector and his ownership of BL, Arundel 285, an important yet neglected Scottish devotional manuscript.[1]

Life

First of all, I should mention but dispel the vivid imaginary portrait of 'Belted Will', invented by Sir Walter Scott in *The Lay of the Last Minstrel*:

> His Bilboa blade, by Marchmen felt,
> Hung in a broad and studded belt:
> Hence, in rude phrase, the Borderers still
> Call'd Noble Howard, *Belted Will*.
> (canto 5, stanza 16)

Meanwhile north of the Border the Scots are vigilant:

> They watch, 'gainst southern force and guile,
> Lest Scroop, or Howard, or Percy's powers,

---

[1] I am much indebted to previous researchers in this field, more particularly Ian Doyle, Richard Ovenden and Cyril Wright.

Threaten Branksome's lordly towers,
From Warkworth, or Naworth, or merry Carlisle.
(canto 1, stanza 6)

Scott's poem is set in the first half of the sixteenth century, and his portrait of Lord William is wholly anachronistic – perhaps harking back to the Flodden Howard – but 'Belted Will' is still alive today, and influences the tourist industry in the north of England.

Lord William Howard was in fact in his early life very much a southerner. Born in 1563, he spent his childhood in Audley End, in Essex. He became a ward of William Cecil, Lord Burghley, after the execution of his father for apparent complicity in the Ridolfi plot of 1572 and for entertaining the misguided notion of marriage to Mary, Queen of Scots. In 1577, he entered St John's College, Cambridge, and during the 1580s and 1590s lived in Enfield Chase, and London. During this time, he became a Catholic, as did his half-brother Philip, with whom he was twice imprisoned in the Tower of London. Yet despite his fervent and open adherence to Catholicism, he showed 'a prudent circumspection' and lived a long life.[2]

[160] Lord William acquired huge estates in the north of England, including Naworth Castle, Cumbria, through his marriage to Elizabeth Dacre (1564–1639). This, despite being very much an arranged marriage, was long, happy and fruitful. A visitor who was entertained hospitably by the couple in 1634 remarked:

> These noble twaine (as it pleased themselves to tell us …) could not make above 25 yeares both togeather, when first they were marryed, that now can make above 140 yeares, and very hearty, well, and merry …[3]

The marriage, in fact, took place in 1577 when Lord William was fourteen, and Elizabeth was thirteen. In 1634, he would have been seventy-one, and she seventy. Lord William did not take possession of his share of the Dacre estates, however, for many years. The reasons for this are many and complicated – prolonged litigation with other members of the Dacre family, the hostility of neighbouring northern families, in particular the Lowthers, and the hostility also of Queen Elizabeth.

King James, by contrast, showed favour to the Howards, and 'protected Lord William all his reign from attempts to prosecute him for recusancy'.[4] From the early 1600s onwards, he and his wife were in permanent residence at Naworth and did much to repair and renovate the castle. The great tower still exists where he housed his library in the topmost chamber, decorated with a fine ceiling brought from another Dacre castle at Kirkoswald, and with religious carvings and a panelled screen

---

2 Howard S. Reinmuth, 'Lord William Howard and His Catholic Associations', *Recusant History*, 12 (1973–74), 226–34 (228); David Mathew, 'The Library at Naworth', in *For Hilaire Belloc: Essays in Honour of his 72nd Birthday*, ed. Douglas Woodruff (London, 1942), pp. 117–30; Richard Ovenden and Stuart Handley, 'Howard, Lord William (1563–1640), Antiquary and Landowner' (2004), *ODNB Online*: http://www.oxforddnb.com.

3 *Selections from the Household Books of the Lord William Howard of Naworth Castle*, ed. Revd George Ornsby, Surtees Society 68 (Durham, 1878), pp. 489 and 311.

4 Reinmuth, 'Howard and His Catholic Associations', p. 227.

from the ruins of Lanercost priory. One is reminded of *Il Penseroso*'s 'high lonely towr', or the tower in which Montaigne lived and studied, his ceiling adorned with humanistic maxims in Latin and Greek. But Lord William, though undoubtedly a scholar, was not solitary or reclusive. He administered his estates, and presided over a large household – seven sons, three daughters, servants, and also a small group of Catholic friends and sympathizers. This included his steward Thomas Widmerpoole, a chaplain, and the Cornish scholar Nicholas Roscarrock whom he had met in the Tower.[5] He was a friend of most of the great antiquaries and bookmen of the period – these included John Stow, and Sir Robert Cotton, whose eldest son married his favourite daughter whom he described as 'the childe that from her infancie never did displease me';[6] and William Camden, who called Howard 'an attentive [**161**] and learned searcher into venerable antiquitie'.[7] In 1599, Camden and Cotton made a visit to the Roman Wall in the company of Sir William, and in later years there are several records of 'great stones' being sent to Cotton from Naworth – presumably inscribed Roman stones from the Wall.[8] It is striking how often and how far afield Lord William travelled, not only to the nearest towns, Carlisle and Newcastle, but to London, and in 1623 – for his health – to 'Spaw'.[9] A few years later (in either 1628 or 1629), he joined a group of Lancashire gentry on pilgrimage to St Winifred's Well at Holywell in Flintshire. The names of the participants – many still familiar as those of old Liverpool Catholic families – are listed in 'A Note of papists and priests assembled on St Winifred's day' in the State Papers.[10]

The Collector

It is widely acknowledged that Lord William Howard possessed one of the important libraries of the period, yet after he died little attempt seems to have been made to keep his printed books and manuscripts together, and they are now dispersed in the great libraries of England and the United States. During his lifetime – in 1629 – he made a gift of approximately fifty items, mainly theological, to St John's College, Cambridge, where he himself had studied.[11] After his death in 1640, a substantial number of his books were 'absorbed' into the collections of his nephew, the second Earl of Arundel.[12] In 1667, the Arundel collection was presented to the Royal Society by the sixth Duke of Norfolk. According to a historian of the family, this was a 'disaster',

---

5   *Nicholas Roscarrock's Lives of the Saints: Cornwall and Devon*, ed. Nicholas Orme, Devon and Cornwall Record Society, n.s. 35 (Exeter, 1992).
6   Reinmuth, 'Howard and His Catholic Associations', p. 230.
7   Reinmuth, 'Howard and His Catholic Associations', p. 234.
8   *Household Books*, ed. Ornsby, pp. 101 and 140.
9   *Household Books*, ed. Ornsby, pp. vii, 202 and 206.
10 *Household Books*, ed. Ornsby, pp. 248, 462–63.
11 For details, see the Special Collections Provenance Index of the Library of St John's College, Cambridge.
12 Richard Ovenden, 'The Libraries of the Antiquaries (*c.*1580–164) and the Idea of a National Collection', in *The Cambridge History of Libraries in Britain and Ireland, Volume 1: To 1640*, ed. Elizabeth Leedham-Green and Teresa Webber (Cambridge, 2006), pp. 526–61 (560).

since the Royal Society paid little attention to the books, and in 1831, 'without consulting the donor's family', sold them to the Library of the British Museum.[13] A number of Lord William's books, however, long remained at Naworth Castle, and a very useful list of the manuscripts still found there in 1697 was completed by a canon of Carlisle, and published in Bernard's *Catalogi Librorum Manuscriptorum Angliae et Hiberniae …* (Oxford, 1697).[14] In the early eighteenth century, a small group of Lord William's manuscripts was purchased from John Warburton, Somerset Herald, by Humfrey Wanley for Robert Harley, first Earl of Oxford, and these as a consequence are now in the Harleian collection of the Brit-[162]ish Library.[15] Many other prints and manuscripts seem to have been taken to Castle Howard, and over the years individual items were sold. Thus a manuscript 'Life of St Cuthbert in English meeter', which figures in Bernard's Catalogue, is later listed among the Castle Howard books, and is still labelled 'Castle Howard' in the old *IMEV* and *Supplement*, but now appears as BL, Egerton MS 3309 in *NIMEV* [2879].[16] Finally, in 1992 the residue of the Naworth collection was bought by the University of Durham. This mainly consists of sixteenth-century printed books, and estate papers, including the extremely valuable 'Household Books'.[17]

If Lord William's books are now so scattered, how is it possible to track them down? There are various clues, of which the most important is his habit of inscribing books with his name in a distinctive squarish hand. This is usually, but not invariably, spelled: *William Howarde of Naworth*. Sometimes this is accompanied by a pen sketch of a rampant lion, as on fol. 1[r] of BL, Harley MS 3836.[18] Occasionally there appears some form of Lord William's motto: *volo sed non valeo*, variously translated as 'I will, but I have not the power', or 'I am willing but unable.' There are other external sources of information, such as the 1697 catalogue mentioned earlier; and purchases recorded in the Household Books, although unfortunately these relate only to the years 1612 to 1640. They record in enormous detail the minutiae of life in a large, wealthy northern household. The payments for books usually occur in what are termed 'My Lord's Parcells', and are often tantalizingly vague. Mostly the books are printed, and, when identifiable, fairly recent publications – for example, *Camden's Remains* in 1623.[19] But occasionally a manuscript is mentioned: so seven shillings and seven pence were paid 'for one olde manuscript' and two other books at Worcester.[20]

What can one say of Lord William's taste as a collector? His primary interests were overwhelmingly religious: in Reinmuth's dry but apt summary: 'there were theological treatises to explain the faith, apologetical works to defend it, devotional

[13] John Martin Robinson, *The Dukes of Norfolk* (Oxford, 1982), pp. 123–24.
[14] See *Household Books*, ed. Ornsby, pp. 469–72.
[15] Cyril E. Wright, *Fontes Harleiani: A Study of the Sources of the Harleian Collection of Manuscripts in the British Museum* (London, 1972), pp. 198–200.
[16] See *Household Books*, ed. Ornsby, pp. 470, 487. For further information: *The Life of St Cuthbert in English Verse*, ed. Revd J. T. Fowler, Surtees Society 87 (Exeter, 1891).
[17] See A. I. Doyle, Untitled Note, *Rare Books Newsletter*, 43 (1993), 16; A. I. Doyle, 'Books of Lord William Howard of Naworth', *Northern Catholic History*, 35 (1994), 67–68.
[18] For a reproduction, see plates opposite page 288 in Wright, *Fontes Harleiani*.
[19] *Household Books*, ed. Ornsby, p. 208.
[20] *Household Books*, ed Ornsby, p. 244.

collections to cultivate it, and liturgical books to celebrate it'.[21] More specifically, he [163] possessed several manuscript lives of the medieval English saints, such as Saint Cuthbert, Saint Thomas a Becket, Saint Edmund, and the unique copy of a Life of Saint William of Norwich to which is attached a life of Saint Godric (now CUL, Add. MS 3037).[22] Lord William also possessed some of the English medieval mystical treatises, notable works by Richard Rolle, and the Wynkyn de Worde print of *The Orchard of Syon* (1519). He was clearly very interested in English history, and possessed numerous chronicles in print or manuscript, including Froissart, Fabian (1559), and a lost manuscript of Hardyng's *Chronicle* that seems unknown to modern scholars. Many of these works were written in Latin, some in English. He not only possessed a Latin manuscript of Higden's *Polychronicon*, apparently written by a John Blyth, but also owned Trevisa's translation of the same work in Caxton's print of 1482.[23]

One remarkable feature of Lord William's collection is the number of fine illuminated manuscripts that he possessed. One of these, the Arundel or Eadui Psalter (BL, Arundel 155), dates from the eleventh century; an inscription records that he bought it in 1592 from John Proctor, who had a shop on Holborn Bridge.[24] Other very famous illuminated English manuscripts of the fourteenth century seem to have passed to him as family treasures or heirlooms – for instance, the Luttrell Psalter (BL, Add. 42130) and the Howard-Fitton Psalter (BL, Arundel 83, pt 1).[25] The De Lisle Psalter, which is now attached to this latter manuscript, was possibly acquired by him in 1590.[26] The annotation that characterizes many of Lord William's books is absent from these illuminated manuscripts, and Richard Ovenden has suggested that this may be a mark of his aesthetic appreciation of their beauty.[27] Lord William was certainly deeply interested not only in Roman antiquities, such as the altars and inscribed stones from Hadrian's Wall, but in medieval works of art. Some of the beautiful artefacts that he preserved may be seen in the Victoria and Albert Museum, such as the Langdale Rosary and the Howard Grace Cup – the latter came to him on the death of his uncle, the Earl of Northampton, in 1614.[28] [164] The Household Books also show that he patronized local artists for heraldic works and portraits of his wife and family.[29]

---

[21] Reinmuth, 'Howard and His Catholic Associations', p. 228.

[22] Ovenden, 'Libraries of the Antiquaries', pp. 533 and 543.

[23] *Household Books*, ed. Ornsby, pp. 486, 481; Ovenden and Handley, 'Howard, Lord William (1563–1640)', p. 453.

[24] Ovenden, 'Libraries of the Antiquaries', pp. 539 and 541.

[25] Lord William's ownership inscription occurs on fol. 1 of the Luttrell Psalter, which came to him via the Fitzalan family, Earls of Arundel: see Lucy Freeman Sandler, *Gothic Manuscripts 1390–1490*, 2 vols, *A Survey of Manuscripts Illuminated in the British Isles*, ed. J. J. G. Alexander (London, 1986), V, no. 107. The Howard-Fitton Psalter has an inscription dated 1591: Sandler, *Gothic Manuscripts*, no. 51.

[26] Sandler, *Gothic Manuscripts*, no. 38.

[27] Ovenden, 'Libraries of the Antiquaries', p. 543. It might also be construed as a sign of respect for their sacred character.

[28] *Gothic: Art for England 1400–1547*, ed. Richard Marks and Paul Williamson (London, 2003), nos 222b and 187; Ovenden, 'Libraries', p. 543.

[29] *Household Books*, ed. Ornsby, p. xlix and *passim*.

What is a little disappointing is that, as far as can be seen, Lord William's collection, unlike that of William Drummond of Hawthornden or other literary figures, does not reveal much evidence of a great love of poetry and imaginative literature. One would expect a gentleman's library at this time to have included many of the great classical writers, and certainly Ovid and Virgil. These, however, seem unrecorded. Yet, interestingly, there is evidence of provision for the education of his children, including his daughter Mary, for whom a Latin primer and 'dictionary poeticall' were purchased, when she was fifteen; also a Latin primer, two dictionaries and Aesop's Fables for his grandson.[30]

As far as medieval English poetry is concerned, the apparent absence of the major works of Chaucer is striking. Lord William's name, however, does appear on the first flyleaf of one very large and diverse manuscript miscellany (Bodleian, Rawlinson C. 86); this contains copies of the Prioress's Tale and the Clerk's Tale.[31] He clearly also had an interest in Gower, more specifically the *Confessio Amantis*. He possessed a copy of the printed edition of 1554 (Berthelet), which was signed, together with his motto and a note on the date of purchase in 1587. He also owned a manuscript of 'Gower's old English poems', which may be the same as a fine manuscript of *Confessio Amantis*, formerly at Castle Howard and now in the Newberry Library, Chicago [Case MS 33.5 (Louis H. Silver Collection)].[32] Lord William Howard owned another manuscript described as 'Lydgate's Book of Sapience. In a hand of the fifteenth century. Very neat, with rubrics and illuminated initials'.[33] This important copy of the *Court of Sapience*, which today is not believed to be the work of Lydgate, is bound together with four prose devotional tracts that would have much appealed to Lord William; now usually known as the Plimpton Manuscript (after a twentieth-century owner), it is owned by Columbia University Library, New York [Plimpton 256].[34]

Another poem that Lord William possessed was undoubtedly the work of Lydgate: this was *The Life of St Edmund*, written 'Antiquo Idiomate Anglicano'.[35] Several copies of this long poem are known, but the most splendid is the richly illuminated manuscript presented to Henry VI, now BL, Harley MS 2278. This was in the royal collection in the early sixteenth century, but there is a divergence of opin-[165]ion among modern scholars as to the identity of the man whose signature appears on the last leaf: 'Audelay baron'. I myself find most plausible the view of Cyril E. Wright and Kathleen Scott that this was Thomas, Baron Audley of Walden (1488–1544), the devoted servant and Lord Chancellor of Henry VIII.[36] Nothing definite is known

---

30 *Household Books*, ed. Ornsby, pp. 484, 109, 232, 343.
31 Julia Boffey and Carol Meale, 'Selecting the Text: Rawlinson C.86 and Some Other Books for London Readers', in *Regionalism in Late Medieval Manuscripts and Texts*, ed. Felicity Riddy (Cambridge, 1991), pp. 143–69.
32 Gower's editor, G. C. Macaulay, however, said very positively that the Castle Howard *Confessio* was not the MS at Naworth: *The Complete Works of John Gower*, 4 vols (Oxford, 1899–1902), II, p. cli.
33 *Household Books*, ed. Ornsby, p. 485.
34 *The Court of Sapience*, ed. Ruth Harvey (Toronto, 1984); *NIMEV* 3406.
35 *Household Books*, ed. Ornsby, p. 470.
36 For the view that the inscription belongs to Thomas Audley, Baron Audley of Walden (1488–1544), see Wright, *Fontes Harleiani*, pp. 55–56; Kathleen Scott, *Later Gothic*

of the manuscript's later history until its acquisition by Robert Harley in 1720. But it is intriguing that Baron Audley's daughter and heir became the second wife of the fourth Duke of Norfolk, and was the mother of Lord William. We know that he acquired a number of manuscripts by inheritance from members of his family, and although Harley 2278 does not now bear Lord William's signature or clear marks of his ownership, it is very much in keeping with his taste for English saints' lives and high-quality illuminated manuscripts.

Scottish Books

Lord William Howard could hardly have lived much closer to Scotland, yet there is no evidence that he was acquainted with Scottish antiquaries or men of letters. It is not unlikely, however, that he knew some of those who came to England, such as Patrick Young (1584–1652), the royal librarian. The Household Books record the purchase of a variety of goods from Scotland – white 'flaning' (flannel), coal, wheat and 'a little gray nag' – but no books. By the end of Lord William's life, relations with Scotland were increasingly hostile: in 1636, two of his sons pursued Scottish horse-thieves whom he termed 'notorious offenders' across the Border; and in 1640 the fear of Scottish invasion forced him to leave Naworth for Greystock Castle, where he died. Yet only nine years later, a Scottish visitor, Anne, Lady Halkett, recorded that she was most hospitably received at Naworth by his son and family.[37]

What evidence is there of interest in specifically Scottish books and manuscripts? One striking instance is provided by entries in the Household [166] Books. In 1624 occurs the payment of 3s 6d for 'the Historie of the Queen of Scots', plausibly interpreted as *Vita Mariae Stuartae Reginae Scotorum*, recently published in Rome by George Con, a Scottish priest and chaplain to Henrietta Maria.[38] A few years later, in 1629 a list of 'My Lord's Parcells' includes many payments for books to Humphrey Robinson, the well-known London bookseller and stationer, and mentions another more expensive Life of Mary, Queen of Scots, that cost 40s. Other payments at this time – 'for one payre of spectacles', and 'for a payre of silver frames for spectacles' – poignantly imply Lord William's deteriorating eyesight, as well as his taste for theologians, such as Bellarmine, Pontus and Jansen.[39]

Manuscripts 1390–1490, 2 vols, *A Survey of Manuscripts Illuminated in the British Isles*, ed. J. J. G. Alexander (London, 1996), VI, no. 78; and *Gothic*, ed. Marks and Williamson, no. 318. For the more recent opinion that the inscription is that of John Touchet, eighth Baron Audley (d. 1559), see James Carley, *The Libraries of Henry VIII* (London, 2000), p. 75. He identifies the manuscript as the 'Lyf of Saint Edmonde' in the Westminster Inventory of 1542, no. 290 and conjectures that it must have 'escaped from the royal collection at some point in the fifteenth century to have been acquired by Audley and then presented to Henry, no doubt at the same time as Royal MS 18.DVI (i.e. 1512)'. This argument is accepted by A. S. G. Edwards, *The Life of St Edmund King and Martyr: A Facsimile of British Library MS Harley 2278* (London, 2004), pp. 14–15.

37 *Household Books*, ed. Ornsby, pp. xxxix, 467, 296–97.
38 *Household Books*, ed. Ornsby, p. 223.
39 *Household Books*, ed. Ornsby, pp. 257–58.

Lord William possessed two important yet very different 'Scottish' manuscripts. The first, strictly speaking, is not Scottish but an English or Anglo-Saxon gospel book of Scottish provenance: Bodleian, MS Lat. Liturg. f. 5. The work is thought to have belonged to Margaret, the Anglo-Saxon princess (c. 1046–93), daughter of 'Edward the Exile', who became queen of Malcolm III, and was canonized in 1249. According to the biography of Margaret written by her chaplain, she loved this book more dearly than any other – 'a gospel-book covered all over with jewels and gold, in which pictures of the four evangelists were embellished with paint mixed with gold'. The manuscript long ago lost the treasure binding that this account implies, but still contains fine portraits of the four evangelists. The later history of the manuscript is complicated, but it may have been one of the five gospel books mentioned in a late fourteenth-century inventory of books at Durham cathedral priory. Lord William himself acquired the book from John Stow, and at a much later period it was bequeathed, along with other manuscripts formerly in his possession, to the parish of Brent Eleigh, a small village in Suffolk, from which the Bodleian Library acquired it in 1887.[40] The appeal of this work to Lord William is not difficult to understand. Quite apart from its antiquity and liturgical content, it is a very handsome manuscript and can be grouped with the other remarkable illuminated manuscripts that he owned.

British Library, MS Arundel 285

The second and undoubtedly Scottish manuscript once in Lord William's possession is British Library, MS Arundel 285,[41] one of the least well-known of the great manuscript miscellanies compiled in Scotland in the fifteenth [**167**] and sixteenth centuries. Everyone working in Scottish studies has heard of the Bannatyne Manuscript and, to a lesser extent, of the Selden, Asloan and Maitland Manuscripts.[42] But who, apart from a few distinguished specialists,[43] has paid much attention to the Arundel Manuscript? One factor perhaps is that it has some resemblance to an anonymous poem – it lacks a social context, a 'local habitation and a name'. Indeed

40 Richard Gameson, 'The Gospels of Margaret of Scotland and the Literacy of an Eleventh-Century Queen', in *Women and the Book: Assessing the Visual Evidence*, ed. Lesley Smith and Jane H. M. Taylor (London, 1997), pp. 149–71; Ovenden, 'Libraries of Antiquaries', pp. 540–41; Rebecca Rushforth, *St Margaret's Gospel-Book* (Oxford, 2007).
41 The British Library has provided a detailed description and a digitized copy of MS Arundel 285: http://www.bl.uk/manuscripts/Viewer.aspx?ref=arundel_ms_285_fs001r
42 Priscilla Bawcutt, 'Manuscript Miscellanies from the Fifteenth to the Seventeenth Century', *English Manuscript Studies 1100–1700*, 12 (2005), 46–73. [See a version of this essay herein (6).]
43 *Devotional Pieces in Verse and Prose from MS Arundel 285 and MS Harleian 6919*, ed. J. A. W. Bennett, STS, 3rd ser. 33 (Edinburgh, 1955); J. A. W. Bennett, 'Scottish Pre-Reformation Devotion: Some Notes on British Library MS Arundel 285', in *So Meny People Longages and Tonges: Philological Essays in Scots and English Presented to Angus McIntosh*, ed. Michael Benskin and M. L. Samuels (Edinburgh, 1981), pp. 299–308; and A. A. MacDonald, 'Passion Devotion in Late-Medieval Scotland', in *The Broken Body: Passion Devotion in Late-Medieval Culture*, ed. A. A. MacDonald, H. N. B. Ridderbos and R. M. Schlusemann (Groningen, 1998), pp. 109–31.

in the past it was variously known, sometimes as the Howard Manuscript, sometimes as the Royal Society Manuscript, and as recently as 1925 this confused Sir William Craigie, who spoke of 'Royal Society MS no. 275' as if it were quite different from Arundel 285.[44] We do not know the name of its first owner or compiler, or its precise date. There is no equivalent to picturesque George Bannatyne, chatting about the plague and his 'mankit and mutillait' sources, or Henry, Lord Sinclair, or Sir Richard Maitland. There is no equivalent either to that great publicizer of the Bannatyne Manuscript, Sir Walter Scott. The manuscript is not owned by a Scottish library too, which has often proved a disincentive to study by Scottish scholars. But the most significant drawback about the Arundel Manuscript, certainly in past centuries, was the nature of its contents, which are exclusively Catholic and devotional, something that would not have endeared it to presbyterian readers. Yet in the mid-twentieth century, there began a great revival of interest in the medieval and Catholic past of Scotland, among both historians and literary scholars. One might have expected that the publication of an edition of this manuscript in 1955 by the very distinguished medievalist J. A. W. Bennett would have had much more impact than it did at the time, or seems to have done so far.[45]

What then is the importance of Arundel 285? Although not huge – containing just 244 leaves – it provides, in Bennett's words, the 'most valuable guide to the practices of private devotion observed in Scotland on the eve of the Reformation.'[46] Bennett suggested that it was probably compiled *c.* 1540, largely on watermark evidence. Nothing comparable now survives from Scotland, though there probably once existed several comparable or smaller collections compiled in the Middle Ages and early sixteenth century, only to be discarded or ruthlessly destroyed by the Reformers. In 2000, Steve Boardman and Michael Lynch remarked, with much justification, that earlier historians of the Scottish church showed more interest in ecclesiastical politics than in religion, and called for a proper assessment 'of the nature of popular piety' in late medieval Scotland.[47] Historians interested in the devo-[168]tional sensibility of that period and the religious cults then flourishing in Scotland should pay more attention to this manuscript.

Scottish literary scholars too were slow to recognize the interest of the Arundel manuscript. David Laing was one of the first to draw upon it for his edition of William Dunbar in 1834. The manuscript contains three poems by Dunbar: one is the unique copy of a poem on confession; another is *The Passion of Christ*; the third is *The Tabill of Confessioun*. The Arundel copy of this last poem, although long neglected by editors, is valuable textually, since it contains more orthodox readings, theologically,

44 *The Asloan Manuscript*, ed. William A. Craigie, 2 vols, STS, 2nd ser. 14, 16 (Edinburgh, 1923–25), II, p. viii.

45 *Devotional Pieces*, ed. Bennett; and the review of Bennett's edition by Priscilla Preston [Bawcutt], *Medium Ævum*, 27 (1958), 45–48.

46 *Devotional Pieces*, ed. Bennett, p. xxiv.

47 Steve Boardman and Michael Lynch, 'The State of Late Medieval and Early Modern Scottish History', in *Freedom and Authority: Historiographical Essays Presented to Grant G. Simpson*, ed. Terry Brotherstone and David Ditchburn (East Linton, 2000), pp. 44–59 (50–52).

than those in the Bannatyne and Maitland versions of Dunbar's poem.[48] Arundel 285 also contains the unique text of Walter Kennedy's longest and most important work, *The Passioun of Christ*. Only recently did this poem and its author emerge from the shadow of Dunbar, in the Scottish Text Society's publication of a complete edition of Kennedy.[49] The manuscript contains another complex work, *The Contemplacioun of Synnaris*, by Friar William of Touris, which seems to have been more popular with contemporary readers than any poem by Dunbar or Kennedy, not only in Scotland but in England also.[50] The relationship between the different witnesses requires further investigation, and a good modern edition is highly desirable. There are, in addition, many short anonymous pieces, some resembling and rivalling poems by Dunbar; a few of these are probably better known to English than Scottish readers, since their publication in Carleton Brown's *Religious Lyrics of the Fifteenth Century* in 1939. They include the best version of a well-known Appeal to Man from the Cross, two impressive poems on the Resurrection, and several ornate Marian lyrics.

Arundel 285 also contains many prose prayers and meditations, largely focusing on the Passion, and 'orisounis' in honour of the Virgin Mary. Bennett's observations on the prose texts have great value, but after fifty years there is room for further investigation of their sources and of many other aspects of the manuscript. One weakness of his edition is that it lacks a glossary, and little is said of the language of the individual pieces.[51] The distinguished lexicographer A. J. Aitken, not surprisingly, had interesting things to say on this topic. One of the poems in rough octosyllabics, the *Fifteen Ois*, is a passion devotion on the last words of Jesus on the Cross.[52] [**169**] There is no known source for this, apart from the prayer in Latin, although other vernacular versions exist in prose (by Caxton) and verse (by Lydgate). Aitken argued that it was the most ancient piece of Scottish verse in the collection, and indeed the oldest known Scottish devotional poem. He noted numerous signs of archaism in the language, such as the rare adverb *tholmudlie* (331), 'patiently'; and other usages in diction, rhymes, and relative pronouns that suggest an early date. He concluded that the language 'agrees' with that of Andrew Wyntoun.[53]

Another prose piece raises very interesting questions, concerning its source and date. This is 'The Lang Rosair', the last item in the concluding section of the manuscript, which is devoted to praise and worship of the Virgin Mary. It consists of prayers to the Virgin, arranged in five decades or groups of ten, interspersed with longer prayers, each followed by the Pater Noster. Bennett noted a general

---

[48] For more detailed information on these texts: *The Poems of William Dunbar*, ed. Priscilla Bawcutt, 2 vols, ASLS, 27, 28 (Glasgow, 1998), I, pp. 136–38 (B 41); pp. 34–38 (B 1); and pp. 261–73 (B 83).

[49] *The Poems of Walter Kennedy*, ed. Nicole Meier, STS, 5th ser. 15 (Woodbridge, 2008).

[50] A. A. MacDonald, 'Political and Religious Instruction in an Eschatological Perspective: *The Contemplacioun of Synnaris* of William of Touris', in *Calliope's Classroom: Studies in Didactic Poetry from Antiquity to the Renaissance*, ed. Annette Harder, Alasdair A. MacDonald and Gerrit J. Reinink (Leuven, 2007), pp. 269–92.

[51] See the Preston [Bawcutt] review of *Devotional Pieces*, *Medium Ævum*, 27 (1958), 45–48.

[52] *Devotional Pieces*, ed. Bennett, pp. 170–81; cf. *IMEV* (1943), 3777.5; TM 1758.

[53] A. J. Aitken, 'A Sixteenth-Century Scottish Devotional Anthology' [review of Bennett, *Devotional Pieces*, 1955], *Scottish Historical Review*, 36.122, part 2 (1957), 147–50 (149).

resemblance to other rosaries, but found no specific source.[54] Mary Erler, however, has pointed out that there exists a printed work to which the Arundel 'Rosary' has a very close verbal resemblance indeed.[55] This is *The Rosary / with the articles of the lyfe and deth of Jesu Chryst / and peticions directe to our Lady*, printed in London in 1537 by John Skot (*STC* 17545.5). This Skot was a different printer from the man of the same name who worked in Edinburgh. The similarities between the two texts are so great that they enable one to solve textual problems in Arundel 285 and supply missing words. One small illustration out of many may be given here. On folio 216^r of the manuscript, there is an obvious absurdity in the text of a petition, which – as is evident if one compares the version in the print – was caused by eyeskip from the first use of 'fynde hym' to a second occurrence, a few lines later:

> Blissit mothir of God, quhome þow did tyne thre dais in Ieruselem, þe tyme of þe pilgramage, and socht him with gret sorrow, and finalie did find him agane in þe kirk of God, be trew confessioun, to my perpetuall consolacioun.[56]

> Blyssed mother of God / whom thou dyd lese thre dayes in Ierusalem the tyme of thy pylgrymage / and sought hym with greate sorowe / and fynally dydest fynde hym in þe temple disputyng with sage doctours / praye for me that I may kepe my soule in the estate of grace. And if I lese [170] hym in any place by deedly synne deseruing dampnacion I may fynde hym agayne in the chirche of god by true [c]onfessyon to my perpetuall consolacyon.

Skot's print, The Rosary, sigs 7^v–8^r.

At first, it seems that we have here a small piece of evidence that might assist in dating the whole manuscript: one might surmise that it was compiled some time after 1537. But, alas, things are not so clear cut. Elsewhere in Skot's print (between sigs 8^r and 9^v), a passage breaks off mid-sentence and lacks three petitions, whereas at the same point the Arundel Manuscript (fols 216^v–217^r)[57] makes good sense and seems complete. One possible explanation is that the 1537 print – of which a sole copy survives in the John Rylands Library, Manchester – represents a defective reprint of an earlier publication by Skot that no longer exists. But, in fact, the textual situation is much more complicated. 'The Rosary' would clearly have been a very desirable text in the 1520s and 1530s in both England and Scotland,[58] and Skot's print had at least two (and possibly more) fore-runners.[59] One of these, the earliest known to me was printed *c.* 1525 at Antwerp by William Vorstermann (*STC* 17544). It is a tiny 16mo book, copiously illustrated, with a very similar title page to Skot's, but the prayers are much briefer, so as to accommodate an image on every page. Yet another 'Rosary in English' was printed by Robert Copland in 1531 (*STC* 17545); my impression is

---

54 *Devotional Pieces*, ed. Bennett, p. xxiii.
55 Robert Copland, *Poems*, ed. Mary C. Erler (Toronto, 1993), pp. 146–47.
56 *Devotional Pieces*, ed. Bennett, p. 325.
57 *Devotional Pieces*, ed. Bennett, pp. 325–26.
58 David McRoberts, 'The Rosary in Scotland', *Innes Review*, 23 (1972), 80–86.
59 All of these prints are available in *Early English Books Online*.

that of the three surviving printed texts this one seems most closely to match the wording of Arundel 285.

Copland's 'Rosary' belongs to a series of small devotional tracts that he published in London between 1522 and 1531; they include other prayers closely related to pieces in Arundel 285, such as the 'Golden Litany' and 'The Psalter of Jesus'.[60] A collection of these tracts is bound together, and [is now held by Aberdeen University Library, (SC) BCL S86 (1–9)]. Unfortunately it is not known how early they were bound in this way, nor precisely when they came to Scotland, although one tract, 'The XV Oos', has an inscription, 'Jean Gordon', that might belong to the sixteenth century.[61] The relation of the Copland tracts to Arundel 285 seems to require further [171] investigation, not only because they provide possible sources or analogues for some of their pieces, but because they and the other prints mentioned earlier also provide the kind of social context for the manuscript that is otherwise lacking. They suggest how strong and how widespread was the demand among pious people of both sexes for these devotional writings in the vernacular throughout Britain in the early sixteenth century.

The overall structure of Arundel 285 also requires more attention than is possible here. According to Bennett, much about the manuscript suggests that its 'copyist was trained in a monastic scriptorium'.[62] This may be true, but I think it is likely to have been compiled for a lay owner rather than a churchman. Its contents are solely in the vernacular, apart from occasional brief Latin phrases in rubrics, such as 'the orisoun callit O clementissime'.[63] Nothing indicates that it was destined for a royal or aristocratic owner. Yet, although not a deluxe manuscript, it does not lack decoration: titles and colophons are usually in red; the beginning of a poem or prayer is often indicated by the use of tall, flourished capitals; and, what is most interesting of all, there are seventeen woodcuts pasted at intervals throughout the manuscript, often marking the beginning of an item. A woodcut of the Scourging [fol. 5^v] thus prefaces Kennedy's *The Passioun of Crist*. This particular woodcut derives from a devotional work printed in Antwerp c. 1505; another has been traced to a work printed in 1510; and a third – with a fine design – has German words on the back, though its source has not been traced.[64]

The woodcuts form one of the most striking and original features of Arundel 285. It can be classed as a 'hybrid', one of those books produced in the late fifteenth and early sixteenth centuries that, in the words of David McKitterick, 'sat, as it were, halfway, part-print, part manuscript'.[65] The tradition of embellishing manuscripts with woodcuts or engravings was particularly strong in Germany and the Low Countries, but there are a number of English examples, several associated with

---

[60] *Devotional Pieces*, ed. Bennett, p. ix.

[61] [For this tract, see Aberdeen University Library, (SC) BCL S86(8).]

[62] *Devotional Pieces*, ed. Bennett, p. ii.

[63] *Devotional Pieces*, ed. Bennett, p. 279.

[64] *Devotional Pieces*, ed. Bennett, pp. xxxii–xxxv.

[65] Review by David McKitterick of *The Woodcut in Fifteenth-Century Europe*, ed. Peter Parshall (2009), *Times Literary Supplement*, 26 February 2010, p. 26.

the Carthusian monastery of Syon.[66] Most of these books, like Arundel 285, are devotional in character – this is not surprising, since the reverent contemplation of an image of Jesus or the Virgin was an important focus for prayer and meditation. For another contemporary Scottish example, one might compare the images in BL, Harley MS 6919, which contains *The Contemplacioun of Synnaris*; these are pen drawings, of course, but possibly derive from engravings.[67] Some of these woodcuts were cut out of books, but others are known to have circulated independently for sale to the devout. Scholars in various disciplines are [172] paying increasing attention to the use, circulation and sources of woodcuts, and this is an aspect of Arundel 285 that would repay investigation.

Conclusion

How did Lord William Howard acquire this manuscript? It is plausible to wonder whether it might have come from the Dacres, with whom he had a double link, through his wife and step-mother, both of whom were named Elizabeth. As Richard Ovenden notes, 'the acquisition of the Dacre estates ... brought new sources of books'.[68] But the only manuscripts from this source of which I am aware are not literary in character – the *Lanercost Cartulary* (now in Cumbria County Record Office), and the *Rotulum of Newminster*.[69] Yet the Dacres had many contacts with Scotland in the fifteenth and sixteenth centuries, some hostile, some amicable. There was an interesting friendship between Gavin Douglas and Thomas Dacre of Gilsland, Warden of the West March, that seems to have been more than a matter of mutual self-interest, and one that survived Flodden. When Douglas died in London in 1522, he was staying in Dacre's house.[70] Similar links and contacts with Scotland in the next generation might have led to the acquisition of the Arundel manuscript by a later member of the Dacre family.

This, however, is no more than speculation, and it seems most probable that Lord William either purchased Arundel 285 or acquired it from a friend. If so, he is likely to have been attracted by the illustrations, even though they are not of exceptional beauty; the devotional subject matter; and the sheer utility of the contents to a practising Catholic. We should never forget that the Arundel manuscript was designed not for a single reading but for repeated, perhaps daily use. It is possible, I think, that Lord William did not realize – at first glance anyway – that the work was Scottish. He may have thought it was written in the northern dialect of English, with which he would be familiar from personal experience. He possessed other northern English works – one example is the fifteenth-century 'Life of St Cuthbert in English meeter' that was mentioned earlier. It is perhaps worth stressing that although the

---

[66] Mary C. Erler, 'Pasted-In Embellishments in English Manuscripts and Printed Books *c*.1480–1533', *The Library*, 6th ser. 14.3 (1992), 185–206 (188); Nigel Palmer, 'Blockbooks, Woodcut and Metalcut Single Sheets', in *A Catalogue of Books Printed in the Fifteenth Century Now in the Bodleian Library*, ed. Alan Coates et al. (Oxford, 2005), I, pp. 1–6.

[67] *Devotional Pieces*, ed. Bennett, p. xxxv.

[68] Ovenden, 'Libraries of the Antiquaries', pp. 547–48.

[69] *Household Books*, ed. Ornsby, pp. lix–lx.

[70] Priscilla Bawcutt, *Gavin Douglas: A Critical Study* (Edinburgh, 1976), pp. 3 and 21.

texts in Arundel 285 are undoubtedly written in Scots, it is, for the most part, in a formal linguistic register that lacks the striking 'low-life' and vernacular Scotticisms that stud Dunbar's *Flyting*.

Whoever compiled this devout devotional work lacked the self-conscious linguistic patriotism of Gavin Douglas, who proclaimed that his translation [**173**] of Virgil was 'Writtin in the langage of Scottis natioun' (*Eneados*, I Prol.103).[71] He is content to follow the older terminology, and thus describes various items as written 'in Inglis': so 'Ane deuoit orisoun till our Lady in Inglis' [fol. 183ᵛ].[72] Even Walter Kennedy says in the Prologue to *The Passioun of Crist* that he is writing 'in Inglis toung' (l. 53). There is nothing remotely nationalistic about this manuscript unless one so regards the inclusion of Saint Giles in a list of universal saints [fol. 124ᵛ].[73] The liturgical references might possibly have displeased James IV or Bishop Elphinstone, since they appear to derive from Sarum, not 'our awin Scottis use'. The compiler of Arundel 285, like the poets Henryson and Dunbar, thus shows no sign of the 'visceral Anglophobia' said to have been prevalent among their compatriots.[74] My impression is that he was supremely uninterested in what is now termed Scottish national identity, and would have regarded it as trivial and unimportant beside the practice and celebration of his faith.

Editorial Note

[a] First published in *Textual Cultures*, 7 (2012), 158–75. Reprinted with the kind permission of *Textual Cultures* and Dr Marta Werner.

---

[71] *Virgil's 'Aeneid' Translated into Scottish Verse by Gavin Douglas*, ed. D. F. C. Coldwell, 4 vols, STS, 3rd Ser. 25, 27, 28, 20 (Edinburgh, 1957–64), II, p. 6.

[72] *Devotional Pieces*, ed. Bennett, p. 283.

[73] *Devotional Pieces*, ed. Bennett, pp. ix and 212.

[74] Roger A. Mason, *Kingship and the Commonweal: Political Thought in Renaissance and Reformation Scotland* (East Linton, 1998), p. 87.

12

Gavin Douglas's *Eneados*:
The 1553 Edition and its Early Owners and Readers

The *Eneados* is Gavin Douglas's longest and most impressive work.[a] A translation of Virgil's *Aeneid*, together with the so-called 'Thirteenth Book' composed by the humanist Maffeo Vegio, it was completed in 1513, while Douglas was provost of St Giles in Edinburgh. Five good manuscripts of the work are extant, all written within forty years of its completion; the earliest and best of these, now owned by Trinity College, Cambridge (MS O.3.12), was written by Douglas's secretary, Matthew Geddes, and provides the basis for David Coldwell's edition for the Scottish Text Society.[1] Scholarly study of the text of the *Eneados* has largely been confined to these manuscripts. But there also survives an edition of the poem, printed at London in 1553 and attributed to the press of William Copland (henceforth 1553), which until recently has received little attention from scholars and strikingly unfavourable assessments. According to Coldwell, it is 'remarkable for its inaccuracies, its partial Anglicizing of the spelling, and its Protestantism' (I, pp, 101–02).[2] Nonetheless, despite its undoubted deficiencies, 1553 has great historical significance. It was published only a few years after the last [74] manuscript of the *Eneados* was completed in November 1547, and it disseminated much wider awareness of the work in the second half of the sixteenth century. What is more, the influence of 1553 continued into later centuries, and may still be detected in subsequent editions of the *Eneados*, such as those of Thomas Ruddiman (1710) and John Small (1874). The present chapter begins with a brief account of the leading characteristics of 1553, but its chief aim is to provide new information about its circulation and readership.

Douglas was much better known during the sixteenth century than Dunbar or Henryson. There is ample evidence to confirm the truth of his prophecy that the *Eneados* would be widely read: 'Throw owt the ile yclepit Albyon / Red sall I be, and sung with mony one' (*Conclusio*, 11–12). Various factors, apart from its poetic excellence, may have contributed to the success of the *Eneados*, such as Douglas's bishopric and his noble birth, as son of one earl of Angus, and uncle to another. Both

---

[1]   See *Virgil's 'Aeneid' Translated into Scottish Verse by Gavin Douglas*, ed. D. F. C. Coldwell, 4 vols, STS, 3rd ser. 30, 25, 27, 28 (Edinburgh, 1957–64). A new and much revised edition of this work has been prepared for the Scottish Text Society by Priscilla Bawcutt and Ian Cunningham. For information about Douglas's life and cultural background, see Priscilla Bawcutt, *Gavin Douglas: A Critical Study* (Edinburgh, 1976).

[2]   References to Coldwell's edition are embedded in the text, either by volume and page (chiefly for the Introduction), or by book, chapter and line (for the translation itself).

of these, revealingly, are mentioned on the title page of 1553: 'THE | xiii Bukes of Eneados of | the famose Poete Virgill | Translatet out of Latyne verses into Scottish me- | tir, bi the Reuerend Fa- | ther in God, May- | ster Gawin Douglas | Bishop of Dunkel, & | vnkil to the Erle | of Angus. Euery | buke hauing hys | perticular | Prologe.' The attribution of this print – a blackletter quarto (*STC* 24797) – to William Copland rests on the evidence of printing types and the close similarity of its title page to his later edition of Douglas's *Palice of Honour* (*STC* 7073).³ The title page of *The Palice of Honour* bears the slogan 'God saue Quene Marye', but 1553 contains no such profession of loyalty to the new monarch, and it is arguable that the date of publication might possibly be narrowed to the first half of the year, in the last months of the reign of Edward VI, who died on 6 July 1553.

The Protestantism for which 1553 is notorious is evident chiefly in the excision of Douglas's references to the Virgin Mary in a number of the Prologues. One instance out of many that may be mentioned is the replacement of a line containing an invocation of Mary – 'Be my laid star, virgyne moder but maik' – by an appeal to Christ: 'Be my lede stere, Christ goddis sone but maik' (III.Prol.42). The doctrine of Purgatory was a similarly sensitive issue: a whole stanza devoted to Purgatory and Limbo (VI.Prol.89–96) is thus omitted in 1553.⁴ But such major modifications of Douglas's text are not confined to religion. There are additions of other new material, notably six lines of verse inserted within Douglas's discussion of Aeneas in Prologue I, between lines 330 and 331. It is likely that whoever composed this passage was also responsible for the numerous notes that are printed in the margins of [**75**] 1553 and have no equivalent in the manuscripts. They are used by their author to provide an elementary commentary on the sense and rhetorical features of the *Aeneid*, laying much stress on the exemplary character of Aeneas: he is a paragon of virtue, an 'exampill and myrrour to euerye prince and nobyl man' (I.Prol.380).⁵ The 1553 edition further departs from the manuscript tradition in another important respect. All the manuscripts have an anomalous and unexplained arrangement of the text: Book II, for instance, begins at *Aeneid* II, line 13, Book VI at VI, line 9, Book VII at VII, line 25, and Book VIII at VIII, line 18. The edition of 1553, however, follows the long-established structure of the *Aeneid*.⁶

All these changes to Douglas's text – excising abhorrent traces of papistical belief and doctrine, placing greater emphasis on the nobility of Aeneas, and re-inserting the traditional book-divisions of the *Aeneid* – seem to represent a conscious editorial policy on the part of Copland. But it is a mistake, I think, to believe that Douglas's

---

3 On Copland's edition of *The Palice of Honour*, see Priscilla Bawcutt, 'Introduction', in *The Shorter Poems of Gavin Douglas*, ed. Priscilla Bawcutt, 2nd edn, STS, 5th ser. 2 (Edinburgh, 2003), pp. xvi–xviii.

4 For further instances of Protestant changes, see Coldwell, I, p. 102.

5 For an interesting discussion of the printed marginal notes, see Jane Griffiths, 'Exhortations to the Reader: The Glossing of Douglas's *Eneados* in Cambridge, Trinity College MS O.3.12', *English Manuscript Studies 1100–1700*, 15 (2009), 185–97; and Jane Griffiths, *Diverting Authorities: Experimental Glossing Practices in Manuscript and Print* (Oxford, 2014), pp. 81–102.

6 Scholarly discussion of this topic has been sparse, but see *Eneados*, ed. Coldwell, I, 54; and Bawcutt, *Gavin Douglas*, pp. 139–40.

language was similarly subjected by him to a deliberate programme for change, and systematically anglicized. Such anglicization seems less a fact than an assumption. In the same way, it was long erroneously believed that the spelling of Copland's *Palice of Honour* was 'more Southron' than that in the Edinburgh edition of 1579.[7] In fact 1553 usually preserves Douglas's distinctive vocabulary, and also retains many of the striking features of Scots spelling and grammar, such as *quh-* for English *wh-*, *-cht* for English *-ght*, *scho* for *she* and present participles ending in *-and*. The language of the marginalia likewise has Scottish characteristics, both in spelling and grammar. Copland's exemplar is not known, but – whether it was a manuscript or even, conjec- turally, a lost Scottish print – he probably reproduced its language much as he found it. The *Eneados* must have been brought to his attention by a Scottish intermediary, and one might conjecture that a Scot who shared Copland's religious sympathies was also involved in its 'editing', or preparation for the press.

Not all copies of 1553 are identical. Some have an extra leaf in gathering X, numbered as fol. clxiii. There is no mention of this by Coldwell, but John Small speaks of 'a separate leaf … afterwards cancelled'.[8] In fact it is the copies without the extra leaf that are defective, since they lack the last two lines of Prologue VII and sixty-eight lines of the first chapter of the following book. [**76**] (It should be noted that this corresponds in the manuscripts not to VII, chapter i, but to VI, chapter xvi, because of their different arrangement of the text within the books.) The error was recognized and corrected by the insertion of a new leaf, but this created a substantial area of empty space. This was then filled by a prose passage, which is interesting in itself but has no authorial justification. (It is available in Coldwell's textual notes at III, pp. 300–01.) There are other omissions of text which do not appear to have been noticed by the printers. One of these is a small section of Book IV. Small suggested that Copland 'from motives of delicacy omits the account of the adventures of Dido and Aeneas' (I, p. clxxix), but this is unconvincing. The omission is so clumsy – it runs across two chapters from IV.iv.65 to IV.v.42 – that it seems to be an accident, perhaps caused by turning over two pages of the copy text rather than one.

The impact of 1553, which appeared just as the manuscript tradition of the *Eneados* was coming to an end, is still not fully recognized. In the first half of the sixteenth century, the *Eneados* circulated chiefly in Scotland. It was dedicated by Douglas to his friend and patron Henry, Lord Sinclair, in the hope 'That Virgill mycht intill our langage be / Red lowd and playn be ʒour lordschip and me, / And other gentill companʒeonys quha sa lyst' (*Directioun*, 85–87; Coldwell, IV, p. 190); it was later owned and copied by minor churchmen, notaries public, lawyers and other members of the Scottish professional classes. The one sign of English awareness of the poem during this period is its influence upon the translations of *Aeneid II* and *IV* by Henry Howard, Earl of Surrey. Since Surrey was executed in 1547, he must have had access to a manuscript.[9] The 1553 print, however, introduced the *Eneados* to a much wider audience, not only in England – as might be expected, given that it was printed in

---

7   See *Shorter Poems of Gavin Douglas*, ed. Bawcutt, pp. xvi–xxvii.

8   See *The Poetical Works of Gavin Douglas*, ed. John Small, 4 vols (Edinburgh, 1874), I, p. clxxx. Further references are given parenthetically.

9   On Surrey's indebtedness to Douglas, which has been much discussed by scholars, see *Henry Howard, Earl of Surrey: Poems*, ed. Emrys Jones (Oxford, 1964), pp. xi–xx, 134–40.

London – but in Scotland also. This may be illustrated in a variety of ways. John Bale's first version of his catalogue of British authors, published in 1548, reveals only a vague knowledge of Douglas's poetry. But his revised and updated version, *Scriptorum Illustrium Majoris Britanniae ... Catalogus* (1559), though far from accurate, is very much better informed, and its entry on Douglas's translation ensured that 1553 entered the later bibliographical tradition.[10] Precisely when 1553 reached Scotland is not known, but it supplied George Bannatyne with [77] three items in his celebrated manuscript anthology, which was completed in 1568. Bannatyne placed eighteen lines of Prologue IX in the moral section of his compilation, Prologue X in the 'ballatis of theoligie' and Prologue IV in the 'Ballatis of luve', and was sufficiently impressed by the marginal notes printed in this edition to draw upon them for his own titles. Prologue IV is thus described as 'Treting of the Incommoditie of luve and Remeid thairof'.[11] The mention of 'fyue Virgilis in Inglis' in a Scottish bookseller's inventory dated 1577 might perhaps refer to Douglas's translation, but it is too vague to be conclusive.[12]

The varied Elizabethan response to the *Eneados*, in the years following its appearance in print, has already been documented by scholars: its influence is visible in Thomas Sackville's Induction to *The Mirror for Magistrates*, which first appeared in 1563; in the same year, Barnabe Googe commended Douglas's 'famous wit in Scottish ryme'; in 1584 Thomas Twyne found fault with the dream vision that introduces Book XIII, and a few years later in 1589 George Puttenham objected to Douglas's use of the word 'fugitive' to describe Aeneas.[13] One of the most thoughtful criticisms of the *Eneados* in this period, however, is perhaps less familiar and should be better known. It comes from the Scottish author, David Hume of Godscroft (1559–1629), who was a remarkably sensitive and wide-ranging reader, as familiar with the classics as with the poetry of his contemporaries Sidney and Daniel. His comments on the *Eneados* cannot be dated precisely, because they occur first in a posthumously printed work, *The History of the Houses of Douglas and Angus* (1644). The Prologues, interestingly, are singled out for special commendation:

> In his Prologues before every Book, where he hath his libertie, he sheweth
> a naturall, and ample vein of of poesie, so pure, pleasant, and judicious, that
> I beleeve there is none that hath written before, or since, but cometh short

---

[10] On Bale's awareness of Douglas and his influence on later cataloguers, see William Geddie, *A Bibliography of Middle Scots Poets*, STS, 1st ser. 61 (Edinburgh, 1912), pp. xliii–liii; and Priscilla Bawcutt, 'Crossing the Border: Scottish Poetry and English Readers in the Sixteenth Century', in *The Rose and the Thistle: Essays on the Culture of Late Medieval and Renaissance Scotland*, ed. Sally Mapstone and Juliette Wood (East Linton, 1998), pp. 59–76 (60–62).

[11] See *The Bannatyne Manuscript*, ed. W. Tod Ritchie, 4 vols, STS, 3rd ser. 5, 22, 23, 26 (Edinburgh, 1928–32), II, p. 113; II, pp. 20–26; and IV, pp. 108–116.

[12] Cf. F. S. Ferguson, 'Relations between London and Edinburgh Printers and Stationers (–1640)', *The Library*, ser. 4, 8.2 (1927), 145–98 (159).

[13] See, for instance, Geddie, *Bibliography*, pp. 235–37; George Puttenham, *The Arte of English Poesie*, ed. Gladys Doidge Willcock and Alice Walker (Cambridge, 1936), pp. 273–74; Bawcutt, *Gavin Douglas*, pp. 197–201.

of him. And in my opinion, there is not such a piece to be found, as is his Prologue to the 8. Book.

It is evident that Hume was using the 1553 print rather than a manuscript, since he later complained that the text is not 'rightly printed and corrected'.[14] [**78**]

1553 had a remarkably long-lasting influence upon the editing of the *Eneados*. It may be detected in the edition attributed to Thomas Ruddiman (1710), which is now justifiably regarded as a landmark of Scottish publishing. The title page proclaims that it is 'a new edition wherein the many errors of the former [that is, 1553] are corrected, and the defects supply'd from an excellent manuscript'. According to the Preface, this manuscript – in fact the Ruthven manuscript [Dc.1.43] owned by Edinburgh University Library – was not discovered until the first forty-five pages were in print; these, and much else in the volume, including the side notes and other material, derive directly from 1553.[15] This is no less true of Small's edition of the *Eneados* (1874), which departs repeatedly from the Elphinstoun Manuscript [EUL, MS Dk.7.49] on which it is said to be based. Small, like Ruddiman, follows 1553 in several respects, not only reinstating the traditional book divisions of the *Aeneid* but also including other features, such as the extraneous lines of verse in Prologue I and what he calls the 'quaint side-notes' (Small, I, p. clxxx).

Many early Scottish poems famous today, such as Robert Henryson's *Fables*, now survive only in manuscript fragments or single copies of prints,[16] but a surprisingly large number of copies of the 1553 *Eneados* are still extant. It is quite mistaken to call it 'one of the scarcest books in Scottish poetry'.[17] In addition to those listed in *STC*, many more are owned by private collectors or various great libraries, principally in Britain and the United States. It is well known that annotations in multiple copies of a single book may provide a valuable supplement to knowledge of its early circulation and reception. Most of the copies of 1553, however, are widely dispersed, and many are not easily accessible. This chapter is largely based on my examination of copies owned by the major scholarly libraries of England and Scotland. But I have, in addition, received images or useful descriptions of other copies through the courtesy of friends, librarians and one very generous private collector. Although this body of evidence is small and far from complete, it usefully enlarges our knowledge of who was handling (if not necessarily closely reading) the *Eneados* in the sixteenth and early seventeenth centuries.

Some early owners of 1553 are little more than names. This is true, sadly, of the two women, probably Scottish but otherwise unidentified, who inscribed 'Anna Gordon' and 'Ianet Williamsone' on the copy owned by the Elizabethan Club (no.

---

[14] For the full text of Hume's comments on Douglas, see *David Hume of Godscroft's The History of the House of Angus*, ed. David Reid, 2 vols, STS, 4th ser. 25, 26 (Edinburgh, 2005), I, pp. 27–28 and II, pp. 477–78.

[15] On Ruddiman's editing, see Douglas Duncan's excellent *Thomas Ruddiman: A Study in Scottish Scholarship of the Early Eighteenth Century* (Edinburgh, 1965).

[16] On early printed texts of the *Fables*, see *The Poems of Robert Henryson*, ed. Denton Fox (Oxford, 1981), pp. l–lvi.

[17] See the unsigned note, 'A Copy of Douglas's *Eneados*', *Studies in Scottish Literature*, 3.3 (1965), 176.

235), at Yale.[18] Little is known for certain about the John Mason [**79**] who donated a copy to Corpus Christi College, Oxford (Δ.12.1), probably in the early seventeenth century, but it seems likely that he was the student of that college who graduated BA in 1599.[19] Another copy, now owned by the National Library of Scotland (H 29.b.53), has a title page with the inscription 'Thomas Duncombe his booke: Amen'. Although he has not been identified, the name sounds English. The same book contains a second inscription in a different and later hand (sig. C8ʳ): 'Thomas Baker is my name and with my pen I wrote this same.'[20] The interest of this is chiefly generic, since parallels to this doggerel rhyme may be found in modern autograph albums and other books: for example, 'Philip Morrey is my name / And with my pen I write the same.'[21] Such inscriptions, which may be designed to deter thieves or simply to celebrate the pleasure of ownership, have a long history. A medieval Bible that is also owned by the National Library of Scotland once belonged to a Scottish notary from Dumfries (fl. 1600), who inscribed it 'Thomas McBurnie with my hand / the worst wryttar in ony land.'[22]

It is possible to say more about other early owners of 1553. Particularly interesting, in view of its early date, is the inscription 'E Layfield 1559', which occurs on the title page of one of two copies now in Innerpeffray Library (Scottish Collection, A 3). This owner is very likely to be the Edward Layfield who was a Cambridge graduate, Fellow of St Catherine's College (c. 1550), rector of Fulham, and prebendary of St Paul's Cathedral from 1575 till his death in 1583.[23] The copy that now belongs to Trinity College, Cambridge (Capell O.2), was presented to the college by the eighteenth-century Shakespeare scholar, Edward Capell (1713–81). An inscription on the title page shows however that its first owner was called 'Wylliam Belasyse'. He is most probably to be identified with the Sir William Belasise (c. 1524–1604) whose main estates were in Yorkshire, who was appointed High Sheriff of York in 1574, and whose funeral monument may be seen in Coxwold parish church.[24] [**80**] William Belasise belonged to a prosperous and upwardly mobile landed family, but I am not aware of further evidence of his cultural tastes. Much more is known about the literary interests of the Thynne family, and in particular those of John Thynne (1512/13–80), who amassed huge estates in the south-west of England, and was the builder of

[18] According to the Yale catalogue, nothing is known of this copy's provenance.
[19] I am grateful to Sebastiaan Verweij, who informed me of this and other copies of 1553 in Oxford college libraries. On Mason, see Joseph Foster, *Alumni Oxonienses: The Members of the University of Oxford 1500–1714*, 4 vols (Oxford, 1891), III, p. 983.
[20] The NLS catalogue reads the surname differently as 'Batir'.
[21] Quoted and discussed in Kevin J. Hayes, *Folklore and Book Culture* (Knoxville, TN, 1997), pp. 89–90.
[22] Edinburgh, NLS, Adv. MS 18.1.2, fol. 288ᵛ. On Thomas McBurnie, see Priscilla Bawcutt, 'The Contents of the Bannatyne Manuscript: New Sources and Analogues', *Journal of the Edinburgh Bibliographical Society*, 3 (2008), 95–133 (108). [See this essay herein.]
[23] See John and J. A. Venn, *Alumni Cantabrigienses*, 8 vols (Cambridge, 1922–54), III, p. 58.
[24] For more details, see W. W. Greg, *Catalogue of Books ... Presented by Edward Capell to Trinity College Library, Cambridge* (Cambridge, 1903), p. 156; and Christine M. Newman, 'Bellasis Family (c.1500–1653)', *ODNB Online*, doi.org./10.10993/ref:odnb/71863.

Longleat House.[25] Among the Longleat archives is an unpublished inventory, entitled 'Sr. John Thinnes books at Longeleate', which was compiled in 1577 (Thynne Papers, 2nd series, 240 01/09/1577). One item runs: 'virgills eneodes in skotishe verse by galbin [sic] douglas'. Kate Harris, the archivist, considers that it is most likely that this refers to the Longleat copy of 1553 (cat. no. 14333), not the fine manuscript of the *Eneados* (MS 252 A), which possibly came to the library at a later date.[26] She points out that the 1577 inventory normally describes manuscripts as 'written'. An interesting example is the Longleat manuscript of John Bellenden's translation of Hector Boece's *History of Scotland* (MS 96): stolen by Thynne from Edinburgh during the English invasion of 1544, as he himself acknowledges on a flyleaf, it is described in the inventory as 'A skottishe cronickll wrighten in skottisshe in wrighten hande'.

A particularly interesting signature occurs on the flyleaf of the copy owned by the Pepys Library, Magdalene College, Cambridge (Print 1652): 'Ed. Waterhous: et amicorum'. Edward Waterhouse (1535–91), who was knighted in 1584, was a friend and correspondent of Sir Philip Sidney and spent much of his career as a distinguished public servant and administrator in Ireland, acting for a time as secretary to Philip's father, Sir Henry Sidney.[27] The words *et amicorum* were a humanistic tag, chiefly employed in the sixteenth century by those who owned learned works written in Latin or Greek.[28] Its use here suggests that Waterhouse placed a high value on the *Eneados*, and was ready to share the book with like-minded friends. A rather different light on Waterhouse's varied literary interests is shed by two manuscripts in the British Library. He was the owner of a collection of Middle English devotional prose texts (MS Harley 1740), and his name also occurs several times – along with those of other persons – in MS Harley 7334. This copy of *The Canterbury Tales* seems [81] to have had several owners in the sixteenth century, but circulated in the late 1550s among a group of young people, who occasionally inscribed its margins with what today might be termed sexual 'banter': so 'Mistress Kimpton is like to have an ill name by Mr Waterhous but she cares not a [?turd]' (81ʳ).[29]

One cultured Scottish owner was the poet William Drummond of Hawthornden, who in 1628 donated his copy, along with many other books, to Edinburgh University Library (De.4.32); a cancelled inscription on the title page shows that it had previously been owned by a 'Iames Levingston'. Disappointingly, it contains no annotations, such as appear in Drummond's copy of *The Faerie Queen*.[30] Edinburgh University Library

---

25 See Mark Girouard, 'Sir John Thynne (1512/13–1580)', *ODNB Online*, doi.org/10.1093/ref:odnb/27421.

26 I am extremely grateful to Dr Harris, who first told me of this inventory. Further information is provided by [John Collins], *A Short Account of the Library at Longleat House, Warminster, Wilts* (London, 1980), pp. 5–7.

27 See Andrew Lyall, 'Sir Edward Waterhouse (1535–1591)', *ODNB Online*, doi.org/10.1093/ref:odnb/28819; and *The Correspondence of Sir Philip Sidney*, ed. Roger Kuin, 2 vols (Oxford, 2012), II, p. 835.

28 See G. D. Hobson, 'Et Amicorum', *The Library*, ser. 5, 4.2 (1949), 87–99.

29 For the details, see The British Library's catalogue, *Explore Archives and Manuscripts*, MS Harley 1740 and MS Harley 7334; also J. M. Manly and E. Rickert, *The Text of the Canterbury Tales*, 8 vols (Chicago, IL, 1940), I, pp. 225–30.

30 On Drummond, see the Robert H. MacDonald, *The Library of Drummond of Hawthornden* (Edinburgh, 1971); and Alastair Fowler and Michael Leslie, 'Drummond's Copy of *The*

possesses another copy of 1553 (De.6.63), which has an inscription 'Tho: Hudson'. This seems most likely (though not of course certain) to be the poet and translator Thomas Hudson, who was active at the court of James VI, and whose Preface to *The Historie of Judith* (1584), a translation of Du Bartas's *La Judit*, commissioned by the king, shows some awareness of Douglas's critical views.[31]

Only a few of these early owners have left some slight indication of their response to the *Eneados*. The inscriptions in the copy now owned by King's College, Cambridge (M 25.32), consist chiefly in the underlining of words, and elementary explicatory marginal notes, chiefly concerning the persons in the *Aeneid*. Dardanus is 'a prince of phrigia wher Troy stode' (labelled sig. H6^v), and Bacchus is 'the god of wyne' (labelled sig. I6^r).[32] The owner's name on the verso of the title page is difficult to decipher, but might perhaps be read as 'andro somervelle'. Douglas suggested that his translation would be useful 'To thame wald Virgill to childryn expone' (*Directioun*, line 43; Coldwell, IV, p. 189). Perhaps this was one of those childish readers whom Douglas himself envisaged.

The copy of 1553 acquired in 2008 by Louisiana State University from the library of the earls of Macclesfield contains annotations very different in scope and importance.[33] The owner's name is written neatly in the cartouche at the [82] at the top of the title page: 'W. Barnesley'. Above it is written the date '1562' in ink of the same colour. Many pages of the text, both Prologues and translation, contain underlinings and marginalia. Those that I have seen appear to be written in a less careful form of the hand on the title page, and suggest a lively and intelligent interest in Douglas's vocabulary. Unusual words in the opening stanzas of Prologue IV are glossed: 'fosteraris' as 'nurses', 'fremmit' as 'vncouthe' and the difficult 'vncorne', which is explained as 'not fully ripe'. Tipped in at the end of the book is a short additional list of words and glosses, some of which are accompanied by their Latin equivalents from the *Aeneid*: 'hamald goddis' (I.ii, line 27) – literally 'household gods' – is accompanied by *Penates*. A full and more detailed inspection of these annotations would clearly be desirable.

Barnesley's notes anticipate the philological interest in Douglas that characterized the seventeenth century. He might be regarded as a less learned and unsystematic forerunner of the great scholar Francis Junius (1591–1677), whose annotated copy of 1553 is now in the Bodleian Library (MS Junius 54) along with his *Index Alphabeticus Verborum Obsoletorum quae occurrunt in Versione Virgilii Aeneadum per Gawenum Douglas* (MS Junius 114). Junius's copy had an earlier owner whose name appears in much abbreviated form in the cartouche on the title page as 'Rgrs Andrs'. He has been plausibly identified as Roger Andrewes, brother of Lancelot Andrewes, one of

Faerie Queene', *Times Literary Supplement*, 4085 (17 July 1981), 821–22.

31 For a modern edition, see *Thomas Hudson's Historie of Judith*, ed. James Craigie, STS, 3rd ser. 14 (Edinburgh, 1941).

32 The book was bequeathed to the college by Jacob Bryant (1715–1804). See K. E. Attar, 'More than a Mythologist: Jacob Bryant as a Book Collector', *The Library*, ser. 7, 3.4 (2002), 351–66.

33 This copy is listed in Sotheby's Sale Catalogue, March 2008, no. 4276. I am grateful to Michael L. Taylor, Assistant Curator in Special Collections at Louisiana State University Library, who sent me several digital images of the work.

the translators of the King James Bible and Master of Jesus College, Cambridge, from 1618 to 1632.[34] Junius makes careful cross-references to Douglas's various uses of a word, and he occasionally notes parallels in Chaucer to such usages as *A per se* (I Prol. line 8), *cryis ho* (III.vi, line 52), and *Partelot* (XII Prol. line 159).[35] He also calls attention to what he calls the *hiatus* between chapters iv and v of Book IV, mentioned above (p. 76). This was also pointed out by another observant reader of a copy of 1553 now in Cambridge University Library (Syn.6.55.9): 'here the translation of 34 verses is wanting, whearin the meting of Aeneas and Dido in the cave, and the description of fame is conteyned'. It is uncertain who made this comment or indeed owned this book in the sixteenth century, although there is a remote possibility that it might have belonged [**83**] to the collector Thomas Knyvett (*c.* 1539–1618).[36] Junius's study of Douglas's vocabulary was extremely influential, and later Oxford scholars drew heavily upon his work. But, as Duncan remarks, 'their interest in Douglas's work was not as a translation of Virgil, much less a production of the Scottish genius, but as a treasury of ancient English words'.[37]

The copy of 1553 now owned by Eton College (Cd.2.3.19) provokes attention, because – according to the useful online catalogue – it contains 'extensive manuscript annotations on the first and last leaves'.[38] But these annotations have nothing to do with the *Eneados*, although they have their own rather bizarre appeal. They reveal two unidentified users of the book, who were less interested in a translation of Virgil than in the usefulness of the blank pages and spaces for note-making. The first writer, presumably a young man, took advantage of the blank verso of the title page directly facing the opening of Prologue I. On it is written a title: 'The diseases of horses', and beneath, in two columns are listed 'the Bottes', 'the Fistula', 'the Staggers', and many other diseases of the eyes, feet, legs and shoulders of horses. Also listed are some noxious recipes for healing these diseases, containing ingredients such as

---

34 See Kees Dekker, 'The Other "Junius" in Oxford, Bodleian Library MS Junius 74: Francis Junius and a Scots Glossary by Patrick Young', *Scottish Language*, 35 (2016), 1–42 (3). There is a scathing account of Roger Andrewes in Adam Nicolson, *God's Secretaries: The Making of the King James Bible* (New York, 2004), pp. 94–95 and 253.

35 For an illustration of Junius's annotations to 1553, see Sally Mapstone, *Scots and Their Books in the Middle Ages and the Renaissance* (Oxford, 1996), p. 20. On Junius's interest in the *Eneados*, see also J. A. W. Bennett, 'The Early Fame of Gavin Douglas's *Eneados*', *Modern Language Notes*, 61.2 (1946), 83–88; and Duncan, *Thomas Ruddiman*, pp. 51–57.

36 The book was included in the important collection formed by John Moore (1646–1714), bishop of Ely, which was bought by George I and presented to Cambridge University. Dr Emily Dourish, Deputy Head of Rare Books in the library, considers the hand similar to that of Bishop Moore, although he 'writes very infrequently in his books'. It is known, however, that Moore acquired many of his early books from the collection of Sir Thomas Knyvett. An entry in the 1618 catalogue of Knyvett's books (no. 1326) reads: 'Virgils Eneides [4°]', and 'according to the later catalogue [dated in or shortly after 1634] this is Gawin Douglas's translation of 1553'. For the details, see David J. McKitterick, *The Library of Sir Thomas Knyvett of Ashwellthorpe, c. 1539–1618* (Cambridge, 1978), p. 148.

37 Duncan, *Thomas Ruddiman*, pp. 51–52.

38 My thanks are due to the archivist of Eton College, Ms Sally Jennings, who supplied me with images of these pages.

lamp oil, sulphur, soot and quicksilver.[39] At the very end of the volume are more inscriptions of a remarkably different character, all written in French, in a different and decorative hand. At the foot of the last page of Douglas's text is the following: 'La bien vostre preste a vous faire plaisir, Helene D'apolonye.' This is the name not of the book's owner but of a once famous literary figure, prominent in Books IX and X of *Amadis de Gaule*. This long chivalric prose romance of Spanish origin received many additions by different authors and translators, and became enormously popular both in France and England particularly in the second half of the sixteenth century.[40] Similarly flowery [84] inscriptions – for example, 'Celuy qui vous desire tout bien et accroissement d'honeur, Le Cheualier de la bergere' – occur on the facing page, and possibly derive from the same work. The writer's motivation is not clear; perhaps this is simply a calligraphic exercise, or more probably an exercise in the art of devising elegant conclusions to letters. *Amadis de Gaule* was at that time regarded not simply as a book of love and chivalry but as a guide to polite manners, including speeches and epistolary compositions.[41]

Another copy of 1553, now belonging to a private collector, also has annotations.[42] None, unfortunately, identifies the first owner, although one hints tantalizingly that the book was a gift: 'of Aeneado [from] your frend Iames D [?]'. The most interesting is written at the end, on the margin beside Douglas's 'Exclamacion aganis detractouris' (sig. bbvii[r]), and consists of a short poem, which begins: 'The night doth rest the toyle / Of workmans wery hand.' It ends with a striking turn in the thought: 'Save I which in my bed / do feele a thowsand waes.' (The final word is difficult to read, but the spelling 'waes', if correct, might indicate a Scottish author.) Quaritch's describes this as 'a twelve-line lyric',[43] but it might better be regarded as consisting of six lines, each containing twelve syllables. The poem is rhetorically ambitious, with a striking five-fold use of anaphora on 'The night', but the many small revisions and corrections suggest an amateur in the act of composition. The verses are not, to my knowledge, recorded in modern scholarly first-line Indexes of Elizabethan and Jacobean Poetry.[44] Such reflections on the difficulty with which sleep comes to a mind that is troubled with pangs of conscience or lack of success in love are not uncommon in Elizabethan

39 The notes may have been copied from a printed work on 'Remedies for Horses', such as that mentioned in Ferguson, 'Relations between London and Edinburgh Printers', p. 177.
40 On the work's popularity, see I. D. Macfarlane, *A Literary History of France: Renaissance France 1470–1589* (London, 1974), pp. 236–37; and John O'Connor, *'Amadis de Gaule' and its Influence on Elizabethan Literature* (New Brunswick, NJ, 1970). William Drummond possessed several volumes: see MacDonald, *Library*, pp. 131–32 and nos 959–62. One of Drummond's Scottish contemporaries, however, strongly disapproved of the 'fabulos faits' of Amadis: see *The Poems of Alexander Hume*, ed. Alexander Lawson, STS, 1st ser. 48 (Edinburgh, 1902), p. 6.
41 See O'Connor, *'Amadis de Gaule'*, p. 23.
42 I am much indebted to the generosity of the owner, who sent me photos of the relevant pages.
43 See the brief account in Bernard Quaritch's catalogue 1125 (1990), item 70.
44 See Margaret Crum, *First-Line Index of English Poetry 1500–1800 in Manuscripts of the Bodleian Library Oxford*, 2 vols (Oxford, 1969); and Steven May and William A. Ringler, *Elizabethan Poetry: A Bibliography and First-Line Index of English Verse, 1559–1603*, 3 vols (New York, 2004).

poetry. But they might well represent this early owner's direct response to Virgilian passages describing how night brings repose to men and beasts (cf. *Aeneid* II, line 268, 'Tempus erat …', or III, line 147, 'Nox erat …'). Equally relevant (and closer at hand in this book) would have been Douglas's own night scene that occupies much of Prologue XIII: [85]

> Owt our the swyre swymmys the soppis of myst,
> The nycht furthspred hir cloke with sabill lyst,
> …
> Still war the fowlis fleis in the air,
> All stoir and catall seysit in thar lair,
> And euery thing, quharso thame lykis best
> Bownys to tak the hailsum nychtis rest.
> (*Eneados*, XIII.Prol.37ff.)

It comes as no surprise that the first owners of the 1553 *Eneados* so far identified were mainly well-educated (though not always wealthy) members of the gentry in England and Scotland: landowners, clergymen, poets, translators, scholars and antiquaries. The annotations are disappointingly scanty. Their most striking feature, evident above all in the comments of Barnesley and Junius, is a fascination with Douglas's language, more particularly the many differences from southern English and the archaism of its vocabulary. The printed version of the *Eneados* continued nonetheless to keep the name of Gavin Douglas alive during a period when the other great Scottish poets, such as Dunbar and Henryson, were virtually forgotten.

This chapter is necessarily limited in scope, and provides only a brief introduction to a rich topic, rather than a full survey. It is designed, however, as a small but warm tribute to Julia Boffey, whose own adventurous research has ranged widely in both manuscript and printed books, and illuminated our understanding of the relationship between Scottish and English literature in the later medieval period. [86]

Editorial Note

a   First published in *Manuscript and Print in Late Medieval and Early Modern Britain: Essays in Honour of Professor Julia Boffey*, ed. Tamara Atkin and Jaclyn Rajsic (Cambridge, 2019), pp. 73–85; and reprinted with the kind permission of Boydell & Brewer.

APPENDIX

The Appendix lists the locations of extant copies of 1553 known to me. In a number of cases, I have been unable to supply shelfmarks.

BRITISH ISLES

Cambridge

University Library, Syn.6.55.9
University Library, O*.11.1 (D)
King's College, M.25.32
Magdalene College, Pepys Library, Print 1652
Trinity College, Capell O.2

Crieff

Innerpeffray Library
Scottish Collection, A 3
Scottish Collection, LD 4

Edinburgh

National Library of Scotland, H.29.b.53
National Library of Scotland, Ry.11.d.2
Signet Library[, 103: a: 33]
University Library, De.4.32
University Library, De.6.63

Glasgow

University Library, Sp Coll BDA1-a.8

Lincoln Cathedral

Wren Library (catalogue, V, 91)

London

BL, G.9722
BL, 78.b.17
University, Senate House Library, Sterling I, 995

Manchester

John Rylands University Library, Spec. Coll. 2039.1

Oxford

Bodleian, MS Junius 54
Christ Church College, OS.1.26
Corpus Christi College, Δ.12.1
Queen's College, Sel.e.244 (1)

St Andrews

University Library, Typ. BL. B53.CV

Warminster

Longleat House, cat. no. 14333

Windsor

Eton College Library, Cd.2.3.19 [**87**]

NORTH AMERICA

Austin, TX

University of Texas, Harry Ransom Center, Pforz 1027.PFz

Baton Rouge, LA

Louisiana State University, Hill Memorial Library[, PA6807 .A5 D6]

Berkeley, CA

Berkeley University, Bancroft Library[, Bancroft PA6807.A1 D6 1553]

Cambridge, MA

Harvard, Houghton Library, Hollis 009644576

Chicago, IL

Newberry Library, Vault Case Y 672.V9147

Montreal, Quebec, Canada

McGill University, PA 6807 A5 D6 1553

New Haven, CT

Yale University, Beinecke Library, Eliz 235

New York

Columbia University[, LODGE 1553 V58 13V STC 24797]
New York Public Library
The Morgan Library, W 09 B

San Marino, CA

Huntington Library, 60190

Washington, DC

Folger Shakespeare Library, HH.211/10

Priscilla Bawcutt: Publications

Elspeth Yeo, A. S. G. Edwards, and Janet Hadley Williams

Publications from 1957 until 1962 were published under the name Priscilla Preston; publications thereafter and continuing are published under the name Bawcutt.

1957

'"The Complaynt of Scotlande": A French Debt', *Notes and Queries*, 202 (1957), 431–32.

1958

Review of: *Devotional Pieces in Verse and Prose from MS. Arundel 285 and MS. Harleian 6919*, ed. J. A. W. Bennett, STS, 3rd ser. 23 (Edinburgh, 1955), *Medium Ævum*, 27 (1958), 45–48.
'Did Gavin Douglas write *King Hart*?', *Medium Ævum*, 28 (1958), 31–47.

1959

'A Note on T. S. Eliot and Sherlock Holmes', *Modern Language Review*, 54.3 (1959), 397–99.
Review of: Ján Šimko, *Word-Order in the Winchester Manuscript and in William Caxton's Edition of Thomas Malory's Morte Darthur (1485) – A Comparison* (Halle, 1957), *Modern Language Review*, 54.2 (1959), 252–53.

1961

Review of: Sir David Lindsay, *Squyer Meldrum*, ed. James Kinsley (London, 1959), *Review of English Studies*, 12.45 (1961), 107–08.

1963

'Gavin Douglas: Some Additions to O.E.D. and D.O.S.T.'. *Notes and Queries*, 10.8 (1963), 289–90.

1964

Review of: Robert Henryson, *Poems*, ed. Charles Elliott (Oxford, 1963), *Notes and Queries*, 11.5 (1964), 197–98.

Ed., *The Palice of Honour* selections, in *Selections from Gavin Douglas*, ed. D. F. C. Coldwell, Clarendon Medieval and Tudor Series (Oxford, 1964), pp. 107–15, 138–42.
'Dunbar's *Tretis of the Tua Mariit Wemen and the Wedo* 185–187 and Chaucer's *Parson's Tale*', *Notes and Queries*, 11.9 (1964), 332–33.

1967

Ed., *The Shorter Poems of Gavin Douglas*, STS, 4th ser. 3 (Edinburgh, 1967).

1968

Review of: Robert Henryson, *The Testament of Cresseid*, ed. Denton Fox (London, 1968), *Notes and Queries*, 15.11 (1968), 435–36.

1969

'The Source of Gavin Douglas's *Eneados* IV. Prologue 92–9', *Notes and Queries*, 16.10 (1969), 366–67.

1970

'Gavin Douglas and Chaucer', *Review of English Studies*, 21.84 (1970), 401–21.
Review of: *Hary's 'Wallace'*, ed. Matthew P. McDiarmid, 2 vols, STS, 4th ser. 4, 5 (Edinburgh, 1968–69), *Medium Ævum*, 39 (1970), 224–28.

1971

'Lexical Notes on Gavin Douglas's *Eneados*', *Medium Aevum*, 40 (1971), 48–55.

1972

'The Lark in Chaucer and Some Later Poets', *The Yearbook of English Studies*, 2 (1972), 5–12.

1973

'Gavin Douglas and the Text of Virgil', *Edinburgh Bibliographical Society Transactions*, 4 (1973), 213–31.
Articles: 'Gavin Douglas', 'William Dunbar', 'Robert Henryson', and '*The Kingis Quair*', *Webster's New World Companion to English Literature*, ed. Arthur Pollard (New York, 1973), pp. 200, 212–14, 324–25, 384.

1974

'Aspects of Dunbar's Imagery', in *Chaucer and Middle English Studies in Honour of Rossell Hope Robbins*, ed. Beryl Rowland (London, 1974), pp. 190–200.

'Douglas and Surrey: Translators of Virgil', *Essays and Studies*, n.s. 27 (1974), 52–67.
'Middle Scots Poets: James I, Henryson, Dunbar, Gavin Douglas and others', in *The New Cambridge Bibliography of English Literature: Volume I, 600–1660*, ed. George Watson, (Cambridge, 1974), cols 651–64.

1975

Review of: Alice S. Miskimin, *The Renaissance Chaucer* (New Haven, CT, 1975), *English Language Notes*, 13 (1975), 140–42.

1976

Gavin Douglas: A Critical Study (Edinburgh, 1976).

1977

'The "Library" of Gavin Douglas', in *Bards and Makars: Scottish Language and Literature; Medieval and Renaissance*, ed. Adam J. Aitken, Matthew P. McDiarmid and Derick S. Thomson (Glasgow, 1977), pp. 107–26.

1978

'Text and Context in Middle Scots Poetry', in *Actes du 2e Colloque de Langue et de Littérature Écossaises (Moyen Age et Renaisssance)*, ed. Jean-Jacques Blanchot and Claude Graf (Strasbourg, 1978), pp. 26–38.
Review of: A. C. Spearing, *Medieval Dream-Poetry* (Cambridge, 1976), *Durham University Journal*, 71, n.s. 40 (1978), 127–28.
Review of: Bengt Ellenberger, *The Latin Element in the Vocabulary of the Earlier Makars Henryson and Dunbar* (Lund, 1977), *Notes and Queries*, 223 (1978), 168–70.
Review of: Joanne Spencer Kantrowitz, *Dramatic Allegory: Lindsay's 'Ane Satyre of the Thrie Estaitis'* (Nebraska, NE, 1975), *Medium Ævum*, 47 (1978), 187–88.

1980

'Bear or Boar in *The Tales of the Five Beasts*?', *Scottish Literary Journal, Supplement*, 13 (1980), 11–12.
Letter: '*Henry V*'. *Times Literary Supplement*, 21 March 1980, 324.
Review of: Robert Wedderburn, *The Complaynt of Scotland* (c. 1550), ed. A. M. Stewart, STS, 4th ser. 11 (Edinburgh, 1979), *Scottish Literary Journal, Supplement* 12, 86–88.

1981

'Henryson's "Poeit of the Auld Fassoun"', *Review of English Studies*, n.s. 32.128 (1981), 429–34.

'Source-Hunting: Some *Reulis and Cautelis*', in *Proceedings of the Third International Conference on Scottish Language and Literature (Medieval and Renaissance)*, ed. Roderick J. Lyall and Felicity Riddy (Stirling/Glasgow, 1981), pp. 85–105.

Review article: 'The Text and Interpretation of Dunbar' [*The Poems of William Dunbar*, ed. James Kinsley. Clarendon Press (Oxford, 1979)], *Medium Ævum*, 50 (1981), 88–100.

Review of: Douglas Gray, *Robert Henryson* (Leiden, 1979), *Medium Ævum*, 50 (1981), 352–53.

1982

'"Venus Starre" in Donne and Douglas', *Notes and Queries*, 29.1 (1982), 15.

'A Crux in *Astrophil and Stella*, Sonnet 21', *Notes and Queries*, 29.5 (1982), 406–08.

Review of: Gregory Kratzmann, *Anglo-Scots Literary Relations 1430–1550* (Cambridge, 1980), *Notes and Queries*, 29.2 (1982), 159–60.

Review of: Gregory Kratzmann, *Anglo-Scots Literary Relations 1430–1550* (Cambridge, 1980), *The Yearbook of English Studies*, 12 (1982), 236–37.

Combined review of: Robert L. Kindrick, *Robert Henryson* (Boston, MA, 1979) and Edmund Reiss, *William Dunbar* (Boston, MA, 1979), *The Yearbook of English Studies*, 12 (1982), 238–40.

1983

'The Art of Flyting' ['Being the lecture given in Edinburgh on 11 November 1982 for the centenary of the Scottish Text Society'], *Scottish Literary Journal*, 10.2 (1983), 5–24.

Review of: Ian Simpson Ross, *William Dunbar* (Leiden, 1981), *Scottish Literary Journal, Supplement*, 18 (1983), 4–6.

Review of: *The Buke of the Sevyne Sagis*, ed. Catherine van Buuren (Leiden, 1982), *Scottish Literary Journal, Supplement* 18 (1983), 6–8.

Review of: *James I of Scotland: 'The Kingis Quair'*, ed. John Norton-Smith (Leiden, 1981), *Medium Ævum*, 52 (1983), 137–38.

1984

'A Note on Sonnet 38', *Shakespeare Quarterly*, 35.1 (1984), 77–79.

Review of: *The King of Tars ed. from the Auchinleck MS, Advocates 19.2.1*, ed. Judith Perryman. Middle English Texts, 12 (Heidelberg, 1980), *The Yearbook of English Studies*, 14 (1984), 303–04.

Review of: *Thomas of Erceldoune*, ed. Ingeborg Nixon, 2 parts (Copenhagen, 1980, 1983), *Scottish Literary Journal, Supplement* 21 (1984), 39–41.

1985

Review of: William Lamb, *Ane Resonyng of ane Scottis and Inglis Merchand betuix Rowand and Lionis*, ed. Roderick J. Lyall (Aberdeen, 1985), *Scottish Literary Journal, Supplement* 22, 2–4.

1986

'Dunbar and an Epigram', *Scottish Literary Journal*, 13.2 (1986), 16–19.

'Dunbar's Christmas Carol', in *Scottish Language and Literature, Medieval and Renaissance: Fourth International Conference 1984; Proceedings*, ed. Dietrich Strauss and Horst W. Drescher, Scottish Studies 4 (Frankfurt am Main, 1986), pp. 381–92.

'Dunbar's Use of the Symbolic Lion and Thistle', *Cosmos: The Yearbook of the Traditional Cosmology Society*, 2: *Kingship* (1986), 83–97 and frontis. illustration.

Letter: 'The Profits of Marriage in Late Medieval Scotland', *Scottish Literary Journal*, 13.1 (1986), 77–78 [concerning terms in Dunbar's *Tua Mariit Wemen and the Wedo* discussed by Eileen Bentsen and S. L. Sanderlin, *Scottish Literary Journal*, 12.2, 1985, 5–18].

Review of: Walter Scheps and J. Anna Looney, *Middle Scots Poets: A Reference Guide to James I of Scotland, Robert Henryson, William Dunbar, and Gavin Douglas* (Boston, 1986), *Scottish Literary Journal, Supplement* 25 (1986), 1–2.

1987

Ed. (with Felicity Riddy), *Longer Scottish Poems: Volume One; 1375–1650* (Edinburgh, 1987).

'*The Copill*: A Crux in *The Kingis Quair*', *Review of English Studies*, 38.150 (1987), 211–14.

'Dunbar: New Light on Some Old Words', in *The Nuttis Schell: Essays on the Scots Language Presented to A. J. Aitken*, ed. Caroline Macafee and Iseabail Macleod (Aberdeen, 1987), pp. 83–95.

Review of: J. A. W. Bennett, *Middle English Literature*, ed. and completed Douglas Gray (Oxford, 1986), *Scottish Literary Journal, Supplement* 27 (1987), 4–7.

1988

'A Miniature Anglo-Scottish Flyting', *Notes and Queries*, 35.4 (1988), 441–44.

'A Medieval Scottish Elegy and its French Original', *Scottish Literary Journal*, 15.1 (1988), 5–13.

'William Dunbar and Gavin Douglas', in *The History of Scottish Literature: Volume 1; Origins to 1660 (Mediæval and Renaissance)*, ed. R. D. S. Jack (Aberdeen, 1988), pp. 73–89.

1989

'Elrich Fantasyis in Dunbar and Other Poets', in *Bryght Lanternis: Essays on the Language and Literature of Medieval and Renaissance Scotland*, ed. J. Derrick McClure and Michael R. G. Spiller (Aberdeen, 1989), pp. 162–78.

1990

'The Commonplace Book of John Maxwell', in *A Day Estivall: Essays on the Music, Poetry and History of Scotland and England ... in Honour of Helena Mennie Shire*, ed. Alisoun Gardner-Medwin and Janet Hadley Williams (Aberdeen, 1990), pp. 59–68.

'Gavin Douglas', *The Spenser Encyclopedia*, ed. A. C. Hamilton et al. (Toronto, 1990), p. 223.

Combined review of: *The Tale of Ralph the Collier: An Alliterative Romance*, ed. Elizabeth Walsh (New York, 1989) and *Rauf Coilȝear* in *Medieval English Romances*, ed. Diane Speed (Sydney, 1989; 2nd edn), *Scottish Literary Journal, Supplement* 33 (1990), 1–3.

1991

'The Earliest Texts of Dunbar', in *Regionalism in Late Medieval Manuscripts and Texts: Essays Celebrating the Publication of 'A Linguistic Atlas of Late Medieval English'*, ed. Felicity Riddy, York Manuscripts Conferences: Proceedings Series (Cambridge, 1991), pp. 183–98.

'A First-Line Index of Early Scottish Verse', *Studies in Scottish Literature*, 26 (1991), 254–70.

1992

Dunbar the Makar (Oxford, 1992).

Ed. (with Felicity Riddy), *Selected Poems of Henryson and Dunbar*, Scottish Classics Series 16 (Edinburgh, 1992).

'Images of Women in the Poems of Dunbar', *Études écossaises*, 1 (1992), 49–58.

1993

'Gavin Douglas (1476–September 1522)', *Sixteenth-Century British Nondramatic Writers*, 1st ser., ed. David A. Richardson, *Dictionary of Literary Biography* 132 (Detroit, 1993), pp. 112–22.

'A New Scottish Poem: On the Literary Interest of Timothy Pont's Map 23', *Scottish Literary Journal*, 20.2 (1993), 5–20.

1994

'The Mystery of *The Spyte of Spaine* (Heirs of Andro Hart, 1628)', *The Bibliotheck*, 19 (1994), 5–22.

'New Light on Gavin Douglas', in *The Renaissance in Scotland: Studies in Literature, Religion, History and Culture Offered to John Durkan*, ed. A. A. MacDonald, Michael Lynch and Ian B. Cowan (Leiden, 1994), pp. 95–106.

1995

'*Pamphilus de Amore* "In Inglish Toung"', *Medium Ævum*, 64.2 (1995), 264–72.

1996

Ed., *William Dunbar: Selected Poems* (London, 1996).

'The Correspondence of Gavin Douglas', in *Stewart Style 1513–1542: Essays on the Court of James V*, ed. Janet Hadley Williams (East Linton, 1996), pp. 52–61.

'An Early Scottish Debate-Poem on Women', *Scottish Literary Journal*, 23.2 (1996), 35–42.

1997

'Editing Dunbar, "The Pompeii of British Poetry"', *ScotLit*, 17 (1997), 1–2.

Entries: 'John Barbour', 'Gavin Douglas', 'William Dunbar', 'Robert Henryson', and 'Sir David Lindsay', in *Discovering Scottish Writers*, ed. Alan Reid and Brian D. Osborne (Hamilton, 1997), pp. 9, 28, 31–32, 45, 52.

'"Nature Red in Tooth and Claw": Bird and Beast Imagery in William Dunbar', in *Animals and the Symbolic in Mediaeval Art and Literature*, ed. L. A. J. R. Houwen, Mediaevalia Groningana 20 (Groningen, 1997), pp. 93–105.

Review of: H. R. Woudhuysen, *Sir Philip Sidney and the Circulation of Manuscripts 1558–1640* (Oxford, 1996), *Rare Books Newsletter*, 56 (1997), 71–74.

Review of: *The Works of Geoffrey Chaucer and 'The Kingis Quair': A Facsimile of Bodleian Library, Oxford, MS Arch. Selden. B. 24*, introd. Julia Boffey and A. S. G. Edwards; app. B. C. Barker-Benfield (Cambridge, 1997), *Rare Books Newsletter*, 57 (1997), 87–90.

1998

Ed. *The Poems of William Dunbar*. 2 vols, Association for Scottish Literary Studies, 27 and 28 (Glasgow, 1998).

'Crossing the Border: Scottish Poetry and English Readers in the Sixteenth Century', in *The Rose and the Thistle: Essays on the Culture of Late Medieval and Renaissance Scotland*, ed. Sally Mapstone and Juliette Wood (East Linton, 1998), pp. 59–76.

Entries: 'William Dunbar', and 'Early Scottish Literature', in *Medieval England: An Encyclopedia*, ed. Paul E. Szarmach, M. Teresa Tavormina, and Joel Rosenthal, Garland Reference Library of the Humanities 907 (New York, 1998), pp. 252–54, 675–77.

Obituary: 'Professor A. J. Aitken', *The Independent*, 18 February 1998, 16.

1999

(With Bridget Henisch), 'Scots Abroad in the Fifteenth Century: The Princesses Margaret, Isabella and Eleanor', in *Women in Scotland c.1100–c.1750*, ed. Elizabeth Ewan and Maureen M. Meikle (East Linton, 1999), pp. 45–55.

'A Golden Age of Poetry', *Scotland's Story*, Part 17, ed. Maxwell Garvie and Anof Scotvand (Glasgow, 1999), 12–14.

2000

'"My bright buke": Women and their Books in Medieval and Renaissance Scotland', in *Medieval Women: Texts and Contexts in Late Medieval Britain; Essays for Felicity Riddy*, ed. Jocelyn Wogan-Browne et al. (Turnhout, 2000), pp. 17–34.

'New Texts of William Dunbar, Alexander Scott and Other Scottish Poets', *Scottish Studies Review*, 1.1 (2000), 9–25.

2001

'On Editing Dunbar', *Folio* [Newsletter, National Library of Scotland], 2 (2001), 5–7.

'Two Cases of Mistaken Identity: Sir David Lyndsay's St. Syith and St Margaret', *Innes Review*, 52.2 (2001), 189–94.

'*King Orphius* and "Opheus Kyng of Portingal"', *Notes and Queries*, 48.2 (2001), 112–14.

'French Connections? From the *Grands Rhétoriqueurs* to Clément Marot', in *The European Sun: Proceedings of the Seventh International Conference on Medieval and Renaissance Scottish Language and Literature*, ed. Graham Caie et al. (East Linton, 2001), pp. 119–28.

'The Boston Public Library Manuscript of John Lydgate's *Siege of Thebes*: Its Scottish Owners and Inscriptions', *Medium Ævum*, 70 (2001), 80–94.

'James VI's Castalian Band: A Modern Myth', *Scottish Historical Review*, 80(2).210 (2001), 251–59.

Review of: *A Palace in the Wild: Essays on Vernacular Culture and Humanism in Late Medieval and Renaissance Scotland*, ed. L. A. J. R. Houwen, A. A. MacDonald and S. L. Mapstone (Leuven, 2000), *Notes and Queries*, 48.3 (2001), 322–23.

'English Books and Scottish Readers in the Fifteenth and Sixteenth Centuries', *Review of Scottish Culture*, 14 (2001–02), 1–12.

2002

Review of: *Sir David Lyndsay: Selected Poems*, ed. Janet Hadley Williams, ASLS, 30 (Glasgow, 2000), *Notes and Queries*, 49.1 (2002), 130–31.

'A Song from the *Complaynt of Scotland*: 'My Hart Is Leiuit on the Land', *Notes and Queries*, 49.2 (2002), 193–97.

Review of: John Higgit, 'The "Murthly Hours": Devotion, Literacy and Luxury in Paris, England and the Gaelic West', *Papers of the Bibliographical Society of America*, 96.2 (2002), 296–98.

2003

Ed., *The Shorter Poems of Gavin Douglas*, 2nd edn, STS, 5th ser. 2 (Edinburgh, 2003).

2004

'Douglas, Gavin (*c.* 1476–1522), Poet and Bishop of Dunkeld', *Oxford Dictionary of National Biography* (2004, rev. 2008), *ODNB Online*: https://doi-org/10.1093/ref:odnb/7882.

'Kennedy, Walter (1455?–1518?), Poet', *Oxford Dictionary of National Biography* (2004), *ODNB Online*: https://doi-org/10.1093/ref:odnb/15395.

'Sempill, Robert (d. 1595?), Poet and Protestant Controversialist', *Oxford Dictionary of National Biography* (2004), *ODNB Online*: https://doi-org/10.1093/ref:odnb/25075.

2005

'Sir Lamwell in Scotland', in *The Scots and Medieval Arthurian Tradition*, ed. Rhiannon Purdie and Nicola Royan (Cambridge, 2005), pp. 83–93.

'*DOST* and the Literary Scholar', in *Perspectives on the Older Scottish Tongue*, ed. Christian Kay and Margaret McKay (Edinburgh, 2005), pp. 5–17.

'Women Talking about Marriage in William Dunbar and Hans Sachs', in *The Medieval Marriage Scene: Prudence, Passion, Policy*, ed. Sherry Roush and Cristelle L. Baskins (Tempe, AZ, 2005), pp. 101–14.

'Manuscript Miscellanies in Scotland from the Fifteenth to the Seventeenth Centuries', in *Older Scots Literature*, ed. Sally Mapstone (Edinburgh, 2005), pp. 189–210.

'Scottish Manuscript Miscellanies from the Fifteenth to the Seventeenth Centuries', *English Manuscript Studies 1100-1700*, 12 (2005), 46–73.

2006

'A Note on the Term "Morality"', *Medieval English Theatre*, 28 (2006), 171–74.

'Writing about Love in Late Medieval Scotland', in *Writings on Love in the English Middle Ages*, ed. Helen Cooney (Basingstoke, 2006), pp. 179–96.

Entry: 'Dunbar, William', in *Key Figures in Medieval Europe: An Encyclopedia*, ed. Richard K. Emmerson (London, 2006), pp. 183–85.

Ed. (with Janet Hadley Williams), *A Companion to Medieval Scottish Poetry* (Cambridge, 2006).

'Introduction: Poets "of this Natioun"', in *A Companion to Medieval Scottish Poetry* (Cambridge, 2006), pp. 1–18 (with Janet Hadley Williams).

'Religious Verse in Medieval Scotland', in *A Companion to Medieval Scottish Poetry* (Cambridge, 2006), pp. 119–31.

2007

'William Dunbar', in *The Edinburgh History of Scottish Literature, 1: From Columba to the Union (until 1707)*, ed. Ian Brown (Edinburgh, 2007), pp. 295–304.

'Dunbar and his Readers: From Allan Ramsay to Richard Burton', *Studies in Scottish Literature*, 35 (2007), 362–81.

2008

Review of: Rebecca Rushworth, *St Margaret's Gospel-book. The Favourite Book of an Eleventh-Century Queen of Scots* (Oxford, 2007), *The Book Collector*, 57.2 (2008), 308–09.

'The Contents of the Bannatyne Manuscript: New Sources and Analogues', *Journal of the Edinburgh Bibliographical Society*, 3 (2008), 95–133.

2009

'A New Poem by Robert Sempill: *The Warning to the Lordis*', *Scottish Literary Review*, 50.1 (2009), 17–49.

'The Authorship of James VI and I's *Amatoria*: The Manuscript Evidence', *English Manuscript Studies 1100–1700*, 15 (2009), 219–36.

2010

'"Mankit and Mutillait": The Text of John Rolland's *The Court of Venus*', in *The Apparelling of Truth: Literature and Literary Culture in the Reign of James VI. A Festschrift for Roderick J. Lyall*, ed. Kevin J. McGinley and Nicola Royan (Newcastle upon Tyne, 2010), pp. 11–29.

2012

Letter: 'The *Eneados*', *Times Literary Supplement*, 4 May 2012, 6.

'Lord William Howard of Naworth (1563–1640): Antiquary, Book Collector, and Owner of the Scottish Devotional Manuscript British Library, Arundel 285', *Textual Cultures*, 7 (2012), 158–75.

'"Holy Words for Healing": Some Early Scottish Charms and their Ancient Religious Roots', in *Literature and Religion in Late Medieval and Early Modern Scotland: Essays in Honour of Alasdair A. MacDonald*, ed. Luuk A. J. R. Houwen (Leuven, 2012), pp. 127–44.

2013

'Editing William Dunbar: Some Afterthoughts on the Decade', in *Fresche fontanis: Studies in the Culture of Medieval and Early Modern Scotland*, ed. Janet Hadley Williams and J. Derrick McClure (Newcastle upon Tyne, 2013), pp. 115–25.

'John Donne: The Scottish Connection', in *James VI and I, Literature and Scotland: Tides of Change, 1567–1625*, ed. David J. Parkinson, Groningen Studies in Cultural Change 47 (Leuven, 2013), pp. 323–38.

2015

'The Source and Significance of a Marginal Inscription in the *Buik of Alexander* (*c.*1580)', *Notes and Queries*, 62.1 (2015), 56–58.

2017

'The Catalogue of Contraries in *The Kingis Quair*, 759–770: Some Emendations', *Notes and Queries*, 64.1 (2017), 19–22.

Foreword, *Premodern Scotland: Literature and Governance 1420–1587; Essays for Sally Mapstone*, ed. Joanna Martin and Emily Wingfield (Oxford, 2017), pp. vii–viii.

2019

'Gavin Douglas's *Eneados*: The 1553 Edition and its Early Owners and Readers', in *Manuscript and Print in Late Medieval and Early Modern Britain*, ed. Tamara Atkin and Jaclyn Rajsic (Cambridge, 2019), pp. 73–87.

2020

Letter: 'Credit to Dunbar', *Times Literary Supplement*, 7 March 2020, 8.

Ed. (with Ian Cunningham), *The Eneados: Gavin Douglas's Translation of Virgil's Aeneid.* Volume I. Introduction and Commentary. STS, 5th ser. 17 (Edinburgh, 2020).

2021

Ed. (with Ian Cunningham), *The Eneados: Gavin Douglas's Translation of Virgil's Aeneid.* Volume II. Books I–VII. STS, 5th ser. 18 (Edinburgh, 2021).

2022

Ed. (with Ian Cunningham), *The Eneados: Gavin Douglas's Translation of Virgil's Aeneid.* Volume III. Books VIII–XIII. STS, 5th ser. 19 (Edinburgh, 2022).

Submitted for Publication

'Single Author Manuscripts: 1500–1603' [working title]. Commissioned for the *Edinburgh History of the Book in Scotland, Volume I: Origins to 1707*, ed. Alastair Mann and Sally Mapstone; now under a new editorial team, Alastair Mann, Joe Marshall, Daryl Green, and Emily Wingfield; General Editor, Bill Bell (Edinburgh University Press).

Priscilla J. Bawcutt
1931–2021

The world of Older Scots studies has suffered an enormous loss in the death of Professor Priscilla Bawcutt, which has come only a few months before what would have been the start of her ninetieth year.[a] Although she published on a wide range of literary, historical, codicological, philological and editorial matters, her name will principally and permanently be linked with two of the most significant figures in the literature of late medieval Scotland: William Dunbar and Gavin Douglas. Her great achievement was to establish trustworthy texts of both these poets, to transform understanding of their works and of the cultural context within which these works arose, and in so doing to lay down secure foundations for future scholarship. It was a huge pleasure to Priscilla that she was at least able to receive the first volume of her edition of the *Eneados* for the Scottish Text Society, though it is ironic and more than sad that she should not live to see the imminent completion of this monumental project, of which she was the prime mover.

The range of literature on which Priscilla worked is impressive. Her interests included English poets (Chaucer, Sidney, Shakespeare, Donne and T. S. Eliot among them), though the poets of Scotland always dominated. In 2001, she was presented with a Festschrift, appropriately entitled *William Dunbar, 'The Nobill Poyet'*. This volume provides a bibliography of her writings to date, including some listed as then forthcoming; more were yet to come, and through the following two decades Priscilla's scholarly activity continued unabated. William Dunbar was long at the forefront of her attention, and she published several minor selections of his poems. In 1991, her study *Dunbar the Makar* appeared and immediately outclassed all previous critical accounts of the poet's life and times. This was followed in 1998 by her complete *The Poems of William Dunbar*, a two-volume work that has superseded all previous editions, and is everywhere accepted as the definitive text.

However, before Priscilla turned to Dunbar, it was with one of his contemporaries that she was principally concerned, and in 1967 she edited *The Shorter Poems of Gavin Douglas* for the Scottish Text Society – reissued in 2003 with a few corrections and some fifty pages of Supplement. This revised volume added to the information earlier presented in a series of articles on the poet and gathered into her *Gavin Douglas: A Critical Study* (1976). The relationship between the *Aeneid* and the *Eneados* was a topic that never ceased to fascinate her, and it is peculiarly fitting that Priscilla's career should be crowned with her edition of Douglas's *magnum opus*.

Priscilla June Bawcutt, *née* Preston, was proud of her Yorkshire origin, though she proceeded as a student to the University of London. In those days, the degree programme was solidly philological, comprising not only the study of the tradition of English literature and the various classical and later European influences thereupon, but also a thorough training in the history of the language, through its West Germanic, Anglo-Saxon, medieval and early modern phases. This integration of literature and language provided an essential bedrock for all her work. Her subsequent long

237

association with the University of Liverpool came through her marriage to Nigel, a specialist in Elizabethan and Jacobean drama; their union was blessed with the birth of a son, himself later also a teacher of English. Priscilla taught only intermittently in the Liverpool English Department, but the University eventually recognized her scholarship by granting her the title of Honorary Professor. Though Priscilla might have wished for a more regularly structured professional appointment, she was able to benefit from her independence, which gave her the time to produce not only the authoritative books already mentioned, but also a steady stream of reviews and articles: *haec otia studia fovent* – as the motto of the University has it.

As a child of the north of England, Priscilla could be diffident towards what she might see as metropolitan fripperies, and an equivalent attitude of curiosity coupled with reserve informed her approach to matters Scottish. Through half a century, no-one contributed more than she to the study of the literature and culture of late medieval and early modern Scotland, in regard to which her position was always that of the dispassionate and impartial observer. She was meticulous and diligent in her research, which was characterized by rationality, precision and the ability to relativize. Although she could be trenchant in combating error, especially where that might have resulted from the indulgence of sentiment, her criticisms were always *ad rem*, never *ad hominem*. Thus, while she was vigorous in the defence of her own views, she was prepared to consider the opinions of others, where these could be justified from the evidence. The death of Priscilla Bawcutt will be greatly lamented by all those interested in Older Scots, by those with whom she collaborated on editorial projects, and especially by those privileged to count themselves among her friends.

Alasdair A. MacDonald

Editorial Note

a First published in *Scottish Literary Review*, 13.1 (2021), 117–19, and reprinted here with kind permission of the Association for Scottish Literature.

Index of Manuscripts

General Index

Cecil, Lord Burghley, guardian
of Lord William as
minor 198
Cotton, Sir Robert, friend 199
Roscarrock, Nicholas, Cornish
scholar-friend 199
Stow, John, friend 199, 204
Widmerpoole, Thomas,
chaplain 199
book collection
catalogue of books at Naworth
in 1697 200
history 201, 209
illuminated 201
literary, English 202
lives 201–03
locations after
dispersal 199–200
religious and
devotional 200–01, 204–20
See also Chaucer, *Court of
Sapience*, Gower, hands,
Index of MSS, London,
miscellanies
Howard Grace Cup 201
Hudson, Thomas, owner, 1553
Eneados 218
Historie of Judith 218
Hume, Alexander 34, 104
Hymnes 103
Hume, David, of Godscroft 6, 214
*History of the Houses of Douglas and
Angus, The* 214–15
Hume, Patrick, of Polwart 34–36
Promine 34
Hutchen, Isabella 59, 59 n.27

IHS, monogram 129
Index of Middle English Verse (Brown
and Robbins) 15, 200
Impossibilia (*adynata*), antifem-
inist 39, 140, 146–47
Inglis, Esther, calligrapher 6, 99
Iphigenia 155
Ireland, John 155, 194

Jack, R. D. S. 23, 29, 32
James I (1394–1437) 131–32, 183

James II (1430–1460) 15, 21
James III (1452–1488) 124, 183
James IV (1473–1513) 47, 97, 166, 183,
210
James V (1512–1542) 4, 44, 136, 144,
192
James VI and I (1566–1625) 2, 34–35,
55, 56, 75, 97, 102, 118, 198, 218
*Essayes of A Prentise in the Divine
Art of Poesie* 172
Reulis and Cautelis 36, 167, 179
James VII (1633–1701) 96
James, M. R. 94–95, 195
*James Carmichaell Collection
of Proverbs in Scots, The* (ed.
Anderson) 172
Jamieson, John, *Etymological
Dictionary* 27
Jansen, Cornelius 203
Jephtha, daughter of 155
Jewel, John 50
John the Reeve 167
Johnson, Samuel 11, 16–17
*Plays of William Shakespeare,
The* 1, 11, 16–17
Rasselas 49
Judgement, Last 51, 81, 82
Junius, Francis, owner, 1553 *Eneados* 7,
218–19
*Index Alphabeticus Verborum
Obsoletorum* 218
Juvenal, *Satire* VIII 193
Juvenalis, Guido 136

Kastner, L. E. 32
Keats, John, *Ode on a Grecian Urn* 25
Kennedie (Kennedy), Walter 43–44,
156, 166, 206
Flyting of Dumbar and Kennedie
(B65) 42, 43, 87, 155, 161, 166
Passioun of Christ, The 6, 78, 206,
208, 210
Kennedy, Quintin, *Litil Breif Tracteit,
Ane* 126, 175, 175 n.9
Kind Kittok ('My gudame wes a gay
wif') 38, 40–41, 52
King Berdok ('Sym of lyntoun') 38–39

Wreittoun, John   104
printers, English
    Copland, Robert   207–08
    Copland, William   6, 211–13
    Day, John   118
    Skot, John   207
Proctor, John, London bookseller   201
Propertius   174–75
prophecy   49–52, 76, 169, 211
Protestantism   50, 96, 104, 108, 118,
    211–12, 136–37, 211–12
    dogma, conformity to   6, 14–15, 75,
        87, 107, 119, 149, 205
protocol books
    of Foular, John   55 n.1
    Selkirk Burgh Court 1557–1575   119
    Selkirk, of Ninian Brydin   130
proverbs   5, 18, 26, 27, 35, 97, 103, 116,
    126, 127, 135–36, 155, 158, 171–73, 174,
    178–79, 191
Psalms see Bible
Purgatory   44, 212
Puttenham, George, Arte of English
    Poesie   214, 214 n.13
Pythagoras   157

Quintin, poet   156, 166

Rabelais, François   51, 52
    Gargantua and Pantagruel   51–52
    Pantagrueline Prognostication   52
Raleigh, Sir Walter
    'Now what is Love'   29
    'Ocean to Cynthia'   17
Ramsay, Allan   12, 17
    Ever Green   12, 24, 66, 113, 131–32
Ramsay, William, book owner   169
Rasselas see Johnson
Ratis Raving   110, 130
Rauf Coil3ear   167
Ravenscroft, Thomas
    Deuteromelia   103
    Pammelia   103
Recueil des Histoires de Troie see Troy
Redford, John   120
    'Walkyng alone Ryght secretly'   120
Reformers see Protestantism
Regiam Majestatem   154

Regimine principum, De   21, 130, 175
    'Quha wald be riche haif ee to
        honowr ay' (extract from)   175
Reidpeth, John   99, 99 n.27, 111
Reidpeth MS
    'Earth upon erthe' (Dunbar)   102
    'In secreit place this hindir nycht'
        (Dunbar)   132
    See also Index of MSS,
        Cambridge
Reson and Sensuallyte see Lydgate
Richard II (1367–1400)   165
Riddy, Felicity   13
riddles   47, 51, 76, 138, 173
Ridolfi plot   198
Ringler, William   3, 103 n.47, 107,
    113–14
Rivers see Woodville
Robin Hood   167
Robb, T. D.   21
Robbins, Rossell Hope   73
Robinson, F. N.   12
Robinson, Humphrey, London
    bookseller   203
Robinson, Walter   60
Roberts, Gareth   80, 81, 82
Robertson, Margaret   100–01, 101
    n.36, 111, 143, 145–47
Robertson MS see Index of MSS,
    Edinburgh
'Robertson sacrister's book
    1602–1622'   125
Robinson, F. N.   12
rogue genre   106, 140
'Roit' or 'Quheill of Tyme' see Abell
Rolland, John   2, 55, 109, 179
    Court of Venus   2, 22, 55–71
    Seuin Seages   5, 22, 55, 174
        und Laus Venerts (Bruce
            miscellany)   66
        and Douce Collection,
            Fragments d.12(11)   65
        and 'Physiognomy'   63–65
Rolle, Richard   201
Rollins, Hyder E.   143
Roman de la Rose, Le   29
Ross, Anthony   154, 169

Tabula in Memoriam

John Archer
Kate Ash-Irisarri
Laurie Atkinson
Peter Auger
John Edward Back
Ruggero Bianchin
Sarah Carpenter
Margaret G. Dareau
Valeria Di Clemente
Marina Dossena
A. S. G. Edwards
Elizabeth Elliott
Elizabeth Ewan
Morna R. Fleming
John Flood
Melissa Furrow
Andrew Galloway
Jonathan Alan Glenn
Rosemary Greentree
Douglas W. Hayes
Janet Hadley Williams
Theo van Heijnsbergen
Julie Hotchin
George Inglis
Pamela King
Joanna Kopaczyk
Emily Lyle
Alasdair A. MacDonald
Margaret A. Mackay
Hector L. MacQueen

Sally Mapstone
Joanna Martin
Pat Mason
Tricia A. McElroy
J. Derrick McClure
J. Craig McDonald
John J. McGavin
Anne M. McKim
Jenna Mead
Nicole Meier
Caroline Palmer
David J. Parkinson
Alessandra Petrina
William Poole
Rhiannon Purdie
John Purser
Jamie Reid-Baxter
Felicity Riddy
Nicola Royan
Patrick Scott
Allison Steenson
Sebastiaan Verweij
Eva Von Contzen
Lawrence Warner
Ian Williams
Eila Williamson
Grace G. Wilson
Emily Wingfield
H. R. Woudhuysen

Trinity College Library, Cambridge
University of Glasgow, Library
University of Stirling, Library